MULTILINGUAL LAW DICTIONARY

MULTILINGUAL LAW DICTIONARY

English — Français — Español — Deutsch

Lawrence Deems Egbert

A.B., Docteur en Droit, University of Paris
Member, District of Columbia Bar

and

Fernando Morales-Macedo

Parliamentary Interpreter
Terminologist, The World Bank

1978
A.W. SIJTHOFF—ALPHEN AAN DEN RIJN
OCEANA PUBLICATIONS, INC.—DOBBS FERRY, N.Y.
NOMOS VERLAGSGESELLSCHAFT—BADEN-BADEN

Library of Congress Cataloging in Publication Data

Egbert, Lawrence Deems, 1897-1977
Multilingual law dictionary.

Bibliography: p.
Includes indexes
1. Law—Dictionaries—Polyglot. I. Morales Macedo, Fernando, joint author. II. Title.
K54.E3 340'.03 77-25072
ISBN 90 286 0267 4 (Sijthoff)
ISBN 90 286 0687 4 (Sijthoff) pbk.
ISBN 0–379–00589–1 (Oceana)
ISBN 0–379–00598–0 (Oceana) pbk.
ISBN 3–7890–0346–8 (Nomos)
ISBN 3–7890–0347–6 (Nomos) pbk.

Printed in The Netherlands.

TO LYN EGBERT

whose beauty of personality
no words of their equivalents
can describe

Table of Contents

Fore Statement

The Nuremberg International Trial of Major Nazi War Criminals involved a long sustained and continuous necessity for communication between members of the legal profession of several tongues. The prosecution was conducted by lawyers of four nations and three languages. While various prosecutors used English, French and Russian, defense counsel, like the defendants, spoke German. Among the judges, three languages were represented and few spoke freely in more than one.

Presentation of the case involved problems of translation and interpretation that I believe are unprecedented in legal history. Every document offered in evidence, and they numbered more than four thousand, as well as the indictment and every order or paper in the case, had to be rendered in four languages. But perhaps the most challenging language task of all was interpretation of oral proceedings in the courtroom. They were almost instantaneously interpreted in four languages, so that whatever language a judge, advocate or witness might speak into the microphone, a version of what he said was immediately available to every auditor upon the earphones in the language of his choice. Every word was also recorded in the language in which it was spoken, to guard against disputes or errors of translation, and each night a complete manuscript of the day's proceedings was made available in four languages.

An effort of this magnitude and of many months' duration brought home to every participant the difficulties that attend accurate translation or quick interpretation. The American legal profession has come to use a sort of shorthand by which a single word or phrase stands for a whole cluster of legal concepts. Words such as 'due process of law,' 'cross examination,' and 'habeas corpus' bring to our minds a complicated background of our own law and practice which does not always have an equivalent in the practice of the British or Continental lawyers. But apart from this discrepancy in legal concepts and backgrounds, which cannot be fully overcome by any lexicon, there are often difficulties in finding the appropriate equivalent by which concepts which two or more professions do hold more or less in common can be adequately identified for communication.

Dr. Lawrence Egbert experienced these difficulties in his editorship of the proceedings of the Nürnberg International Trial for publication in different languages, to which he brought special educational qualifications. Out of his travail in editing the transcripts was born the idea of a dictionary of legal words and phrases designed to give French and

German equivalents, where possible, for the terms familiarly used by English-speaking lawyers. Close relations with the professions of Spanish-speaking lawyers of our own hemisphere suggested addition of that language.

Whenever communication is undertaken between English-speaking members of the profession and those whose speech is Spanish, French or German, this dictionary will be found useful. It does not purport to be an encyclopedia of four systems of law. It undertakes to furnish in short and convenient form equivalent foreign words and phrases for the ideas an English-speaking lawyer is most likely to wish to convey to his foreign professional brother.

Certainly to facilitate understanding between our own legal profession and those of other languages is not only an end worthy in itself, but is also a considerable means to cultivation of that broader assault upon barriers to understanding which may interfere with amicable relations and friendly intercourse between nations.

Robert H. Jackson
Justice, United States Supreme
Court, 1941-1954

Preface

Anyone who has participated in an international conference, a negotiation between two or more States, or the proceedings of an international tribunal (whether on the Bench or at the Bar), is aware of the difficulty involved in translation and even more in interpretation. Translation and interpretation are not identical although the most skillful **translator** seeks to **interpret** the thought of the speaker to the listener. The same is true when it is a matter of rendering a written text into another language.

The problem of rendering into another language the technical significance of **legal** terms is especially difficult as the experience at the International Court of Justice in The Hague, despite the excellence of the personnel of the Registry, testifies. As stated in the Introduction, there is no equivalent term in French, German or Spanish – to give just one example – for 'due process of law' which is such an important concept in American constitutional law. As the Introduction also points out, where there is no exact equivalent of an English legal concept, 'a brief explanation (definition) of its meaning' is given in the other three languages.

Legal contacts of multinational corporations and their counsel have multiplied. Many leading law firms are involved in negotiating bilingual or multilingual contracts. Many new multipartite treaties regulating problems of private international law ('conflicts of law' to an American lawyer) require study, and since translations of treaty texts are by no means always exact, counsel is forced to study texts in both or several languages to be sure that what he understands in his own tongue is exactly reproduced in a meeting of minds with another lawyer whose native language is different.

Philip C. Jessup
Judge, International Court of Justice, 1961-1970

Foreword

Grateful acknowledgement is made to all who contributed to this volume:

For his contribution of the Preface, Dr. Philip C. Jessup, former Professor of International Law at Columbia University, United States Ambassador-at-Large, Judge on the International Court of Justice, and distinguished scholar and author.

For extensive work on the German text, Edmund Jann, Chief of the European Division of the Law Library of Congress; for certain Spanish terms, Isidoro Zanotti of the Organization of American States and Armando E. Gonzales of the Law Library of Congress; and for proofing French terms, Hélène Vernier Thatcher and Joan Crook.

For work on the definitions of selected terms (Appendix I), Kathleen Montague, attorney in the Office of Legislative Counsel of the United States House of Representatives, and Patricia Murphy Zissu, Legal Counsel, American Broadcasting Company.

For useful comments on Selected References on Legal Literature (Appendix III), Helen Philos, Librarian of the American Society of International Law, and Edmund Jann of the Law Library of Congress.

For checking the accuracy of the reference data on the United Nations (Appendix IV), the United Nations Terminology Section, the Austrian and German Embassies, the Office of the Permanent Observer of the Federal Republic of Germany to the United Nations, and the European Communities Delegation.

For typing the final draft of the basic text of the Dictionary and the French and Spanish indexes, Yetlie Kern; for typing the German index, Ingrid Taylor.

For meticulous care and skillful workmanship in producing the final text of the Dictionary, Peter Dijkstra and other members of the staff of the A.W. Sijthoff International Publishing Company.

The authors also express their deep appreciation of the encouragement given by many lawyers, language specialists, law librarians and international organizations, especially the Inter-American Bar Association through its Secretary-General, John Dahlgren.

It is hoped that users of the Dictionary will find help in their work and will extend their indulgence for its imperfections, relying on Boswell's statement in his Life of Dr. Johnson (Vol. II, p. 189) that 'Dictionaries are like watches, the worst is better than none, and the best cannot be expected to go quite true.'

Introduction

This multilingual law dictionary has been prepared primarily to assist practicing lawyers, legal scholars, and language specialists in their professional work. Its aim is to give equivalents of legal terms and related English language terms in the French, Spanish and German languages, when the concepts of these terms are the same or similar. If the concept of any given English term does not exist in the law and practice of French, German or Spanish speaking countries, a brief explanation (definition) of its meaning is given in each of these languages.

Although it is impossible to satisfy the varying needs of lawyer, interpreter and translator, and to convey fully the equivalents of the concepts of so many terms in a dictionary of readily useable size, every attempt has been made to achieve this goal.

The lawyers who have participated with us in the drafts of these terms or in checks of these drafts have had wide experience in the field of legal terminology and in foreign law and comparative law through studies, teaching, writing, participation in international conferences (as lawyers or language specialists) or through work in international organizations. We are keenly aware of the fact that such terms as 'habeas corpus' and 'due process of law' would require a legal encyclopedia to explain fully the complicated background of the legal concepts involved. To provide some knowledge in depth, appendix material has been included, as indicated below.

Appendix I contains a list of definitions in English.
Appendix II lists a few much-used American, English, French, Spanish and German law dictionaries and also gives the titles of numerous bilingual dictionaries useful to lawyers.
Appendix III provides a guide to the law and literature of many countries.
Appendix IV gives a list of the members of the United Nations and a list of U.N. organs and related agencies because of their widespread and important activities. We regret that space does not permit the inclusion of similar data for other important international organizations, such as the Council of Europe and the Organization of American States.

Introduction

Ce dictionnaire juridique en quatre langues a pour but essentiellement de servir aux avocats en exercice, aux juristes, ainsi qu'aux traducteurs et interprètes pour leurs travaux. Il a pour but également de fournir en français, espagnol et allemand les expressions juridiques qui correspondent à celles employées en anglais lorsqu'elles obeissent à un concept identique ou semblable. Si le concept d'un terme quelconque en anglais n'existe pas dans le droit ou la pratique courante de pays de langue française, espagnole ou allemande, ce dictionnaire prévoit une explication succinte (définition) de son sens dans chacune des langues.

Bien qu'il soit impossible de faire face aux multiples besoins de l'avocat, de l'interprète ou du traducteur, et de reproduire entièrement les équivalences de concept d'un aussi grand nombre de termes dans un dictionnaire qui soit facilement maniable, tous les efforts ont été faits pour y parvenir d'aussi près que possible.

Les juristes qui ont collaboré avec nous pour rédiger ces expressions, ou pour les vérifier, possèdent une riche expérience dans le domaine de la terminologie juridique et du droit de divers pays ainsi qu'en matière de droit comparé, grâce à leurs études, enseignements, écrits, participation aux conférences internationales (en tant que juristes ou linguistes) ou par le rôle qu'ils ont joué aupres des organismes internationaux. Nous sommes pleinement conscients du fait que des termes tels 'habeas corpus' et 'due process of law' exigeraient une encyclopédie juridique pour expliquer en détail les bases compliquées des concepts juridiques en jeu. Toutefois, pour faciliter la recherche, nous avons inclus dans cet ouvrage les annexes suivantes:

Annexe I: Définitions en anglais de termes choisis.
Annexe II: Liste des dictionnaires juridiques américains, anglais, français, espagnols et allemands d'usage courant ainsi que les titres de nombreux dictionnaires bilingues utiles aux juristes.
Annexe III: Donne les indications sur le droit et ses publications de droit dans divers pays.
Annexe IV: Contient la liste des pays membres des Nations Unies, la liste des organismes affiliés particulièrement intéressants en raison de leurs activités à la fois importantes et étendues.

Nous regrettons que par faute d'espace nous n'ayons pu insérer des renseignements semblables en ce qui concerne d'autres organisations internationales de haute portée telles que le Conseil de l'Europe et L'Organisation des Etats Américains.

Introducción

Este diccionario jurídico en cuatro idiomas ha sido elaborado esencialmente para facilitar las labores profesionales de abogados en ejercicio, juristas y lingüistas. Su objetivo es ofrecer en español, francés y alemán equivalencias de términos jurídicos y expresiones afines que se usan en idioma inglés cuando los conceptos de dichos términos son idénticos o similares. Si el concepto de cualquier término en inglés no existiera en jurisprudencia de países de habla española, francesa o alemana, presentamos en ese caso una explicación sucinta (definición) de su significación en cada uno de esos idiomas.

Aunque resulte imposible atender a las múltiples necesidades de abogados, intérpretes o traductores y expresar exactamente los equivalentes de los conceptos de tantos términos en un diccionario de tamaño razonable, sin embargo, nos hemos esforzado de alcanzar esa meta.

Los juristas que nos han prestado su colaboración en la selección y verificación de los términos poseen una amplia experiencia en el campo de la terminología júridica, del derecho de distintos países merced a sus estudios, labor docente o publicaciones, participación en conferencias internacionales (como delegados o asesores lingüisticos) o por su labor en el seno de organismos internacionales. Nos damos perfectamente cuenta que tales términos como 'habeas corpus' y 'due process of law' exigirían una enciclopedia jurídica para explicar detalladamente los antecedentes de los conceptos jurídicos involucrados. A fin de brindar información complementaria hemos incluido los anexos siguientes:

Anexo I. Definiciones en inglés de los términos.
Anexo II. Lista de algunos diccionarios jurídicos de uso corriente en países de habla inglesa, española, francesa o alemana, así como los títulos de diccionarios bilingües para uso de profesionales.
Anexo III. Guía sobre el derecho y las publicaciones de distinto países.
Anexo IV. Lista de los países miembros de las Naciones Unidas; una lista de los organismos de las N.U. y entidades afiliadas.

Lamentamos que por falta de espacio no hayamos podido incluir datos similares para otras organizaciones internacionales importantes como la Organización de Estados Americanos y el Consejo de Europa.

Vorwort

Dieses vier-sprachige Rechtswörterbuch soll, vor allem, dem Rechtsanwalt, Rechtsgelehrten und Sprachspezialisten in ihren beruflichen Arbeit behilflich sein. Der Zweck dieses Wörterbuch ist, die englische Rechtsterminologie und verwandte Fachausdrücke auf Französisch, Spanisch und Deutsch wiederzugeben, falls den ausländischen Ausdrücken gleiche, oder zumindest ähnliche Begriffe zugrunde liegen. Wenn der Begriff eines englischen Rechtsausdrucks im Recht und in der Praxis eines französischen-, spanisch- oder deutschsprechenden Landes nicht existiert, wird eine kurze Erklärung (Definition) seiner Bedeutung in jeder dieser Sprachen gegeben.

Obwohl es unmöglich ist, den verschiedenen Bedürfnissen des Rechtsanwalts, Dolmetschers und Übersetzers gleichermassen zu entsprechen, und den Begriffen so vieler Rechtsausdrücke in einem viersprachigen Wörterbuch von brauchbarer Länge völlig gerecht zu werden, wurde keine Mühe erspart, diese Ziele zu erreichen.

Die Rechtsanwälte, die mit uns an der Abfassung oder Überprüfung dieser Ausdrücke arbeiteten, haben aufgrund ihrer Studien, Lehrtätigkeit, Publikationen, Teilnahme an internationalen Konferenzen (als Rechtsanwälte oder Sprachspezialisten) oder durch ihre Arbeit bei internationalen Organisationen, langjährige Erfahrung auf dem Gebiet der Rechtsterminologie und im ausländischen und vergleichenden Recht. Wir sind uns dessen vollkommen bewusst, dass Konzepte wie 'habeas corpus' oder 'due process of law' einer Rechtsenzyklopädie bedürften, um den Ursprung und die Geschichte dieser komplizierten Begriffe völlig klar zu machen. Das unten erwähnte Material in Anhang soll deshalb eine tiefer gehende Kenntnis dieser Begriffe übermitteln.

Anhang I enthält eine Liste von Definitionen in der englischen Sprache.
Anhang II verweist auf oft-verwendete amerikanische, englische, französische, spanische und deutsche Rechtswörterbücher und gibt auch die Titel zahlreicher zweisprachiger Wörterbücher, die für Rechtsanwälte besonders nützlich sind.
Anhang III soll als Handbuch für das Recht und die Rechtsliteratur vieler Länder dienen.

Schliesslich befindet sich am Ende des Anhangs eine Liste der Vereinten Nationen und deren Spezialorganisationen, die aufgrund ihrer wichtigen und weitverbreiteten Tätigkeit unerlässlich erschien. Leider konnten wegen Raummangels ähnliche Angaben für andere wichtige internationale Organisationen, wie der Europarat oder die Organisation Amerikanischer Staaten, nicht eingeschlossen werden.

Explanatory Note

The dictionary consists of a carefully selected list of legal terms grouped under key words. Meanings in English, French, Spanish and German are given for each term. Following the basic text are alphabetical indexes for each language except English. The English section of the basic text has been arranged alphabetically and numbered consecutively. Words related to the key word are indented and alphabetized under that word; verbs are alphabetized separately at the end of each group. Thus 'Hearsay evidence,' number 2369, is one of the several words indented under 'Evidence,' number 2353, and 'To adduce evidence,' number 2390, appears after the words other than verbs indented under 'Evidence.'

In the indexes, terms are alphabetized according to the key word which is placed above each term and is not numbered unless it appears independently in the dictionary. The indexes enable readers in any one of these languages to find equivalents in any of the other languages. For example a reader, thinking in Spanish of the word 'Derecho' and seeking the German equivalent, can turn to the Spanish alphabetical index and after the word 'Derecho' he will find the number where the equivalents in the other three languages are given. If he happens to think of the word 'Ley' he will find the number after that word also and by the same process find the same equivalents.

Note Explicative

Le dictionnaire se compose d'une liste de termes légaux soigneusement choisis groupés autour de mots clefs. Le sens en anglais, espagnol, français et allemand est donné pour chaque terme. A la suite du texte de base vous trouverez des tables alphabétiques pour chaque langue excepté l'anglais. La section anglaise du texte de base a été arrangée alphabétiquement et numérotée consécutivement. Les mots se rattachant au mot clef sont hors-marge et alphabétisés au dessous de ce mot; les verbes sont alphabétisés séparément à la fin de chaque groupe. Ainsi 'Preuve par ouï-dire', numéro 2369, est l'un des termes hors-marge au dessous de 'Moyens de preuve; preuve', numéro 2353, et 'Apporter la preuve', numéro 2390, se trouve au bout de la liste de mots autres que des verbes hors-marge au dessous de 'Moyens de preuve; preuve'.

Dans les index, les termes sont alphabétisés selon le mot clef qui est placé au dessous de chaque terme et n'est pas numéroté à moins qu'il apparaisse indépendamment dans le dictionnaire. Les index permettent aux lecteurs de n'importe quelle langue de trouver des équivalents dans n'importe laquelle des autres langues. Par exemple, un lecteur, pensant en espagnol au mot 'Derecho' et cherchant l'équivalent allemand, peut consulter l'index alphabétique espagnol, et après le mot 'Derecho' il trouvera le numéro où les équivalents sont donnés dans les trois autres langues. S'il pense au mot 'Ley' il trouvera également le numéro après ce mot, et par le même moyen trouvera les mêmes équivalents.

Nota Aclaratoria

El diccionario consiste en una lista cuidadosamente seleccionada de términos legales agrupados por palabras claves. Cada vocablo tiene su significado en inglés, español, francés y alemán. Siguiendo los textos básicos hay índices alfabéticos para cada idioma excepto inglés. La sección inglesa del texto básico ha sido ordenada alfabéticamente y enumerada consecutivamente. Las palabras relacionadas con el término clave son individualizadas y alfabetizadas bajo tal término; los verbos son alfabetizados separadamente al fin de cada grupo. Así 'Prueba por referencia', número 2369, es una de varias palabras colocadas bajo 'Prueba; evidencia', número 2353, y 'Aducir una prueba; aducir como prueba', número 2390, aparecen al final de las palabras que no son verbos, colocadas bajo 'Prueba; evidencia'.

En los índices, los términos son alfabetizados de acuerdo a la palabra clave que se coloca sobre cada término y no es numerada a menos que aparezca independientemente en el diccionario. Los índices permiten a los lectores de cualquiera de estos idiomas, encontrar equivalentes en cualquiera de los otros idiomas. Por ejemplo, un lector que piense en español sobre la palabra 'Derecho' y busque el equivalente alemán puede recurrir al índice alfabético español y después de la palabra 'Derecho' encontrará el número donde se dan los equivalentes en los otros tres idiomas. Si es que piensa en la palabra 'Ley', encontrará el número después de esa palabra también y por el mismo procedimiento encontrará los mismos equivalentes.

Erklärung

Das Wörterbuch besteht aus einer sorgfältig ausgewählten Reihe juristischer Fachausdrücke, die nach Stichwörtern eingeteilt sind. Neben jedem englischen Ausdruck erscheint die spanische, französische und deutsche Übersetzung. Verzeichnisse in alphabetischer Folge für jede Sprache, mit Ausnahme des Englischen, folgen dem Haupttext. Der englische Teil des Haupttextes is alphabetisch angeordnet und fortlaufend numeriert. Ausdrücke, deren Bedeutung mit der des Stichwortes in Zusammenhang steht, sind unter jedem Stichwort angeführt; sie sind alphabetisch geordnet und eingerückt. Zeitwörter erscheinen am Schluss jeder Gruppe in getrennter alphabetischer Anordnung. Zum Beispiel: 'Zeugnis auf Grund von Hörensagen' (Nummer 1458) is einer der eingerücketen Ausdrücke unter 'Beweismittel' (Nummer 1448) und 'Beweise liefern' (Nummer 1470) erscheint am Schluss der Nicht-Zeitwörter, eingerückt unter 'Beweismittel'.

In den Verzeichnissen erscheinen die Ausdrücke in alphabetischer Folge unter dem Stichwort, welches dem betreffenden Ausdruck vorangeht; die Stichwörter sind nicht numeriert, es sei denn, dass sie selbständig im Wörterbuch vorkommen. Auf diese Weise kann der Leser für jeden Ausdruck einer Sprache einen gleichwertigen Ausdruck in jeder der drei anderen Sprachen finden. Sucht der Leser z.B. die deutsche Übersetzung für das spanische Wort 'Derecho', so braucht er nur im spanischen alphabetischen Verzeichnis nachzuschlagen, wo er hinter 'Derecho' die findet; sieht er dann unter dieser Nummer im Hauptteil nach, so findet er dort die englische, französische und deutsche Übersetzung von 'Derecho'. Sollte er im spanischen Verzeichnis unter 'Ley' statt unter 'Derecho' nachsehen, so verweist ihn die auch hinter 'Ley' erscheinende Zahl auf dieselbe Stelle im Hauptteil und somit auf dieselben Entsprechungen in den drei anderen Sprachen.

A

1. **abandonment**
abandon (m); désistement (m) d'une demande (d'instance)
abandono (m); desamparo (m); desistimiento (m) (de una apelación)
Aufgabe (f); Verzicht (m) auf; Klagerücknahme (f)

2. **to abandon**
abandonner; se désister
abandonar: desamparar; desistir
aufgeben; verzichten auf

3. **abatement**
atténuation (f); réduction (f); annulation (f)
atenuación (f); reducción (f); anulación (f)
Milderung (f); Ermässigung (f); Abschaffung (f)

4. **to abate**
atténuer; réduire; annuler
disminuir; rebajar; anular
mildern; ermässigen; abschaffen; beseitigen

5. **abdication**
abdication (f); renonciation (f)
abdicación (f); renuncia (f)
Abdankung (f); Verzicht (m) auf

6. **to abdicate**
abdiquer; renoncer
abdicar; renunciar
abdanken; verzichten auf

7. **abduction**
détournement (m); enlèvement (m)
abducción (f); rapto (m); secuestro (m)
Entführung (f)

8. **to abduct**
détourner; enlever
raptar; secuestrar
entführen

9. **abetment**
instigation (f); appui (m); encouragement (m)
instigación (f)
Anstiftung (f); Beihilfe (f); Hilfe (f)

10. **abettor**
instigateur (m); provocateur (m)
fautor (m); inductor (m); instigador (m)
Anstifter (m); Gehilfe (m); Helfer (m)

11. **to abet**
encourager; inciter à; provoquer à
incitar; inducir; instigar
anstiften; helfen

12. **abeyance**
condition (f) suspensive
inacción (f) transitoria; suspensión (f)
Aufschub (m)

13. **to hold in abeyance**
tenir sous condition suspensive
dejar en suspenso (pendiente)
aufschieben; in der Schwebe halten

14. **abide by, to**
observer; se soumettre à
atenerse a; someterse a
sich fügen (unterwerfen); verharren bei

15. **ability**
habilité (f)
aptitud (f)
Fähigkeit (f)

16. **abjure, to**
renoncer à
renunciar
abschwören

17. **abode**
demeure (f); habitation (f); résidence (f)
habitación (f); residencia (f)
Wohnsitz (m); Aufenthaltsort (m)

18. **abolishment; abolition**
abolition (f); abrogation (f)
abolición (f); derogación (f)
Abschaffung (f); Aufhebung (f)

19. **to abolish**
abolir; supprimer
abolir; derogar
abschaffen; aufheben

20. **abortion**
avortement (m)
aborto (m)
Abtreibung (f)

21. **abortive**
avorté; échoué
abortivo; fallido
fehlgeschlagen; ergebnislos

22. **above-mentioned**
susmentionné
antedicho
oben erwähnt

23. **abridgement**
abréviation (f); restriction (f)
abreviación (f); compendio (m)
Abkürzung (f); Abriss (m); Auszug (m)

24. **to abridge**
abréger; restreindre
abreviar; compendiar
abkürzen

25. **abrogation**
abrogation (f); annulation (f)
abrogación (f); anulación (f)
Aufhebung (f); Ausserkraftsetzung (f)

26. **to abrogate**
abroger; annuler
abolir; abrogar
aufheben; ausser Kraft setzen; annulieren

27. **absconder**
contumace (m, f); contumax (m); fugitif (m); défaillant (m)
contumaz (m); fugitivo (m); prófugo (m)
Nichterschienener (m); Flüchtiger (m)

28. **to abscond**
évader la justice; s'enfuir
esconderse; evadir la justicia
fliehen; sich der Festnahme entziehen; flüchten

29. **absence**
absence (f); non-comparution (f)
ausencia (f); no comparecencia (f)
Abwesenheit (f); Nichterscheinen (n)

30. **absence without leave (AWOL)**
absence (f) illégale
ausencia (f) sin permiso (m)
unerlaubtes Ausbleiben (n); eigenmächtige Entfernung (f)

31. **absent**
absent
ausente
abwesend

32. **on leave of absence**
en congé
en uso de licencia
auf Urlaub

33. **absolute**
absolu; définitif
absoluto; definitivo
absolut; unbeschränkt; uneingeschränkt

34. **absolve, to**
absoudre; affranchir; dégager
absolver; dispensar
entbinden; freisprechen; lossprechen

35. **abstention**
abstention (f)
abstención (f)
Enthaltung (f)

36. **to abstain**
s'abstenir
abstenerse
sich enthalten

37. **abstract**
abstrait (m); abrégé (m); résumé (m)
abstracto (m); compendio (m); resumen (m)
Abriss (m); Auszug (m); Zusammenfassung (f)

38. **to abstract**
abréger; résumer
epitomar; resumir
abstrahieren; zusammenfassen; verallgemeinern; entwenden

39. **abstraction**
détournement (f); vol (m)
abstracción (f); hurto (m)
Entwendung (f); Abstraktion (f); Verallgemeinerung (f)

40. **abuse**
abus (m); injures (f, pl); mauvais traitement (m)
abuso (m); injuria (f); maltrato (m)
Missbrauch (m); Beleidigung (f); Misshandlung (f)

41. **abuse of discretion**
excès (m) de pouvoir
abuso (m) de poder discrecional
Ermessensmissbrauch (m)

42. **abusive**
abusif; insultant
abusivo; insultante
missbräuchlich; beleidigend

43. **to abuse**
abuser; injurier; maltraiter
abusar de; injuriar; maltratar
missbrauchen; beleidigen; misshandlen

44. **abutment**
borne (f); confins (m, pl)
linde (m); confín (m)
Angrenzen (n)

45. **abutting**
adjacent; contigu
limítrofe; colindante
angrenzend; benachbart

46. **to abut**
confiner; être contigu
confinar; lindar
angrenzen

47. **acceleration**
accélération (f)
aceleración (f)
Beschleunigung (f)

48. **to accelerate**
accélérer; hâter
acelerar
beschleunigen

49. **acceptance**
acceptation (f); consentement (m)
aceptación (f); allanamiento (m)
Annahme (f); Zustimmung (f)

50. **acceptable**
acceptable; agréable
aceptable
annehmbar

51. **acceptor**
accepteur (m); tiré (m)
aceptador (m); aceptante (m)
Akzeptant (m)

52. **acceptor for honor**
avaliste (m); intervenant (m)
aceptador (m) por intervención (f)
Ehrenakzeptant (m)

53. **conditional, qualified acceptance**
acceptation (f) conditionnelle
aceptación (f) condicional
bedingte Annahme (f)

54. **constructive acceptance**
acceptation (f) établie par déduction
aceptación (f) implícita
stillschweigende Annahme (f)

55. **to accept**
accepter; consentir
aceptar
akzeptieren; annehmen

56. **access**
accès (m); droit (m) de passage
acceso (m)
Zugang (m); Zugangsrecht (n)

57. **accession**
accession (f)
accesión (f)
Eintritt (m); Beitritt (m); Zutritt (m)

58. **to accede**
accéder; entrer en fonctions
acceder; entrar en funciones
beitreten; beipflichten

59. **accessory; accessary**
complice (m)
cómplice (m)
Mittäter (m); Helfershelfer (m)

60. **accessory after the fact**
complice par assistance
cómplice encubridor de un crimen cometido
Helfershelfer; Hehler

61. **accessory before the fact**
complice par instigation
cómplice instigador de un crimen
Mittäter; Gehilfe

62. **accident**
accident (m)
accidente (m)
Unfall (m)

63. **accidental**
accidentel; fortuit
accidental; casual
zufällig

64. **fatal accident**
fatalité (f)
fatalidad (f)

tödlicher Unfall (m)
65. **unavoidable accident**
accident (m) inevitable
accidente (m) inevitable
unvermeidlicher Unfall (m)
66. **acclamation**
acclamation (f)
aclamación (f)
Zuruf (m)
67. **accommodation**
ajustement (m); complaisance (f)
acomodamiento (m); ajuste (m)
Anpassung (f); Beilegung (f); Gefälligkeit (f)
68. **to accommodate**
accommoder; ajuster; obliger
acomodar; adaptar; ajustar
unterbringen; anpassen; beilegen
69. **accompanying**
concomitant de; ci-joint
que acompaña
Begleit-
70. **accomplice**
complice (m)
cómplice (m)
Komplize (m); Mittäter (m)
71. **accomplishments**
réalisations (fpl)
realizaciones (fpl)
Fertigkeiten (fpl)
72. **accord**
accord (m)
acuerdo (m)
Einigung (f); Einverständnis (n)
73. **accord and satisfaction**
novation (f) exécutée
arreglo (m) de una disputa (f)
vergleichsweise Erfüllung (f)
aussergerichtlicher Vergleich (m)
74. **according to in accordance with**
conformément à; d'après; selon
conforme a; de acuerdo con; según
gemäss; laut, nach
75. **account**
compte (m); exposé (m)
cuenta (f); informe (m)
Rechnung (f); Bericht (m); Konto (n)
76. **account book**
livre (m) de comptes
libro (m) de contabilidad
Rechnungsbuch (n)
77. **account stated**
arrêté (m) de comptes
cuenta (f) convenida
Rechnungsausgleich (m)
78. **accounts payable**
créancier divers (mpl)
cuentas (fpl) por pagar
Verbindlichkeiten (fpl); Passiva (fpl)
79. **accounts receivable**
dettes (f, pl) actives
cuentas (f, pl) en cobranza
Forderungen (f, pl); Aktiva
80. **blocked account**
compte (m) bloqué
cuenta (f) congelada
Sperrkonto (n)
81. **charge account**
compte de crédit (à la clientèle)
cuenta (f) abierta
Kundenkreditkonto (n)
82. **expense account**
compte (m) de frais
cuenta (f) para gastos (m)
Spesenkonto (n)
83. **joint account**
compte (m) collectif, conjoint
cuenta (f) conjunta, mancomunada
Gemeinschaftskonto (n)
84. **on account**
à compte
a cuenta
auf Rechnung
85. **overdrawn account**
compte désaprovisionné
cuenta sobregirada
überzogenes Konto
86. **to close an account**
arrêter un compte
cerrar una cuenta
ein Konto schliessen
87. **to keep accounts**
tenir les comptes
llevar cuentas
Bücher, Rechnung führen
88. **to open an account**
ouvrir un compte

abrir una cuenta
ein Konto eröffnen

89. **to take into account**
tenir compte
tener en cuenta
in Erwägung ziehen

90. **accountable**
responsable
responsable
verantwortlich

91. **accountancy; accounting**
comptabilité (f)
contabilidad (f)
Buchführung (f); Rechnungsführung (f)

92. **accountant**
agent, expert -comptable (m)
contador (m)
Buchführer (m); Rechnungsführer (m)

93. **certified public accountant (CPA)**
expert-comptable (m)
contador (m) público
Bücherrevisor (m)

94. **accreditation**
accréditement (m)
crédito (m)
Beglaubigung (f)

95. **to accredit**
accréditer
acreditar
akkreditieren bei; bevollmächtigen

96. **accretion**
accroissement (m)
acrecencia (f)
Zuwachs (m) durch Anschwemmung (f); Zuwachs (m); Erbzuwachs (m); Anlandung (f)

97. **accrual**
accumulation (f)
acumulación (f)
Zuwachs (m); Anfall (m); Auflaufen (n)

98. **accrual of a right**
naissance (f) d'un droit
surgimiento (m) de un derecho (m)
Rechtserwerb (m)

99. **accrued**
acquis; cumulé
acumulado
angefallen; aufgelaufen

100. **accumulation**
cumul (m)
acumulación (f)
Anhäufung (f)

101. **to accumulate**
accumuler
acumular
anhäufen

102. **accuracy**
précision (f)
precisión (f)
Genauigkeit (f)

103. **a high degree of accuracy**
une mesure élevée de justesse, précision
un alto grado de precisión
ein hoher Grad an Genauigkeit

104. **accusation**
accusation (f); inculpation (f)
acusación (f)
Anklage (f); Beschuldigung (f)

105. **accused**
accusé (m); inculpé (m)
acusado (m); procesado (m)
Angeklagter (m); Beschuldigter (m)

106. **accuser**
accusé (m); inculpé (m)
acusador (m); denunciante (m)
Ankläger (m)

107. **false accusation**
accusation (f) calomnieuse; fausse accusation (f)
acusación (f) falsa; calumnia (f)
falsche Anschuldigung (f)

108. **to accuse**
accuser; incriminer; inculper
acusar; inculpar
anklagen; beschuldigen

109. **to acquit the accused**
acquitter l'accusé
absolver al acusado
von einer Anklage freisprechen

110. **achievement**
accomplissement (m); réalisation (f)
logro (m); realización (f)
Leistung (f)

111. **to achieve**
aboutir à; accomplir; parvenir à

acabar; llevar a cabo; realizar
ausführen; leisten; erreichen

112. **acknowledgement**
récépissé (m); reconnaissance (f)
acuse (m) de recibo (m); reconocimiento (m)
Anerkennung (f)

113. **to acknowledge**
aviser de; reconnaître
acusar recibo; reconnocer
anerkennen

114. **acquaintance**
connaissance (f)
conocimiento (m); conocido (m)
Kenntnis (f); Bekanntschaft (f)

115. **to acquaint**
aviser de; faire savoir; informer
enterar; familiarizar; informar
bekanntmachen; mitteilen

116. **acquiescence**
acquiescement (m); consentement (m)
aquiescencia (f); asenso (m);
Beistimmung (f); Einwilligung (f)

117. **to acquiesce**
acquiescer; céder; se soumettre
allanarse; consentir
einwilligen; zugeben; sich fügen

118. **acquisition**
acquisition (f)
adquisición (f)
Erwerb (m)

119. **acquired**
acquis
adquirido
erworben

120. **to acquire**
acquérir
adquirir
erwerben

121. **acquisitive**
apte à apprendre
adquisitivo
habsüchtig; gewinnsüchtig

122. **acquittal**
acquittement (m); décharge (f)
absolución (f); descargo (m)
Freispruch (m)

123. **to acquit**
acquitter
absolver
freisprechen

124. **acquittance**
décharge (f) d'une dette
descargo (m) de una deuda (f)
Quittung (f); Entlastung (f); Schuldbefreiung (f)

125. **act**
acte (m); action (f); fait (m); loi (f)
acción (f); acto (m); hecho (m); ley (f)
Akt (m); Handlung (f); Tat (f); Gesetz (n)

126. **act of Congress (U.S.A.)**
décision, loi, du Congrès
ley del Congreso
Gesetz des Kongresses; Kongressbeschluss

127. **act of God**
force majeur (f)
fuerza mayor (f)
höhere Gewalt (f)

128. **act of state**
acte (m) de gouvernement
acto (m) de dominio
Hoheitsakt (m); Regierungshandlung (f)

129. **authentic act**
acte (m) authentique
acto (m) auténtico
beglaubigte Urkunde (f)

130. **enabling act**
décret (m) d'exécution
ley (f) de autorización
Ermächtigungsgesetz (n)

131. **final act**
acte (f) final
acta (f) final
Schlussakte (f)

132. **overt act**
acte (m) manifeste
acto (m) evidente
offenkundige Handlung (f)

133. **unfriendly act**
acte (m) inamical
acto (m) hostil
unfreundlicher Akt (m)

134. **unlawful act**
acte illicite
acto ilícito
rechtswidrige Handlung

135. **to act**

agir
actuar
handeln; tätig sein

136. **action (at law)**
action (f) en justice; demande (f) judiciaire plainte
acción (f); demanda (f); proceso (m)
Klage (f)

137. **action for damages**
action en dommages-intérêts (m, pl)
demanda (f) por daños (m, pl) y perjuicios (m, pl)
Schadenersatzklage (f)

138. **action for infringement of right**
assignation (f) en contrefaçon (f)
demanda (f) por violación (f) de patente (f)
Patentverletzungsklage (f)

139. **action for libel**
action (f) en diffamation (f)
demanda (f) por difamación (f)
Beleidigungsklage (f)

140. **action in rem**
action (f) réelle
acción (f) contra la cosa (f)
dingliche Klage (f)

141. **action of assumpsit**
action (f) en reconnaissance de dette
acción (f) por incumplimiento (m) de promesa (f)
Erfüllungsklage (f)

142. **action of covenant**
action (f) en dommages-intérêts pour inexécution de contrat
acción (f) judicial por incuplimiento (m) de contrato
eine aus einem Vertrag (m) zustehende Klage

143. **action of debt**
action (f) personnelle
acción (f) en cobro (m) de dinero (m)
Klagespruch (m) auf Zahlung; Schuldklage (f)

144. **action of detinue**
action (f) possessoire (en réintégration)
acción (f) derivada de la retención (f) ilegal de bienes
Besitzklage (f); Klage (f) auf Herausgabe

145. **action of ejectment**
action (f) d'expulsion
acción (f) de desahucio (m)
Räumungsklage (f)

146. **action of replevin**
action de revendication
acción de revindicación
Anfechtungsklage wegen unzulässiger Pfändung

147. **action of trespass**
action de transgression
acción de transgresión
Besitzstörungsklage

148. **action of trover**
action en restitution
acción para recuperar
Bereicherungsklage

149. **action on the case**
action *ex delicto*
acción *ex delicto*
Schadenersatzklage aus widerrechtlichen Handlungen

150. **actionable**
actionnable; sujet à procès
que da lugar a acción,.proceso
klagbar

151. **civil action**
action au civil
acción civil
bürgerlicher Rechtsstreit

152. **common law action**
action de droit commun
acción bajo derecho común
Klage nach dem Gewohnheitsrecht

153. **criminal action**
action criminelle
acción criminal
strafrechtliche Verfolgung

154. **right of action**
droit d'ester
derecho (m) de acción (f)
Klagerecht (n)

155. **to bring an action against**
intenter une action, un procès, contre
entablar pleito; acusar (penal); demandar (civil)

jemand klagen; gegen jemand Klage erheben

156. **activist**
activiste
activista
Aktivist

157. **activities**
fonctions (fpl); occupations (fpl)
actividades (fpl); ocupaciones (fpl)
Tätigkeiten (fpl); Wirksamkeit (f)

158. **gainful activities**
activités lucratives
actividades lucrativas
Berufstätigkeit(en); Erwerbstätigkeit

159. **actual**
réel; véritable
real; efectivo
gegenwärtig; wirklich

160. **actuary**
actuaire (m)
actuario (m)
Rechnungssachverständiger (m); Versicherungsmathematiker (m)

161. **addendum**
supplément (m)
suplemento (m)
Nachtrag (m); Zusatz (m)

162. **addict**
personne (f) adonnée à
adicto
Süchtiger

163. **drug addict**
toxicomane (m)
drogadicto (m)
Rauschgiftsüchtiger (m)

164. **addition**
addition (f)
suplemento (m)
Hinzufügung (f)

165. **to add**
adjouter
añadir
hinzufügen

166. **address**
adresse (f); allocution (f); discours (m)
dirección (f); alocución (f); discurso (m)
Adresse (f); Anschrift (f); Ansprache (f)

167. **address of welcome**
discours de bienvenue
discurso de bienvenida
Begrüssungsansprache

168. **business address**
adresse de bureau
dirección del negocio
Geschäftsadresse

169. **closing address**
discours de clôture
discurso de clausura
Schlussvortrag

170. **opening address**
allocution d'ouverture
discurso de apertura
Eröffnungsansprache

171. **radio address**
discours à la radio
discurso por radio
Rundfunkansprache

172. **television address**
discours télévisé
discurso televisado
Fernsehansprache

173. **to give an address**
prononcer un discours
pronunciar un discurso
eine Ansprache halten

174. **adduce, to**
alléguer; offrir
aducir; rendir
beibringen

175. **ademption**
révocation (f)
revocación (f)
Entziehung (f); Wegnahme (f); Widerruf (m) Erlöschen (n) eines Legats

176. **adequacy**
caractère (m) adéquat; suffisance (f)
calidad (f) de adecuado; suficiencia (f)
Angemessenheit (f)

177. **adequate**
adéquat; suffisant
adecuado; suficiente

angemessen; hinreichend

178. **adherence**
adhérence (f)
adherencia (f)
Anhänger (f); Mitgliedschaft (f); Zugehörigkeit (f)

179. **to adhere to**
adhérer à
adherirse
beitreten

180. **adhesion**
adhésion (f)
adhesión (f)
Beitritt (m)

181. **adjacent adjoining**
adjacent; contigu
adyacente; contiguo
angrenzend; anliegend

182. **adjournment**
ajournement (m); renvoi (m)
aplazamiento (m); suspensión (f)
Vertagung (f); Aufschub (m)

183. **to adjourn**
ajourner; renvoyer
aplazar; diferir
vertagen; aufschieben

184. **to adjourn sine die**
ajourner *sine die*
aplazar *sine die*
auf unbestimmte Zeit vertagen

185. **adjudication**
adjudication (f); jugement (m)
adjudicación (f); fallo (m)
richterliche Entscheidung (f); Rechtsspruch (m); Zuerkennung (f)

186. **to adjudicate; to adjudge**
adjuger; décider par jugement
adjudicar; fallar
entscheiden, zuerkennen

187. **adjustment**
ajustement (m); arrangement (m)
ajuste (m); arreglo (m)
Berichtigung (f); Schlichtung (f)

188. **to adjust**
arranger; régler
ajustar; acomodar
beilegen; berichtigen

189. **administration**
administration (f); gestion (f); régie (f)
administración (f); dirección (f); gobierno (m)

190. **administration cum testamento annexo**
administration *cum testamento annexo*
administración *cum testamento anexo*
gerichtlich angeordnete Testamentsvollstreckungsbestellung *cum testamento annexo*

191. **administration of a bankrupt's estate**
administration d'une faillite
administración de una quiebra
Konkursverwaltung

192. **administration of an oath**
prestation (f) d'un serment (m)
prestación (f) de juramento (m)
Vereidigung (f)

193. **administration of justice**
administration de justice
administración de justicia
Justizverwaltung; Rechtspflege

194. **administrative**
administratif
administrativo
verwaltungsmässig; Verwaltungsadministration

195. **Administrator**
administrateur (m); gérant (m)
administrador (m); gerente (m)
Administrator (m); Verwalter (m)

196. **administrator de bonis non**
nouvel administrateur d'une succession
nuevo albacea en una sucesión; administrador designado para distribuir los bienes en herencia
gerichtlich neu bestellter Testamentsvollstrecker

197. **administratix**
administratrice (f)
adminstradora (f)
Verwalterin (f)

198. **public administration**
administration public
administración pública
öffentliche Verwaltung

199. **the administration (U.S.A.)**
l'exécutif; le gouvernement

el ejecutivo (m); el gobierno (m)
Die Regierung (f)

200. **to administer**
administrer; gérer
administrar
verwalten

201. **admissibility**
admissibilité (f); recevabilité (f)
admisibilidad (f)
Zulässigkeit (f)

202. **admissible**
admissible; recevable
admisible
zulässig

203. **admission**
admission (f); reconnaissance (f)
admisión (f); reconocimiento (m)
Aufnahme (f); Geständnis (n)

204. **admission against interest**
aveu à l'encontre de son intérêt
admisión desventajosa
nachteiliges Geständnis

205. **admission of guilt**
reconnaissance (f) de culpabilité (f)
admisión (f) de culpabilidad (f); confesión (f)
Geständnis der Schuld; Eingeständnis (n)

206. **admission under duress**
aveu (m) sous coercition (f)
confesión (f) bajo coacción (f)
Geständnis (n) unter Zwang (m)

207. **on his own admission**
de son propre aveu
de motu proprio
auf Grund seines freiwilligen Zugeständnisses

208. **to admit**
admettre; reconnaître
admitir; conceder
eingestehen, zugeben

209. **admonition**
admonestation (f); réprimande (f); avertissement (m)
admonición (f); advertencia (f)
Ermahnung (f); Verweis (m); Warnung (f)

210. **to admonish**
exhorter; faire une remontrance
advertir; amonestar
ermahnen; verweisen; warnen

211. **adolescence**
adolescence (f)
adolescencia (f)
jugendliches Alter (n)

212. **adolescent**
adolescent
adolescente
jugendlich; Jugendlicher

213. **adoption**
adoption (f)
adopción (f)
Adoption (f); Annahme (f); Annahme an Kindes Statt

214. **adopted**
adopté
adoptado
adoptiert; angenommen

215. **to adopt**
accepter; adopter
adoptar; prohijar
adoptieren; annehmen; an Kindes Statt annehmen

216. **adult**
adulte (m)
adulto (m)
Erwachsene(r) (m); erwachsen

217. **adulteration**
adultération (f); falsification (f)
adulteración (f); falsificación (f)
Fälschung (f); Verfälschung (f)

218. **adulterated**
adultéré; falsifié
adulterado; falsificado
verdorben; verfälscht

219. **to adulterate**
adultérer; falsifier
adulterar; viciar
verderben; verfälschen

220. **adultery**
adultère (m)
adulterio (m)
Ehebruch (m)

221. **adulterer**
adultère (m)
adúltero (m)
Ehebrecher (m)

222. **adulteress**

adultère (f)
adúltera (f)
Ehebrecherin (f)

223. **adulterous**
adultère
adúltero
ehebrecherisch

224. **to comit adultery**
commettre un adultère
cometer adulterio
Ehebruch begehen

225. **advance**
avance (f); hausse (f); progrès (m)
avance (m); progreso (m)
Vorschuss (m); Beförderung (f)

226. **in advance**
d'avance
por adelantado
vorher; im voraus

227. **to advance**
avancer; hausser
acelerar; avanzar
befördern; vorstrecken

228. **advancement**
avancement (m); progrès (m)
promoción (f); progreso (m)
Beförderung (f); Fortschritt (m)

228a. **advantage**
avantage (m); profit (m)
ventaja (f); lucro (m)
Vorteil (m)

229. **adventure**
entreprise (f)
empresa (f)
gewagtes Unternehmen (n); Wagnis (n)

230. **adversity**
adversité (f)
adversidad (f)
Unglück (n)

231. **adverse**
adverse; contraire
adverso; contrario
feindlich; ungünstig

232. **advertisement**
annonce (f); avis (m)
anuncio (m); aviso (m)
Annonce (f); Inserat (n); Anzeige (f)

233. **advertised**
annoncé
anunciado
annonciert; inseriert

234. **to advertise**
annoncer; faire de la réclame
anunciar; avisar
annoncieren; Reklame machen

235. **advertising**
publicité (f); réclame (f)
propaganda (f); publicidad (f)
Werbung (f); Reklame (f)

236. **advice**
avis (m); conseil (m)
aviso (m); consejo (m); asesoramiento (m)
Rat (m); Ratschlag (m); Gutachten (n)

237. **advisedly**
à dessein; après mûre considération
deliberadamente; cuerdamente
mit Bedacht; vorsätzlich

238. **adviser; advisor**
conseiller (m)
asesor (m)
Berater (m); Gutachter (m)

239. **on the advice of**
d'après l'avis de
según el consejo de
auf Rat

240. **as may, shall, be deemed advisable**
ainsi qu'on le jugera convenable
según sea aconsejable
wie es für zweckmässig erachtet wird

241. **to advise**
aviser; conseiller; informer
aconsejar; asesorar
beraten; benachrichtigen

242. **to consider it advisable to**
estimer qu'il aurait lieu de
considerarlo aconsejable
es für ratsam halten

242a. **advisable**
convenable; opportun
conveniente; prudente
klug; rätlich; zweckmässig

243. **advisement**
considération (f)
consideración (f)
Betrachtung (f)

244. **under advisement**

sous considération (f)
en tela (f) de juicio (m)
in Erwägung (f)

245. **advisory**
consultatif
consultivo
beratend

246. **advocate**
avocat (m); avoué (m)
abogado (m); defensor (m)
Advokat (m); Rechtsanwalt (m)

247. **to advocate**
plaider; soutenir; suggérer
abogar; defender
vertreten; verteidigen

248. **aeronautics**
aéronautique (f)
aeronáutica (f)
Aeronautik (f)

249. **aeronaut**
aéronaute (m)
aeronauta (m)
Aeronaut (m)

250. **civil aeronautics**
aéronautique civile
aeronáutica (f) civil
Zivilluftfahrt (f); Zivilflugwesen (n)

251. **affect, to**
affecter; influer sur, toucher
afectar; influir en; impresionar
betreffen; beeinflussen; beeinträchtigen

252. **affidavit**
attestation (f); déclaration (f) par écrit; sous serment (m)
declaración (f) escrita bajo juramento (m)
schriftliche Erklärung (f); eidesstattliche Versicherung (f)

253. **affidant**
déposant (m); celui qui fait un affidavit
declarante (m); deponente (m)
Aussteller (m) einer eidesstattlichen Versicherung (f)

254. **affiliation**
affiliation (f); rattachement (m)
afiliación (f); adhesión (f)
Angliederung (f); Anschluss (m)

255. **affiliated**
affilié; associé
afiliado; miembro
angegliedert; angeschlossen

256. **to be affiliated with**
être affilié à; être associé avec
estar afiliado a; ser miembro de
angegliedert; angeschlossen sein an

257. **affinity**
alliance (f)
afinidad (f)
Verschwägerung (f); geistige Verwandtschaft (f)

258. **affirmation**
affirmation (f)
afirmación (f)
Bestätigung (f); Versicherung (f)

259. **affirmative**
affirmatif
afirmativo
bestätigend; versichernd

260. **affray**
bagarre (f); rixe (f)
pendencia (f); riña (f)
Raufhandel (m); Schlägerei (f)

261. **affreightment**
affrètement (m)
fletamento (m)
Befrachtung (f)

262. **affront**
affront (m); offense (f)
insulto (m); ofensa (f)
grobe Beleidigung (f); Beschimpfung (f)

263. **to affront**
faire affront à; offenser
ofender; insultar
beleidigen; beschimpfen

264. **aforementioned (aforesaid)**
susmentionné; susdit
antes mencionado; antedicho
vorerwähnt

265. **aforenamed**
susmentionné
ya mencionado
obengenannt

266. **aforethought**
prémedité
premeditado
vorbedacht

267. **aftermath**
conséquences (fpl)
consecuencias (fpl)
die Folgen (fpl); die Konsequenzen (fpl)

268. **age**
âge (m); époque (f); ère (f)
edad (f); época (f); período (m)
Alter (n); Zeitalter (n)

269. **age of consent**
âge nubile
edad núbil
Mündigkeitsalter (n)

270. **age of discretion**
âge de raison
edad de discreción
unterscheidungsfähiges Alter

271. **age of retirement**
âge de la retraite (m)
edad jubilación (f)
Pensionsalter (n)

272. **full, legal age**
majorité (f)
mayoría (f)
Mündigkeit (f)

273. **of legal age**
majeur
mayor de edad
volljährig; mündig

274. **under legal age**
mineur
menor de edad
minderjährig

275. **to come of age**
atteindre la majorité
alcanzar a la mayoría
volljährig werden

276. **agency**
agence (f); mandat (m); service (f)
agencia (f); oficina (f); gestión (f)
Agentur (f); Dienststelle (f); Stelle (f)

277. **administrative agency**
administration (f)
administración (f)
Amtsstelle (f)

278. **employment agency**
bureau (m) de placement
agencia (f) de empleos
Arbeitsamt (n); Dienstvermittlung (f)

279. **agenda**
ordre du jour (m); programme de travaux (m)
orden del día (m); temario (m)
Tagesordnung (f); Verhandlungsgegenstände (mpl)

280. **agenda item**
point (m) de l'ordre du jour
punto (m) del orden del día
Punkt (m) der Tagesordnung

281. **approved agenda**
ordre du jour définitif
orden del día definitivo
endgültige Tagesordnung

282. **provisional agenda**
ordre du jour provisoire
orden del día provisional
vorläufige Tagesordnung

283. **to adopt the agenda**
adopter l'ordre du jour
aprobar el orden del día
die Tagesordnung annehmen

284. **to appear on the agenda**
figurer à l'ordre du jour
figurar en el orden del día
auf der Tagesordnung stehen

285. **to discuss the agenda**
délibérer sur l'ordre du jour
deliberar sobre el orden del día
über die Tagesordnung beraten

286. **to draw up the agenda**
dresser l'ordre du jour
fijar el orden del día
die Tagesordnung aufstellen

287. **to include in (on) the agenda**
insérer dans l'ordre du jour
insertar en el orden del día
in die Tagesordnung einfügen oder aufnehmen

288. **to remove (withdraw) from the agenda**
rayer, retirer de l'ordre du jour
retirar, suprimir del orden del día
von der Tagesordnung absetzen (streichen)

289. **agent**
agent (m); mandataire (m); représentant (m)
agente (m); mandatario (m); representante (m)
Agent (m); Geschäftsführer (m); Vertreter (m)

290. **accredited agent (representative)**
représentant attitré
representate autorizado
beglaubigter Bevollmächtigter (m)

291. **commission agent**
commissionnaire (m)
comisionado (m)
Kommissionär (m)
292. **consular agent**
agent consulaire (m)
agente consular (m)
Konsularagent (m)
293. **del credere agent**
commissionnaire du croire (m)
agente del credere (m)
Bürge (m); Delkrederekommissionär (m)
294. **diplomatic agent**
agent diplomatique (m)
agente diplomático (m)
diplomatischer Vertreter (m) oder Agent (m)
295. **general, universal agent**
agent général
agente general
Generalbevollmächtigter
296. **insurance agent**
courtier d'assurances (m)
corredor de seguros (m)
Versicherungsagent (m)
297. **sole agent**
agent exclusif
agente (distribuidor) exclusivo
Alleinvertreter
297a. **special agent**
agent limité à un acte déterminé
agente de poder limitado
Sonderbevollmächtigter
298. **aggravation**
circonstance (f) aggravante
circunstancia (f) agravante
Verschärfung (f); erschwerender Umstand (m)
299. **aggravation**
aggravant
agravante
erschwerend
300. **to aggravate**
aggraver
agravar
erschweren
301. **aggregate**
ensemble (m); masse (f); total (m)
conjunto (m); colección (f); totalidad (f)
Anhäufung (f); Ansammlung (f); Gesamtheit (f)
302. **in the aggregate**
en masse; en somme
en total
im ganzen; insgesamt
303. **aggression**
agression (f)
agresión (f)
Angriff (m); Überfall (m)
304. **act of aggression**
acte d'agression
acto de agresión
Angriffshandlung
305. **aggressive**
agressif
agresivo
aggressiv
306. **aggressor**
agresseur (m)
agresor (m)
Angreifer (m)
307. **aggrieved**
affligé; lésé
agraviado
in seinem Recht; verletzt
308. **agitator**
agitateur (m); meneur (m)
incitador (m); perturbador (m)
Aufwiegler (m)
309. **agreement**
accord (m); consentement (m); convention (f)
acuerdo (m); convenio (m); convención (f)
Abkommen (n); Übereinstimmung (f); Vertrag (m)
310. **agreed as follows**
ont convenu comme suit
ha, han convenido lo siguiente
haben die folgende Vereinbarung getroffen
311. **amicable agreement**
accord à l'amiable
arreglo amistoso; transacción amistosa
gütlicher Vergleich
312. **armistice agreement**
convention (f) d'armistice
convenio (m) de armisticio
Waffenstillstandsabkommen (n)

313. **as may be agreed upon**
dont il serait convenu
según se convenga
je nach Vereinbarung

314. **as per agreement**
comme il a été convenu
de acuerdo con lo convenido
laut Vertrag

315. **barter agreement**
contrat (m) commutatif
acuerdo (m) de compensación
Tauschvertrag (m)

316. **bilateral agreement**
accord (m) bilatéral
acuerdo (m) bilateral
zweiseitiger Vertrag (m)

317. **by mutual agreement**
à l'amiable, d'un commun accord
de mutuo acuerdo
nach gegenseitiger Vereinbarung; durch beiderseitiges Abkommen

318. **clearing agreement**
accord de clearing
acuerdo de clearing
Clearingabkommen; Verrechnungsabkommen

319. **executive agreement**
convention (f) exécutive
convenio (m) ejecutivo
Regierungsabmachung (f)

320. **express agreement**
consentement (m) formel
acuerdo (m) expreso
ausdrückliche Abmachung (f)

321. **Gentlemen's agreement**
Gentlemen's agreement
acuerdo de caballeros
freiwillige Vereinbarung

322. **multilateral agreement**
accord multilatéral, plurilatéral
acuerdo multilateral
mehrseitiger Vertrag

323. **oral agreement**
accord verbal
acuerdo verbal
mündliche Vereinbarung

324. **standstill agreement**
accord de suspension
acuerdo para la suspensión de un contrato o procedimiento
Stillhalteabkommen

325. **tacit agreement**
convention tacite
convenio tácito
stillschweigende Vereinbarung

326. **trade agreement**
accord commercial; traité de commerce
acuerdo, convenio comercial
Handelsabkommen; Handelsvertrag

327. **unilateral agreement**
accord unilatéral
acuerdo unilateral
einseitiger Vertrag

328. **unless otherwise agreed**
sauf stipulation contraire
salvo pacto en contrario
vorbehaltlich abweichender Vereinbarung

329. **working agreement**
modus vivendi
modus vivendi
modus vivendi; Arbeitsabkommen

330. **written agreement**
convention en écrit
acuerdo escrito
schriftliches Abkommen

331. **to abide by the terms of an agreement**
se conformer aux clauses d'un accord
sujetarse a los términos del convenio
die Vertragsbestimmungen befolgen

332. **to agree**
être d'accord; s'accorder
acordar; convenir
übereinstimmen; zustimmen; vereinbaren

333. **to come to an agreement**
aboutir à un accord; arriver à une entente
llegar a un acuerdo
zu einer Übereinstimmung gelangen

334. **aid**
aide (f); secours (m)
ayuda (f); auxilio (m)
Hilfe (f)

335. **financial aid**
assistance financière
asistencia, ayuda financiera; subsidio
finanzielle Unterstützung; Finanzhilfe
336. **legal aid**
assistance légale
asistencia legal
Rechtshilfe
337. **aide-memoire**
aide-mémoire (m)
memorandum (m)
Denkschrift (f)
338. **aider and abettor**
complice (m)
cómplice (m)
Mittäter (m); Komplize (m)
339. **aim**
but (m); objet (m)
meta (f); objeto (m)
Ziel (n)
340. **air**
air (m)
aire (m)
Luft (f)
341. **aircraft**
aéronef (m)
aeronave (f)
Luftfahrzeug (n)
342. **air force**
forces aériennes (fpl)
fuerzas aéreas (fpl)
Luftwaffe (f)
343. **airlift**
pont (m) aérien
puente (m) aéreo
Luftbrücke (f)
344. **airport**
aéroport (m)
aeropuerto (m)
Flughafen (m)
345. **air raid**
raid (m) aérien
bombardeo (m) aéreo
Luftangriff (m)
346. **airspace**
espace (m) aérien
espacio (m) aéreo
Luftraum (m)
347. **alcoholic**
alcoolique (m)
alcohólico (m)
Alkoholiker (m)
348. **alderman**
conseiller (m) municipal
concejal (m); consejero (m) municipal; regidor (m)
Stadtrat (m)
349. **alias**
alias (m); autrement dit
alias (m); conocido por
alias (n); sonst ... genannt
350. **to go under several aliases**
avoir plus d'un nom d'emprunt
tener varios nombres supuestos
falsche Namen führen
351. **alibi**
alibi (m)
coartada (f)
Alibi (n)
352. **to establish an alibi**
prouver un alibi
probar una coartada
ein Alibi nachweisen
353. **to produce an alibi**
fournir un alibi
presentar una coartada
ein Alibi beibringen
354. **alien**
étranger (m)
extranjero (m)
Ausländer (m)
355. **alien enemy**
ressortissant (m) ennemi
extranjero (m) enemigo
Staatsangehöriger (m) einer feindlichen Macht; feindlicher Ausländer
356. **resident alien**
étranger immigré
extranjero residente
Ausländer mit Aufenthaltsgenehmigung
357. **alien property custodian**
administrateur séquestre de biens étrangers
custodio de propiedad extranjera
Verwalter ausländischen Vermögens
358. **alienation**

aliénation (f)
enajenación (f)
Veräusserung (f); Entfremdung (f)

359. **alienation of affection**
aliénation, détournement d'affection
enajenación de afectos
Entfremdung der Zuneigung

360. **alienation of property**
aliénation de biens
enajenación de bienes
Eigentumsveräussung; -übertragung

361. **mental alienation**
aliénation mentale
enajenación mental
Geistesgestörtheit

362. **to alienate**
aliéner
enajenar
entfremden; veräussern

363. **alimony**
pension alimentaire
pensión alimenticia
Alimente; Unterhalt

364. **to pay alimony**
fournir des aliments
pagar alimentos
Unterhalt gewähren, zahlen

365. **allegation**
allégation (f)
alegato (m); alegación (f)
Angabe (f); Behauptung (f)

366. **alleged**
prétendu
alegado
angeblich; vorgeblich

367. **to allege**
alléguer; prétendre
alegar
aussagen; behaupten

368. **allegiance**
allégeance (f); fidélité (f)
fidelidad (f); lealtad (f)
Treuepflicht (f); Treueverhältnis (n)

369. **to swear allegiance**
prêter serment d'allégeance, de fidélité
jurar fidelidad
den Treueid ablegen; Treue schwören

370. **alliance**
alliance (f)
alianza (f)
Allianz (f)

371. **Alliance for Progress**
Alliance pour le Progrès
Alianza para el Progreso
Allianz für den Fortschritt

372. **allocation; allotment**
affectation (f); allocation (f)
asignación (f)
Anweisung (f); Zuteilung (f)

373. **to allocate; to allot**
affecter; allouer
asignar
anweisen; zuteilen

374. **allonge**
allonge (f)
añadido (m)
Allonge (f)

375. **allowance**
allocation (f); autorisation (f); pension (f)
concesión (f); pensión (f); permiso (m)
Bewilligung (f); Anerkennung (f); Vergütung (f)

376. **allowance for necessaries**
pension alimentaire
pensión alimenticia
Alimente; Unterhalt

377. **entertainment allowance**
frais de représentation
gastos de representación
Dienstauswandsentschädigung

378. **per diem allowance**
indemnité (f) journalière
viático (m)
Tagegeld (n)

379. **subsistence allowance**
indemnité de séjour
indemnización por desplazamiento
Aufenthaltsvergütung (f)

380. **tax allowance**
dégrèvement (m)
deducción (f)
Steuerbegünstigung (f)

381. **traveling allowance**

frais de route
gastos de viaje
Reisekostenvergütung

382. **to make allowance for**
tenir compte de
tener en cuenta
zugutehalten

383. **to allow**
autoriser; permettre
autorizar; permitir
bewilligen; erlauben

384. **alluvion; alluvium**
alluvión (m)
aluvión (m)
Alluvion (n); Anschwemmung (f)

385. **Ally**
allié (m)
aliado (m)
Alliierter (m); Verbündeter (m)

386. **allied**
allié
aliado
alliiert; verbündet

387. **Allied and Associated Powers**
Puissances alliées et associées
Potencias Aliadas y Asociadas
Alliierte und Assoziierte Mächte

388. **alms**
aumône (f)
limosna (f)
Almosen (n)

389. **almshouse**
asile (m) d'indigents
asilo (m) de pobres
Armenhaus (n)

390. **alteration**
altération (f); modification (f)
alteración (f); modificación (f)
Änderung (f); Veränderung (f)

391. **to alter**
changer; remanier
alterar
ändern; verändern

392. **altercation**
altercation (f); dispute (f)
altercación (f); disputa (f)
Wortwechsel (m)

393. **alternat**
alternat (m)
alternancia (f)
Alternat (n)

394. **alternate**
substitut (m); suppléant (m)
substituto (m); suplente (m, f)
Ersatzmann (m); Stellvertreter (m)

395. **alternative**
alternative
alternativo
Alternative

396. **amalgamation**
fusion (f); mélange (m)
amalgama (f)
Fusion (f); Verschmelzung (f)

397. **to amalgamate**
fusionner; mélanger
amalgamar
verschmelzen

398. **amanuensis**
secrétaire (à la main)
amanuense (m)
Amanuensis (m)

399. **ambassador**
ambassadeur (m)
embajador (m)
Botschafter (m)

400. **ambassador-at-large**
ambassadeur itinérant
embajador visitador
Sonderbotschafter

401. **to accredit an ambassador**
accréditer un ambassadeur
acreditar a un embajador
einen Botschafter beglaubigen

402. **ambiguity**
ambiguité (f); équivoque (f)
ambigüedad (f); equívoco (m)
Zweideutigkeit (f)

403. **ambiguous**
ambigu; équivoque
ambiguo
zweideutig

404. **latent ambiguity**
ambiguité latente
ambigüidad latente
latente Zweideutigkeit

405. **amelioration**
amélioration (f)
mejoramiento (m)
Verbesserung (f)

406. **to ameliorate**
améliorer
mejorar

verbessern
407. **amenable**
responsable
responsable
verantwortlich
408. **amendment**
amendement (m)
enmienda (f)
Abänderung (f); Zusatzantrag (m)
409. **as amended**
ainsi modifié
como fué enmendado
wie ergänzt; wie richtiggestellt
410. **to adopt an amendment**
accepter un amendement
aceptar una enmienda
einen Ergänzungs- Abänderungs- antrag anerkennen
411. **to amend**
amender; rectifier
enmendar; corregir
ergänzen; verbessern; richtigstellen
412. **amends**
compensation (f); dédommagement (m)
compensación (f); recompensa (f)
Schadenersatz (m); Vergütung (f)
413. **to make amends**
dédommager; réparer
dar cumplida satisfacción
Schadenersatz leisten
414. **amercement**
amende (f); peine (f)
multa (f)
Geldstrafe (f)
415. **amicable**
amiable
amigable; amistoso
freundlich; freundschaftlich
416. **amity**
amitié (f); bons rapports (m, pl)
amistad (f); harmonía (f)
Freundschaft (f); gute Beziehungen (f, pl)
417. **amnesty**
amnistie (f)
amnistía (f)
Amnestie (f)
418. **to grant amnesty to**
amnistier
amnistiar
amnestieren
419. **amortization**
amortissement (m)
amortización (f)
Amortisation (f); Tilgung (f)
420. **to amortize**
amortir
amortizar
amortisieren; tilgen
421. **amount**
montant (m); quantité (f); somme (f)
cantidad (f); monto (m); suma (f)
Betrag (m); Summe (f); Bestand (m)
422. **amount in controversy, in dispute**
somme en litige
suma en litigio
Streitbetrag
423. **to amount to**
valoir; se monter à
valer; ascender a
betragen; sich belaufen auf
424. **analogy**
analogie (f)
analogía (f)
Analogie (f)
425. **analagous**
analogue
análogo
analog
426. **analysis**
analyse (f)
análisis (m)
Analyse (f)
427. **analyst**
analyste (m)
analizador (m)
Analytiker (m)
428. **analytical**
analytique
analítico
analytisch
429. **to analyse**
analyser
analizar
analysieren
430. **anarchy**
anarchie (f)

anarquía (f)
Anarchie (f)

431. **anarchist**
anarchiste (m)
anarquista (m)
Anarchist (m)

432. **ancestry**
ancêtres (mpl); race (f)
linaje (m); prosapia (f)
Vorfahren (m); Ahnen (mpl)

433. **ancestor**
ancêtre (m); aïeul (m)
antepasado (m)
Vorfahre (m); Ahne (m)

434. **ancestral**
héréditaire
solariego
angestammt

435. **lineal ancestor**
ascendant (m) en ligne directe
ascendiente (m) directo
Vorfahre in gerader Linie

436. **ancient lights**
vues anciennes; servitude (f) de jour
servidumbre (f) de luces
Recht (n) auf Licht; Licht- und Fensterrecht (n)

437. **ancient writings**
documents de 30 ans ou plus
documentos de más de 30 años de edad
alte Urkunden

438. **ancillary**
subordonné
subordinado
untergeordnet

439. **angary**
angarie (f)
angaria (f)
Angarienrecht (n)

440. **anguish**
angoisse (f)
angustia (f)
Angst (f)

441. **mental anguish**
torture (f) mentale
tortura (f) mental
seelisches Leiden (n)

442. **animus**
esprit (m); intention (f)
ánimo (m)
Absicht (f); Geist (m)

443. **annexation**
annexion (f)
anexión (f)
Annexion (f); Einverleibung (f)

444. **annex**
annexe (f)
anexo (m)
Anhang (m); Nachtrag (m)

445. **to annex**
annexer; ajouter
anexar; añadir
annektieren; einverleiben

446. **annihilation**
anéantissement (m); destruction (f)
aniquilación (f)
Vernichtung (f)

447. **to annihilate**
anéantir; détruire
aniquilar
vernichten

448. **annotation**
annotation (f)
anotación (f)
Anmerkung (f); Kommentar (m)

449. **to annotate**
annoter
anotar
mit Anmerkungen versehen; kommentieren

450. **announcement**
annonce (f); communication (f); proclamation (f)
declaración (f); prospecto (m)
Ankündigung (f)

451. **announcement of death**
avis (m) de décès (m)
aviso (m) de defunción (f)
Todesanzeige (f)

452. **announcement of marriage**
faire-part (m) de mariage (m)
aviso de matrimonio (m)
Heiratsanzeige (f)

453. **annuity**
annuité (f); rente (f)
anualidad (f); renta (f)
Annuität (f); Rente (f)

454. **annuitant**
rentier (m)

pensionista (m); rentista (m, f)
Rentner (m); Rentenempfänger (m)

455. **government annuity**
rente sur l'Etat
pensión anual del gobierno
Staatsrente

456. **life annuity**
rente viagère
pensión, renta vitalicia
Lebensrente; Leibrente

457. **annulment**
annulation (f); cassation (f)
anulación (f); casación (f)
Aufhebung (f); Ungültigkeitserklärung (f)

458. **to annul**
annuler; casser
anular
aufheben; für ungültig erklären

459. **anonymity**
anonymat (m)
anonimato (m)
Anonymität (f)

460. **anonymous**
anonyme
anónimo
namenlos; anonym

461. **answer**
réplique (f); réponse (f)
réplica (f); respuesta (f)
Antwort (f); Klagebeantwortung (f)

462. **answer to a charge**
réfutation d'une accusation (f)
descargo (m)
Klagebeantwortung (f)

463. **answerable**
responsable
responsable
verantwortlich

464. **to answer**
répliquer; repondre
comparecer; responder
antworten; beantworten

465. **antecedent**
antécédent
antecedente
vorhergehend; früher

466. **antecedents**
antécédents (mpl)
antecedentes (mpl)
vorhergehende Umstände (mpl); Vorgeschichte (f)

467. **antedate, to**
antidater
antedatar; retrotraer
vor- oder zurückdatieren

468. **anticipation**
anticipation (f); expectative (f)
anticipación (f); expectación (f)
Vorgreifen (n); Vorwegnahme (f)

469. **anticipatory**
anticipé; par anticipation
anticipado; que anticipa
vorwegnehmend; in Vorwegnahme von

470. **to anticipate**
anticiper; s'attendre à
anticipar, anticiparse
vorgreifen; vorwegnehmen

471. **apartheid**
ségregation (f) raciale
segregación (f) racial
Rassentrennung (f)

472. **apology**
excuse (f)
excusa (f)
Entschuldigung (f)

473. **apparent**
apparent; évident; manifeste
aparente; evidente
scheinbar; augenscheinlich; offenbar

474. **appeal**
appel (m); pourvoi (m) en cassation (f); recours (m)
apelación (f); recurso (m)
Berufung (f); Beschwerde (f); Revision (f)

475. **appelant**
appelant (m)
apelante (m)
Beschwerdeführer (m)

476. **appellee**
intimé (m)
demandado (m); apelado (m)
Berufungsbeklagter (m)

477. **ground for appeal**
motif (m) d'appel (m)
motivo (m) de apelación (f)
Rechtsmittelbegründung (f)

478. **right of appeal**
droit de recours (m)

derecho de recurso (m)
Berufungsrecht (n)

479. **without appeal**
sans recours
sin recurso
in letzter Instanz; ohne Rechtsmittel, Berufungsmöglichkeit

480. **to appeal**
faire, interjeter appel; se pourvoir en cassation
apelar; recurrir a
appellieren; Berufung einlegen

481. **to dimiss an appeal**
rejeter l'appel
desechar un recurso de apelación
eine Berufung verwerfen

482. **appearance (in court)**
comparution (f)
comparecencia (f)
Erscheinen (n) (vor Gericht)

483. **special appearance**
comparution aux seules fins de contester la compétence du tribunal
comparecencia exclusivamente para objetar la competencia del tribunal
Erscheinen vor Gericht zum Zweck der Zuständigkeitsbestreitung

484. **appeasement**
apaisement (m)
apaciguamiento (m)
Beschwichtigung (f)

485. **to appease**
apaiser
apaciguar
beschwichtigen

486. **appendix**
annexe (f); appendice (m)
anexo (m); apéndice (m)
Anhang (m); Anlage (f)

487. **to append**
ajouter; annexer; joindre à
añadir; anexar
beiflügen

488. **appertaining to**
appartenant, relevant, à
perteneciente, relativo, a
zustehend; sich beziehend auf

489. **applicability**
portée (f)
aplicabilidad (f)
Anwendbarkeit (f)

490. **applicable**
applicable
aplicable
anwendbar

491. **when applicable**
chaque fois qu'il convient
cuando sea aplicable
wenn anwendbar

492. **application**
demande (f); requête (f)
petición (f); solicitud (f)
Antrag (m); Gesuch (n)

493. **applicant**
candidat (m); demandeur (m)
solicitante (m); aspirante (m)
Antragsteller (m); Bewerber (m)

494. **upon application**
sur demande
a solicitud
auf Antrag

495. **to apply in writing**
présenter une requête écrite
presentar una solicitud por escrito
schriftlich ansuchen

496. **to grant an application**
admettre, faire droit à, une requête
conceder una solicitud
einem Antrag stattgeben

497. **to make an application**
faire une demande; présenter une requête
hacer, presentar, una solicitud
beantragen; einen Antrag stellen

498. **appointment**
désignation (f); engagement (m)
designación (f); nombramiento (m)
Ernennung (f); Bestellung (f)

499. **appointee**
personne désignée
nombrado
Ernannter

500. **to appoint**
designer comme; nommer
designar; nombrar
ernennen; bestimmen

501. **apportionment**
partage; répartion
prorrateo (m); repartición (f)
proportionelle Verteilung (f); Zuteilung (f)

502. **to apportion**
partager; répartir
prorratear; repartir
verhältnismässig verteilen; zulen

503. **appraisal; appraisement**
estimation (f); évaluation (f)
estimación (f); valuación (f); tasación (f)
Schätzung (f); Bewertung (f)

504. **appraiser**
commissaire-priseur (m); expert (m)
avaluador (m); tasador (m)
Abschätzer (m); Taxator (m)

505. **to appraise**
estimer; évaluer
estimar; valuar; tasar
abschätzen; taxieren

506. **appreciation**
appréciation (f); hausse (f) de valeurs (fpl)
aprecio (m); incremento (m)
Schätzung (f)

507. **to appreciate**
apprécier
apreciar
schätzen

508. **apprehension**
appréhension (f); arrestation (f)
crainte (f)
aprehensión (f); captura (f); temor (m)
Festnahme (f); Verhaftung (f); Furcht (f)

509. **apprehension of a criminal**
arrêt d'un criminel, délinquant
arresto, detención de un criminal, delincuente
Festnahme eines Verbrechers

510. **apprehensive**
craintif
aprehensivo
furchtsam

511. **to apprehend**
arrêter; craindre
aprehender; temer
festnehmen; verhaften

512. **apprenticeship**
apprentissage (m)
aprendizaje (m)
Lehrzeit (f)

513. **apprentice**
apprenti (m)
aprendiz (m)
Lehrling (m)

514. **apprise, to**
mettre au courant
informar
in Kenntnis setzen

515. **approbation**
approbation (f)
aprobación (f)
Billigung (f)

516. **appropriate**
approprié; convenable
apropiado; apto
angemessen

517. **appropriation**
affectation (f) de crédit (m), fonds (mpl)
asignación (f) de fondos (mpl)
(Geld) Bewilligung (f)

518. **to appropriate**
affecter; approprier
asignar
bewilligen; bestimmen

519. **approval**
agrément (m); approbation (f); assentiment (m)
aprobación (f); sanción (f)
Billigung (f); Zustimmung (f)

520. **to approve**
approuver; donner son assentiment
aprobar; dar el visto bueno
billigen; zustimmen

521. **approximation**
approximation (f)
aproximación (f)
Angleichung (f)

522. **approximate**
approximatif
aproximado
annähernd; ungefähr

523. **appurtenance**
appartenance (f); droit (m) accéssoire
dependencia (f); pertenencia (f)

Zubehör (n)

524. **arbitrary**
arbitraire
arbitrario
willkürlich

525. **arbitration**
arbitrage (m)
arbitraje (m)
Schiedsverfahren (n)

526. **arbitrable**
susceptible d'arbitrage
arbitrable
für ein Schiedsverfahren geeignet

527. **arbitral award; arbitrament**
sentence (f) arbitrale
laudo (m) arbitral
Schiedsspruch (m)

528. **arbitrator; arbiter**
arbitre (m); amiable compositeur (m)
arbitrador (m); árbitro (m)
Schiedsrichter (m)

529. **commercial arbitration**
arbitrage commercial
arbitraje comercial
Handelsschiedsgerichtbarkeit

530. **to arbitrate**
arbitrer
arbitrar
schiedsgerichtlich entscheiden; schlichten

531. **archives**
archives (fpl)
archivos (mpl)
Archiv (n); Urkundensammlung (f)

532. **archivist**
archiviste (m)
archivero (m)
Archivar (m)

533. **area**
aire (f); étendue (f); surface (f)
área (f); espacio (m); superficie (f)
Bereich (n); Gebiet (n)

534. **area of agreement**
marge (f), portée d'accord
puntos (mpl) no controvertidos
Bereich des Abkommens (n)

535. **area of disagreement**
marge (f); (portée) de désaccord
puntos (mpl) controvertidos
strittiger Punkt (m)

536. **areas of responsibility**
zones de responsabilité (f)
áreas de responsabilidad (f)
Verantwortungsbereich (m)

537. **argument**
argument (m); discussion (f); controverse (f)
argumento (m); discusión (f); controversia (f)
Argument (n); Beweisgrund (m); Streitfrage (f)

538. **arguable**
disputable
controvertible
diskutierbar

539. **oral argument**
plaidoirie (f)
alegato (m)
mündliches Verfahren (n); Plädoyer (n)

540. **to argue**
débattre; discuter; exposer
argüir; discutir; disputar
argumentieren; bestreiten; begründen; erörtern

541. **to argue for**
plaider en faveur de
argumentar por
Gründe anführen für

542. **argumentative**
argumentateur
argumentador; arguyente
polemisch; streitsüchtig

543. **armistice**
armistice (m)
armisticio (m)
Waffenstillstand (m)

544. **arms; armament**
armement (m)
armamentos (m, pl)
Rüstung (f)

545. **armed forces**
force (f) armée (f)
fuerzas (fpl) armadas
Streitkräfte (fpl); Bundeswehr (f)

546. **armed resistance**
résistance (f) armée

resistencia (f) armada
bewaffneter Widerstand (m)

547. **arms race**
course (f) aux armaments
carrera (f) a los armamentos
Wettrüsten (n)

548. **limitation of armaments**
limitation (f) des armements
limitación (f) de armamentos
Rüstungsbeschränkung (f)

549. **to bear arms**
porter des armes; servir dans l'armée
portar armas; llevar las armas
Waffen tragen; beim Militär dienen

550. **army**
armée (f)
ajército (m)
Armee (f); Heer (n)

551. **arraignment**
mise (f) en accusation
acusación (f); denuncia (f)
Anklage (f)

552. **to arraign**
mettre en accusation; traduire en justice
acusar; denunciar
anklagen; in den Anklagestand versetzen

553. **arrangement**
accord (m); entente (f)
arreglo (m); disposición (f)
Abkommen (n); Übereinkommen (n)

554. **interim arrangements**
dispositions (fpl); provisoires
disposiciones (fpl) provisorias
vorläufiges Abkommen

555. **array**
liste (f) des jurés (mpl)
lista (f) de los jurados (mpl)
Dienstliste (f) der Geschworenen, Schöffen (mpl)

556. **arrears; arrearages**
arriérés (mpl)
atrasos (mpl)
Rückstände (mpl)

557. **arrest**
arrestation (f)
arresto (m); detención (f)
Haft (f); Festnahme (f); Verhaftung (f)

558. **under arrest**
en état d'arrestation
detenido; preso
in Haft

559. **wholesale arrests**
arrestations en masse
arresto en masa
Massenverhaftungen

560. **to arrest; to put under arrest**
arrêter
arrestar; detener
festnehmen; verhaften

561. **to resist arrest**
résister à une arrestation
resistir a la autoridad
der Verhaftung Widerstand leisten

562. **arson**
incendie (m) volontaire
incendio (m) doloso
Brandstiftung (f)

563. **art**
art (m)
arte (m, f)
Kunst (f)

564. **fine arts**
beaux arts
bellas artes
schöne Künste

565. **industrial arts**
arts industriels
artes industriales
Kunstgewerbe

566. **prior art; patent law**
antériorité (f)
arte (m) anterior
Stand (m) der Technik (f)

567. **article**
article; clause (f)
artículo (m); cláusula (f)
Artikel (m); Paragraph (m)

568. **articles of association, of incorporation**
statuts (m) d'une société (f)
estatutos (mpl), de una sociedad (f)
Gründungsprotokoll (n)

569. **artificial**
artificiel

artificial
künstlich

570. **ascertainment**
vérification (f)
averiguación (f)
Ermittlung (f); Feststellung (f)

571. **ascertainable**
vérifiable
averiguable
bestimmbar

572. **to ascertain**
arriver à savoir; vérifier
averiguar; informarse; verificar
ermitteln; sich vergewissern

573. **ascribe, to**
imputer;
atribuir
zuschreiben

574. **aspect**
aspect (m)
aspecto (m)
Aspekt (m); Seite (f)

575. **aspersion**
diffamation (f)
difamación (f)
Verleumdung (f); Ehrenbeleidigung (f)

576. **to cast aspersion on**
diffamer
difamar
verleumden; beleidigen

577. **asportation**
emport (m) d'un objet (m) volé
acarreo (m) de bienes (mpl) robados
widerrechtliche Wegschaffung (f) einer fremden Sache (f)

578. **assailant**
assaillant (m); agresseur (m)
asaltador (m); agresor (m)
Angreifer (m)

579. **assassination**
assassinat (m)
asesinato (m)
Mord (m); Ermordung (f)

580. **assassin**
assassin (m)
asesino (m)
Mörder (m)

581. **to assassinate**
assassiner
asesinar
ermorden

582. **assault**
assaut (m); attaque (f); menaces (f, pl)
asalto (m); ataque (m); amenaza (f)
tätlicher Angriff (m); Gewalttätigkeit (f)

583. **aggravated assault**
actes (m) de violence (f) caractérisés
acometimiento (m) grave
tätliche Beleidigung (f)

584. **assault and battery**
voies (mpl) de fait; coups (mpl) et blessures (fpl)
vías (fpl) de hecho (m)
Körperverletzung (f); gewalttätiger Angriff (m)

585. **assault with a deadly weapon**
attaque armée
asalto a mano armada
tötlicher Angriff mittels einer Waffe

586. **assault with intent to commit a felony**
voies de fait avec intention criminelle
asalto con intención criminal
vorsätzlicher schwere Körperverletzung

587. **criminal, indecent assault**
attentat (m) à la pudeur (f)
atentado (m) contra la moral (f)
Sittlichkeitsverbrechen (n)

588. **to assault**
se livrer à des voies de fait
amenazar; asaltar
tätlich angreifen

589. **assembly**
assemblée (f)
asamblea (f)
Versammlung (f)

590. **general assembly**
assemblée générale
assamblea general
Generalversammlung

591. **legislative assembly**
assemblée (f) législative; parlement (m)
cuerpo (m) legislativo; parlamento (m)

gesetzgebende Versammlung (f); Parlament (n)
592. **right of assembly**
droit de réunion
derecho de asamblea, de reunión
Versammlungsrecht (n)
593. **unlawful assembly**
attroupement (m) séditieux
reunión (f) ilegal
illegale Versammlung (f)
594. **assent**
approbation (f); assentiment (m)
aprobación (f); asentimiento (m)
Einwilligung (f); Zustimmung (f)
595. **mutual assent; consent**
commun accord (m)
mutuo acuerdo (m)
gegenseitiges Einvernehmen (n)
596. **to assent**
approuver; donner son assentiment
approbar; sentir
einwilligen; zustimmen
597. **assertion**
assertion (f)
aserción (f)
Behauptung (f)
598. **to assert**
affirmer; déclarer
afirmar; mantener
behaupten
599. **assessment**
imposition (f); répartition (f); assiete (f)
amillaramiento (m); derrama (f); fijación (f)
Einschätzung (f); Feststellung (f); Veranlagung (f)
600. **assessor**
juge (m) assesseur; repartiteur (m)
amillarador (m); tasador (m)
Assessor (m); Steuerabschätzer (m)
601. **to assess**
coter; évaluer; imposer
amillarar; avaluar; tasar
einschätzen; besteuern; veranlagen
602. **assets**
actif (m); avoirs (mpl); biens (mpl); patrimoine (m)
activo (m); bienes (mpl); patrimonio (m)
Aktiva; Eigentum; Vermögen
603. **assets and liabilities**
actif (m) et passif (m)
activo (m) y pasivo (m)
Aktiva (npl) und Passiva (npl); Soll (n) und Haben (n)
604. **business assets**
fonds (mpl) de commerce (m)
fondos (mpl) commerciales
Betriebsvermögen (n)
605. **capital assets**
biens de capital
bienes de capital
Anlagevermögen
606. **frozen assets**
avoirs bloqués
fondos congelados
blockierte Gelder (npl); eingefrorene Guthaben (npl)
607. **liquid assets**
avoirs disponibles; disponibilités
activo líquido
bares Vermögen; verfügbares Guthaben
608. **personal assets**
biens mobiliers
bienes muebles
bewegliches Vermögen
609. **real assets**
biens immobiliers
bienes raíces
Immobiliarvermögen
610. **tangible assets**
valeurs matérielles
fondos convertibles en dinero o valores
greifbare Werte
611. **assignment**
assignation (f); cession (f); endossement (m); transfer (m)
asignación (f); cesión (f); traslación (f) de dominio (m)
Abtretung (f); Anweisung (f); Übertragung (f); Zession (f)
612. **assignee**
bénéficiaire (m); cessionnaire (m); mandataire (mpl)
apoderado (m); cesionario (m);

síndico (m)
Bevollmächtigter (m); Zessionar (m)

613. **assignment for benefit of creditors**
cession en faveur des créditeurs (mpl)
cesión de bienes para beneficio de acreedores (mpl)
(ausserkonkursrechtliche) Geschäftsabwicklung durch privatgeschäftlich bestellten Vertreter

614. **assignor**
cédant (m); disposant (m)
cedente (m); cesionista (m, f)
Abtreter (m); Zedent (m)

615. **assigns**
ayants (mpl) droit
cesionarios (mpl); sucesores (mpl)
Rechtsnachfolger (mpl)

616. **to assign**
assigner; céder; transférer
asignar; ceder; traspasar
abtreten; übertragen; zedieren

617. **assistance**
aide (f); assistance (f); secours (m)
auxilio (m); ayuda (f); socorro (m)
Beistand (m); Hilfe (f); Unterstützung (f)

618. **assistant**
auxiliaire (m); adjoint (m)
auxiliar (m); ayudante (m)
Gehilfe (m); Assistent (m)

619. **mutual assistance**
assistance mutuelle
asistencia, ayuda mutua
gegenseitiger Beistand

620. **to assist**
aider
auxiliar; ayudar
beistehen; helfen

621. **association**
association (f)
asociación (f)
Verein (m); Genossenschaft (f)
Verband (m)

622. **associate**
associé (m); adjoint (m)
asociado (m); socio (m)
Gesellschafter (m); Teilhaber (m)

623. **bar association**
ordre (m) des avocats (mpl)
colegio (m) de abogados (mpl)
Rechtsanwaltkammer (f)

624. **benelovent, charitable, association**
association de bienfaisance (f)
asociación de beneficencia (f)
Wohltätigkeitsverein (m)

625. **unincorporated association**
association sans personnalité civile
sociedad no inscrita en registros
eine nicht ins Handelsregister eingetragene Gesellschaft

626. **to associate**
s'associer
asociarse; unirse
einen Verein, eine Gesellschaft, gründen

627. **assumpsit** (see **action** of assumpsit)

628. **assumption**
présomption (f); supposition (f)
presunción (f); suposición (f)
Voraussetzung (f); Annahme (f)

629. **assumed**
faux; supposé
fingido; supuesto
vorausgesetzt; angenommen

630. **assumption of risk**
acceptation (f) de risque (m)
asunción (f) del riesgo (m)
Risikoübernahme (f)

631. **to assume**
assumer; supposer; s'arroger
asumir; presumir; suponer; arrogarse
voraussetzen; annehmen; übernehmen

632. **asylum**
asile (m); hospice (m)
asilo (m); refugio (m)
Asyl (n)

633. **diplomatic asylum**
asile diplomatique
asilo diplomático

diplomatisches Asyl
634. **inmate of a lunatic asylum**
aliéné (m) interné
recluso (m) de un manicomio (m)
Insasse (m) einer Irrenanstalt (f)
635. **lunatic asylum**
maison (f) d'aliénés (mpl)
manicomio (m)
Irrenanstalt (f)
636. **orphanasylum; orphanage**
orphelinat (m)
orfanato (m)
Waisenhaus (n)
637. **territorial asylum**
asile (m) territorial
asilo (m) territorial
Territorialasyl (n)
638. **atmosphere**
ambiance (f); climat (m)
medio (m) ambiente; clima (m)
Stimmung (f); Klima (n); Atmosphäre (f)
639. **atomic energy**
énérgie atomique
energía atómica
Atomenergie (f)
640. **atrocity**
atrocité (f)
atrocidad (f)
Greueltat (f)
641. **attaché**
attaché (m)
agregado (m)
Attaché (m)
642. **attachment** (see also **writ** of attachment)
annexe (f); mainmise (f); saisie-arrêt (f)
embargo (m); secuestro (m)
Beschlagnahme (f); Pfändung (f)
643. **attachment of real property**
saisie d'immeubles (mpl)
secuestro de inmuebles (mpl)
Zwangsvollstreckung (f) in das unbewegliche Vermögen
644. **to attach**
attacher; saisir
atribuir; embargar; secuestrar
pfänden; in Beschlag nehmen
645. **attack**
attaque (f)
ataque (m)
Angriff (m)
646. **collateral attack**
allégation de nullité radicale
acción colateral; alegato de nulidad
Angriff auf ein Urteil ausserhalb des betreffenden Verfahrens
647. **surprise attack**
attaque par surprise
ataque por sorpresa
Überfall
648. **to attack**
attaquer
atacar
angreifen
649. **attainder** (see also **bill of attainder**)
extinction de droits civils et politiques
extinción de derechos civiles; muerte civil
Verlust der bürgerlichen und politischen Rechte infolge Urteils
650. **attainment**
capacité (f)
adquisición (f)
Fertigkeit (f); Kenntnis (f)
651. **attempt**
essai (m); tentative (f)
tentativa (f)
Versuch (m)
652. **criminal attempt**
attentat (m)
atentado (m)
verbrecherischer Anschlag (m)
653. **attendance**
audience (f); assistance (f); présence (f)
auditorio (m); asistencia (f)
Zubehörschaft (f); Anwesenheit (f); Teilnahme (f)
654. **to attend**
assister; être présent; prendre part
asistir; estar presente; tomar parte
besuchen; teilnehmen an
655. **attention**
attention (f)
atención (f)

Aufmerksamkeit (f)

656. **to call attention to**
signaler; souligner
llamar la atención sobre
Aufmerksamkeit lenken auf

657. **to pay attention**
tenir compte
prestar atención
Aufmerksamkeit schenken

658. **attenuation**
atténuation (f)
atenuación (f)
Verminderung (f)

659. **attestation**
attestation (f)
atestación (f)
Bescheinigung (f); Zeugnis (n)

660. **attested**
certifié
certificado
beglaubigt

661. **to attest**
attester
atestar
bescheinigen; bezeugen; beglaubigen

662. **attorney**
avocat (m); avoué (m); procureur (m)
abogado (m); apoderado (m); procurador (m)
Anwalt (m); Bevollmächtigter (m)

663. **Attorney-General (U.S.A.)**
Ministre de la Justice; Procureur-Général
Ministro de Justicia; Procurador General
Justizminister; Generalstaatsanwalt

664. **district attorney**
procureur (m) de la République
fiscal (m)
Staatsanwalt (m)

665. **patent attorney; lawyer**
avocat spécialisé en brevets (mpl)
abogado de patentes (mpl)
Patentanwalt (m)

666. **state's attorney (U.S.A.)**
procureur
abogado fiscal
Staatsanwalt eines Einzelstaates

667. **attornment**
reconnaissance par un locataire des droits d'un nouveau propriétaire
reconocimiento por el arrendatario de los derechos del nuevo propietario
Anerkennung eines neuen Gutsherrn

668. **attrition**
attrition (f)
atrición (f)
Zermürbung (f)

669. **auction**
vente (f) aux enchères (fpl)
remate (m); subasta (f)
Auktion (f); Versteigerung (f)

670. **auctioneer**
commissaire-priseur (m)
subastador (m)
Auktionator (m); Versteigerer (m)

671. **to knock down at auction**
adjuger au dernier enchérisseur
adjudicar en subasta
bei einer Auktion zuschlagen

672. **to put up for auction**
mettre aux enchères
poner a pública subasta
öffentlich versteigern

673. **audience**
audience (f)
audiencia (f)
Audienz (f)

674. **audit**
vérification (f) des comptes (mpl)
intervención (f) y ajuste (m) de cuentas (fpl)
Buchprüfung (f); Rechnungsprüfung (f)

675. **auditor**
commissaire (m) aux, verificateur des, comptes
auditor (m), interventor (m) de cuentas (fpl)
Buchprüfer (m); Rechnungsprüfer (m)

676. **to audit**
apurer; vérifier
intervenir, revisar, una cuenta

prüfen
677. **augmentation**
augmentation (f)
aumento (m)
Zuwachs (m)
678. **to augment**
augmenter
aumentar
vergrössern
679. **autarchy**
autarchie (f)
autarquía (f)
Autarkie (f); wirtschaftliche Selbstgenügsamkeit (f)
680. **authentication**
authentification (f)
autenticación (f)
Beglaubigung (f); Legalisierung (f)
681. **authentic**
authentique
auténtico
authentisch
682. **authenticity**
authenticité (f)
autenticidad (f)
Authentizität (f); Echtheit (f)
683. **to authenticate**
authentifier
autenticar
beglaubigen
684. **author**
auteur (m)
autor (m)
Urheber (m); Verfasser (m)
685. **authoritarian**
autoritaire
autoritario
autoritär
686. **authority**
autorité (f); pouvoir (m); source (f)
autoridad (f); poder (m)
Autorität (f); Gewalt (f); Vollmacht (f)
687. **abuse of authority**
abus d'autorité
abuso de autoridad
Amtmissbrauch
688. **apparent authority**
autorité apparente
autoridad aparente
stillschweigende Vollmacht; Rechtsscheinvollmacht; scheinbare Vertretungsmacht
689. **assumption of authority**
présomption d'autorité; prise de pouvoir
arrogación de facultades, de poder
Amtsanmassung
690. **delegation of authority**
délégation de pouvoir
delegación de autoridad
Bevollmächtigung
691. **having equal authority**
ayant même authorité; faisant également loi
con igual autoridad
mit gleicher Vollmacht; gleicherweise massgebend
692. **local authorities**
collectivités (f) publiques territoriales
autoridades locales (fpl)
Ortsbehörden (fpl)
693. **parental authority**
puissance paternelle
patria potestad'
elterliche, väterliche Gewalt
694. **public authority**
autorité publique
autoridad pública
öffentliche Gewalt
695. **reviewing authority**
autorité chargée de vérifications
autoridad fiscalizadora
Überprüfungsinstanz
696. **usurpation of authority**
empiètement d'autorité
ursurpación de autoridad
rechtswidrige Anmassung der Befugnis
697. **to be authoritative**
faire foi, loi; être péremptoire
ser autoritatativo; hacer fe
massgebend sein
698. **to have authority**
avoir autorité, pouvoir; être autorisé
tener autoridad; ser autorizado
ermächtigt sein; bevollmächtigt sein

699. **authorization**
autorisation (f)
autorización (f)
Bevollmächtigung (f)
700. **authorized**
agréé; homologué
autorizado
ermächtigt; autorisiert; berechtigt sein
701. **duly authorized**
dûment autorisé
debidamente autorizado
ordnungsgemäss; ausgewiesen
702. **to authorize**
autoriser
autorizar
bevollmächtigen; ermächtigen
703. **to be authorized**
être autorisé
estar autorizado
berechtigt sein zu
704. **autocracy**
autocratie (f)
autocracia (f)
Autokratie (f)
705. **autocrat**
autocrate (m, f)
autócrata (m, f)
Autokrat (m)
706. **autocratie**
autocratique
autocrático
autokratisch
707. **automation**
automation (f)
automatización (f)
Automation (f)
708. **autonomy**
autonomie (f)
autonomía (f)
Autonomie (f); Selbstregierung (f); Selbständigkeit (f)
709. **autonomous**
autonome
autónomo
autonom; sich selbst regierend
710. **autopsy**
autopsie (f)
autopsia (f)
Leichenbeschau (f); Abduktion (f)
711. **to perform an autopsy**
autopsier; faire une autopsie
practicar una autopsia
Leichenschau, Leichenöffnung vornehmen
712. **autrefois acquit**
précédemment acquitté
ya absuelto
früher freigesprochen
713. **auxillary**
auxiliaire (m)
auxiliar (m)
mitwirkend; Hilfs- (m)
714. **availability**
disponibilité (f)
disponibilidad (f)
Verfügbarkeit (f); Nutzbarkeit (f)
715. **available**
disponible
disponible
erhältlich; zugänglich; zur Verfügung stehend; verfügbar
716. **without avail**
inutilement
inútilmente
vergeblich
717. **to make available**
mettre à la disposition
poner a disposición
zugänglich machen; zur Verfügung stellen
718. **aval**
aval (m)
aval (m)
Wechselbürgschaft (f)
719. **average**
avarie (f); moyenne (f)
avería (f); promedio (m)
Havarie (f); Durchschnitt (m)
720. **averment**
affirmation (f); déclaration (f)
afirmación (f); declaración (f)
Versicherung (f); Behauptung (f)
721. **to aver**
affirmer; déclarer
afirmar; declarar
versichern; behaupten
722. **aversion**
aversion (f); répugnance (f)
aversión (f); repugnancia (f)
Abneigung (f); Widerwille (m)
723. **avoidance**
résiliation (f); annulation (f);

rescision (f)
evasión (f); evitación (f); anulación (f)
Vermeidung (f); Aufhebung (f); Widerruf (m)

724. **avoidable**
évitable
evitable
vermeidlich

725. **to avoid**
éviter
evitar
vermeiden; aufheben

726. **avowal**
aveu (m); déclaration (f)
confesión (f); reconocimiento (m)
Bekenntnis (n)

727. **to avow**
avouer; déclarer
confesar; reconocer
bekennen

728. **avulsion**
avulsion (f)
avulsión (f)
Abschwemmung (f)

729. **award**
récompense (f); décernement (m)
recompensa (f); adjudicación (f)
Preis (m); Belohnung (f); Urteil (n)

730. **to award**
adjuger; conférer
adjudicar; conferir
(durch Schiedspruch, Urteilspruch) zuerkennen

731. **(the) ayes and nayes (noes)**
les voix pour et contre
votos a favor y votos en contra
die Stimmen für und gegen

B

732. **backward**
arriéré
atrasado
rückständig

733. **background**
historique (m)
antecedentes (mpl)
Hintergrund (m); Geschichte (f)

734. **backlog**
travaux (mpl) en attente (f)
trabajo (m) acumulado, atrasado
Arbeitsrückstand (m)

735. **baggage**
bagages (mpl)
equipaje (m)
Gepäck (n)

736. **bail**
caution (f)
fianza (f); caución (f)
Kaution (f); Bürgschaft (f)

737. **bail bond**
engagement signé par la caution
escritura de fianza
Kautionsschein (m)

738. **on bail**
sous caution
bajo fianza
gegen Kaution

739. **to furnish, give, bail**
fournir caution
prestar fianza
Kaution leisten

740. **to release on, admit to, bail**
mettre en liberté sous caution
poner en libertad bajo fianza
gegen Kaution freilassen

741. **bailiff**
huissier (m)
alguacil (m)
Büttel (m); Gerichtsvollzieher (m)

742. **bailment**
dépôt (m)
depósito (m)
Hinterlegung (f); Kaution (f)

743. **bailee**
dépositaire (m) de biens (mpl)
depositario (m)
Verwahrer (m); Depositar (m)

744. **bailor**
déposant (m); prêteur (m)
fiador (m)
Hinterleger (m); Deponent (m)

745. **balance**

balance (f); équilibre (m); solde (m)
equilibrio (m); saldo (m)
Gleichgewicht (n); Bilanz (f); Saldo (m)

746. **balance sheet**
bilan (m) d'inventaire (m)
balance (m)
Bilanz (f); Rechnungsabschluss (m)

747. **ballast**
lest (m)
lastre (m)
Ballast (m)

748. **ballistics**
balistique (f)
balística (f)
Ballistik (f)

749. **ballot**
scrutin (m) secret; vote (m)
balota (f); cédula (f) de voto (m)
geheime Abstimmung (f); Stimmzettel (m)

750. **ballot box**
urne (f) électorale
urna (f) electoral
Wahlurne (f)

751. **single ballot**
scrutin à un tour
votación en una sola vez
Abstimmung mit einem einzigen Wahlgang

752. **ban**
interdiction (f)
prohibición (f)
Verbot (n)

753. **banned**
interdit
prohibido
verboten

754. **banned by censor**
interdit par la censure
prohibido por la censura
von der Zensur verboten

755. **to ban**
interdire
prohibir
verbieten

756. **bandit; brigand**
bandit (m); brigand (m)
bandido (m); bandolero (m)
Bandit (m); Strassenräuber (m)

757. **banishment**
bannissement (m); expulsion (f)
destierro (m); deportación (f)
Verbannung (f)

758. **to banish**
bannir; expulser
desterrar; deportar
ausweisen; verbannen

759. **bank**
banque (f)
banco (m)
Bank (f)

760. **bank account**
compte (m) en banque
cuenta (f) bancaria
Bankkonto (n); Bankguthaben (n)

761. **bank credit**
crédit (m) en banque
crédito (m) bancario
Bankkredit (m)

762. **bank failure**
faillite (f) bancaire
quiebra (f) bancaria
Bankrott, Zahlungsunfähigkeit (f) einer Bank

763. **bank note**
billet (m) de banque
billete (m) de banco
Banknote (f)

764. **banker**
banquier (m)
banquero (m)
Bankier (m)

765. **mortgage bank**
banque hypothécaire
banco hipotecario
Hypothekenbank

766. **reserve bank**
banque de réserve
banco de reserva
Reservebank

767. **savings bank**
caisse (f) d'épargne (f)
banco, caja de ahorro (m)
Sparkasse (f)

768. **bankruptcy**
faillite (f); liquidation (f) judiciaire
bancarrota (f); quiebra (f)
Bankrott (f); Konkurs (m)

769. **adjudication in bankruptcy**

jugement déclaratif de faillite
adjudicación en quiebra
Konkurserklärung (f)

770. **administrator in bankruptcy**
liquidateur (m) judiciaire; syndic (m) de faillite
liquidador (m); síndico (m)
Konkursverwalter (m)

771. **bankrupt**
failli; insolvable
fallido; insolvente
bankrott; in Konkurs

772. **bankrupt person**
banqueroutier (m)
insolvente (m)
der Gemeinschuldner (m); der Insolvente (m)

773. **discharge in bankruptcy**
réhabilitation (f) d'un failli (m)
rehabilitación (f) del quebrado (m)
Entlastung (f) eines Gemeinschuldners (m)

774. **involuntary bankruptcy**
banqueroute involontaire
quiebra involuntaria
unfreiwilliger Konkurs

775. **petition in bankruptcy**
requête (f) des créanciers (mpl)
petición (f) de quiebra
Antrag (m) auf Eröffnung (f) des Konkursverfahrens (n)

776. **receiver, referee, trustee in bankruptcy**
syndic d'une faillite
síndico de una quiebra
Konkursverwalter

777. **voluntary bankrupt**
failli volontaire
quebrado voluntario
freiwilliger Konkursschuldner

778. **to be adjudicated bankrupt**
être déclaré en faillite
ser declarado en quiebra
bankrott erklärt werden

779. **to adjudicate someone bankrupt**
mettre quelqu'un en faillite
declarar a alguien en quiebra
jem. bankrott erklären

780. **to file a bill in bankruptcy**
présenter une requête de mise en faillite
declararse en quiebra
Konkurs anmelden

781. **to go into bankruptcy**
courir à la faillite
ir a la quiebra
Konkurs machen; in Konkurs gehen

782. **bar**
barreau (m); obstacle (m) légal
foro (m); obstáculo (m) legal
Rechtsanwaltschaft (f); rechtliches Hindernis (n)

783. **to bar**
exclure; interdire
excluir; prohibir
verbieten; ausschliessen

784. **to be admitted to the bar**
être admis, inscrit au barreau
ser reconocido como abogado
zur Anwaltschaft zugelassen werden

785. **bargain**
bonne affaire (f); occasion (f)
ganga (f)
Gelegenheitskauf (m); vorteilhaftes Geschäft (n)

786. **bargain and sale**
contrat (m) de vente (f) avec transfert (m) immédiat
contrato (m) de compraventa (f) inmediata
Kaufvertrag (m) mit sofortiger Eigentumsübertragung (f)

787. **collective bargaining**
négotiations (fpl) collectives
negociación (f) colectiva
Tarifverhandlungen (fpl)

788. **barratry; barretry**
baraterie (f); incitation (f) aux litiges (mpl)
baratería (f)
Baratterie (f); gewohnheitsmässiges, schikanöses Prozessieren (n)

789. **barrister**
avocat (m) à la Cour
abogado (m) ante los tribunales
Rechtsanwalt (m); Advokat (m)

790. **barter**
échange (m); troc (m)

cambio (m); trueque (m)
Tausch (m)

791. **to barter**
faire du troc; troquer
cambiar; trocar
tauschen

792. **base; basis**
base (f); fondement (m)
base (f); fundamento (m)
Grundlage (f); Basis (f)

793. **air base**
base aérienne
base aérea
Luftstützpunkt

794. **basic**
fondamental
fundamental
grundsätzlich

795. **legal basis**
fondement juridique
fundamento jurídico
Rechtsgrundlage

796. **on the basis of**
en se fondant sur
en base a
auf Grund von

797. **bastardy**
bâtardise (f)
bastardía (f)
uneheliche Geburt (f)

798. **bastard**
bâtard (m); enfant (m) naturel
bastardo (m); hijo (m) natural
uneheliches Kind (n); Bastard (m)

799. **battery**
voies (fpl) de fait (m)
agresión (f)
tätlicher Angriff (m)

800. **bawdy house**
maison (f) de tolérance (f)
burdel (m); lupanar (m)
Bordell (m)

801. **bear**
baissier (m)
bajista (m)
Baissier (m)

802. **bearer**
porteur (m); titulaire (m)
portador (m)
Inhaber (m)

803. **begging**
mendicité (f)
mendicidad (f); pordioseo (m)
Betteln (n); Bettelei (f)

804. **beggar**
mendiant (m)
mendigo (m); pordiosero (m)
Bettler (m)

805. **to beg**
mendier
mendigar
betteln

806. **behalf; on behalf of**
au nom de; en faveur de
en nombre de; por
in Namen, zugunsten von

807. **behavior**
comportement (m); conduite (f)
comportamiento (m); conducta (f)
Verhalten (n); Führung (f)

808. **during good behavior**
tant qu'il aura bonne conduite
mientras observa buena conducta
solange er sich wohl verhält

809. **belief**
conviction (f); croyance (f)
convencimiento (m); creencia (f)
Glaube (m); Überzeugung (f)

810. **to believe**
croire; estimer
creer
glauben

811. **to the best of one's knowledge and belief**
en toute conscience
a su leal saber y entender
nach bestem Wissen und Gewissen

812. **belligerency**
belligérance (f)
beligerancia (f)
Kriegszustand (m)

813. **belligerent**
belligérant (m)
beligerante (m, f)
Kriegfuhrender (m)

814. **bench**
magistrature (f)
magistratura (f)
Gerichtshof (m)

815. **The Bench and the bar**
La magistrature (f) et le barreau (m)
La magistratura (f) y el foro (m)
Richter (mpl) und Anwälte (mpl)

816. **beneficial**
avantageux; utile
útil; ventajoso
nützlich; zuträglich

817. **beneficiary**
bénéficiaire (m)
beneficiario (m)
Begünstigter (m) (aus einem Versicherungsvertrag); Empfänger (m) einer Erbschaft (f)

818. **benefit**
profit (m); avantage (m)
provecho (m); ventaja (f)
Gewinn (m); Vorteil (m)

819. **benefit of the doubt**
bénéfice (m) du doute (m)
beneficio (m) de la duda (f)
im Zweifelsfall (m) zugunsten (des Angeklagten)

820. **fringe benefits**
avantages accessoires
beneficios marginales
(freiwillige) Sozialleistungen (fpl); Nebenleistungen (fpl)

821. **to benefit by**
tirer profit de
beneficiar de
Nutzen ziehen aus

822. **bequest**
legs (m)
legado (m)
Legat (n); Vermächtnis (n)

823. **to bequeath**
léguer
legar
vermachen

824. **bestiality; buggery; sodomy**
bestialité (f); sodomie (f)
bestialidad (f); sodomía (f)
Bestialität (f); Sodomie (f)

825. **bet**
pari (m)
apuesta (f)
Wette (f)

826. **to bet**
parier
apostar
wetten

827. **betrayal**
perfidie (f); trahison (f)
perfidia (f); traición (f)
Treubruch (m); Verrat (m)

828. **to betray**
trahir
traicionar
verraten

829. **betrothal**
fiançailles (fpl)
esponsales (mpl); noviazgo (m)
Verlöbnis (n); Verlobung (f)

830. **betrothed**
fiancé (m); fiancée (f)
novio (m); novia (f); prometido (m); prometida (f)
der (die) Verlobte (m, f)

831. **bias**
parti (m) pris; penchant (m); préjugé (m)
parcialidad (f); propensión (f); prejuicio (m)
Vorurteil (n); Voreingenommenheit (f)

832. **bid**
enchère (f); appel (m) d'offre (f); soumission (f)
licitación (f); oferta (f)
Angebot (n); Submission (f)

833. **bidder**
enchérisseur (m)
postor (m); licitador (m)
Bieter (m); Submittent (m)

834. **highest bidder**
plus offrant
licitador (m) más alto
Höchstbieter (m)

835. **to bid**
faire une offre; mettre une enchère
entrar en licitatión
ein Angebot machen

836. **bigamy**
bigamie (f)
bigamia (f)
Bigamie (f); Doppelehe (f)

837. **bigamist**
bigame (m)
bígamo (m)
Bigamist (m)

838. **bilateral**
bilatéral
bilateral
bilateral; zweiseitig; gegenseitig

839. **bill**
affiche (f); facture (f); billet (m) de banque (f); projet (m) de loi
cartel (m) de anuncios (mpl); factura (f); billete (m) de banco (m); proyecto (m) de ley (f)
Rechnung (f); Banknote (f); Gesetzentwurf (m); Plakat (n)

840. **accommodation bill**
billet (m), effet (m), traite (f) de complaisance
pagaré (m); letra (f) de favor
Gefälligkeitswechsel (m)

841. **appropriation bill**
projet (m) de loi de finances
proyecto (m) de ley sobre finanzas
Gesetzesvorlage (f) zur Bewilligung (f) von Geldern

842. **bill in equity**
recours (m) d'équité (f)
recurso (m) de equidad (f)
Klageschrift (f) in Billigkeitsrecht (n)

843. **bill of attainder**
acte législatif prononçant l'extinction (f) des droits civils
decreto de extinción (f) de derechos civiles
Dekret über den Verlust (m) des Vermögen und der Bürgerrechte

844. **bill of exceptions**
écrit (m) de récusation (f)
nota (f) de recusación (f)
Beschwerde (f) gegen eine Gerichtsentscheidung (f)

845. **bill of exchange**
lettre (f) de change (m)
letra (f) de cambio (m)
Wechsel (m); Tratte (f)

846. **bill of health**
patente (f) de santé (f)
certificado (m) de buena salud (f)
Gesundheitszeugnis (n)

847. **bill of indictment**
acte d'accusation (f)
acusación (f) formal
Anklageschrift (f)

848. **bill of lading**
connaissement (m)
conocimiento (m) de embarque (m)
Konnossement (n); Frachtbrief (m)

849. **bill of particulars**
énumération (f) de demandes (fpl); résumé (m) des charges (fpl)
escrito (m) pormenorizado
schriftliche Darlegung (f) von Einzelheiten (fpl) des Tatbestandes (m)

850. **bill of peace**
demande (f) pour éviter plusieurs litiges (mpl)
solicitud (f) de prevención de litigios (mpl) múltiples
Klage (f) auf Rechtsschutz (m) gegen wiederholte schikanöse Klagen

851. **bill of rights**
déclaration (f) des droits
declaración (f) de derechos
Grundrechte (mpl)

852. **bill of sale**
contrat (m) de vente (f) pour des biens mobiliers
contrato (m) de compraventa (f) de bienes muebles
Kaufvertrag (m)

853. **bill quia timet**
demande de protection contre dommages (mpl) éventuels
solicitud de protección contra daños (mpl) eventuales
Klage auf Rechtsschutz gegen erwartete Schadenszufügung (f)

854. **deficiency bill**
loi ouvrant des crédits (mpl) complémentaires
ley de créditos (mpl) suplementarios
Nachtragsetat (zur Deckung eines Defizits)

855. **due bill**

reconnaissance (f) de dette (f)
reconocimiento (m) de deuda (f)
fällige Rechnung (f)

856. **legislative bill**
projet (m) de loi
proyecto (m) de ley
Gesetzentwurf (m)

857. **true bill**
mise en accusation par jury
acusación aprobada por el gran jurado
von der grand jury für begründet erklärte Anklage

858. **bills and notes**
effets (mpl) de commerce; valeurs (fpl) négociables
efectos, títulos(mpl) negociables
Handelspapiere (f); Wertpapiere (npl)

859. **binding**
obligatoire
obligatorio
verbindlich

860. **legally binding**
obligeant légalement
capaz de obligar legalmente
rechtsverbindlich

861. **to be binding upon**
être obligatoire pour
ser obligatorio para
verbindlich sein für

862. **to bind**
astreindre; lier
juntar; obligar
binden

863. **bipartite**
biparti
bipartito
zweiseitig; in doppelter Ausfertigung

864. **birth**
naissance (f)
nacimiento (m)
Geburt (f)

865. **birthright**
droit de naissance; patrimoine (m)
derechos de nacimiento (m)
Geburtsrecht (n)

866. **blackmail**
chantage (m)
chantaje (m)
Erpressung (f)

867. **blasphemy**
blasphème (m)
blasfemia (f)
Gotteslästerung (f)

868. **blockade**
blocus (m)
bloqueo (m)
Blockade (f)

869. **pacific blockade**
blocus pacifique
bloqueo pacífico
friedliche Blockade

870. **paper blockade**
blocus théorique, fictif
bloqueo en el papel
Papierblockade; verhängte, aber unwirksam gebliebene Blockade

871. **to blockade**
faire le blocus
bloquear
blockieren; sperren

872. **board**
comité (m); commission (f); conseil (m)
concejo (m); consejo (m); junta (f)
Amt (n); Ausschuss (m); Rat (m)

873. **board of directors**
conseil (m) d'administration (f)
junta (f) directiva; directorio (m)
Aufsichtsrat (m)

874. **board of education**
conseil d'enseignement
junta de educación
Schulaufsichtsbehörde; Schulpflegschaft

875. **board of examiners**
jury (m) d'examen (m)
jurado (m) de examinadores (mpl)
Prüfungskommission (f)

876. **board of review**
commission (f) de vérification (f)
junta (f) revisadora
Berufungsauschuss (m)

877. **board of supervisors**

conseil (m) d'administration (f)
junta (f) de administración (f)
Aufsichtsrat (m)

878. **Board of Trade**
Chambre, Ministère de Commerce
Cámara, Ministerio de Comercio
Handelskammer

879. **board of trustees**
conseil de gestion
consejo de gerencia
Kuratorium

880. **draft board**
conseil de révision (f)
junta de reclutamiento (m)
Rekrutierungsamt (m)

881. **body**
corps (m)
cuerpo (m)
Körperschaft (f); Gesellschaft (f)

882. **administrative body**
corps (m) administratif
cuerpo (m) administrativo
Behörde (f); Verwaltungsorgan (n)

883. **advisory body**
organe (m) consultatif
organismo (m) consultativo
Beirat (m)

884. **auxiliary body**
organe auxiliaire
organismo auxiliar
Hilfsorgan (n)

885. **body politic**
le gouvernement; l'Etat
cuerpo político; el Estado
Regierung (f); Staat (m)

886. **celestial bodies**
corps célestes
cuerpos celestiales
Himmelskörper

887. **corporate body; body corporate**
personne civile, morale
persona moral
juristische Person; Gesellschaft

888. **governing bodies**
autorités dirigeantes
autoridades dirigentes
leitende Behörden

889. **legislative body**
corps législatif
cuerpo legislativo
gesetzgebendes Organ; Parlament

890. **sound in body and mind**
sain de corps et d'esprit
sano de cuerpo y alma
bei guter physischer und geistiger Gesundheit

891. **to act as a body**
agir d'ensemble
proceder de acuerdo
gemeinsam vorgehen

892. **bogus**
factice; simulé
espurio; falso
falsch

893. **bomb**
bombe (f)
bomba (f)
Bombe (f)

894. **atom, atomic, bomb**
bombe atomique
bomba atómica
Atombombe

895. **hydrogen bomb**
bombe à hydrogène
bomba de hidrógeno
Wasserstoffbombe

896. **bombardment**
bombardement (m)
bombardeo (m)
Bombardierung (f); Beschiessung (f)

897. **bond**
bon (m); lien (m)
bono (m); lazo (m)
Schuldschein (m); Obligation (f); Schuldverschreibung (f)

898. **bondholder**
obligataire (m); porteur (m) d'obligations (fpl)
tenedor (m) de bonos (mpl)
Obligationsinhaber (m)

899. **bondsman**
garant (m)
fiador (m)
Bürge (m)

900. **bottomry bond**
contrat (m) à la grosse (f) aventure
contrato (m) a la gruesa (f)

Bodmereibrief (m); Schiffswechsel (m)

901. **government bond**
bon du Trésor
bono de Tesorería
Staatspapier

902. **bonus**
bonification (f); prime (f)
bonificación (f)
Extradividende (f); Zulage (f); Prämie (f)

903. **book**
livre (m)
libro (m)
Buch (n)

904. **bookkeeping**
comptabilité (f); tenue (f) des livres
contabilidad (f); teneduría (f) de libros
Buchführung (f); Buchhaltung (f)

905. **bookkeeper**
comptable (m); teneur (m) de livres
contador (m); tenedor (m) de libros
Buchhalter (m)

906. **boom**
hausse (f) rapide; boom (m)
auge (m); prosperidad (f)
Hausse (f)

907. **bootlegger**
contrebandier (m) d'alcool (m)
contrabandista (m) de licores (mpl)
Alkoholschmuggler (m)

908. **booty**
butin (m)
botín (m)
Beute (f)

909. **border**
frontière (f)
frontera (f)
Grenze (f)

910. **borrower**
emprunteur (m)
prestatario (m)
Entleiher (m); Kreditnehmer (m)

911. **to borrow**
emprunter
pedir prestado; hacer empréstito
borgen; entleihen; Kredit aufnehmen

912. **bottleneck**
goulet, goulot (m) d'étranglement (m); embouteillage (m)
estrangulamiento (m); congestión (f) del tráfico (m)
Engpass (m) (der Produktion); Verkehrsstockung (f)

913. **boundary**
frontière (f)
confín (m); límite (m)
Grenze (f)

914. **rectification of boundaries**
action (f) en bornage (m)
rectificación (f) de fronteras (fpl)
Grenzberichtigung (f)

915. **bounty**
gratification (f); prime (f)
generosidad (f); prima (f)
Freigebigkeit (f); Prämie (f)

916. **boycott**
boycottage (m)
boicoteo (m)
Boykott (m)

917. **to boycott**
boycotter
boicotear
boykottieren

918. **bracket**
tranche (f)
clase (f); grupo (m)
Gruppe (f); Klasse (f)

919. **age bracket**
tranche d'âge
grupo de edad
Altersklasse

920. **income bracket**
tranche de revenue
grupo de ingresos
Einkommensgruppe

921. **brawl**
tapage (m); rixe (f)
alboroto (m); pendencia (f)
Prügelei (f); Schlägerei (f)

922. **breach**
infraction (f); rupture (f); violation (f)

infracción (f); rompimiento (m); violación (f)
Bruch (m); Verletzung (f)

923. **breach of authority**
abus d'autorité, de pouvoir
abuso de autoridad, de poder
Missbrauch der Amtsgewalt

924. **breach of confidence, faith, trust**
rupture (f) de confiance (f)
abuso (m) de confianza (f)
Vertrauensbruch (m)

925. **breach of contract**
inexécution (f), rupture (f) de contrat
violación (f) de contrato
Vertragsbruch (m)

926. **breach of international law**
violation du droit international
violación del derecho internacional
Verletzung des Völkerrechts

927. **breach of the peace**
atteinte à la paix publique; délit contre l'ordre public
desorden en la vía pública; escándalo público
Friedensbruch; Ruhestörung

928. **breach of promise**
rupture de promesse
violación de promesa
Nichteinhaltung eines Versprechens

929. **breach of warranty**
rupture de garantie
violación de garantía
Verletzung der Gewährleistungspflicht

930. **breaking and entering**
pénétration (f) par effraction (f)
violación (f) de domicilio (m)
Einbruch (m)

931. **bribery**
subornation (f)
soborno (m)
Bestechung (f)

932. **bribe**
pot-de-vin (m)
soborno (m)
Bestechungsgeld (n)

933. **briber**
suborneur (m)
sobornador (m)
Bestechender (m); Bestecher (m)

934. **to accept a bribe**
accepter un pot-de-vin
aceptar un soborno
sich bestechen lassen

935. **to bribe**
suborner
sobornar
bestechen

936. **brief**
exposé (m); mémoire (m)
informe (m); escrito (m)
Schriftsatz (m)

937. **brief for the defense**
dossier (m) de plaidoirie (f)
informe (m) de la defensa (f)
Verteidigungsschriftsatz (m)

938. **brief for the prosecution**
réquisitoire (m)
informe (m) de la acusación (f)
Anklageschriftsatz (m)

939. **trial brief**
dossier (m) d'audience (f)
expediente (m)
Verhandlungsakten (mpl)

940. **to brief**
exposer les faits; informer
informar; instruir
informieren; unterrichten

941. **brigand** (see **bandit,** No. 755)

942. **broadcast**
diffusion (f); émission (f)
radiodifusión (f)
Rundfunksendung (f)

943. **brokerage**
courtage (m)
corretaje (m)
Maklergeschäft (n); Maklergebühr (f)

944. **broker**
courtier (m)
corredor (m)
Makler (m)

945. **brothel**
bordel (m); maison close, de tolérance
burdel (m); lupanar (m)
Bordell (m)

946. **budget**
budget (m)

presupuesto (m)
Budget (n); (Staats)Haushalt (m); Haushaltsplan (m)

947. **to balance the budget**
équilibrer le budget
equilibrar el presupuesto
den (Staats)Haushalt ins Gleichgewicht bringen

948. **buggery** (see **bestiality,** No. 824)

949. **bull**
spéculateur (m) à la hausse (f)
alcista (m)
Haussier (m)

950. **bulletin**
bulletin (m)
boletín (m)
Amtsblatt (n); Bekanntmachung (f)

951. **bulletin board**
tableau (m) d'affichage (m)
tablero (m) de anuncios (mpl)
Anschlagetafel (f); das schwarze Brett (n)

952. **bullion**
or, argent en barre
oro, plata en barras
Gold oder Silber in Barren

953. **bureau**
administration (f); bureau (m)
dirección (f); oficina (f)
Amt (n); Büro (n)

954. **burglary**
cambriolage (m); vol avec effraction (f)
robo (m) con escalamiento (m)
Einbruch diebstahl (m)

955. **burglar**
cambrioleur (m)
ladrón (m)
Einbrecher (m)

956. **burial**
enterrement (m)
entierro (m)
Beerdigung (f)

957. **burial ground** (see **cemetery,** No. 1059)

958. **business**
affaire (f); métier (m); occupation (f)
comercio (m); profesión (f); ocupación (f)
Geschäft (n); Beruf (m); Beschäftigung (f)

959. **big business**
les grandes entreprises (fpl)
negocio (m) en gran escala (f)
Grossbetrieb (m); Grossunternehmen (n)

960. **business-like**
professionnel
profesional
geschäftsmässig; sachlich

961. **businessman**
homme (m) d'affaires (fpl)
comerciante (m); hombre (m) de negocios (mpl)
Geschäftsmann (m); Kaufmann (m)

962. **to do, transact business**
faire des affaires
hacer negocios; negociar
Geschäfte betreiben (machen); geschäftliche Beziehungen haben mit . . .

963. **buyer**
acheteur (m)
comprador (m)
Käufer (m)

964. **to buy and sell on commission**
faire du (le) courtage
trabajar a comisión
gegen Provision kaufen und verkaufen

965. **to buy at marked-down prices**
acheter au rabais (m)
comprar con rebaja (f)
mit Rabatt (m) kaufen

966. **to buy on credit**
acheter à crédit, à terme
comprar al fiado
auf Kredit kaufen

967. **by-laws**
règlements (mpl); status (mpl)
estatuto (m); reglamento (m)
Satzungen (fpl); Verordnungen (fpl)

968. **by-product**
sous-produit (m)
producto (m) secundario; derivados (mpl)
Nebenprodukt (n)

C

969. **Cabinet**
Conseil (m) des Ministres (mpl)
Consejo (m) de Ministros (mpl)
Kabinett (n); Ministerrat (m)
970. **cabotage**
cabotage (m)
cabotaje (m)
Küstenschiffahrt (f)
971. **calculation**
calcul (m)
cálculo (m)
Kalkulation (f); Berechnung (f)
972. **to calculate**
calculer
calcular
kalkulieren; berechnen
973. **calumny**
calomnie (f)
calumnia (f)
Verleumdung (f)
974. **campaign**
campagne (f)
campaña (f)
Kampagne (f); Wahlkampf (m); Feldzug (m)
975. **cancellation**
annulation (f); résiliation (f); résolution (f)
cancelación (f); rescisión (f)
Annullierung (f); Aufhebung (f); Streichung (f)
976. **to cancel**
annuler; résilier
cancelar; rescindir
annullieren
977. **candidature**
candidature (f)
candidatura (f)
Kandidatur (f)
978. **candidate**
candidat (m)
candidato (m)
Kandidat (m); Anwärter (m)
979. **canon**
canon (m); décret (m)
canón (m); regla (f)
Regel (f); Grundsatz (m); Prinzip (n)
980. **canvassing**
sollicitation (f)
solicitación (f)
Werbetätigkeit (f)
981. **canvassing of votes**
sollicitation (f) de suffrages (mpl)
solicitación (f) de votos (mpl)
Stimmenwerbung (f)
982. **capacity**
capacité (f); qualité (f)
capacidad (f); habilidad (f)
Fähigkeit (f); Kapazität (f)
983. **in an advisory capacity**
à titre consultatif
en calidad de asesor
in beratender Eigenschaft
984. **in an official capacity**
à titre officiel
con carácter oficial
in amtlicher Eigenschaft
985. **in a private capacity**
à titre non officiel
de carácter particular
in nichtamtlicher Eigenschaft
986. **in the capacity of**
à titre, en qualité de
en calidad de
in der Eigenschaft als
987. **legal capacity**
capacité légale
capacidad legal
Rechtsfähigkeit; juristische Eigenschaft
988. **capias** (see **writ of capias**, No. 6276)
989. **capital**
la capitale; le capital; fonds (m)
la capital; el capital; fondos (mpl)
Hauptstadt (f); das Kapital (n)
990. **movement of capital**
mouvements de capitaux
flujos de capital
Kapitalverkehr; -bewegung
991. **paid-up capital**
capital versé
capital pagado
eingezahltes Kapital
992. **subscribed capital**

capital souscrit
capital suscrito
gezeichnetes Kapital

993. **to capitalize**
capitaliser
capitalizar
kapitalisieren; mit Kapital ausstatten

994. **capitalism**
capitalisme (m)
capitalismo (m)
Kapitalismus (m)

995. **capitalist**
capitaliste
capitalista
Kapitalist

996. **capitulation**
capitulation (f)
capitulación (f)
Kapitulation (f)

997. **to capitulate**
capituler
capitular
kapitulieren

998. **capitulations**
régime des capitulations
régimen de capitulaciones
Kapitulationen

999. **caption**
en-tête (f); intitulé (m)
título (m)
Überschrift (f); Legende (f)

1000. **captivity**
captivité (f)
cautiverio (m)
Gefangenschaft (f)

1001. **captive**
captif (m); prisonnier (m)
cautivo (m); prisionero (m)
Gefangener (m)

1002 **capture**
arrestation (f); capture (f)
arresto (m); captura (f)
Gefangennahme (f); Erbeutung (f)

1003. **to capture**
arrêter; capturer; s'emparer
apresar; capturar; prendar
gefangennehmen; erbeuten

1004. **care**
attention (f); diligence (f); soin (m); garde (f)
atención (f); cuidado (m); diligencia (f); custodia (f)
Aufmerksamkeit (f); Sorgfalt (f); Pflege (f); Obhut (f); Sorge (f)

1005 **careful**
soigneux
cuidadoso
sorgfältig

1006. **due care**
diligence (f)
diligencia (f)
angemessene, übliche Sorgfalt (f)

1007. **carelessness**
insouciance (f); négligence (f)
descuido (m); imprudencia (f)
Fahrlässigkeit (f)

1008. **careless**
insouciant; négligent
descuidado; negligente
fahrlässig

1009. **to handle with care**
traiter avec soin
manejar con cuidado
mit Sorgfalt behandeln

1010. **cargo**
cargaison (f); chargement (m)
carga (f); cargamento (m)
Fracht (f); Ladung (f)

1011. **carnal knowledge**
rapports (mpl) sexuels
relaciones (fpl) sexuales
Geschlechtsverkehr (m)

1012. **carriage of goods**
transport (m) de marchandises (fpl)
transporte (m) de mercancías (fpl)
Gütertransport (m)

1013. **carrier**
transporteur (m)
transportador (m)
Spediteur (m)

1014. **common carrier**
transporteur public
empresa de transporte público
(gewerbsmässiger) Frachtführer; öffentliches Transportunternehmen

1015. **private carrier**
transporteur privé
transportador particular

privates Transportunternehmen

1016. **carte blanche**
carte (f) blanche
carta (f) blanca
unbeschränkte Vollmacht (f)

1017. **cartel**
cartel (m)
cartel (m)
Kartell (n)

1018. **cartoon**
caricature (f)
caricatura (f)
Karikatur (f)

1019. **case** (see also **action on the case**)
affaire (f); cause (f); procès (m)
caso (m); causa (f); proceso (m)
Rechtssache (f); Prozess (m); Rechtsstreit (m)

1020. **borderline case**
cas (m) indéterminé
caso (m) dudoso
Grenzfall (m)

1021. **case at bar, under consideration**
affaire; procès
caso ante el tribunal
schwebender Rechtsfall (m)

1022. **case in point, in question**
cas d'espèce
caso aplicable
betreffender Rechtsfall

1023. **hypothetical case**
affaire hypothétique
caso hipotético
hypothetischer Rechtsfall

1024. **leading case**
cas d'espèce faisant autorité
caso considerado como precedente
Präzedenzfall

1025. **moot case**
affaire à débattre
caso académico
hypothetischer Fall

1026. **substance of the case**
fond (m) du procès
fondo (m) de la cuestión
wesentlicher Tatbestand (m)

1027. **written statement of the case**
mémoire (m)
memoria (f)
Memorandum (n)

1028. **to bring a case before the court**
saisir un tribunal d'une affaire
entablar proceso; proceder en justicia
eine Sache vor Gericht bringen

1029. **to conduct one's own case**
plaider soi-même sa cause
defender su propia causa
sich selbst vertreten

1030. **to decide a case**
statuer
fallar un caso
in einer Rechtssache entscheiden

1031. **to dismiss a case**
poser une fin de non-recevoir (m); signer un non-lieu (m)
desechar, desestimar una acción
die Klage abweisen; das Verfahren (n) einstellen

1032. **to plead a case**
plaider une cause
argumentar un caso
eine Rechtssache vertreten

1033. **to review a case**
revoir un procès
revisar un caso
einen Prozess überprüfen

1034. **to try a case**
poursuivre en justice
conocer una causa
einen Fall verhandeln

1035. **casebook**
recueil (m) de jurisprudence
libro (m) conteniendo casos selectos clasificados
Entscheidungssammlung (f)

1036. **cash**
argent comptant; espèces (fpl)
efectivo (m)
Bargeld (n); Barzahlung (f)

1037. **cash on delivery (C.O.D.)**
paiement à la livraison (f)
pago contra entrega (f)
Zahlung gegen Nachnahme (f)

1038. **cash on hand**
argent (m) liquide; disponibilités (fpl)
efectivo (m) en caja (f)
Kassenbestand (m)

1039. **cashier**
caissier (m)
cajero (m)
Kassierer (m)

1040. **petty cash**
argent (m) pour menus frais (mpl)
caja (f) chica
geringe Beträge (mpl); Handkasse (f)

1041. **to pay in cash**
payer en espèces (fpl)
pagar en efectivo (m)
in Bargeld (n) zahlen

1042. **casual**
accidentel; fortuit
casual; fortuito
gelegentlich; zufällig; beiläufig; zwanglos

1043. **casualty**
accident (m); victime (f) d'accident ou de guerre
accidente (m); víctima (f) de un accidente; baja (f) (en la guerra)
Unfall (m); Opfer (n) eines Unfalls; Tote und Verwundete

1044. **catalogue**
catalogue (m)
catálogo (m)
Katalog (m)

1045. **caucus**
comité (m) électoral
camarilla (f) política; conventículo (m)
Versammlung (f) von Wählern (mpl) (von Parteiführern), (U.S.); ortlicher Parteiausschuss (Br.)

1046. **causation**
causalité (f)
causalidad (f)
Verursachung (f)

1047. **chain of causation**
rapport (m) de causalité
nexo (m) causal
Kausalzusammenhang (m)

1048. **cause**
cas (m); cause (f); motif (m); procès (m)
caso (m); causa (f); pleito (m); razón (f)
Prozess (m); Sache (f); Ursache (f)

1049. **cause of action**
recours (m) en justice
derecho a entablar demanda (f)
Klagegrund (m)

1050. **good cause**
motif (m) suffisant
motivo (m) suficiente
triftiger oder guter Grund (m)

1051. **cause célèbre**
cause (f) célèbre
causa (f) célebre
Sensationsprozess (m)

1052. **probable cause**
des présomptions (fpl) sérieuses
indicios (mpl) racionales
wahrscheinliche Ursache (f)

1053. **proximate cause**
cause immédiate
causa inmediata
unmittelbare Ursache

1054. **to cause**
causer
causar
verursachen

1055. **to show cause**
démontrer, donner des raisons
motivar; presentar los motivos
Gründe angeben; begründen

1056. **caveat**
notification (f) d'opposition (f)
advertencia (f); amonestación (f)
von Gericht (n) erhobener Einspruch (m); Verwahrung (f)

1057. **cease-fire**
cessez-le-feu (m)
cese (m) de combate (m)
Waffenruhe (f); Feuereinstellung (f)

1058. **cell**
cellule (f)
celda (f); calabozo (m)
Zelle (f)

1059. **cemetery (burial ground)**
cimetière (m)
cementerio (m)

Friedhof (m)
1060. **censorship**
censure (f)
censura (f)
Zensur (f)
1061. **censor**
censeur (m)
censor (m)
Zensor (m)
1062. **to censor**
censurer
censurar
zensurieren
1063. **censure**
blâme (m)
censura (f)
Tadel (m); Rüge (f); Tadelsmotion (f); Misstrauensvotum (n)
1064. **to censure**
blâmer; critiquer
criticar; culpar
tadeln; rügen
1065. **census**
recensement (m)
censo (m); empadronamiento (m)
Volkszählung (f); Zensus (m)
1066. **certainty**
certitude (f)
certidumbre (f)
Gewissheit (f)
1067. **certificate**
certificat (m)
certificado (m)
Zeugnis (n); Bescheinigung (f)
1068. **certificate of birth**
certificat (m), extrait (m) d'acte (m) de naissance (f)
partida (f) de nacimiento (m)
Geburtsschein (m)
1069. **certificate of civil status**
extrait des actes de l'état civil
certificación del registro civil de personas
Personenstandsurkunde (f)
1070. **certificate of death**
acte, certificat de décès (m)
certificado de defunción (f)
Totenschein (m)
1071. **certificate of incorporation**
certificat d'inscription d'une société
escritura (f) de constitución de una sociedad anónima
Korporationsurkunde (f)
1072. **certificate of marriage**
acte, certificat de mariage
certificado de matrimonio
Heiratsschein
1073. **certificate of service**
attestation (f) de services; certificat de travail (m)
certificado (m) de servicio; hoja (f) de servicios
Arbeitsbescheinigung (f); Zeugnis (n)
1074. **medical certificate**
certificat médical
certificado médico
ärztliches Zeugnis
1075. **mortgage certificate**
inscription (f) hypothécaire
título (m) hipotecario
Hypothekenbrief (m); Pfandbrief (m)
1076. **certification**
certification (f)
certificación (f)
Bescheinigung (f)
1077. **duly certified**
dûment certifié
debidamente certificado
öffentlich beglaubigt
1078. **to certify**
certifier
certificar
bescheinigen
1079. **certiorari** (see **writ of certiorari**, No. 6277)
1080. **cession**
cession (f); transfert (m)
cesión (f) traspaso (m)
Abtretung (f); Überlassung (f)
1081. **to cede**
céder; transférer
ceder; traspasar
abtreten; überlassen
1082. **chairmanship**
présidence (f)
presidencia (f)
Vorsitz (m)
1083. **acting chairman**
président provisoire
presidente provisional

stellvertretender Vorsitzender

1084. **cochairman**
co-président (m)
copresidente (m)
gemeinschaftlicher Vorsitzender (m)

1085. **honorary chairman**
président honoraire
presidente honorario
Ehrenpräsident

1086. **the chair**
la présidence (f); le président (m)
la presidencia (f); el presidente (m)
der Vorsitz (m)

1087. **under the chairmanship of**
sous la présidence de
bajo la presidencia de
unter dem Vorsitz von

1088. **to address the chair**
s'addresser au président
dirigirse al presidente
sich an den Vorsitzenden wenden

1089. **to take the chair**
assumer, prendre la présidence
asumir la presidencia
den Vorsitz übernehmen

1090. **challenge**
récusation (f)
recusación (f); tacha (f)
Ablehnung (f) (von Geschworenen) (mpl)

1091. **challenge for cause**
récusation motivée
recusación con causa
Ablehnung unter Angabe bestimmter Gründe

1092. **challenge to the array**
récusation de tous les jurés
objeción a todo el jurado
Ablehnung der ganzen Geschworenenbank

1093. **challenge to the polls**
récusation de chaque juré individuellement
recusación a los jurados individualmente
Ablehnung der einzelnen Geschworenen

1094. **peremptory challenge**
récusation sans motif déclaré
recusación sin motivo declarado
Ablehnung ohne Angabe der Gründe

1095. **right of challenge**
droit de récusation
derecho de recusar
Ablehnungsrecht

1096. **to challenge**
récuser
recusar; tachar
ablehnen

1097. **chamber**
chambre (f)
cámara (f)
Kammer (f); Sitzungssaal (m); Richterzimmer (n)

1098. **chamber of commerce**
chambre de commerce
cámara de comercio
Handelskammer (f)

1099. **Chamber of Deputies**
Chambre des Députés
Cámara de Diputados
Deputiertenkammer; Unterhaus

1100. **death, lethal chamber**
chambre de l'exécution
cámara letal
Todeskammer

1101. **chambers**
cabinet (m) du juge
sala (f) del juez
Richterzimmer (f)

1102. **champerty**
maintien d'un procès par un tiers intéressé
mantenimiento de una demanda por tercera parte con interés creado
Klage auf Erfolgshonorar eines Dritten

1103. **chance**
chance (f); occasion (f)
casualidad (f); ocasión (f); posibilidad (f)
Aussicht (m); Chance (f)

1104. **last clear chance**
dernière occasion évidente
última oportunidad evidente
letzte Rettungschance

1105. **chancellery**

chancellerie (f)
cancillería (f)
Kanzlei (f)

1106. **chancellor**
chancelier (m)
canciller (m)
Kanzler (m)

1107. **Chancellor of the Exchequer**
Ministre des Finances
Ministro de Hacienda
Finanzminister (m)

1108. **chancery**
équité (f)
equidad (f)
Kanzleigericht (n)

1109. **change**
altération (f); changement (m); petite monnaie (f)
alteración (f); cambio (m); dinero (m) suelto; sencillo (m)
Änderung (f); Tausch (m); Kleingeld (n)

1110. **to change hands**
changer de propriétaire
cambiar de dueño
in andere Hände übergehen

1111. **channel**
détroit (m); voie (f)
estrecho (m); cauce (m)
Fahrrine (f); Kanal (m); Weg (m)

1112. **diplomatic channel**
voie diplomatique
vía diplomática
diplomatischer Weg

1113. **official channels**
voie hiérarchique
tramitación oficial
Dienstweg

1114. **to go through channels**
suivre la voie hiérarchique
tramitar
den Instanzenweg gehen

1115. **character**
caractère (m); réputation (f)
carácter (m); reputación (f)
Charakter (m); Wesen (n)

1116. **characteristic**
caractéristique (f); particularité (f)
característica (f)
Kennzeichen (n); charakteristisches

1117. **characterization**
caractérisation (f); description (f)
caracterización (f); descripción (f)
Charakterisierung (f); Kennzeichnung (f)

1118. **to characterize**
caractériser; décrire
caracterizar; describir
charakterisieren; kennzeichnen

1119. **charge**
charge (f); accusation (f); obligation (f); prix (m)
cargo (m); acusación (f); obligación (f); precio (m)
Anklage (f); Beschuldigung (f)

1120. **additional charges**
frais (mpl) supplémentaires
costos (mpl) adicionales
zusätzliche Kosten (pl)

1121. **charged with**
accusé de
acusado de
beschuldigt; angeklagt

1122. **free of charge**
gratuit; à titre gracieux
gratis
unentgeltlich

1123. **investigation of charges**
examen des chefs (mpl) d'accusation
investigación de los cargos (mpl)
Voruntersuchung (f)

1124. **on a charge of**
sous l'inculpation de
acusado de
unter Anklage

1125. **specification of charges**
énumération (f) des chefs d'accusation
enumeración (f) de los cargos contra un acusado
Anklagepunkt (m)

1126. **to become a public charge**
tomber à la charge de l'Etat
convertirse en carga pública
unter soziale Fürsorge geraten

1127. **to charge with**
accuser de; incriminer
acusar de; incriminar
jdn. anklagen

1128. **to make charges**

retenir des chefs d'accusation
formular la acusación
jdm. etwas vorwerfen

1129. **to sustain charges**
soutenir l'accusation
sostener los cargos
Anklage aufrechterhalten

1130. **chargé d'affaires**
chargé (m) d'affaires
encargado (m) de negocios
Geschäftsträger (m)

1131. **chart**
schéma (m); tableau (m)
diagrama (m); tabla (f)
Tabelle (f); graphische Darstellung (f); (geographische) Karte (f)

1132. **charter**
charte (f); statuts (mpl)
convenio (m) constitutivo; estatutos (mpl)
Satzung (f); Statut (n)

1133. **chartering**
affrètement (m)
fletamento (m)
Charter (m)

1134. **charter party**
charte-partie (f)
contrato (m) de fletamento (m)
Chartepartie (f)

1135. **to charter**
affréter
fletar
chartern

1136. **chattels**
biens mobiliers (mpl)
bienes muebles, personales (mpl); enseres (mpl)
bewegliche Sachen (fpl); bewegliches Vermögen (n)

1137. **incorporeal chattels**
choses en action
bienes inmuebles
Forderungen (fpl)

1138. **personal chattels**
biens mobiliers
bienes muebles
bewegliche Sachen

1139. **real chattels**
biens immobiliers
bienes inmuebles, raíces
unbewegliche Sachen

1140. **cheating**
escroquerie (f); fraude (f); tromperie (f)
estafa (f); engaño (m)
Betrug (m)

1141. **to cheat**
escroquer; frauder
defraudar; engañar
betrügen

1142. **check**
chèque (m); contrôle (m); vérification (f)
cheque (m); control (m); freno (m); verificación (f)
Scheck (m); Einhalt (m); Kontrolle (f)

1143. **blank check**
chèque en blanc
cheque en blanco
Blankoscheck

1144. **cancelled check**
chèque barré, annulé
cheque cancelado
bezahlter und retournierter Scheck

1145. **cashier's check**
chèque émis sur le cassier d'une banque
cheque de caja
eine von der Bank auf sich selbst ausgestellter Scheck

1146. **certified check**
chèque certifié
cheque certificado
bestätigter Scheck

1146a. **crossed check (G.B.)**
chèque barré
cheque cruzado, rayado
Verrechnungscheck

1147. **checkbook**
carnet de chèques
libreta de cheques
Scheckbuch

1148. **traveller's check**
chèque de voyage, de traveller
cheque de viajero
Reisescheck

1149. **to cash a check**
encaisser, toucher un chèque
cobrar un cheque
einen Scheck einlösen

1150. **to check**

contrôler; vérifier
controlar; verificar
kontrollieren; nachprüfen

1151. **to make out a check (on an account)**
émettre, tirer un chèque
extender, librar un cheque
einen Scheck ausstellen oder ausschreiben

1152. **to utter a forged check**
faire circuler un faux chèque
emitir un cheque falso
einen gefälschten Scheck ausgeben

1153. **checks and balances**
éléments d'équilibre des pouvoirs
equilibrio de los poderes públicos
gegenseitige Überwachung der Trennung der Gewalten

1154. **chicanery**
chicanes (fpl)
trapacería (f)
Schikane (f)

1155. **chief**
chef (m)
jefe (m)
Leiter (m)

1156. **child**
enfant (m)
niño (m)
Kind (n)

1157. **adopted child**
enfant (m) adoptif
niño (m) adoptivo
Adoptivkind (n)

1158. **illegitimate, natural child**
enfant illégitime, naturel
niño ilegítimo, natural
uneheliches Kind

1159. **chose in action**
droit incorporel
derecho de acción
Forderungsrecht

1160. **circuit**
ressort (m) d'un tribunal
circuito (m)
Gerichtsbezirk (m)

1161. **circular**
circulaire (f)
circular (f)
Zirkular (n); Rundschreiben (n)

1162. **circulation**
circulation (f)
circulación (f)
Umlauf (m)

1163. **circumstances**
circonstances (fpl)
circunstancias (fpl)
Umstände (mpl)

1164. **according to the circumstances**
selon les circonstances
de acuerdo con las circunstancias
nach den Umständen

1165. **aggravating circumstances**
circonstances aggravantes
circunstancias agravantes
erschwerende Umstände

1166. **circumstances beyond control**
circonstances indépendantes de la volonté
circunstancias fuera de control
unabwendbarer Umstand

1167. **extenuating, attenuating, mitigating circumstances**
circonstances atténuantes
circunstancias atenuantes
mildernde Umstände

1168. **unforeseen circumstances**
circonstances imprévisibles
caso fortuito imprevisto
unvorhergesehene Umstände

1169. **citation**
citation (f); référence (f)
citación (f); cita (f)
Vorladung (f); Zitat (n)

1170. **to cite**
faire comparaître; se référer
citar; referirse a
vorladen; zitieren

1171. **citizenship**
citoyenneté (f)
ciudadanía (f)
Staatsbürgerschaft (f)

1172. **citizen**
citoyen (m)
ciudadano (m)
Staatsbürger (m)

1173. **city**
ville (f)
ciudad (f)
Stadt (f)

1174. **City Hall**

Hôtel (m) de ville (f); mairie (f)
ayuntamiento (m); municipio (m)
Rathaus (n)

1175. **civil service**
administration (f)
servicio (m) civil
Staatsdienst (m)

1176. **civil servant**
fonctionnaire (m)
funcionario (m)
Staatsbeamter (m)

1177. **civilian**
civil
civil
Zivilist

1178. **claim**
demande (f); plainte (f); réclamation (f)
demanda (f); petición (f); reclamación (f)
Anspruch (m); Behauptung (f); Forderung (f)

1179. **adverse claim**
prétention de tiers qui s'oppose à la demande du requérant
reclamación de tercero sobre bienes embargados
entgegenstehender Anspruch eines Dritten; Gegenforderung

1180. **assignment of claim**
transfert (m) d'une créance (f)
transferencia (f) de reclamación (f)
Forderungsabtretung (f)

1181. **claimant**
demandeur (m); plaignant (m)
demandante (m, f); reclamante (m, f)
Anspruchsberechtigter (m); Kläger (m) (Forderungsberechtigter)

1182. **false claim**
demande (f) mal, non fondée
demanda (f) injustificada
unberechtigter Anspruch (m)

1183. **multifariousness of claims**
confusion de plusieurs demandes indépendantes en une action
diversidades en la demanda
unzulässige Verbindung mehrerer Klagen in einer Klageschrift

1184. **prior claim**
demande antérieure
derecho preferente
älterer Anspruch

1185. **rightful claimant**
ayant droit (m)
demandante (m, f) legítimo
Anspruchsberechtigter (m)

1186. **abatement of claims**
réduction (f) ou annulation (f) de prétentions (fpl)
reducción (f) o anulación (f) de pretenciones (fpl)
Ermässigung (f) des Anspruchs (m)

1187. **to claim**
demander; réclamer; revendiquer
demandar; pedir; reclamar
beanspruchen; fordern; verlangen

1188. **to collect a claim**
toucher une créance (f)
obtener el pago de una deuda, demanda
eine Forderung (f) eintreiben

1189. **to set up a claim**
faire valoir ses droits; faire une réclamation (f)
establecer una demanda (f); hacer valer un derecho
einen Anspruch (m) geltend machen

1190. **to waive a claim**
renoncer à ses droits
renunciar a una demanda
auf einen Anspruch verzichten

1191. **clandestine**
clandestin; secret
clandestino; secreto
geheim; heimlich

1192. **clarification**
clarification (f)
aclaración (f); clarificación (f)
Klärung (f)

1193. **to clarify**
clarifier
aclarar; clarificar

klarstellen
1194. **clarity**
clarté (f)
claridad (f)
Klarheit (f)
1195. **class**
catégorie (f); classe (f)
categoría (f); clase (f)
Kategorie (f); Klasse (f)
1196. **classification**
classement (m); classification (f)
clasificación (f)
Einordnung (f); Klassifikation (f)
1197. **classified**
classé
clasificado
klassifiziert
1198. **to classify**
classer; classifier
clasificar
einordnen; klassifizieren
1199. **clause**
clause (f); disposition (f)
cláusula (f); estipulación (f)
Klausel (f); Abschnitt (m); (Vertrags-) Bestimmung (f)
1200. **arbitration clause**
clause compromissoire
cláusula compromisoria
Schiedsgerichtsklausel
1201. **attestation clause**
clause de certification
cláusula de certificación
Beglaubigungsklausel
1202. **enacting clause**
dispositif de mise en vigueur d'une loi
cláusula declarando la vigencia de la ley
Inkrafttretungsklausel
1203. **escape clause**
clause échappatoire
cláusula escapatoria
Ausweichklausel
1204. **general participation clause**
clause de participation générale
cláusula de participación general
Allbeteiligungsklausel
1205. **gold clause**
clause d'or
cláusula del oro
Goldklausel
1206. **most-favored-nation clause**
clause de la nation la plus favorisée
cláusula de la nación más favorecida
Meistbegünstigungsklausel
1207. **optional clause**
clause facultative
cláusula facultativa
Fakultativklausel
1208. **saving clause**
clause d'exemption (f), de sauvegarde (f)
cláusula de excepción (f), salvedad (f)
Ausnahmebestimmung (f); Vorbehaltsklausel (f)
1209. **standard clause**
clause de style
cláusula usual
Stilklausel
1210. **clearance**
autorisation (f); permission (f)
descarga (f); despacho (m)
Verzollung (f)
1211. **customs clearance**
formalités (fpl) douanières
formalidades (fpl) aduaneras
Zollabfertigung (f)
1212. **security clearance (U.S.A.)**
approbation (f) de la qualification (f) de la personne (f)
sanción (f) de garantía de la persona (f)
Unbedenklichkeitserklärung (f)
1213. **clearing**
clearing (m); compensation (f)
clearing (m); compensación (f)
Clearing (n); Verrechnungsverfahren (n)
1214. **clearinghouse**
banque (f) de virement (m)
cámara (f) de compensación (f)
Abrechnungsstelle (f)
1215. **clemency**
clémence (f); grâce (f)
clemencia (f)
Gnade (f); Milde (f)
1216. **petition of clemency**
recours (m) en grâce
petición (f) de clemencia

Gnadengesuch (n)
1217. **clerk**
commis (m); greffier (m); vendeur (m); employé (m)
empleado (m) de oficina (f); escribano (m) vendedor (m)
Leiter (m) der Gerichtskanzlei (f); Verkäufer (m); kaufmännischer Angestellte(r) (m); Gerichtsreferendar (m)
1218. **client**
client (m)
cliente (m)
Klient (m)
1219. **climate**
ambiance (f); climat (m)
ambiente (m); clima (m)
Klima (n)
1220. **cloture**
clôture (f)
clausura (f)
Schluss (m) (der Debatte) (fpl)
1221. **clue**
clef (f); indice (m)
índice (m); pista (f)
Schlüssel (m); Anhaltspunkt (m)
1222. **to give a clue**
mettre sur la voie
dar un indicio
Aufschluss geben
1223. **coalition**
coalition (f)
coalición (f)
Koalition (f)
1224. **code**
code (m)
código (m)
Gesetzbuch (n)
1225. **civil code**
code civil
código civil
bürgerliches Gesetzbuch
1226. **code of civil procedure**
code de procédure civile
código de procedimiento civil
Zivilprozessordnung
1227. **code of criminal, penal procedure**
code d'instruction criminelle
código de procedimiento penal
Strafprozessordnung
1228. **commercial code**
code de commerce
código de comercio
Handelsgesetzbuch
1229. **criminal, penal code**
code pénal
código penal
Strafgesetzbuch
1230. **military code**
code de justice militaire
código militar
Militärgesetzbuch
1231. **codicil**
codicille (m)
codicilo (m)
Kodizill (n)
1232. **codification**
codification (f)
codificación (f)
Kodifizierung (f)
1233. **to codify**
codifier
codificar
kodifizieren
1234. **coercion**
coercition (f); contrainte (f)
coacción (f); coerción (f); compulsión (f)
Zwang (m)
1235. **coercive**
coercitif
coactivo; coercitivo
zwingend
1236. **to coerce**
contraindre
coaccionar
zwingen
1237. **coexistence**
coexistence (f)
coexistencia (f); convivencia (f)
Koexistenz (f)
1238. **peaceful coexistence**
coexistence pacifique
convivencia pacífica
friedliche Koexistenz (f)
1239. **cogency**
force (f); validité (f)
fuerza (f); lógica (f)
Stichhaltigkeit (f); Beweiskraft (f)
1240. **cognizance**
connaissance (f)
conocimiento (m)

Anerkenntnis (n); gerichtliches Erkenntnis (n)

1241. **cohabitation**
cohabitation (f)
cohabitación (f)
Beiwohnung (f)

1242. **to cohabit**
cohabiter
cohabitar
beiwohnen

1243. **coin**
pièce (f) de monnaie (f)
moneda (f) acuñada
Münze (f)

1244. **false coiner**
faux monnayeur (m)
falsificador (m) de monedas
Falschmünzer (m)

1245. **collapse**
écroulement (m)
fracaso (m)
Zusammenbruch (m)

1246. **to collapse**
écrouler
fracasar
zusammenbrechen

1247. **collate, to**
collationner; comparer
comparar; cotejar
kollationieren; vergleichen

1248. **collateral**
collatéral (m); nantissement (m); sûreté (f) subsidiaire
colateral (m); garantía (f)
Neben-; zusätzliche Deckung (f)

1249. **collection**
rassemblement (m); réception (f)
recopilación (f); recaudación (f)
Eintreibung (f); Kollektion (f)

1250. **for collection**
en recouvrement
en cobranza
zum Inkasso

1251. **to collect**
percevoir; recouvrer; recueillir
recaudar; recoger
einsammeln; eintreiben; einkassieren

1252. **collective bargaining**
négociation (f) d'un contrat (m) collectif
negociación (f) para la contratación (f) colectiva
Tarifverhandlungen (fpl)

1253. **collision**
abordage (m); collision (f)
choque (m); colisión (f)
Kollision (f); Zusammenstoss (m)

1254. **collusion**
collusion (f)
colusión (f)
Kollusion (f)

1255. **colonization**
colonisation (f)
colonización (f)
Kolonisation (f)

1256. **colony**
colonie (f)
colonia (f)
Kolonie (f)

1257. **to colonize**
coloniser
colonizar
kolonisieren

1258. **color**
couleur (f); droit (m) apparent
color (m); pretexto (m)
Farbe (f); Anschein (m); Vorwand (m)

1259. **color of office**
usurpation (f) de fonctions (fpl)
usurpación (f) de funciones (fpl)
rechtswidrige Amtsübernahme (f)

1260. **combatant**
combattant (m)
combatiente (m)
Kombattant (m)

1261. **combine**
cartel (m); consortium (m); entente (f) industrielle
acuerdo (m), grupo industrial
Kartell (m); Verband (m)

1262. **comity**
courtoisie (f)
cortesía (f)
Höflichkeit (f); gutes Einvernehmen (n)

1263. **commencement**
commencement (m)
comienzo (m)
Anfang (m)

1264. **to commence**
commencer
comenzar
anfangen

1265. **commentator**
commentateur (m)
comentador (m)
Kommentator (m)

1266. **comments**
critique (f); observations (fpl)
crítica (f); observaciones (fpl)
Anmerkungen (fpl); Kritik (f); Bemerkungen (fpl)

1267. **commerce**
commerce (m)
comercio (m)
Handel (m)

1268. **inter-state commerce**
commerce entre Etats
comercio entre Estados
zwischenstaatlicher Handel

1269. **commission**
brevet (m); commission (f); perpétration (f)
comisión (f); encargo (m); perpetración (f)
Kommission (f); Begehung (f)

1270. **commission merchant**
commissionnaire (m)
comisionista (m)
Kommissionär (m)

1271. **commission of enquiry**
commission (f) d'enquête (f)
comisión (f) de investigación (f)
Untersuchungskommission (f)

1272. **commissioner**
commissaire (m); membre (m) d'une commission
comisario (m); miembro (m) de una comisión
Kommissionär (m); Mitglied (m) einer Kommission

1273. **on commission**
sur commission
en comisión
in Kommission

1274. **commitment**
emprisonnement (m); internement (m); engagement (m)
encarcelamiento (m); internación (f); compromiso (m)
Überweisung (f) an eine Anstalt (f); Verpflichtung (f); Verübung (f)

1275. **commitments**
engagements (mpl); obligations (fpl)
compromisos (mpl); promesas (fpl)
Verpflichtungen (fpl)

1276. **to commit for trial**
mettre en accusation (f)
dictar auto (m) de procesamiento (m)
dem Gericht (n) zur Aburteilung (f) einliefern

1277. **to commit to prison**
écrouer; mettre en prison
dictar auto de prisión; encarcelar
ins Gefängnis einliefern

1278. **committee**
comité (m); curateur (m) (d'un aliéné)
comité (m); curador (m) (de enajenado mental)
Ausschuss (m); Vormund (m) (eine Geisteskranken)

1279. **appropriations committee**
comité de repartition du fonds du budget
comité de asignación de fondos del presupuesto
Bewilligungsausschuss

1280. **committee of experts**
comité d'experts
comité de expertos
Sachverständigenausschuss

1281. **committee on credentials**
comité de vérification des pouvoirs
comité de credenciales
Vollmachtenprufungsausschuss

1282. **committee on nominations**
comité des candidatures, nominations
comité de candidaturas, postulaciones
Nominierungsausschuss

1283. **drafting committee**
comité de rédaction
comité de redacción

Redaktionsausschuss

1284. **executive committee**
comité exécutif
comité ejecutivo
Vollzugsausschuss

1285. **finance committee**
comité financier
comité financiero
Finanzausschuss

1286. **foreign affairs committee**
commission des affaires étrangères
comité de asuntos extranjeros
Ausschuss für auswärtige Angelegenheiten

1287. **permanent, standing, committee**
comité permanent
comisión permanente
ständiger Ausschuss

1288. **reception committee**
comité d'accueil
comité de acogida
Empfangskomitee

1289. **steering committee**
comité de direction
comité de dirección
Lenkungsausschuss

1290. **working committee**
comité de travail
comité de trabajo
Arbeitsausschuss

1291. **sub-committee**
sous-comité
subcomité
Unterausschuss

1292. **to appoint a committee**
nommer un comité
nombrar un comité
einen Ausschuss einsetzen

1293. **commodity**
marchandise (f); produit (m)
mercancía (f); producto (m)
Artikel (m); Ware (f)

1294. **common**
commun
común (m)
gemeinsam; gewöhnlich

1295. **commonwealth**
communauté; commonwealth (m)
mancomunidad de naciones
Gemeinschaft (f); Commonwealth (n)

1296. **communication**
communication (f)
comunicación (f)
Mitteilung (f); Nachricht (f)

1297. **confidential, privileged communications**
communications sous le sceau du secret
comunicaciones bajo secreto
vertrauliche Mitteilungen

1298. **means of communication**
moyens (mpl) de communication (f)
medios (mpl) de comunicación (f)
Kommunikationsmittel (n)

1299. **to communicate**
communiquer
comunicar
mitteilen; sich in Verbindung setzen mit

1300. **communiqué**
communiqué (m)
informe (m) oficial
amtlicher Bericht (m)

1301. **community**
communauté (f)
cuerpo (m) social
Gemeinschaft (f); Gemeinde (f)

1302. **community of interest**
intérêt (m) commun
interés (m) común
Interessengemeinschaft (f)

1303. **commutation**
commutation (f)
conmutación (f)
Unwandlung (f)

1304. **compact**
accord (m)
convenio (m)
Vertrag (m)

1305. **company**
compagnie (f); société (f) commerciale
compañía (f); sociedad (f)
Gesellschaft (f); Handelsgesellschaft (f)

1306. **affiliated company**
filiale (f); société (f) affiliée
compañía (f) asociada, afiliada

Tochtergesellschaft (f)

1307. **insurance company**
compagnie (f) d'assurance (f)
compañía (f) de seguros (mpl)
Versicherungsgesellschaft (f)

1308. **joint stock company**
société (f) anonyme, par actions (fpl)
compañía (f) por acciones (fpl); sociedad anónima
Aktiengesellschaft (f)

1309. **limited liability company**
société à responsabilité limitée
sociedad de responsabilidad limitada
Gesellschaft mit beschränkter Haftung

1310. **non-profit company**
société sans but lucratif
sociedad sin fines lucrativos
Gesellschaft, die keinen Erwerbszweck verfolgt

1311. **public utility company**
société d'utilité publique
empresa de servicios públicos
öffentlicher Versorgungsbetrieb

1312. **winding up of a company**
liquidation d'une société
liquidación de una sociedad
Liquidation einer Gesellschaft

1313. **compatible**
compatible
compatible
vereinbar

1314. **compensation**
indemnité (f); dédommagement (m); réparation (f)
indemnización (f)
Entschädigung (f); Vergütung (f)

1315. **to compensate**
indemniser; dédommager
indemnizar
entschädigen; vergüten

1316. **competence; competency**
compétence (f)
competencia (f)
Zuständigkeit (f); Fähigkeit (f)

1317. **competent**
compétent
competente
zuständig; fähig

1318. **competition**
concurrence (f)
concurrencia (f); competencia (f)
Konkurrenz (f); Preisausschreiben (n)

1319. **unfair competition**
concurrence déloyale
competencia desleal
unlauterer Wettbewerb (m)

1320. **compilation**
compilation (f); recueil (m); rassemblement (m)
compilación (f); recopilación (f)
Sammlung (f); Zusammenstellung (f)

1321. **to compile**
compiler; recueillir; rassembler
compilar; recopilar
sammeln; zusammenstellen

1322. **complaint**
demande (f); plainte (f)
demanda (f); queja (f)
Beschwerde (f); Klage (f)

1323. **complainant**
demandeur (m); plaignant (m)
demandante (m)
Kläger (m); Beschwerdeführer (m)

1324. **to complain**
demander
demandar
sich beschweren

1325. **to lodge a complaint**
porter plainte; déposer, formuler une plainte
formular una queja; presentar una demanda
Beschwerde einreichen; Klage erheben

1326. **completion**
accomplissement (m)
terminación (f)
Erfüllung (f); Vollendung (f)

1327. **to complete**
compléter
completar
vollenden

1328. **compliance**
soumission (f); conformité (f)
conformidad (f); cumplimiento (m)
Einwilligung (f); Genehmigung (m); Erfüllung (f)

1329. **to comply with**
se soumettre à
cumplir con
befolgen

1330. **complicity**
complicité (f)
complicidad (f)
Mittäterschaft (f)

1331. **component**
composant (m)
componente (m)
Bestandteil (m)

1332. **component parts**
parties (fpl) composantes
partes (fpl) componentes
Bestandteile (mpl)

1333. **comprehensive**
compréhensif
comprensivo
umfassend

1334. **compromis**
accord d'arbitrage
acuerdo de arbitraje
Schiedsvertrag

1335. **compromise**
compromis (m); transaction (f)
compromiso (m); transacción (f)
Kompromiss (n); Vergleich (m)

1336. **to compromise**
faire un compromis; transiger; compromettre
transar; transigir; comprometer
vergleichen; kompromittieren

1337. **comptroller**
contrôleur (m)
contralor (m)
Rechnungsprüfer (m)

1338. **compulsion**
contrainte (f)
compulsión (f)
Zwang (m)

1339. **compulsory**
obligatoire
obligatorio
obligatorisch

1340. **to compel**
contraindre
compeler
zwingen

1341. **computation**
calcul (m)
cálculo (m)
Berechnung (f)

1342. **to compute**
calculer
calcular
berechnen

1343. **computer**
ordinateur (m)
computadora (f)
Komputer (m)

1344. **concealment; place of concealment**
cachette (f); recel (m)
encubrimiento (m) ocultación (f)
Geheimhaltung (f); Verheimlichung (f)

1345. **to conceal**
receler
encubrir; ocultar
geheimhalten; verheimlichen

1346. **concept**
notion (f)
noción (f)
Begriff (m)

1347. **concern**
établissement (m); inquiétude (f); intérêt (m)
negocio (m); inquietud (f); preocupación (f); interés (m)
Unternehmen (n); Sorge (f); Interesse (n)

1348. **going concern**
affaire (f) en bonne marche
empresa (f) en buen funcionamiento
gutgehendes Geschäft (n)

1349. **to whom it may concern**
à ceux qu'il appartient; à qui de droit
a quien pueda interesar
an alle, die es angeht

1350. **to concern**
inquiéter; intéresser
inquietar; interesar
angehen; betreffen

1351. **concession**
concession (f)
concesión (f)
Konzession (f); Zugeständnis (n)

1352. **to concede**
concéder
conceder
zugestehen

1353. **concessions**
franchises (fpl)
franquicias (fpl)
Konzessionen (fpl)
1354. **conciliation**
conciliation (f)
conciliación (f)
Versöhnung (f)
1355. **to conciliate**
concilier
conciliar
versöhnen
1356. **conclusion**
conclusion (f)
conclusión (f)
Abschluss (m)
1357. **conclusion of fact**
conclusion (f) tirée des faits (mpl) prouvés
fundamento (m) basado en hechos (mpl) comprobados
Tatsachenfeststellung (f)
1358. **conclusion of law**
conclusion (f) applicant la loi aux faits
fundamento (m) basado en la ley, derecho
Rechtsfolgerung (f)
1359. **conclusive**
concluant; décisif
concluyente; decisivo
schlüssig; überzeugend
1360. **to conclude**
conclure
concluir
schliessen; abschliessen (Vertrag)
1361. **concordat**
concordat (m)
concordato (m)
Konkordat (n)
1362. **concurrence**
accord (m); assentiment (m)
acuerdo (m); concurrencia (f)
Übereinstimmung (f); Zusammenwirken (n)
1363. **concurrent**
concourant; simultané
concomitante; concurrente
übereinstimmend; zusammenwirkend
1364. **concurrently**
concurremment; conjointement
simultáneamente
gleichzeitig (mit)
1365. **to concur in**
concourir à; se mettre d'accord
coincidir; convenir
übereinstimmen; beistimmen
1366. **condemnation**
condamnation (f); expropriation (f)
condenación (f); expropiación (f)
Verurteilung (f); Enteignung (f)
1367. **to condemn**
condamner; exproprier
condenar; expropiar
verurteilen; enteignen
1368. **condition**
condition (f)
condición (f)
Bedingung (f); Klausel (f)
1369. **basic condition**
condition fondamentale
condición básica
Grundbedingung
1370. **condition precedent**
condition suspensive
condición suspensiva
aufschiebende Bedingung
1371. **condition subsequent**
condition résolutoire
condición resolutiva
auflösende Bedingung
1372. **conditional**
conditionnel
condicional
bedingt
1373. **express condition**
condition expresse
condición expresa
ausdrückliche Bedingung
1374. **implied condition**
condition tacite
condición tácita
stillschweigende Bedingung
1375. **condominium**
condominat (m)
condominio (m)
Kondominium (n)
1376. **condonation**
pardon (m)
condonación (f)
Verzeihung (f)

1377. **to condone**
pardonner
condonar
verzeihen

1378. **conducive to**
favorable à
conducente
dienlich; förderlich

1379. **conduct**
conduite (f); gestion (f); maniement (m)
conducta (f); gestión (f)
Betragen (n); Verhalten (n); Führung (f)

1380. **disorderly conduct**
conduite (f) désordonnée; débauche (f)
conducta (f) desordenada; escándalo (m)
ungehöriges Betragen (n)

1381. **good conduct**
bonne conduite
buena conducta
gutes Betragen

1382. **confederation**
confédération (f)
confederación (f)
Staatenbund (m)

1383. **conference**
conférence (f); entretien (m)
conferencia (f); entrevista (f)
Konferenz (f); Sitzung (f)

1384. **roundtable conference**
conférence de table ronde
conferencia de mesa redonda
Konferenz am runden Tische

1385. **summit conference**
conférence au sommet
conferencia (en la cumbre) de jefes de gobierno
Gipfeltreffen

1386. **to confer upon**
accorder; conférer à
conferir; dar a
verleihen

1387. **to confer with**
conférer avec
conferenciar
verhandeln (mit)

1388. **confession**
aveu (m)
confesión (f)
Geständnis (n)

1389. **confession and avoidance**
admission de faits spécifiés avec contestation de leur admissibilité
reconocimiento de hechos con denegación de responsabilidad
Anerkennung spezifischer Tatsachen unter Ablehnung ihrer Zulassung zum Beweis

1390. **to confess**
avouer; se reconnaître coupable
confesar
gestehen

1391. **to make a full confession**
faire des aveux complets
confesar plenamente
ein umfassendes Geständnis ablegen

1392. **confidential**
confidentiel
confidencial
vertraulich

1393. **confinement**
détention (f); réclusion (f)
detención (f); reclusión (f)
Haft (f); Freiheitsstrafe (f)

1394. **close confinement**
réclusion (f)
reclusion (f) rigurosa
strenge Haft (f)

1395. **solitary confinement**
emprisonnement (m) cellulaire
encarcelamiento (m) incomunicado
Einzelhaft (f)

1396. **to confine**
consigner; détenir
confinar; encerrar
beschränken; einsperren; gefangenhalten

1397. **confirmation**
confirmation (f)
confirmación (f)
Bestätigung (f)

1398. **to confirm**
confirmer
confirmar
bestätigen

1399. **confiscation**
confiscation (f)
confiscación (f)

Konfiszierung (f)
1400. **to confiscate**
confisquer
confiscar
konfiszieren
1401. **conflict**
conflit (m)
conflicto (m)
Konflikt (m)
1401a. **conflict of laws** (see **private international law,** No. 3441)
1402. **to conflict with**
être en désaccord avec
estar en conflicto con
in Widerspruch stehen
1403. **confrontation**
confrontation (f)
careo (m)
Konfrontation (f)
1404. **to confront**
confronter
carear
konfrontieren
1405. **Congress**
Congrès (m); Parlement (m)
Congreso (m); Parlamento (m)
Kongress (m); Parlament (n)
1406. **congressman**
membre (m) du Congrès; député (m)
miembro (m) del Congreso; diputado (m)
Kongressmitglied (m); Abgeordneter (m)
1407. **conjugal**
conjugal
conyugal
ehelich
1408. **connivance**
connivence (f)
connivencia (f)
strafbares Einverständnis (n)
1409. **to connive**
être de connivence
estar de connivencia
zur Begehung eines Verbrechens sträflich zusammenwirken
1410. **conquest**
conquête (f)
conquista (f)
Eroberung (f)
1411. **to conquer**
conquérir
conquistar
erobern
1412. **consanguinity**
consanguinité (f); parenté (f)
consanguinidad (f); parentesco (m)
Blutsverwandtschaft (f); Verwandtschaft (f)
1413. **consensus**
avis (m) majoritaire; consensus (m)
consenso (m)
Übereinstimmung (f) der Ansichten (f)
1414. **consent**
agrément (m); consentement (m)
consentimiento (m)
Einwilligung (f); Zustimmung (f)
1415. **by common consent**
d'un commun accord (m)
de común acuerdo (m)
mit allgemeiner Zustimmung (f)
1416. **with the tacit consent of**
avec le consentement (m) tacite de
con el consentimiento (m) tácito de
mit stillschweigender Einwilligung (f)
1417. **to consent**
consentir
consentir
einwilligen
1418. **consequence**
conséquence (f)
consecuencia (f)
Folge (f)
1419. **consideration**
cause (f); considération (f)
causa (f); consideración (f)
Erwägung (f); Beweggrund (m)
1420. **in consideration of**
compte-tenu de; en considération de
a cambio de; considerando
in Anbetracht
1421. **under consideration**
envisagé
en consideración
in Erwägung
1422. **valuable consideration**

titre (m) onéreux
causa (f) onerosa
angemessene Gegenleistung (f)

1423. **to consider**
considérer; envisager
considerar; contemplar
betrachten; erwägen

1424. **consignment**
consignation (f); envoi (m)
consignación (f)
Konsignation (f); Versendung (f)

1425. **consignee**
consignataire (m); destinataire (m)
consignatario (m)
Konsignatar (m); (Waren-)Empfänger (m)

1426. **consignor**
consignateur (m); expéditeur (m)
consignador (m)
Konsignant (m); Sender (m)

1427. **to consign**
consigner
consignar
in Konsignation geben; versenden

1428. **consolidation**
consolidation (f)
consolidación (f)
Konsolidierung (f)

1429. **to consolidate**
consolider
consolidar
konsolidieren

1430. **consortium**
consortium (m)
consorcio (m)
Konsortium (n)

1431. **conspiracy**
complot (m); conspiration (f)
conspiración (f); conjuración (f)
geheime Abrede (f); Verschwörung (f)

1432. **conspiracy in restraint of trade**
plan concerté visant à restreindre le commerce
confabulación para restringir el comercio
geheime Abrede zur Wettbewerbsbeschränkung

1433. **conspirator**
conspirateur (m)
conspirador (m)
Verschwörer (m)

1434. **to conspire**
comploter; conspirer
conspirar
sich verschwören

1435. **constabulary**
corps (m) des agents (mpl) de police (f)
guardia (f) civil
Polizei (f)

1436. **constable**
gardien (m) de la paix
policía (f)
Polizist (m)

1437. **county constabulary**
gendarmerie (f)
gendarme (m)
Gendarmerie (f)

1438. **rural constable**
garde-champêtre (m)
alguacil (m)
Gendarm (m)

1439. **constituency**
collège (m) électoral; électeurs (mpl)
distrito (m) electoral; electorado (m)
Wahlkreis (m); Wählerschaft (f)

1440. **constituent**
constituant; électeur (m)
constituyente; elector (m)
wesentlich Wähler (m); Vollmachtgeber (m)

1441. **constitution**
constitution (f)
constitución (f)
Verfassung (f)

1442. **constitutional limitations**
limitations constitutionnelles
limitaciones constitucionales
verfassungsrechtliche Beschränkungen

1443. **constitutionality**
constitutionnalité (f)
constitucionalidad (f)
Verfassungsmässigkeit (f)

1444. **constitute, to**
constituer
constituir
konstituieren

1445. **construction**
explication (f); interprétation (f)
explicación (f); interpretación (f)
Auslegung (f); Interpretation (f)
1446. **constructive**
constructif
constructivo
konstruktiv
1447. **to construe**
expliquer; interpréter
explicar; interpretar
deuten; auslegen
1448. **consulate**
consulat (m)
consulado (m)
Konsulat (n)
1449. **consul**
consul (m)
cónsul (m)
Konsul (m)
1450. **vice-consul**
vice-consul (m)
vicecónsul (m)
Vizekonsul (m)
1451. **consultation**
consultation (f)
consulta (f)
Beratung (f); Rücksprache (f)
1452. **to consult**
consulter
consultar
um Rat fragen; (sich) beraten
1453. **consultant**
conseiller (m) technique
consultor (m)
Berater (m)
1454. **consummation**
consommation (f); accomplissement (m)
consumación (f); cumplimiento (m)
Vollziehung (f); Vollendung (f)
1455. **consummated**
achevé
consumado
vollzogen
1456. **to consummate**
achever; accomplir
consumar
vollziehen; vollenden
1457. **consumption**
consommation (f)
consunción (f)
Verbrauch (m)
1458. **consumer**
consommateur (m)
consumidor (m)
Verbraucher (m)
1459. **contemporaneous**
contemporain
contemporáneo
zeitgenössisch
1460. **contempt**
délit (m) d'audience (f); manque (m) de respect (m); mépris (m)
contumacia (f); desacato (m); rebeldía (f)
Missachtung (f); Nichtbefolgung (f) gerichtlicher Anordnungen (fpl); Ungebühr (f); Schande (f)
1461. **contempt of court**
outrage (m) au tribunal
desacato (m) al tribunal
Ungebühr (f) von Gericht
1462. **contemptible**
méprisable
despreciable
verachtenswert
1463. **contention**
différend (m); prétention (f)
contención (f); disputa (f)
Behauptung (f); Streit (m)
1464. **bone of contention**
sujet de dispute
sujeto de disputa
Streitgegenstand
1465. **contentious**
contentieux
contencioso
streitig; strittig
1466. **to contend**
discuter; prétendre
contender; disputar
behaupten; streiten
1467. **contents**
contenu (m)
contenido (m)
Inhalt (m)
1468. **table of contents**
table (f) des matières (fpl)
índice (m) general; tabla (f) de materias (fpl)

Inhaltsverzeichnis (n)

1469. **contest**
conflit (m); lutte (f)
conflicto (m); disputa (f)
Streit (m); Wettbewerb (m)

1470. **to contest**
contester; disputer
contestar; disputar
anfechten; bestreiten

1471. **context**
contexte (m)
contexto (m)
Zusammenhang (m)

1472. **in this context**
dans cet ordre d'idées
en este contexto
in diesem Zusammenhang

1473. **contiguous**
contigu
contiguo
angrenzend

1474. **continental shelf**
plateau (m) continental
zócalo (m) continental; plataforma (f) submarina
Kontinentalsockel (m); Festlandssockel (m)

1475. **contingency**
contingence (f); éventualité (f)
contingencia (f); eventualidad (f)
möglicher Fall (m); Zufälligkeit (f)

1476. **contingent**
aléatoire; contingent
contingente; eventual
eventuell; Kontingent

1477. **continuance**
ajournement (m); continuation (f)
aplazamiento (m); continuación (f)
Aufschub (m); Vertagung (f)

1478. **continuation**
continuation (f); suite (f)
continuación (f)
Fortsetzung (f)

1479. **to continue**
continuer
continuar
fortsetzen

1480. **continuous voyage**
voyage (m) continu
viaje (m) continuado
ununterbrochene Seereise (f) oder Fahrt (f)

1481. **contraband**
contrebande (f)
contrabando (m)
Konterbande (f)

1482. **contraband of war**
contrebande de guerre
contrabando de guerra
Kriegskonterbande

1483. **contract**
contrat (m)
contrato (m)
Vertrag (m)

1484. **bilateral contract**
contrat bilatéral
contrato bilateral
zweiseitiger Vertrag

1485. **by private contract**
sous seing privé
por contrato privado
durch Privatvertrag

1486. **contract of sale**
contrat de vente (f)
contrato de compraventa (f)
Kaufvertrag (m)

1487. **contractual**
contractuel
contractual
vertraglich

1488. **employment contract**
contrat de travail (m)
contrato de trabajo (m)
Anstellungsvertrag (m)

1489. **marriage contract**
contrat de mariage (m)
contrato matrimonial, nupcial
Ehevertrag

1490. **multilateral contract**
contrat multilatéral, plurilatéral
contrato multilateral
mehrseitiger Vertrag

1491. **nude contract; nudum pactum**
contrat à titre gratuit
contrato sin causa
unentgeltlicher Vertrag

1492. **quasi contract**
quasi-contrat (m)
cuasicontrato (m)
Quasivertrag (m)

1493. **third party beneficiary contract**
stipulation (f) pour autrui
contrato en beneficio de terceros
Vertrag zu Gunsten eines Dritten

1494. **unenforceable contract**
contrat sans force obligatoire
contrato que no se puede complir
klagloser Vertrag; nicht durch Klage erzwingbarer Vertrag

1495. **void contract**
contrat nul et non avenu
contrato nulo
nichtiger Vertrag

1496. **to contract**
contracter
contratar
einen Vertrag abschliessen; kontrahieren

1497. **to enter into a contract**
passer un contrat
cerrar un contrato
eine Verbindlichkeit eingehen

1498. **to terminate, void, a contract**
résilier un contrat
anular un contrato
einen Vertrag auflösen

1499. **contractor**
entrepreneur (m); contractant (m)
contratista (m)
Kontrahent (m); Unternehmer (m)

1500. **independent contractor**
contractant indépendant
contratante independiente
selbständiger Unternehmer

1501. **contradiction**
contradiction (f)
contradicción (f)
Widerspruch (m)

1502. **contradiction in terms**
contradiction dans les termes
contradicción de términos
innerer Widerspruch

1503. **to contradict**
contredire
contradecir
widersprechen

1504. **contravention**
contravention (f); infraction (f)
contravención (f); infracción (f)
Verletzung (f); Zuwiderhandlung (f); Ordnungswidrigkeit (f)

1505. **to contravene**
contrevenir à
contravenir
zuwiderhandeln

1506. **contribution**
contribution (f); apport (m)
contribución (f)
Beitrag (m); Kontribution (f)

1507. **contribution in kind**
apport (m) en nature
contribución (f) en especie
Naturalleistung (f)

1508. **contributory**
contribuant
contribuyente
beitragend

1509. **to contribute**
contribuer
contribuir
beitragen

1510. **control**
contrôle (m)
control (m)
Kontrolle (f); Aufsicht (f)

1511. **birth control**
contrôle des naissances
planificación familiar
Geburtenkontrolle

1512. **price control**
contrôle des prix
control de precios
Preisüberwachung

1513. **rent control**
réglementation (f) des loyers
reglamentación (f) de alquileres
Mieterschutz (m)

1514. **to control**
contrôler
controlar
kontrollieren; überwachen

1515. **controversy**
controverse (f)
controversia (f)
Kontroverse (f)

1516. **controversial**
controversable; discuté
contencioso; controvertible

streitig; umstritten

1517. **contumacy**
contumace (f); défaut (m)
contumacia (f); desacato (m)
Kontumaz (n); Nichterscheinen (n) vor Gericht (m)

1518. **contumacious**
contumace
contumaz
kontumazial; ungehorsam gegen gerichtliche Vorladung

1519. **convention**
accord (m); convention (f)
convención (f); convenio (m)
Kongress (m); Versammlung (f); Parteitag (m)

1520. **constitutional convention**
assemblée (f) constituante
asamblea (f) constitucional
verfassungsgebende Versammlung (f)

1521. **to convene**
convoquer; se réunir
convocar; reunirse
einberufen; zusammentreten; sich versammeln

1522. **conversion**
conversion (f); détournement (m)
conversión (f); apropiación (f) ilícita
widerrechtliche Verwendung (f); unrechtmässige Veräusserung (f); Umwandlung (f)

1523. **equitable conversion**
ameublissement (m)
canje (m) teórico de inmuebles (mpl) por muebles (mpl) y vice-versa, por equidad para facilitar cumplimiento de una cláusula contractual o testamentaria
Unwandlung (f) von unbeweglichem in beweglich Vermögen (n) (und umgekehrt)

1524. **to convert**
détourner; opérer une conversion
apropiarse ilícitamente; convertir
widerrechtlich verwenden; konvertieren (Währung); unwandeln

1525. **conveyance**
aliénation (f) de propriété (f) foncière; transfert (m)
traslación (f) de dominio (m); traspaso (m)
Abtretung (f); Übertragung (f)

1526. **to convey**
aliéner; transférer
transferir; traspasar
abtreten; übertragen

1527. **conviction**
condamnation (f); conviction (f)
condena (f); convicción (f)
Schuldigerklärung (f); Verurteilung (f)

1528. **convict**
condamné (m)
reo (m) convicto
Verurteilter (m)

1529. **convicted**
condamné
condenado
verurteilt; überführt

1530. **prior conviction**
condamnation antérieure
convicción anterior
Vorstrafe (f)

1531. **to be convicted of**
être reconnu coupable de
ser condenado por
verurteilt werden wegen

1532. **to convict**
condamner; reconnaître coupable
condenar
verurteilen; überführen

1533. **convince, to**
convaincre; persuader
convencer; persuadir
überzeugen

1534. **convoy**
convoi (m); escorte (f)
convoy (m); escolta (f)
Geleit (n); Bedeckung (f)

1535. **cooperation**
coopération (f); concours (m)
cooperación (f)
Mitwirkung (f); Zusammenarbeit (f)

1536. **cooperative**
coopératif
cooperativo

mitwirkend; kooperativ; Genossenschafts-

1537. **cooperative society**
la (société) coopérative
la (sociedad) cooperativa
Genossenschaft (f); Konsumverein (m)

1538. **to cooperate**
coopérer
cooperar
zusammenarbeiten

1539. **coordination**
coordination (f)
coordinación (f)
Koordinierung (f)

1540. **coordinator**
coordinateur (m)
coordinador (m)
Koordinator (m)

1541. **to coordinate**
coordonner
coordinar
koordinieren

1542. **coparcenary**
succession (f) par indivis
herencia (f) conjunta
gemeinschaftliches Eigentum (n) (durch Erbschaft (f))

1543. **coparcener**
propriétaire (m) indivis
coheredero (m)
Miteigentümer (m) (durch Erbschaft)

1544. **copy**
copie (f); exemplaire (m); numéro (m)
copia (f); ejemplar (m); número (m)
Abschrift (f); Ausfertigung (f); Exemplar (n); Kopie (f)

1545. **authentic copy**
copie (f) authentifiée
copia (f) auténtica
authentisches Exemplar (n)

1546. **certified, true, copy**
copie conforme
copia auténticada, fiel
öffentlich beglaubigte Abschrift

1547. **photostatic copy**
photocopie
fotocopia
Photokopie

1548. **to copy**
faire une copie
sacar copia
abschreiben; kopieren

1549. **copyright**
droit (m) d'auteur (m)
derechos (mpl) de autor (m)
Urheberrecht (n)

1550. **infringement of a copyright**
contrefaçon (f) du droit d'auteur
violación (f) del derecho de autor
Urheberrechtsverletzung (f)

1551. **to copyright**
déposer les droits d'auteur
registrar los derechos de autor
Urheberrecht erwerben

1552. **co-respondent**
complice (m) d'adultère (m)
codemandado (m) en casos (mpl) de adulterio (m)
Mitbeklagter (m) in einem Ehescheidungsprozess (m)

1553. **coroner**
enquêteur (m)
pesquisidor (m)
amtlicher Leichenbeschauer (m)

1554. **coroner's inquest**
enquête (f) en cas de mort violente ou suspecte
indagatoria (f) de pesquisidor
amtliche Leichenschau (f) Leichenöffnung (f)

1555. **corporate**
ayant la personnalité morale
perteneciente a una sociedad anónima
gesellschaftlich; Gesellschafts-

1556. **body corporate**
personne morale; corps constitué
persona jurídica
juristische Person

1557. **corporation**
société (f) anonyme
sociedad (f) anónima; empresa (f)
Aktiengesellschaft (f)

1558. **charitable, eleemosynary, corporation**
société de bienfaisance (f)

sociedad de beneficencia (f)
Wohltätigkeitsgesellschaft (f)
1559. **limited (Ltd.) corporation**
société anonyme à responsabilité (f) limitée
sociedad de responsabilidad (f) limitada
Gesellschaft mit beschränkter Haftung (f)
1560. **municipal corporation**
municipalité (f)
municipalidad (f)
Stadtgemeinde (f)
1561. **to incorporate**
constituer, mettre en société
constituir una sociedad anónima
eine Gesellschaft errichten oder amtlich eintragen
1562. **corporeal**
corporel
corpóreo
körperlich; materiell
1563. **corpse**
cadavre (m)
cadáver (m)
Leiche (f)
1564. **correction**
correction (f); rectification (f) d'erreur (f)
corrección (f); rectificación (f)
Berichtigung (f); Verweis (m)
1565. **to correct**
corriger
corregir
berichtigen
1566. **corroboration**
confirmation (f); corroboration (f)
confirmación (f); corroboración (f)
Bestätigung (f); Bekräftigung (f)
1567. **in corroboration of**
à l'appui de
en prueba de
zur Bestätigung, Unterstützung von
1568. **to corroborate**
confirmer; corroborer
confirmar; corroborar
bestätigen; bestärken
1569. **corruption**
corruption (f)
corrupción (f)
Bestechlichkeit (f); Bestechung (f)
1570. **to corrupt**
corrompre
corromper
bestechen
1571. **cosigner**
cosignataire (m)
cofirmante (m)
Mitunterzeichner (m)
1572. **costs**
frais (mpl)
costas (fpl)
Kosten (fpl)
1573. **cost of living**
coût (m) de la vie (f)
costo (m) de la vida (f)
Lebenshaltungskosten (f)
1574. **cost of production**
coût (m) de production (f)
costo (m) de producción (f)
Herstellungskosten (f); Erzeugungskosten (f)
1575. **cost of the war**
charges (fpl) de la guerre (f)
costo (m) de la guerra (f)
Kriegskosten (f)
1576. **overhead costs, charges, expenses**
frais (mpl) généraux
gastos (mpl) generales
allgemeine Unkosten (fpl); Generalunkosten (fpl)
1577. **council**
conseil (m)
concejo (m); consejo (m)
Rat (m); Ratsversammlung (f)
1578. **cabinet council**
conseil de cabinet
consejo de gabinete, ministros
Ministerrat (m); Kabinettssitzung (f)
1579. **Council of State**
Conseil d'Etat
Consejo de Estado
Staatsrat
1580. **councillor**
conseiller (m)
consejero (m)
Rat (m); Ratsmitglied (m)

1581. **counsel**
avocat (m); conseiller (m); conseil (m)
abogado (m); consejero (m); concejo (m)
Anwalt (m); Rechtsvertreter (m); Rat (m)

1582. **chief of counsel**
procureur (m) général
abogado (m) principal
Hauptankläger (m)

1583. **counsel for the defense; defense counsel**
défenseur (m)
defensor (m)
Verteidiger (m)

1584. **counsel for the prosecution**
Le Ministère Public
acusador
Staatsanwalt

1585. **counselor of embassy**
conseiller (m) d'ambassade (f)
consejero (m) de embajada (f)
Botschaftsrat (m)

1586. **to be represented by counsel**
comparaître par avoué
comparecer representado por letrado, abogado
durch einen Anwalt vertreten sein

1587. **to designate a counsel**
choisir, désigner un défenseur
nombrar a un abogado
einen Verteidiger bestellen

1588. **countenance, to**
approuver; favoriser
apoyar; aprobar
unterstützen; begünstigen

1589. **counter**
contre
contra
wider; gegen

1590. **to run counter to**
aller à l'encontre de
oponerse
zuwiderlaufen

1591. **countercharge**
contre-accusation (f)
reconvención (f)
Gegenklage (f)

1592. **counterclaim**
demande (f) reconventionnelle; reconvention (f)
contrarreclamación (f); reconvención (f)
Gegenanspruch (m); Widerklage (f)

1593. **counterfeit; counterfeiting**
contrefaçon (f)
falsificación (f)
Fälschung (f)

1594. **counterfeiter**
contrefacteur (m); faux-monnayeur (m)
falsificador (m)
Falschmünzer (m)

1594a. **to counterfeit**
contrefaire; falsifier
falsificar; forjar
falschmünzen; fälschen

1595. **countermand, to**
contremander; révoquer
dar contraorden; revocar
abbestellen; widerrufen

1596. **counter-memorial**
contre-mémoire (m)
contramemorial (m)
Klageabweisungsantrag (m)

1597. **counterpart**
duplicat (m)
duplicado (m)
Gegenstück (n)

1598. **counter-proposal**
contre-proposition (f)
contraproposición (f)
Gegenvorschlag (m)

1599. **countersignature**
contreseing (m)
refrendata (f); refrendo (m)
Gegenzeichnung (f)

1600. **to countersign**
contresigner
refrendar
gegenzeichnen

1601. **country**
pays (m)
país (m)
Land (m)

1602. **country of origin; mother country**
pays d'origine
país de origen

Ursprungsland (n)
1603. **coup d'état**
coup d'Etat
golpe de Estado
Staatsstreich (m)
1604. **coupon**
bon (m); coupon (m)
cupón (m)
Kupon (m)
1605. **court**
cour (f); tribunal (m)
corte (f); tribunal (m)
Gericht (n); Gerichtshof (m)
1606. **by leave of court**
par autorisation du tribunal
con autorización del tribunal
mit Genehmigung des Gerichts
1607. **court costs, fees**
frais de justice
costas judiciales
Gerichtskosten
1608. **courthouse**
palais de justice
palacio de justicia
Gerichtsgebäude
1609. **court record**
acte (m) du tribunal (m); compte rendu (m) d'audience (f)
autos (mpl); sumario (m)
Gerichtsprotokoll (n)
1610. **court reporter**
sténographe (m) parlementaire
taquígrafo (m) de actas (fpl)
Protokollführer (m)
1611. **courtroom**
salle d'audience
sala de audiencia
Gerichtssaal
1612. **court ruling**
décision (f) du juge
providencia (f) de juez
richterlicher Entscheid (m)
1613. **in open court**
en audience publique; à huis ouvert
en audiencia pública
in öffentlicher Gerichtssitzung
1614. **to address the court**
s'adresser au tribunal
dirigirse al tribunal
dem Gericht vortragen
1615. **to clear the court**
faire évacuer la salle
despejar la sala
den Gerichtssaal räumen lassen
1616. **to hold court**
tenir audience
hallarse el tribunal en sesión
eine Gerichtsverhandlung abhalten
1617. **to settle a case out of court**
arranger une affaire à l'amiable
transar un pleito
(einen Rechtsstreit) aussergerichtlich beilegen
1618. **to sit in camera, behind closed doors**
délibérer à huis clos
reunirse en sesión secreta
eine geschlossene Sitzung abhalten
1619. **courts**
cours (fpl) de justice; tribunaux (mpl)
cortes (fpl); tribunales (mpl)
Gerichte (npl)
1620. **administrative court**
tribunal administratif
tribunal administrativo
Verwaltungsgericht
1621. **admiralty court**
l'amirauté
tribunal de almirantazgo
Admiralitätsgericht
1622. **army, military court**
tribunal militaire
tribunal militar
Militärgericht
1623. **Central American Court of Justice**
Cour de Justice de l'Amérique Centrale
Tribunal de Justicia Centro-Americano
Zentralamerikanischer Gerichtshof
1624. **civil court**
tribunal civil
tribunal civil
Zivilgericht
1625. **court-martial**
conseil de guerre; cour martiale
consejo de guerra; corte marcial

Kriegsgericht; Standgericht

1626. **court of appeals; appellate court**
cour d'appel
tribunal de apelación
Appellationsgericht; Berufungsgericht; Oberlandesgericht (Germany)

1627. **court of arbitration**
cour d'arbitrage
tribunal de arbitraje
Schiedsgericht

1628. **court of assizes** (see **nisi prius court**)

1629. **court of cassation**
cour de cassation
corte de casación
Kassationsgerichthof (France); Bundesgerichtshof (Germany)

1630. **court of chancery, equity**
court d'équité
tribunal de equidad
Kanzleigericht

1631. **court of claims**
tribunal qui juge les réclamations contre le gouvernement
tribunal para juicios contra el gobierno
Gericht, das die Zuständigkeit besitzt, Klagen gegen die Regierung zu entscheiden

1632. **court of customs and patent appeals**
cour d'appel pour les cas de douane et de brevets
tribunal de apelación en materia aduanal y de patentes
Berufungsgericht in Zoll- und Patentsachen

1633. **court of domestic relations**
tribunal d'affaires de famille
juzgado de relaciones familiares
Spezialgericht für Familienrechtssachen

1634. **court of equity**
tribunal qui applique l'équité
tribunal de equidad
Gericht, das nach Regeln der Billigkeit urteilt

1635. **court of first instance, common pleas**
tribunal de première instance
tribunal de primera instancia
Gericht erster Instanz

1635a. **Court of Justice of the European Communities**
Cour de Justice des Communautés Européennes
Tribunal de Justicia de las Comunidades Europeas
Gerichtshof der Europäischen Gemeinschaften

1636. **court of last resort**
cour de dernière instance
tribunal de última instancia
Gericht der höchsten Instanz

1637. **court of original jurisdiction**
tribunal de première instance
tribunal de primera instancia
Gericht der ersten Instanz

1638. **court of record**
tribunal dont les actes et la procédure font l'objet de procès verbaux
tribunal de registro, de autos
ordentliches Gericht

1639. **criminal court**
cour d'assises
tribunal penal
Strafgericht

1640. **district court**
tribunal fédéral de première instance
tribunal federal de primera instancia
Bezirksgericht; Gericht erster Instanz

1641. **domestic, national court**
tribunal national
tribunal nacional
innerstaatliches Gericht

1642. **European Court of Human Rights**
Cour européenne de droits humains
Tribunal Europeo de Derechos Humanos
Europäischer Gerichtshof für Menschenrechte

1643. **federal court**
cour fédérale
tribunal federal

Bundesgericht

1644. **Inter-American Court of Justice**
Cour inter-américaine de Justice
Tribunal Inter-Americano de Justicia
Interamerikanischer Gerichtshof

1645. **International Court of Justice**
Cour de Justice Internationale
Corte Internacional de Justicia
Internationaler Gerichtshof

1646. **juvenile, children's court**
tribunal des mineurs
tribunal de menores
Jugendgericht

1647. **military court**
tribunal militaire
tribunal militar
Militärgericht

1648. **municipal court**
cour municipale
tribunal municipal
Stadtgericht; Bezirksgericht

1649. **nisi prius court; court of assizes**
tribunal civil de première instance; tribunal d'instance (section contentieuse)
tribunal civil de primera instancia
Amtsgericht (Abteilung Zivilsachen)

1650. **Permanent Court of Arbitration**
Cour Permanente d'Arbitrage
Corte Permanente de Arbitraje
Ständiger Schiedsgerichtshof

1651. **Permanent Court of International Justice**
Cour Permanente de Justice Internationale
Tribunal Permanente de Justicia Internacional
Ständiger Internationaler Gerichtshof

1652. **police court**
tribunal de simple police
tribunal de policía
Polizeigericht

1653. **prize court**
tribunal des prises
tribunal de presas
Prisengericht

1654. **probate court**
tribunal qui connaît des testaments
tribunal testamentario
Nachlassgericht

1655. **provost court**
tribunal militaire
tribunal militar
Feldgericht

1656. **special court**
tribunal d'exception spécial
tribunal especial
Sondergericht

1657. **supreme court**
cour suprême
corte suprema
oberster Gerichtshof

1658. **surrogate court**
tribunal des homologations, successions
tribunal testamentario
Gericht für Nachlass- und Pflegeschaftssachen

1659. **covenant**
contrat (m); convention (f); pacte (m)
convenio (m); pacto (m)
Vertrag (m); Pakt (m); Satzung (f)

1660. **Covenant of the League of Nations**
Pacte de la Société des Nations
Convenio de la Liga de las Naciones
Völkerbundssatzung

1661. **covenant running with the land**
servitude foncière
obligación ligada con los bienes raíces
Verpflichtungen, die mit dem Eigentum an einem Grundstück verbunden sind

1662. **restrictive covenant**
stipulation limitant l'usage
estipulación limitando el uso
einschränkende Abmachung (Klausel)

1663. **solemn covenant**

contrat solennel
contrato solemne
feierliche Vereinbarung

1664. **to covenant**
s'engager
pactar
einen Vertrag abschliessen

1665. **coverture, under**
en puissance de mari; mariée
estado de la mujer casada
verheiratete Frau

1666. **create, to**
créer
crear
schaffen; kreieren

1667. **credentials**
lettres (fpl) de créance
credenciales (fpl)
Beglaubigungsschreiben (n)

1668. **presentation of credentials**
remise des lettres de créance
presentación de credenciales
Überreichung des Beglaubigungsschreibens

1669. **credibility**
crédibilité (f)
credibilidad (f)
Glaubwürdigkeit (f)

1670. **credible**
digne de foi
fidedigno
glaubwürdig

1671. **credit**
crédit (m); croyance (f)
crédito (m)
Kredit (m); Glaubwürdigkeit (f)

1672. **creditor**
créancier (m)
acreedor (m)
Gläubiger (m)

1673. **crime**
délit (m); crime (m)
delito (m); crimen (m)
Verbrechen (n)

1674. **attempt to commit a crime**
attentat criminel
atentado criminal
Versuch einer strafbaren Handlung

1675. **commission of crimes**
perpétration de crimes
perpetración de crímenes
Begehung von Verbrechen

1676. **crime wave**
recrudescence de criminalité
ola de crímenes
zeitweise grosse Steigerung der Anzahl von Verbrechen

1677. **crimes against humanity**
crimes contre l'humanité
crímenes contra la humanidad
Verbrechen gegen die Menschheit

1678. **crimes against the peace**
crimes contra la paix
crímenes contra la paz
Verbrechen gegen den Frieden

1679. **to compound a crime, felony**
fermer les yeux sur un délit contre rémunération
cerrar los ojos sobre un delito contra remuneración
ein Verbrechen wegen erhaltener Entschädigung nicht verfolgen

1680. **criminality**
criminalité (f)
criminalidad (f)
Kriminalität (f)

1681. **criminal**
criminel (m)
criminal (m)
Verbrecher (m)

1682. **dangerous criminal**
criminel dangereux
criminal peligroso
gefährlicher Verbrecher

1683. **habitual criminal**
récidiviste (m)
delincuente (m) habitual
Gewohnheitsverbrecher (m)

1684. **to harbor a criminal**
recéler un criminel
encubrir un criminal
einem Verbrecher obdach gewähren

1685. **criminology**
criminologie (f)
criminología (f)
Kriminologie (f)

1686. **criminologist**
criminologiste (m)
criminólogo (m)
Kriminologe (m)

1687. **criterion**
critère (m); criterium (m)
criterio (m)
Kriterium (n); Prüfstein (m)

1688. **critical**
critique; urgent
crítico; urgente
kritisch

1689. **criticism**
critique (f); censure (f)
crítica (f); censura (f)
Kritik (f)

1690. **critic**
critique (m)
crítico (m)
Kritiker (m)

1691. **crook**
filou (m); voyou (m)
estafador (m)
Gauner (m)

1692. **cross-examination**
interrogatoire (m) contradictoire
contrainterrogatorio (m); repregunta (f)
Kreuzverhör (n)

1693. **to cross-examine**
contre-interroger
contrainterrogar; repreguntar
ins Kreuzverhör nehmen

1694. **cross-reference**
renvoi (m)
remisión
Kreuzverweis (m)

1695. **crowd**
foule (f); attroupement (m)
muchedumbre (f); masa (f) popular
Gedränge (n); Menschenmenge (f)

1696. **unruly crowd**
attroupement (m)
muchedumbre (f) incontrolable
aufrührerische Menschenmenge (f)

1697. **cruelty**
cruauté (f)
crueldad (f)
Grausamkeit (f)

1698. **cruel**
cruel
cruel
grausam

1699. **culpability**
culpabilité (f)
culpabilidad (f)
Schuldhaftigkeit (f)

1700. **culpable**
coupable
culpable
schuldig

1701. **culprit**
coupable (m, f); prévenu (m)
culpable (m); reo (m)
Angeklagter (m); Beschuldigter (m); Schuldiger (m)

1702. **cumulation**
accumulation (f)
acumulación (f)
Anhäufung (f); Realkonkurrenz (f)

1703. **cumulative**
cumulatif
cumulativo
kumulativ

1704. **curb, to**
mettre un frein à
poner freno a
beschränken; dämpfen

1705. **curfew**
couvre-feu (m)
toque (m) de queda (f)
Ausgehverbot (n); Ausgehsperre (f)

1706. **currency**
monnaie (f)
moneda (f)
Währung (f); Umlaufsmittel (n)

1707. **devaluation of currency**
dévaluation (f) monétaire
devaluación (f) de la moneda
Abwertung (f)

1708. **foreign currency**
devise (f), monnaie (f) étrangère
moneda (f) extranjera
Fremdwährung (f) Devisen (fpl)

1709. **hard currency**
monnaie forte, convertible
moneda convertible
harte Währung

1710. **local currency**
monnaie locale
moneda local
Landeswährung

1711. **soft currency**
monnaie faible, non-convertible
moneda inconvertible
weiche Währung

1712. **current**
courant; en vigueur
corriente; en vigor
gegenwärtig; laufend

1713. **curtailment**
diminution (f); restriction (f)
rebaja (f); reducción (f)
Kürzung (f); Beschränkung (f)

1714. **to curtail**
diminuer; restreindre
reducir; restringir
kürzen; beschränken

1715. **curtesy**
douaire ou usufruit (m) marital du veuf sur les biens-fonds de l'épouse
derechos del hombre en la propiedad raíz de su difunta esposa
Niessbrauchrecht des Witwers am Grundbesitz seiner verstorbenen Frau

1716. **custody**
détention (f); internement (m)
custodia (f)
Gewahrsam (m); Haft (f)

1717. **custodian**
gardien (m)
custodio (m)
Verwalter (m); Verwahrer (m)

1718. **in custody**
en état d'arrestation, d'internement
bajo custodia
in Gewahrsam oder Haft

1719. **preventive custody**
détention (f), prison (f) préventive
prisión (f) preventiva; secuestro (m) judicial
Vorbeugungshaft (f); Sicherung (f)

1720. **protective custody**
détention protectrice
custodia protectiva
Schutzhaft

1721. **to release from custody**
libérer; relâcher
libertar
aus der Untersuchungshaft entlassen; die Untersuchungshaft aufheben

1722. **to remand a prisoner in custody**
remettre un prisonnier en état d'arrestation
continuar la detención de un preso
einen Gefangenen in die Untersuchungshaft zurückbringen

1723. **custom**
coutume (m); moeurs (fpl)
costumbre (f); uso (m)
Gewohnheit (f); Sitte (f); Brauch (m)

1724. **customary**
habituel
consuetudinario
gewöhnlich; üblich

1725. **customer**
client (m)
cliente (m, f)
Kunde (m)

1726. **customs**
douane (f)
aduana (f)
Zoll (m)

1727. **customhouse**
douane (f)
aduana (f)
Zollamt (n)

1728. **customs regulations**
règlements douaniers
reglamentos de aduana
Zollbestimmungen

1729. **customs union**
union (f) douanière
unión (f) aduanera
Zollunion (f)

1730. **exempt from customs**
exempt de droits de douane
libre de derechos de aduana
zollfrei

1731. **cut**
coupe (f); diminution (f)
corte (m); reducción (f)
Herabsetzung (f); Kürzung (f)

1732. **cut-throat**
coupe-jarret (m)
asesino (m)

Halsabschneider (m)

1733. **cycle**
cycle (m)
ciclo (m)
Zyklus (m)

1734. **trade cycle**
cycle économique; conjoncture (f)
ciclo económico; coyuntura (f)
Wirtschaftszyklus; Konjunktur (f)

1735. **cy-pres doctrine**
doctrine d'après laquelle les intentions d'un testateur doivent être observées aussi exactement que possible
doctrina que interpreta los contratos o documentos escritos conforme a la intención de las partes contratantes
Doktrin, nach der schriftliche Willenserklarungen nach dem wirklichen Willen des Erblassers auszulegen sind

D

1736. **damage**
dommage (m); préjudice (m); tort (m); dégâts (mpl)
daño (m); perjuicio (m)
Schaden (m) durch unerlaubte Handlung (f)

1737. **damages**
dommage; dommages-intérêts (mpl)
daño (m); pérdida (f); perjuicio (m)
Beschädigung (f); Schaden (m); Schadensersatz (m)

1738. **actual damages**
dommage effectif
daños efectivos
tatsachlicher Schaden

1739. **compensatory damages**
dédommagement (m)
indemnización (f)
Schadenersatz (m); Ersatz des tatsachlichen Schadens

1740. **exemplary damages**
dommages-intérêts punitifs
daños punitivos
vershärfter Schadensersatz

1741. **liquidated damages**
dommages-intérêts dont le montant est prévu
daños cuyo monto ha sido fijado
verträglich im voraus festgestellte Schadenssumme

1742. **measure of damages**
évaluation du montant des dommages-intérêts
evaluación de daños
Masstab der Berechnung von Schadensersatz

1743. **nominal damages**
dommages-intérêts symboliques
indemnización simbólica
nomineller Schaden

1744. **punitive damages**
réparation d'un préjudice moral
sanción pecuniaria por daños morales
Schadensersatz für unerlaubte Handlungen

1745. **quantum of damages**
quantum des dommages-intérêts
monto de daños
Höhe des Schadens

1746. **substantial damages**
réparation d'un préjudice réel
indemnización por daños reales
hoher Schadensersatz

1747. **unliquidated damages**
dommages-intérêts non-évalués
indemnización no determinada
nicht im voraus vertraglich festgestellte Schadenssumme

1748. **to assess the amount of damages**
déterminer, fixer le montant des dommages-intérêts
determinar el monto de la indemnización
den Schaden abschätzen

1749. **to be liable for damages**
être tenu des dommages-intérêts
ser responsable por los daños causados
schadenersatzpflichtig sein

1750. **to claim damages**
réclamer des dommages-intérêts
reclamar daños y perjuicios
auf Schadenersatz klagen

1751. **to damage**
endommager
dañar
Schaden zufügen

1752. **to sue for damages**
poursuivre en dommages-intérêts
demandar por daños y perjuicios
auf Schadensersatz klagen

1753. **damaging**
nuisible
perjudicial
schädlich

1754. **danger**
danger (m)
peligro (m); riesgo (m)
Gefahr (f)

1755. **danger of war**
menace (f) de guerre
peligro (m) de guerra
Kriegsgefahr (f)

1756. **dangerous**
dangereux
peligroso
gefährlich

1757. **imminent danger**
danger imminent
peligro inminente
drohende Gefahr

1758. **data**
données (fpl); faits (mpl)
datos (mpl)
Angaben (fpl); Daten (npl)

1759. **data processing**
traitement (m) de données (fpl); informatique (f)
elaboración (f) de datos (mpl)
Datenverarbeitung (f)

1760. **date**
date (f)
fecha (f)
Datum (n)

1761. **due date**
date d'échéance
fecha de vencimiento
Fälligkeitsdatum

1762. **effective date**
date en vigueur
fecha efectiva
Zeitpunkt des Inkraftretens

1763. **to date**
à ce jour
hasta la fecha
bis heute; bisher

1764. **days of grace**
jours de grâce (f)
días de gracia (f)
Gnadenfrist (f); Aufschub (m)

1765. **deadline**
date limite; délai imposé
fecha límite; límite absoluto.
äusserstes Datum; Stichtag

1766. **deadlock**
impasse (f)
situación (f) sin salida (f)
ausweglose Situation (f)

1767. **dealings**
opérations (fpl)
transacciones (fpl)
Transaktionen (fpl)

1768. **dealer**
marchand (m)
comerciante (m, f)
Händler (m)

1769. **dean**
doyen (m)
decano (m)
Dekan (m)

1770. **death**
décès (m); mort (f)
muerte (f); defunción (f)
Tod (m)

1771. **accidental death**
mort accidentelle
muerte por accidente
Tod durch Unfall

1772. **dead**
mort (m)
muerto (m)
tot (m)

1773. **death by poison**
mort par empoisonnement
muerte mediante veneno
Tod durch Gift

1774. **in contemplation of death**
en prévision de la mort
en previsión de fallecimiento
in Hinblick auf den Tod

1775. **at, on, the point of death**
à l'article de mort
en artículo de muerte
in den letzten Zügen liegen

1776. **under pain of death**
sous peine de mort
bajo pena de muerte
bei Todesstrafe

1777. **violent death**
mort violente
muerte violenta
gewaltsamer Tod

1778. **to die**
mourir
morir; fallecer
sterben

1779. **debetable**
contestable; discutable
discutible; disputable
diskutierbar; streitig

1780. **debauchery (debauch)**
débauche (f)
libertinaje (m)
Ausschweifung (f)

1781. **to debauch**
débaucher; séduire
corromper; seducir
ausschweifen; verführen; verleiten

1782. **debenture**
obligation (f); reconnaissance (f) de dette (f)
obligación (f); reconocimiento (m) de deuda (f)
Schuldverschreibung (f); Obligation (f)

1783. **debenture holder**
obligataire (m)
tenedor (m) de obligaciones (fpl)
Inhaber (m) einer Schuldverschreibung (f); Obligationär (m)

1784. **debit**
débit (m)
débito (m); saldo (m) deudor
Debet (m); Soll (n)

1785. **to debit**
débiter
cargar en cuenta
belasten

1786. **debt**
dette (f)
deuda (f)
Schuld (f)

1787. **acknowledgement of debt**
reconnaissance de dette
reconocimiento de deuda
Schuldanerkenntnis

1788. **active debt**
dette portant intérêt
deuda que devenga interés
ausstehende Schuld

1789. **adjudication of debts**
répartition de dettes
repartición de las deudas
urteilsmässig festgestellte Schuldverhältnisse

1790. **bad debt**
créance irrécouvrable
deuda incobrable
uneinbringliche Forderung

1791. **floating debt**
dette flottante
deuda flotante
schwebende Schuld

1792. **debt due**
créance exigible
deuda vencida
fällige Schuld

1793. **funded debt**
dette consolidée
deuda consolidada
konsolidierte Schuld

1794. **national, public, debt**
dette publique
deuda pública
Staatsschuld

1795. **recoverable debt**
créance recouvrable
deuda recobrable
einbringliche Forderung

1796. **unfunded debt**
créance non-consolidée
deuda no consolidada
schwebende Schuld; nicht konsolidierte Schuld

1797. **unsecured debt**
créance sans garantie
deuda sin garantía

ungedeckte Schuld

1798. **to discharge a debt**
s'acquitter d'une dette
pagar, saldar una deuda
eine Schuld bezahlen

1799. **to fund a debt**
consolider une dette
consolidar una deuda
eine Schuld decken

1800. **to repudiate a debt**
dénier une dette
repudiar una deuda
eine Schuld nicht anerkennen

1801. **debtor**
débiteur (m)
deudor (m)
Schuldner (m)

1802. **judgment debtor**
débiteur en vertu d'un jugement
deudor por juicio
Urteilsschuldner

1803. **decease**
décès (m); mort (f)
fallecimiento (m); muerte (f)
Hinscheiden (n); Tod (m)

1804. **deceased**
décédé
fallecido
verstorben

1805. **decedent**
défunt (m)
difunto (m)
Erblasser (m)

1806. **deceit; deception**
dol (m); tromperie (f)
engaño (m); fraude (m)
arglistige Täuschung (f); Betrüg (m)

1807. **deceitful**
dolosif; trompeur
engañoso; falso
betrügerisch; hinterlistig

1808. **to deceive**
tromper
engañar
betrügen

1809. **decision**
décision (f)
decisión (f)
Entscheidung (f)

1810. **admonitory decision**
décision de cour d'appel
fallo de tribunal de apelación
Appellentscheidung

1811. **decisive**
décisif
decisivo
entscheidend

1812. **to decide**
décider; statuer sur
decidir; fallar
beschliessen; entscheiden

1813. **declaration**
déclaration (f)
declaración (f)
Erklärung (f)

1814. **customs declaration**
déclaration en douane
declaración de aduana
Zolldeklaration; Zollerklärung

1815. **declaration of war**
déclaration de guerre
declaración de guerra
Kriegserklärung

1816. **dying declaration**
déclaration d'un mourant
declaración de un moribundo
Erklärung eines Sterbenden

1817. **false declaration**
fausse déclaration
declaración falsa
unrichtige Erklärung

1818. **to declare**
déclarer
declarar
erklären

1819. **decoy**
leurre (m)
señuelo (m)
Köder (m)

1820. **decree**
arrêt (m); arrêté (m); décret (m)
auto (m); decreto (m); ley (f)
Urteil (n); Verordnung (f); Erlass (m)

1821. **decree nisi**
décision provisoire
fallo condicional
vorläufiges Urteil

1822. **interlocutory decree**
jugement interlocutoire
auto interlocutorio
Zwischenurteil

1823. **decree-law**
décret-loi (m)
decreto-ley (m)
gesetzvertretende Verordnung (f); Verordnung (f) mit Gesetzkraft (f)

1824. **deduction**
conséquence (f); déduction (f)
deducción (f); inferencia (f)
Ableitung (f); Folgerung (f)

1825. **to deduce**
déduire
deducir
ableiten; folgern

1826. **to deduct**
rabattre
rebajar
abziehen

1827. **deed**
acte (m); titre (m)
hecho (m); título (m) legal; escritura (f)
Tat (f); Dokument (n); Urkunde (f); Übertragungsurkunde (f)

1828. **deed of conveyance**
titre de transfert de propriété
escritura de traspaso
Abtretungsurkunde

1829. **deed of sale**
contrat de vente
escritura de compraventa
Kaufvertrag

1830. **deed of trust**
acte de fidéicommis
escritura de fideicomiso
Übertragungsurkunde eines Treuhandvertrages

1831. **quitclaim deed**
acte transférant le titre par renonciation
escritura de pago y finiquito
Grundstückskaufvertrag

1832. **defamation**
diffamation (f)
difamación (f)
Verleumdung (f)

1833. **to defame**
diffamer
difamar
verleumden

1834. **default**
défaut (m); non comparution (f)
incumplimiento (m); quebrantamiento (m)
Nichterscheinen (n); Nichterfüllung (f)

1835. **by default**
par défaut
en rebeldía
durch Versäumnis, in Abwesenheit

1836. **defaulter**
contumax (m); défaillant (m)
contumaz (m); rebelde (m)
säumiger Schuldner (m); Zahlungsunfähiger (m)

1837. **to default**
faire défaut; ne pas comparaître
faltar; no comparecer
seinen Verpflichtungen nicht nachkommen; zum Termin nicht erscheinen

1838. **defeasance**
annulation (f); contre-lettre (f)
anulación (f); revocación (f)
Aufhebung (f); Annullierung (f)

1839. **defeasible**
annulable
anulable
aufhebbar

1840. **defects**
défauts (mpl)
defectos (mpl)
Mängel (mpl); Fehler (mpl)

1841. **defect of form**
défaut de forme
defecto de forma
Formmangel

1842. **defect of substance**
défaut matériel
defecto material
Substanzmangel

1843. **defective**
défectueux
defectuoso
mangelhaft

1844. **hidden, latent, defects**
défauts, vices cachés
vicios ocultos
verborgene Mängel

1845. **inherent defects**
défauts inhérents

vicios inherentes
anhaftende Mängel

1846. **defendant**
accusé (m)
acusado (m)
Beklagter (m)

1847. **to be named as a defendant**
être mis en accusation
ser acusado, demandado
angeklagt werden

1848. **to find for the defendant**
rendre un verdict en faveur de l'accusé
dictar sentencia en favor del acusado
eine Klage abweisen

1849. **defense**
défense (f)
defensa (f)
Verteidigung (f)

1850. **civil defense**
défense passive
defensa civil
Zivilverteidigung

1851. **defensible**
défendable
defendible
verfechtbar; haltbar

1852. **to conduct one's own defense**
présenter sa propre défense
asumir su propia defensa en un juicio
seine eigene Verteidigung führen

1853. **to defend**
défendre
defender
verteidigen

1854. **defiance**
défi (m)
desafío (m)
Herausforderung (f); Trotz (m)

1855. **to defy**
défier
desafiar
herausfordern Trotz bieten

1856. **deficiency**
manque (m)
deficiencia (f)
Mangel (m)

1857. **deficient**
déficient; défectueux
deficiente; defectuoso
unzureichend; mangelhaft

1858. **deficit**
déficit (m)
déficit (m)
Defizit (m); Fehlbetrag (m)

1859. **to make up a deficit**
combler un déficit
reparar un déficit
ein Defizit ausgleichen

1860. **defilement**
souillure (f)
profanación (f); mancha (f)
Beschmutzung (f); Schändung (f)

1861. **to defile**
souiller
manchar
beschmutzen; schänden

1862. **definite**
déterminé
definido
bestimmt

1863. **definition**
définition (f)
definición (f)
Definition (f)

1864. **to define**
définir
definir
definieren

1865. **definitive**
définitif
definitivo
bestimmt; entgültig

1866. **defraud, to**
frauder
defraudar
betrügen

1867. **defunct**
défunt (m)
difunto (m); fallecido (m)
Verstorbene (m, f)

1868. **degradation**
dégradation (f)
degradación (f)
Degradierung (f)

1869. **to degrade**
dégrader
degradar
degradieren

1870. **degree**

diplôme (m); mesure (f)
título (m); cuantía (f)
akademischer Grad (m); Mass (n)

1871. **delay**
remise (f); retard (m)
demora (f); tardanza (f)
Aufschub (m); Verzug (m)

1872. **to delay**
accorder une remise; retarder
demorar; retardar
aufschieben; verzögern

1873. **delegation**
délégation (f)
delegación (f)
Delegation (f); Abordnung (f); Vollmachtsübertragung (f)

1874. **delegate**
délégué (m)
delegado (m)
Delegierter (m); Abgeordneter (m)

1875. **list of delegates**
tableau (m) des délégués
lista (f) de delegados
Verzeichnis (n) der Delegierten

1876. **to delegate**
déléguer
delegar
delegieren; bevollmächtigen

1877. **deleterious**
nocif
nocivo
schädlich

1878. **deletion**
annulation (f); suppresion (f); rature (f)
anulación (f); supresión (f)
Tilgung (f); Streichung (f); Ausmerzung (f)

1879. **to delete**
effacer; rayer; biffer
borrar; suprimir; tachar
tilgen; streichen; ausmerzen

1880. **deliberation**
délibération (f)
deliberación (f)
Überlegung (f)

1881. **deliberate**
délibéré
deliberado
bedacht; bedachtsam

1882. **deliberately**
intentionnellement; à dessein
deliberadamente
vorsätzlich

1883. **to deliberate**
délibérer; réfléchir
deliberar
überlegen; bedenken

1884. **delict**
délit (m)
delito (m)
Delikt (m)

1885. **delinquency**
délinquence (f); faute (f)
delincuencia (f)
Verbrechen (n); Kriminalität (f)

1886. **delinquent**
délinquant (m)
delincuente (m)
Verbrecher (m)

1887. **juvenile delinquency**
délinquence de mineurs
delincuencia juvenil
Jugendkriminalität (f)

1888. **delivery**
livraison (f); remise (f); tradition (f)
cesión (f); entrega (f); traspaso (m)
Lieferung (f); Übergabe (f)

1889. **to deliver**
livrer; remettre
entregar; traspasar
abliefern; übergeben

1890. **demand**
demande (f); exigence (f)
demanda (f); exigencia (f)
Nachfrage (f); Verlangen (n)

1891. **formal demand**
demande formelle
requerimiento
Antrag (m)

1892. **payable on demand**
exigible sur demande
pagadero contra demanda
zahlbar bei Sicht (f)

1893. **to demand**
exiger; requérir
exigir; requerir
fordern; verlangen

1894. **demarcation**
abornement (m); démarcation (f)
demarcación (f); limitación (f)

Abgrenzung (f)

1895. **line of demarcation**
ligne (f) de démarcation
línea (f) de demarcación
Grenzlinie (f)

1896. **demise**
cession (f); décès (m)
cesión (f); muerte (f)
Ableben (n); Tod (m)

1897. **democracy**
démocratie (f)
democracia (f)
Demokratie (f)

1898. **demonstration**
manifestation (f); démonstration (f)
manifestación (f); demostración (f)
Demonstration (f); Verführung (f)

1899. **demonstrable**
évident
demostrable
beweisbar

1900. **demonstrator**
manifestant (m)
manifestante (m)
Demonstrant (m)

1901. **mass demonstration**
manifestation en masse
manifestación en masa
Massendemonstration (f)

1902. **to demonstrate**
démontrer; manifester
demostrar; manifestar
demonstrieren

1903. **demurrer**
exception (f); fin (f) de non-recevoir (m); objection (f)
excepción (f); objeción (f)
Rechtseinwand (m); Einrede (f)

1904. **to demur**
présenter une objection
presentar una excepción
Einwände oder Einwendungen erheben

1905. **denial**
dénégation (f); refus (m)
denegación (f); desmentido (m)
Ableugung (f); Verneinung (f); Dementi (n)

1906. **to deny**
dénier; rejeter
negar; denegar; rehusar
ableugnen; dementieren

1907. **denunciation**
dénonciation (f)
denunciación (f); denuncia (f)
Denunziation (f); Anzeige (f)

1908. **to denounce**
dénoncer
denunciar
denunzieren; anzeigen

1909. **department**
département (m); direction (f); ministère (m)
departamento (m); dirección (f); ministerio (m)
Abteilung (f); Amt (n); Ministerium (n)

1910. **departure**
départ (m); déviation (f)
desviación (f); partida (f)
Abreise (f); Abweichung (f)

1911. **to depart**
partir; sortir
desviarse; partir
abfahren; abreisen

1912. **dependent**
dépendant (m); personne (f) à la charge
dependiente (m); persona (f) a cargo
Angehöriger (m); Unterhaltsberechtigter (m)

1913. **deponent**
signataire (m) d'un affidavit (m); témoin (m) déposant
declarante (m); deponente (m)
beeidigter Zeuge (m)

1914. **deportation**
déportation (f)
deportación (f)
Deportation (f)

1915. **wholesale deportation**
déportation massive
deportación en masa
Massendeportation (f)

1916. **to deport**
déporter
deportar
deportieren

1917. **deposit**
dépôt (m); versement (m)

depósito (m)
Einlage (f); Einzahlung (f); Anzahlung (f)

1918. **depositor**
déposant (m)
depositador (m)
Einleger (m); Einzahlender (m)

1919. **to deposit**
faire un dépôt
depositar
Geld (n) bei einer Bank (f) deponieren oder einzahlen; deponieren

1920. **deposition**
déposition (f)
deposición (f)
eidliche schriftliche Aussage (f)

1921. **to depose**
déposer
deponer
eine eidliche schriftliche Aussage machen

1922. **depravity**
corruption (f)
corrupción (f)
Verderbtheit (f)

1923. **depreciation**
dépréciation (f)
depreciación (f)
Entwertung (f); Abschreibung (f)

1924. **depreciation of currency**
dépréciation des valeurs
depreciación de valor corriente
Geldenwertung

1925. **to depreciate**
diminuer la valeur de
bajar de precio
entwerten

1926. **depression**
crise (f) économique; dépression (f)
crisis (f) económica; depresión (f)
wirtschaftliche Depression (f); Krise (f)

1927. **deprivation**
perte (f); privation (f)
pérdida; privación (f)
Verlust (m); Entzug (m)

1928. **to deprive**
déposséder; priver
despojar; privar
von etwas ausschliessen; entziehen

1929. **deputy**
adjoint (m); député (m); suppléant (m)
adjunto (m); diputado (m); suplente (m)
Abgeordneter (m); Stellvertreter (m); Vertreter (m)

1930. **derelict**
objet abandonné; épave (f)
objeto abandonado; derrelicto (m)
herrenlose Sache; Wrack (n)

1930a. **dereliction**
abandon (m)
abandono (m)
Besitzaufgabe (f)

1931. **derogation**
atteinte (f); dérogation (f)
derogación (f)
Beeinträchtigung (f); Herabsetzung (f)

1932. **derogatory**
dérogatoire
derogatorio
nachteilig; herabsetzend

1933. **to derogate**
déroger à; porter atteinte à
derogar
beeinträchtigen; abweichen von

1934. **descent**
descendance (f); dévolution (f) successorale
descendencia (f); sucesión (f) hereditaria
Abstammung (f); Zufallen (n) von Besitz (m) durch Erbschaft (f)

1935. **descendant**
descendant (m)
descendiente (m)
Machkomme (m)

1936. **to descend from**
descendre de; être issue de
descender de
abstammen von

1937. **description**
description (f)
descripción (f)
Beschreibung (f)

1938. **to describe**
décrire
describir
beschreiben

1939. **desecration**
profanation (f)
profanación (f)
Entweihung (f)

1940. **to desecrate**
profaner
profanar
entweihen

1941. **desertion**
abandon (m); désertion (f)
abandono (m); deserción (f)
Verlassen (n)

1942. **deserter**
déserteur (m)
desertor (m)
Fahnenflüchtiger (m); Deserteur (m)

1943. **to desert**
abandonner; déserter
abandonar; desertar
desertieren; verlassen

1944. **design**
intention (f)
intención (f)
Absicht (f)

1945. **designation**
désignation (f)
designación (f)
Bezeichnung (f)

1946. **to designate**
désigner
designar
bezeichnen

1947. **destitution**
dénuement (m)
indigencia (f)
Armut (f); Elend (n)

1948. **destitute**
dénué
indigente
mittellos

1949. **destruction**
destruction (f)
destrucción (f)
Zerstörung (f)

1950. **to destroy**
détruire
destruir
zerstören

1951. **detainer** (see **writ of detainer,** No. 6273)

1952. **detective**
agent (m) de sûreté (f); détective (m)
detective (m)
Detektiv (m); Geheimpolizist (m)

1953. **detention**
détention (f)
detención (f)
Haft (f)

1954. **detention on remand; preventive detention**
détention préventive
detención preventiva
Untersuchungshaft

1955. **illegal detention**
détention illégale
detención ilegal
ungesetzliche Haft

1956. **to detain illegally**
détenir illégalement
detener ilegalmente
rechtswidrig in Haft halten

1957. **determination**
détermination (f)
determinación (f)
Bestimmung (f)

1958. **to determine**
déterminer
determinar
bestimmen

1959. **detinue** (see **action of detinue,** No. 144)

1960. **detriment**
détriment (m); dommage (m); préjudice (m)
daño (m); detrimento (m); perjuicio (m)
Nachteil (m); Schaden (m)

1961. **detrimental**
nuisible; préjudiciable
perjudicial
nachteilig; schädlich; zum Nachteil

1962. **to be detrimental to**
porter préjudice à
ser perjudicial a
nachteilig, schädlich sein

1963. **devaluation**
dévaluation (f)

devalorización (f)
Abwertung

1964. **devastation**
dévastation (f)
devastación (f)
Verwüstung (f)

1965. **to devastate**
dévaster
devastar
verwüsten

1966. **development**
développement (m)
desarrollo (m)
Entwicklung (f)

1967. **to develop**
développer
desarrollar
entwickeln

1968. **devest, to** (see **to divest,** No. 2097)

1969. **deviation**
déviation (f)
desvío (m); desviación (f)
Abweichung (f)

1970. **to deviate**
dévier
desviarse
abweichen

1971. **device**
dispositif (m); moyen (m)
dispositivo (m); medio (m)
Vorrichtung (f); Gerät (n)

1972. **devise**
disposition (f) testamentaire; legs (m) immobilier
legado (m) de bienes raíces
Vermächtnis (n) von Grundbesitz (m)

1973. **devisee**
bénéficiaire (m); légataire (m)
legatario (m) de bienes raíces
Vermächtnisnehmer (m) (von Grundbesitz)

1974. **devisor**
disposant (m); testateur (m)
testador (m) que lega bienes raíces
Vermächtnisgeber (m) oder Erblasser (m) (von Grundbesitz)

1975. **to devise**
léguer
legar bienes raíces
Grundbesitz vermachen

1975a. **devolution**
dévolution (f)
devolución (f)
Erbschaftsanfall (m)

1976. **dictatorship**
dictature (f)
dictadura (f)
Diktatur (f)

1977. **dictator**
dictateur (m)
dictador (m)
Diktator (m)

1978. **dictum**
opinion (f) d'un juge n'ayant pas autorité de chose jugé
conclusión (f); dicho (m)
Diktum (n); richterlicher Ausspruche (m) (nicht findend)

1979. **difference**
différence (f)
diferencia (f)
Unterschied (m)

1980. **to differ**
différer
diferir
sich unterscheiden; anderer Meinung (f) sein

1981. **digest**
abrégé (m); digeste (m); recueil (m); résumé (m)
digesto (m); recopilación (f); resumen (m)
Auszug (m); Gesetzessammlung (f); Digesten (Pandekten)

1982. **to digest**
faire un recueil; résumer
abreviar; recopilar
zusammenfassen; kompilieren

1983. **dilatory**
dilatoire
dilatorio
dilatorisch

1984. **dilemma**
dilemme (m)
dilema (m)
Dilemma (n)

1985. **diligence**
diligence (f)
diligencia (f)
Fleiss (m)

1986. **diligent**

diligent
diligente
fleissig

1987. **diminution**
diminution (f)
disminución (f)
Verminderung (f)

1988. **diplomacy**
diplomatie (f)
diplomacia (f)
Diplomatie (f)

1989. **dean of the diplomatic corps**
doyen (m) du corps diplomatique
decano (m) del cuerpo diplomático
Doyen (m) des diplomatischen Korps

1990. **diplomat; diplomatist**
diplomate (m)
diplomático (m)
Diplomat (m)

1991. **diplomatic**
diplomatique
diplomático
diplomatisch

1992. **diplomatic conference**
conférence diplomatique
conferencia diplomática
diplomatische Konferenz

1993. **diplomatic immunity**
immunité diplomatique
inmunidad diplomática
diplomatische Immunität

1994. **diplomatic note**
note diplomatique
nota diplomática
diplomatische Note

1995. **diplomatic relations**
relations diplomatiques
relaciones diplomáticas
diplomatische Beziehungen

1996. **to enter the diplomatic service**
entrer dans la diplomatie
entrar en la carrera diplomática
in den diplomatischen Dienst eintreten

1997. **direction**
administration (f); instruction (f)
administración (f); instrucción (f)
Direktion (f); Anordnung (f)

1998. **direct**
direct
directo
direkt

1999. **to direct**
diriger
dirigir
anordnen; anweisen

2000. **directive**
circulaire (f); directive (f); instruction (f)
dirección (f); instrucción (f)
Anweisung (f); Richtlinie (f); Weisung (f)

2001. **director**
directeur (m)
director (m)
Direktor (m)

2002. **executive director; director general**
directeur général
director general
Generaldirektor

2003. **directorate**
direction (f); conseil (m) d'administration (f)
dirección (f); junta (f)
Direktorium (n); Vorstand (m)

2004. **disability**
incapacité (f); invalidité (f)
incapacidad (f); invalidez (f)
Rechtsunfähigkeit (f); Arbeitsunfähigkeit (f)

2005. **permanent disability**
invalidité (f)
incapacidad (f) permanente
dauernde Arbeitsunfähigkeit (f); Invalidität (f)

2006. **disadvantage**
désavantage (m); inconvénient (m)
desventaja (f); menoscabo (m)
Nachteil (m)

2007. **disadvantageous**
désavantageux
desventajoso
nachteilig

2008. **disagreement**
désaccord (m)
desacuerdo (m)
Meinungsverschiedenheit (f)

2009. **to disagree**
être en désaccord

estar en desacuerdo
nicht übereinstimmen; verschiedener Meinung (f) sein

2010. **disapproval; disapprobation**
désapprobation (f)
desaprobación (f)
Missbilligung (f)

2011. **to disapprove**
désapprouver
desaprobar
missbilligen

2012. **disarmament**
désarmement (m)
desarme (m)
Abrüstung (f)

2013. **disarmanent conference**
conférence (f) de désarmement
conferencia (f) de desarme
Abrüstungskonferenz (f)

2014. **to disarm**
désarmer
desarmar
abrüsten

2014a. **disavowal**
désaveu (m); répudiation (f)
denegación (f); repudiación (f)
Ableugung (f); Nichtanerkennung (f)

2014b. **to disavow**
désavouer; répudier
denegar; repudiar
ableugnen; nichtanerkennen

2015. **disbarment of a lawyer**
radiation (f) d'un avocat
desaforo (m)
Streichung (f) von der Anwaltsliste (f)

2016. **to disbar a lawyer**
radier, rayer un avocat du barreau
desaforar
von der Anwaltsliste streichen

2017. **disbursement**
débours (m); frais (mpl)
desembolso (m); gasto (m)
Auslage (f); Ausgabe (f)

2018. **to disburse**
débourser
desembolsar
auslegen; ausgeben

2019. **discharge**
décharge (f); renvoi (m); résiliation (f); libération (f)
descarga (f); desempeño (m); despido (m); liberación (f)
Bezahlung (f); Entlassung (f); Entlastung (f); Freilassung (f)

2020. **disclaimer**
désistement (m); renonciation (f) à un droit
abandono (m); renuncia (f)
Anspruchsverzicht (m); Widerruf (m)

2021. **to disclaim**
renoncer à; se désister de; désavouer
abandonar; renunciar
dementieren; leugnen

2022. **disclosure**
divulgation (f); révélation (f)
divulgación (f); revelación (f)
Enthüllung (f)

2023. **to disclose**
divulguer; révéler
divulgar; revelar
enthüllen

2024. **discontinuance**
abandon (m); arrêt (m); cessation (f)
cesación (f); sobreseimiento (m)
Einstellung (f); Unterbrechung (f); Zurückziehung (f)

2025. **to discontinue**
discontinuer
descontinuar; discontinuar
einstellen; aufhören; zurückziehen

2026. **discord**
discorde (f)
discordia (f)
Uneinigkeit (f)

2027. **discordant**
discordant
discordante
uneinig

2028. **discount**
escompte (m); rabais (m)
descuento (m); rebaja (f)
Diskont (m); Rabatt (m)

2029. **at a discount**
au rabais
al descuento

unter Pari (n)
2030. **to discount**
escompter; invalider
descontar; rebajar
diskontieren; nicht mitrechnen
2031. **discovery**
communication (f) des pièces (fpl); découverte (f)
acción (f) *ad exhibendum*; descubrimiento (m)
Zugänglichmachung (von Beweismitteln); Entdeckung (f)
2032. **discredit**
discrédit (m)
descrédito (m)
Misstrauen (n); Misskredit (m)
2033. **to discredit**
discréditer
desacreditar
diskreditieren; anzweifeln
2034. **discrepancy**
divergence (f); contradiction (f)
discrepancia (f); variante (f)
Widerspruch (m); Zwiespalt (m)
2035. **discretion**
discrétion (f)
discreción (f)
Ermessen (n)
2036. **discretionary**
discrétionnaire
discrecional
nach freiem Ermessen
2037. **discrimination**
discrimination (f); discernement (m); partialité (f)
discernimiento (m); discriminación (f); parcialidad (f)
Diskriminierung (f); Unterscheidung (f); Parteilichkeit (f)
2038. **to discriminate against**
désavantager
discriminar en contra
diskriminieren gegen; benachteiligen
2039. **discussion**
débats (mpl); discussion (f)
debate (m); discusión (f)
Diskussion (f)
2040. **discussion groups**
cercles (mpl) d'études (fpl)
grupos (mpl) de estudio (m)
Diskussionsgruppen (fpl)
2041. **informal discussions**
discussions officieuses
discusiones informales
zwangslose Diskussionen
2042. **under discussion**
en discussion
en discusión
zur Erörterung stehend
2043. **to discuss**
discuter
discutir
besprechen
2044. **disfranchisement**
perte (f), privation (f), des droits civiques
privación (f) de los derechos civiles
Entziehung (f) des Wahl (f) oder Bürgerrechts (n)
2045. **to disfranchise**
priver des droits civiques (de l'électorat)
privar del derecho electoral
Wahl- oder Bürgerrechte entziehen
2046. **dishonor**
déshonneur (m); non-paiement (m)
deshonor (m); falta (f) de pago (m)
Ehrlösigkeit (f); Nichteinlösung
2047. **disinheritance**
déshéritement (m)
desheredación (f)
Enterbung (f)
2048. **to disinherit**
déshériter
desheredar
enterben
2049. **dismemberment**
démembrement (m)
desmembración (f)
Zerstückelung (f)
2050. **to dismember**
démembrer
desmembrar
zerstückeln
2051. **dismissal**
congédiement (m); renvoi (m); rejet (m)
despido (m); destitución (f)
Entlassung (f); Abweisung (f)

2052. **to dismiss**
congédier; débouter; rejeter
despedir; destituir; rechazar
entlassen; abweisen

2053. **disorder**
désordre (m)
desorden (m)
Unordnung (f)

2054. **disparagement**
dénigrement (m); dépréciation (f)
menosprecio (m)
Herabsetzung (f); Verachtlichmachung (f)

2055. **to disparage**
dénigrer; déprécier
desacreditar; menospreciar
herabsetzen; verächtlich machen

2056. **dispatch**
célérité (f); envoi (m); promptitude (f)
despacho (m); expedición (f); prontitud (f)
Absendung (f); Promptheit (f)

2057. **dispensation**
dispense (f)
dispensa (f)
Dispens (f)

2058. **to dispense with**
se dispenser de; se passer de
hacer caso omiso de; renunciar a
dispensieren; verzichten auf

2059. **displaced persons**
réfugiés et déportés (mpl)
refugiados y deportados (mpl)
Flüchtlinge und Verschleppte (mpl)

2060. **disposal**
disposition (f); élimination (f)
disposición (f); enajenación (f)
Verfügung (f); Beseitigung (f)

2061. **to dispose of**
disposer (de)
disponer
über etwas verfügen; sich einer Sache entledigen

2062. **disposition**
caractère (m); cession (f)
genio (m); cesión (f)
Naturell (n); Zession (f) oder Abtretung (f); Übertragung (f)

2063. **testamentary disposition**
cession testamentaire
cesión testamentaria
letztwillige Verfügung

2064. **dispossession**
dépossession (f)
desposeimiento (m)
Enteignung (f)

2065. **to dispossess**
déposséder
desposeer
enteignen

2066. **dispute**
contestation (f); différend (m)
controversia (f); disputa (f)
Disput (m); Streit (m)

2067. **to dispute**
contester
disputar
bestreiten

2068. **to settle disputes**
régler les différends
resolver disputas
Streitigkeiten beilegen

2069. **amount in dispute, in controversy**
somme en litige
suma en litigio
eingeklagter Betrag

2070. **disqualification**
inhabilité (f)
inhabilitación (f); descalificación (f)
Disqualifizierung (f)

2071. **to disqualify**
disqualifier
inhabilitar; descalificar
disqualifizieren

2072. **disseizin**
dépossession (f) illégitime
usurpación (f) ilegítima
widerrechtliche Besitzergreifung (f)

2073. **dissemination**
dissémination (f)
diseminación (f)
Verbreitung (f)

2074. **to disseminate**
disséminer
diseminar
verbreiten

2075. **dissent**
dissentiment (m)
disensión (f)
Meinungsverschiedenheit (f)

2076. **dissenter**
dissident (m)
disidente (m)
Dissident (m)

2077. **dissenting opinion**
opinion (f) dissidente
opinión (f) disidente
abweichende Meinung (f)

2078. **to dissent**
exposer une opinion dissidente
disentir
anderer Meinung sein

2079. **dissolution**
dissolution (f)
disolución (f)
Auflösung (f)

2080. **to dissolve**
dissoudre
disolver
auflösen

2081. **distinction**
distinction (f)
distinción (f)
Unterschied (m); Auszeichnung (f)

2082. **distinctive**
distinctif
distintivo
unterschiedlich; kennzeichnend; charakteristisch

2083. **distortion**
déformation (f)
falseamiento (m)
Verdrehung (f); Entstellung (f)

2084. **to distort**
déformer
falsear
verdrehen; entstellen

2085. **distraint**
saisie (f); saisie-exécution (f)
embargo (m); retención (f)
Pfändung (f); Zwangsvollstreckkung (f)

2086. **to distrain**
saisir
embargar; retener
pfänden; zwangsvollstrecken

2087. **distress**
saisie (f); détresse (f)
embargo (m); miseria (f)
Beschlagnahme (f); Pfändung (f); Notlage (f)

2088. **distribution**
distribution (f); répartition (f)
distribución (f); repartición (f)
Verteilung (f); Verbreitung (f)

2089. **geographical distribution**
répartition géographique
distribución geográfica
geographische Verteilung

2090. **to distribute**
distribuer; répartir
distribuir; repartir
verteilen; verbreiten

2091. **distributor**
concessionnaire (m)
concesionario (m)
Konzessionär (m)

2092. **district**
district (m); région (f)
distrito (m); región (f)
Bezirk (m); Kreis (m)

2093. **disturbance**
émeute (f); trouble (m) apporté à l'ordre public
disturbio (m); desorden (m)
Ruhestörung (f); Störung (f)

2094. **to disturb**
déranger; troubler
distraer; perturbar
stören

2095. **divergence**
divergence (f)
divergencia (f)
Divergenz ( )

2096. **diversity**
diversité (f)
diversidad (f)
Verschiedenheit (f)

2097. **divest, to; to devest**
dépouiller de; dévêtir
despojar; desposeer
verzichten auf; entkleiden

2098. **dividend**
dividende (m)
dividendo (m)
Dividende (f)

2099. **division**
division (f); répartition (f)
división (f); repartición (f)

Abteilung (f); Division (f)
2100. **to divide**
diviser; répartir
dividir; repartir
dividieren; teilen
2101. **divorce**
divorce (m)
divorcio (m)
Scheidung (f)
2102. **divorce a mensa et thoro**
séparation (f) de corps
divorcio (m) limitado
Trennung (f) von Tisch und Bett
2103. **divorce a vinculo matrimonii**
divorce absolu
divorcio absoluto
Aufhebung der Ehe; Ehescheidung
2104. **ground for divorce**
motif (m) de divorce
causa (f) de divorcio
Scheidungsgrund (m)
2105. **petition for a divorce**
demande (f) en divorce
demanda (f) de divorcio
Scheidungsklage (f)
2106. **to divorce**
divorcer
divorciar
scheiden
2107. **to seek a divorce**
demander le divorce
solicitar el divorcio
Scheidung begehren
2108. **dock for prisoners**
banc (m) des accusés (mpl)
barra (f), banquillo (m) de acusados (mpl)
Anklagebank (f)
2109. **docket**
rôle (m); sommaire (m); liste (f); extrait (m)
lista (f) de casos (mpl); orden (m) del día
Liste (f) von Urteilen (npl)
2110. **doctrine**
doctrine (f)
doctrina (f)
Doktrin (f)
2111. **document**
acte (m); document (m)
documento (m)
Aktenstück (n); Dokument (n); Urkunde (f)
2112. **basic documents**
documentation (f) essentielle
documentos (mpl) fundamentales, básicos
wesentliche Dokumente (npl)
2113. **body of a document**
contenu (m) d'un document
contenido (m) de un documento
Inhalt (m) der Urkunde
2114. **restricted document**
document à circulation restreinte
documento de carácter reservado
nur für den Dienstgebrauch
2115. **to document**
documenter
documentar
mit Urkunden belegen
2116. **Doe, John (Richard Roe)**
Monsieur un Tel
Fulano de Tal
N.N. (fingiertes Rechtssubjekt)
2117. **domain**
domaine (m); propriété (f) foncière
dominio (m); propiedad (f)
Domäne (f); Gebiet (n)
2118. **public domain, property**
domaine public
dominio público
öffentliches Eigentum
2119. **domicile**
domicile (m)
domicilio (m)
Domizil (n); Wohnsitz (m)
2120. **legal domicile**
domicile légal
domicilio legal
rechtlicher Wohnsitz
2121. **marital domicile**
domicile conjugal
domicilio conyugal
ehelicher Wohnsitz
2122. **donation**
donation (f)
donación (f)
Schenkung (f)

2123. **donee**
donataire (m)
donatario (m)
Schenkungsempfänger (m)
2124. **donor**
donateur (m)
donante (m)
Schenkungsgeber (m)
2125. **to donate**
faire une donation
donar
schenken
2126. **dormant**
dormant; latent
durmiente; latente
unbenützt; ungebraucht
2127. **double-cross, to**
trahir; vendre (un complice)
traicionar
verraten (einen Mitschuldigen)
2128. **doubt**
doute (m)
duda (f)
Zweifel (m)
2129. **beyond reasonable doubt**
au-delà de tout doute raisonnable
fuera de toda duda razonable
über berechtigten Zweifel hinaus
2130. **doubtful**
douteux; incertain
dudoso; incierto
unsicher; zweifelnd
2131. **doubtless**
sans aucun doute
sin duda
ohne Zweifel
2132. **to doubt**
douter
dudar
bezweifeln
2133. **downgrading**
déclassement (m)
descenso (m) de categoría (f)
niedrigere Einstufung (f)
2134. **dowry**
dot (f)
dote (f)
Mitgift (n)
2135. **dower**
douaire (m)
herencia (f) de la viuda (f)
Witwenteil (m)
2136. **draft**
conscription (f); lettre (f) de change (m); plan (m); projet (m) de loi (f); brouillon (m)
conscripción (f); letra (f) de cambio (m); plan (m); anteproyecto (m) de ley (f); borrador (m)
Einberufung (f) zum Militär (n); Tratte (f); Entwurf (m); Gesetzentwurf (m)
2137. **rough draft**
avant-projet (m)
bosquejo (m)
erster Entwurf (m)
2138. **to draft**
détacher; tirer une traite; émettre une lettre de change; faire un plan, un projet de loi; rédiger
reclutar; girar una letra; hacer un borrador, un proyecto de ley; redactar
einberufen; einen Wechsel (m) ausstellen; auswählen; auf jemanden ziehen; entwerfen; einen Gesetzentwurf vorbereiten
2139. **drawback**
remboursement (m) des droits (mpl) (d'importation); inconvénient (m)
reintegro (m) de derechos (mpl) (de aduana); inconveniente (m)
Ausführprämie (f); Nachteil (m)
2140. **drawee of a bill of exchange**
le tiré d'un effet négociable, d'une lettre de change
librado, girado de una letra de cambio
Bezogener beim Wechsel
2141. **drawer of a bill of exchange**
le tireur d'un effet négociable
librador, girador de una letra de cambio
Aussteller eines Wechsels
2142. **drugs**
narcotique (m); stupéfiants (mpl)
narcóticos (mpl); drogas (fpl)
Betäubungsmittel (n)

2143. **drunkenness**
ébriété (f); ivresse (f)
borrachera (f); embriaguez (f)
Trunkenheit (f)

2144. **drunk**
ivre
ebrio
betrunken

2145. **drunkard**
ivrogne (m)
borrachín (m)
Betrunkener (m)

2146. **due**
dû; échu; exigible
debido; vencido
fällig; gebührend; zustehend

2147. **to fall due**
venir à échéance
vencer
fällig werden

2148. **duel**
duel (m)
duelo (m)
Duell (n)

2149. **duly**
dûment
debidamente
pünktlich

2150. **dumping**
bourrage (m) du marché (m); dumping (m)
saturación (f) de mercado (m); dumping (m)
Preisdrückung (f); Dumping (n)

2151. **dungeon**
cachot (m)
calabozo (m)
Kerker (m)

2152. **duplicity**
duplicité (f)
duplicidad (f)
Duplizität (f)

2153. **duration**
durée (f)
duración (f)
Dauer (f)

2154. **duress**
coercition (f); contrainte (f); pression (f)
coacción (f); compulsión (f)
Zwang (m); Nötigung (f); Druck (m)

2155. **under duress**
sous la contrainte
bajo coacción, compulsión
unter Zwang

2156. **duty**
devoir (m); droit (m) de douane (f)
deber (m); derecho (m) de aduana (f)
Pflicht (f); Zoll (m)

2157. **customs duty**
droit de douane
derechos de aduana
Zollgebühr

2158. **dutiable**
taxable
imponible
zollpflichtig

2159. **duty free**
libre à l'entrée; exempt de droits
exento de derechos
zollfrei

2160. **export duty**
taxe (f) à l'exportation (f)
derecho (m) de exportación (f)
Ausfuhrzoll (m)

2161. **import duty**
taxe à l'importation
derecho de importación
Einfuhrzoll (m)

E

2162. **earnings**
gains (mpl); profits (mpl); salaire (m)
entradas (fpl); ganancias (fpl); ingresos (mpl)
Einkommen (n); Gewinn (m); Verdienst (m)

2163. **earphones**
écouteurs (mpl)
audífonos (mpl)
Kopfhörer (m)

2164. **easement**
servitude (f)
servidumbre (f)
Servitut (f); Dienstbarkeit (f)

2165. **affirmative, positive easement**
servitude active
servidumbre positiva
aktive Dienstbarkeit

2166. **negative easement**
servitude passive
servidumbre negativa
passive Dienstbarkeit

2167. **eavesdropping**
écoute (f) aux portes
escucha (f) a las puertas
Lauschen (n); Abhören (n)

2168. **eavesdropper**
écouteur (m) aux portes
el que escucha a las puertas
Horcher (m); Lauscher (m)

2169. **to eavesdrop**
écouter aux portes
escuchar a las puertas
an der Tür hörchen; lauschen; am Schlüsselloch hörchen; abhören

2170. **economy**
économie (f)
economía (f)
Wirtschaft (f)

2171. **economical**
économique
económico
ökonomisch; wirtschaftlich

2172. **economics**
sciences économiques
ciencias económicas
Wirtschaftswissenschaften

2173. **economist**
économiste (m)
economista (m)
Wirtschaftler (m)

2174. **planned economy**
économie dirigée
economía planificada
Planwirtschaft

2175. **political economy**
économie politique
economía política
Volkswirtschaftslehre

2176. **to economize**
économiser
economizar
sparsam wirtschaften

2177. **edict**
édit (m)
edicto (m)
Erlass (m)

2178. **edition**
édition (f)
edición (f)
Auflage (f)

2179. **editor**
rédacteur (m)
redactor (m)
Redakteur (m)

2180. **to edit**
corriger; éditer
editar; redactar
redigieren

2181. **education**
éducation (f); enseignement (m)
educación (f); enseñanza (m)
Erziehung (f); Bildung (f)

2182. **legal education**
enseignement du droit
enseñanza del derecho
juristisches Studium

2183. **to educate**
instruire
instruir
erziehen; bilden

2184. **efface, to**
effacer; oblitérer
borrar; obliterar
auslöschen; tilgen

2185. **effect**
effet (m)
efecto (m)
Folge (f); Wirkung (f)
2186. **effective; effectual**
effectif; en vigueur
efectivo; eficaz; en vigor
wirksam; mit Wirkung vom; in Kraft
2187. **effects**
effets
efectos
Habe (n)
2188. **to effect**
effectuer
efectuar
bewirken
2189. **to take effect**
entrer en vigueur
entrar en vigor, en vigencia
in Kraft treten
2190. **effectiveness; efficiency**
effet (m) utile; efficacité (f)
eficacia (f); eficiencia (f)
Leistungsfähigkeit (f); Wirksamkeit (f)
2191. **efficient**
efficient
eficiente
leistungsfähig
2192. **ejectment** (see also **action of ejectment**)
éviction (f)
desahucio (m); lanzamiento (m); expulsión (f)
Vertreibung aus dem Besitz
2193. **to eject**
évincer
desahuciar; expeler
aus dem Besitz vertreiben
2194. **election**
élection (f)
elección (f); comicios (mpl)
Wahl (f)
2195. **election booth**
isoloir (m)
cabina (f) electoral
Wahlzelle (f)
2196. **election returns**
résultats (mpl) d'une élection
resultados (mpl) de una elección
Wahlergebnisse (n)
2197. **electoral college**
collège électoral
colegio electoral
Wahlkollegium (n)
2198. **elector**
électeur (m)
elector (m)
Wahlmann (m)
2199. **electorate**
corps (m), district (m) électoral
electorado (m)
Wählerschaft (f)
2200. **uncontested election**
élection (f) sans opposition (f)
candidatura (f) única
Wahl ohne Gegenkandidat (m)
2201. **to elect**
élire
elegir
wählen
2202. **to hold elections**
organiser des élections
celebrar elecciones
Wahlen abhalten
2203. **electrocution** (see **death penalty**)
électrocution (f)
electrocución (f)
Hinrichtung (f) im elektrischen Stuhl (m)
2204. **to electrocute**
électrocuter
electrocutar
hinrichten im elektrischen Stuhl
2205. **eleemosynary**
bienfaisant; charitable
caritativo; de caridad
wohltätig
2206. **elements**
éléments (mpl)
elementos (mpl)
Elemente (npl)
2207. **eligibility**
éligibilité (f)
elegibilidad (f)
Wählbarkeit (f)
2208. **eligible**
éligible
elegible
wählbar
2209. **emancipation**
émancipation (f)

emancipación (f)
Emanzipation (f)

2210. **to be emancipated**
être émancipé
ser emancipado
emanzipiert sein

2211. **to emancipate**
émanciper
emancipar
emanzipieren

2212. **embargo**
embargo (f)
embargo (f)
Embargo (n)

2213. **embassy**
ambassade (f)
embajada (f)
Botschaft (f)

2214. **embezzlement**
détournement (m) de fonds (mpl)
desfalco (m); peculado (m)
Unterschlagung (f); Veruntreuung (f)

2215. **embezzler**
détourneur (m) de fonds
desfalcador (m)
Veruntreuer (m)

2216. **to embezzle**
commettre un détournement de fonds
desfalcar
unterschlagen; veruntreuen

2217. **emblements; growing crops**
fruits de la terre; récoltes sur pied
frutos cultivados
natürliche Früchte; Früchte auf dem Halm

2218. **embracery**
subornation (f) d'un juré
tentativa (f) de influenciar un jurado
Bestechung (f)

2219. **emergency**
cas d'urgence; crise (f)
emergencia (f)
Notstand (m)

2220. **state of emergency**
état de crise
estado de emergencia
Ausnahmezustand

2221. **in case of emergency**
en cas de nécessité
en caso de emergencia
im Notfall

2222. **emigration**
émigration (f)
emigración (f)
Emigration (f); Auswanderung (f)

2223. **emigrant**
émigrant
emigrante
Emigrant

2224. **to emigrate**
émigrer
emigrar
emigrieren; auswandern

2225. **eminent domain**
domaine éminent
dominio eminente
Obereigentum des Staates am Grundbesitz

2226. **emolument**
émolument (m)
emolumento (m)
Bezuge (m)

2227. **empire**
empire (m)
imperio (m)
Weltreich (n)

2228. **employment**
emploi (m); travail (m); occupation (f)
empleo (m); ocupación (f)
Anstellung (f); Beschäftigung (f)

2229. **employee**
employé (m)
empleado (m)
Angestellter (m); Arbeitnehmer (m)

2230. **employer**
patron (m)
patrón (m); patrono (m)
Arbeitgeber (m)

2231. **employment agency, bureau**
bureau de placement
agencia de empleos
private Stellenvermittlung; Arbeitsamt

2232. **gainful employment**
emploi lucratif
empleo provechoso, lucrativo
einträgliche Beschäftigung

2233. **to employ**

employer
emplear
anstallen; beschäftigen

2234. **to seek employment**
chercher un emploi
buscar empleo
Arbeit suchen

2235. **empowered**
autorisé
autorizado; facultado
bevollmächtigt

2236. **to empower**
donner pouvoir, procuration
autorizar; facultar; dar poder
bevollmächtigen

2237. **enable, to**
mettre en état de; rendre capable de
hacer posible que; habilitar
befähigen; ermächtigen

2238. **enactment**
promulgation (f)
promulgación (f) de una ley
Inkraftsetzung (f), Verabschiedung (f) eines Gesetzes (n)

2239. **to enact**
promulguer
dar una ley; promulgar
ein Gesetz verabschieden; verordnen; öffentlich bekanntmachen; in Kraft setzen

2240. **enclosure; inclosure**
pièce (f) jointe; clôture (f)
anexo (m); recinto (m)
Einfriedung (f); Beilage (f)

2241. **to enclose**
joindre; clore; entourer
incluir; circundar; encerrar
einfrieden; beilegen

2242. **encroachment**
atteinte (f); empiètement (m)
intrusión (f); usurpación (f)
Eingriff (m); Übergriff (m)

2243. **to encroach**
empiéter
usurpar
eingreifen

2244. **encumbrance; incumbrance**
charge (f); hypothèque (f); servitude (f)
gravamen (m); impedimento (m); servidumbre (f)
Belastung (f) eines Grundstücks (n); Hypothek (m); Dienstbarkeit (f)

2245. **to encumber**
grever; hypothéquer
gravar; impedir
ein Grundstück belasten

2246. **endanger, to**
mettre en danger
poner en peligro
in Gefahr bringen; gefährden

2247. **endorsement; indorsement**
appui (m); endossement (m)
endoso (m); respaldo (m)
Giro (n); Indossament (n)

2248. **endorsee**
endossataire (m); tiers (m) porteur
endosatario (m)
Indossat(ar) (m)

2249. **endorsement in blank**
endossement en blanc
endoso en blanco
Blankoindossament

2250. **endorser**
endosseur (m)
endosador (m)
Indossant (m)

2251. **qualified endorsement**
endossement avec clauses restrictives
endoso condicional
bedingtes Indossament

2252. **to endorse**
approuver; endosser
apoyar; endosar
indossieren; girieren

2253. **endowment**
dot (f); fondation (f)
dote (f); fundación (f)
Aussteuer (f); Stiftung (f)

2254. **to endow**
doter; fonder
dotar; fundar
aussteuern; stiften

2255. **enemy**
ennemi (m)
enemigo (m)
Feind (m)

2256. **enforcement**
exécution (f); mise (f) en vigueur (f)

ejecución (f); aplicación (f)
Durchführung (f); Inkraftsetzung (f)

2257. **enforceable**
exécutoire
ejecutable
klagbar

2258. **to enforce**
faire respecter; mettre en vigueur
ejecutar; hacer cumplir
durchführen; durchsetzen; erzwingen

2259. **engagement**
engagement (m); fiançailles (fpl); occupation (f)
compromiso (m); esponsales (mpl); obligación (f)
Verpflichtung (f); Verlöbnis (n); Beschäftigung (f)

2260. **to engage**
engager
comprometer; tomar a servicio
anstellen; beschäftigen

2261. **enjoin, to**
enjoindre; prescrire
mandar; prohibir
Anweisung erteilen; bestimmen

2262. **enjoyment**
jouissance (f); possession (f)
uso (m); usufructo (m)
Genuss (m); Niessbrauch (m)

2263. **quiet enjoyment**
paisible jouissance
posesión quieta
ungestörter Genuss

2264. **enlistment**
engagement (m); enrôlement (m)
alistamiento (m); enganche (m)
Anwerbung (f); Einstellung (f)

2265. **to enlist**
appeler sous les drapeaux; engager
alistar; alistarse
sich anwerben lassen; anwerben

2266. **enquiry; inquiry**
enquête (f)
investigación (f)
Untersuchung (f)

2267. **to enquire**
enquêter; rechercher; demander
investigar; inquirir
nachforschen; untersuchen

2268. **enrichment**
enrichissement (m)
enriquecimiento (m)
Bereicherung (f)

2269. **unjust enrichment**
enrichissement sans cause
enriquecimiento torticero, sin causa
ungerechtfertigte Bereicherung

2270. **enslavement**
asservissement (m)
reducción (f) a esclavitud (f)
Versklavung (f)

2271. **to enslave**
asservir
esclavizar
versklaven

2272. **entailment**
substitution d'héritiers (d'un bien)
vinculación
Übertragung eines Gutes als Fideikommiss

2273. **to entail**
substituer (un bien) des héritiers
vincular
ein Gut jdm. als Fideikommiss vererben

2274. **entente**
entente (f)
entente (f)
Bündnis (n)

2275. **enterprise**
entreprise (f)
empresa (f)
Unternehmen (n)

2276. **entirety**
totalité (f)
totalidad (f)
Gesamtheit (f)

2277. **entity**
entité (f)
entidad (f)
Wesen (n)

2278. **legal entity**
personne juridique, morale
persona jurídica
juristische Person

2279. **entrapment**
piège (m)

añagaza (f)
Verleitung (f)

2280. **entry**
entrée (f)
entrada (f)
Eintritt (m)

2281. **forcible, unlawful entry**
violation de domicile
allanamiento de morada
Hausfriedensbruch

2282. **to enter**
entrer
entrar
eintreten in

2283. **envoy**
envoyé (m)
enviado (m)
Gesandter (m)

2284. **equality**
égalité (f)
igualdad (f)
Gleichheit (f)

2285. **equal**
égal
igual
gleich

2286. **equality before the law**
égalité devant la loi
igualdad ante la ley
Gleichheit vor dem Gesetz

2287. **sovereign equality**
égalité souveraine
igualdad soberana
souveräne Gleichheit

2288. **equilibrium**
équilibre (m)
equilibrio (m)
Gleichgewicht

2289. **equity**
équité (f)
equidad (f)
Billigkeitsrecht (n)

2290. **equitable**
équitable
equitativo
unparteiisch

2291. **equity of redemption**
droit de rachat d'un débiteur hypothécaire
derecho de rescate
Recht auf Zurückzahlung einer Hypothek

2292. **equity maxims**
maximes d'équité
máximas de equidad
Maximen des Billigkeitsrechts

2293. **between equal equities the law will prevail**
entre équités égales, le droit strict prévaut
la ley prevalecerá sobre dos principios de equidad en materias iguales
zwischen gleichen, sich aus dem Billigkeitsrecht ergebenden Rechten ist das strenge Recht Ausschlaggebend

2294. **equity acts in personam**
l'équité porte sur le droit des personnes
la equidad actúa *in personam*
das Billigkeitsrecht wirkt *in personam*

2295. **equity aids the vigilant, not the indolent**
l'équité vient au secours du diligent, et non pas à celui de l'indolent
la equidad asiste al diligente, no al indolente
das Billigkeitsrecht hilft der sorgfältigen, nicht der nachlässigen Person

2296. **equity follows the law**
l'équité respecte la loi
la equidad está subordinada a la ley
das Billigkeitsrecht folgt dem strengen Recht

2297. **equity imputes an intent to fulfill an obligation**
l'équité présume l'intention de remplir une obligation
la equidad presupone la intención de cumplir una obligación
das Billigkeitsrecht setzt die Absicht des Schuldners (des Verpflichteten) voraus, seine Verpflichtung zu erfüllen

2298. **equity is equality**
l'équité, c'est l'égalité
equidad es igualdad
Aequitas bedeutet Gleichheit

2299. **equity looks to intent rather than form**
l'équité se soucie de l'intention plutôt que de la forme
la equidad considera más la intención que la forma
das Billigkeitsrecht trägt eher der Absicht als der Form Rechnung

2300. **equity regards that as done which ought to be done**
l'équité considère comme chose faite ce qui aurait dû l'être
la equidad considera lo hecho como que debió ser
das Billigkeitsrecht betrachtet das, was getan werden soll, als getan

2301. **he who comes into equity must come in with clean hands**
celui qui recherche l'équité doit avoir la conscience tranquille
quien busca equidad debe tener la conciencia tranquila
wer das Billigkeitsrecht in Anspruch nehmen will, muss ein gutes Gewissen haben, muss reine Hände haben

2302. **he who seeks equity must do equity**
celui qui recherche l'équité doit l'exercer
el que busca amparo en la equidad debe practicarla
wer **Aequitas** sucht, muss **Aequitas** üben

2303. **equivalent**
équivalent
equivalente
gleichwertig

2304. **equivocation**
équivocation (f); tergiversation (f); équivoque (m)
equívoco (m); tergiversación (f)
Ausflucht (f); Doppelsinn (m)

2305. **equivocal**
équivoque
equívoco
zweideutig

2306. **errata**
errata (mpl)
fe de erratas (fpl)
Druckfehlerverzeichnis (npl)

2307. **error**
erreur (f)
error (m)
Irrtum (m)

2308. **clerical error**
erreur d'écriture, de plume
error de pluma
Schreibfehler

2309. **erroneous**
erroné; faux
erróneo
irrig; irrtümlich

2310. **escape**
évasion (f); fuite (f)
fuga (f); huida (f); escape (m)
Entweichen (n); Flucht (f)

2311. **to escape**
s'enfuir; s'évader
escapar(se); huir(se)
entweichen; entfliehen

2312. **escheat**
dévolution (f) d'un bien à l'Etat; déshérence (f)
reversión (f) de bienes (mpl) abintestatos al Estado
Heimfall (m) von Grundstücken (npl) an den Staat

2313. **escrow**
garantie (f) bloquée
plica (f); garantía (f) bloqueada
eine einem Dritten anvertraute bedingte Urkunde (f); bedingte Hinterlegung (f)

2314. **espionage**
espionnage (m)
espionaje (m)
Spionage (f)

2315. **essence**
essence (f); fond (m)
esencia (f); fondo (m)
Wesen (n)

2316. **essential**
essentiel
esencial
wesentlich

2317. **establishment**
établissement (m)
establecimiento (m)
Gründung (f)

2318. **to establish**
établir
establecer
gründen; einrichten

2319. **estate**
domaine (f); propriété (f) foncière; succession (f)
bienes raíces (mpl); propiedades (fpl); herencia (f)
Besitztum (n); Landbesitz (m); Vermögen (n); Nachlass (m)

2320. **administrator of an estate**
administrateur (m) légal
albacea (m)
Vermögensverwalter (m)

2321. **bankrupt's estate**
masse (f) en faillite (f)
masa (f) de la quiebra (f)
Konkursmasse (f)

2322. **contingent estate**
propriété dépendant d'un événement incertain
propiedad contingente
Eigentum, dessen Wirkungen von einem künftigen Ereignis abhängen

2323. **estate at will**
bail (m) révocable au plaisir (m) des parties (fpl)
posesión (f) terminable por locator (m) o locatario (m)
von den Parteien (fpl) jederzeit kündbares Besitzrecht

2324. **estate by sufferance**
possession à titre précaire
posesión por tolerancia
fehlerhaftes, wenn auch rechtmässig erworbenes Grundeigentum

2325. **estate for years**
possession (f) pour une période déterminée
posesión (f) por tiempo fijo
auf bestimmte Zeit festgelegtes Besitzrecht

2326. **estate in fee simple**
propriété tenue sans restriction
propiedad en dominio pleno
unbeschränkt vererbliches Grundeigentum

2327. **estate in fee tail**
bien substitué
propiedad limitada al donatario y sus herederos directos
Grundbesitz, der an alle männlichen ehelichen Abkömmlinge vererblich ist

2328. **estate pur autre vie**
possession pendant la vie d'autrui
dominio por vida de otra persona
Eigentum für die Dauer des Lebens eines Dritten

2329. **freehold estate**
franc-fief (m)
dominio (m) absoluto de propiedad
Landbesitz

2330. **future estate**
bien à venir (m)
propiedad (f), participación (f) o interés (m) en el futuro
Eigentums oder anderes Vermögensrecht

2331. **life estate**
biens (mpl) en viager
dominio (m) durante la vida
Landbesitz (n) auf Lebenszeit (f)

2332. **misappropriation of an estate**
détournement (m) de patrimoine (m), succession (f)
malversación (f) de una herencia (f)
Unterschlagung (f) eines Nachlasses (m)

2333. **residuary estate**
montant de la succession après déductions
heredad residuaria
Restnachlass

2334. **to break up an estate**
morceler un domaine, une succession
dividir una herencia
einen Nachlass teilen

2335. **estimate**
estimation (f); évaluation (f)
estimado (m); tasa (f); cálculo (m)
Abschätzung (f); Schätzung (f)

2336. **to estimate**
estimer; évaluer

estimar; tasar; calcular
abschätzen; schätzen

2337. **estoppel**
exception (f); fin (f) de non-recevoir (m); irrecevabilité (f)
impedimento (m); acción (f) innegable
Hemmung (f) des Klageanspruchs (n)

2338. **to estop**
empêcher; soulever une exception
impedir; anular
hemmen; hindern

2339. **estovers**
droit (m) d'affouage (m)
derecho (m) a cortar árboles
Brennholzrecht (n)

2340. **estrangement**
aliénation (f); éloignement (m)
enajenamiento (m); alejamiento (m)
Entfremdung (f)

2341. **to estrange**
aliéner; éloigner
enajenar; alejar
entfremden; abspenstig machen

2342. **ethical**
éthique; moral
ético; moral
ethisch; moralisch

2343. **evaluation**
évaluation (f)
avalúo (m)
Wertbestimmung (f)

2344. **to evaluate**
évaluer
evaluar; avaluar
bewerten

2345. **evasion**
évasion (f)
evasión (f)
Umgehung (f)

2346. **evasive**
évasif
evasivo
ausweichend

2347. **tax evasion**
évasion de taxe (f)
evasión tributaria
Steuerhinterziehung (f)

2348. **to evade**
s'évader; s'échapper
evadir
ausweichen; umgehen

2349. **event**
événement (m); cas (m)
evento (m); caso (m)
Ereignis (n)

2350. **eventual**
éventuel
eventual
endlich; möglich

2351. **eviction**
dépossession (f); éviction (f); expulsion (f)
desahucio (m); desalojo (m); evicción (f)
Eviktion (f); Räumung (f)

2352. **to evict**
déposséder; évincer; expulser
desahuciar; desalojar; excluir
einen Mieter (Pächter) zur Kaumung zwingen; jdn. aus dem Besitz vertreiben

2353. **evidence**
moyens (mpl) de preuve; preuve (f)
evidencia (f); prueba (f)
Beweismittel (n)

2354. **admissibility of evidence**
recevabilité (f) d'une preuve
admisibilidad (f) de prueba
Zulässigkeit (f) von Beweismitteln

2355. **best evidence**
meilleure preuve possible
la mejor prueba
Hauptbeweismittel

2356. **character evidence**
témoignage (m) de moralité (f)
testimonio (m) de reputación (f)
Leumundszeugnis (n)

2357. **circumstancial evidence**
preuve indirecte, par indices (mpl) ou présomption (f)
indicios (mpl); prueba (f) indiciaria
Indizienbeweis (m)

2358. **competent evidence**
preuve admissible, recevable
prueba admisible
zulässiges Beweismaterial

2359. **concealment of evidence**
dissimulation (f) de preuves
ocultamiento (m) de prueba
Verhehlung (f) von Beweismaterial

2360. **conclusive evidence**
preuve décisive, concluante
prueba concluyente, decisiva
schlüssiges Beweismaterial

2361. **conflicting evidence**
témoignage contradictoire
testimonio contradictorio
widersprechende Zeugenaussagen

2362. **corroborating evidence**
preuve corroborative
prueba corroborativa
bestätigender Beweis

2363. **cumulative evidence**
preuve cumulative
prueba cumulativa
kumulatives Beweismaterial

2364. **destruction of evidence**
destruction de preuve
destrucción de pruebas
Vernichtung von Beweismitteln

2365. **direct evidence**
preuve directe
prueba directa
direkter Beweis

2366. **documentary evidence**
preuve documentaire
prueba documental
Urkundenbeweis

2367. **extrinsic evidence**
preuve extrinsèque
prueba (extrínseca) de otra fuente
aüsserer Beweis

2368. **fabrication of evidence**
falsification de preuve
falsificación de prueba
Fälschung des Beweises

2369. **hearsay evidence**
preuve par ouï-dire (m)
prueba por referencia (f)
Zeugnis auf Grund von Hörensagen

2370 **inadmissibility of evidence**
irrecevabilité d'une preuve
inadmisibilidad de prueba
unzulässiger Beweis

2371. **incompetent evidence**
témoignage incompétent
prueba incompetente
inkompetenter, unbrauchbarer Beweis

2372. **incriminating evidence**
pièces (fpl) à conviction (f)
pieza (f) de acusación (f)
Belastungsmaterial (n)

2373. **intrinsic evidence**
preuve intrinsèque
prueba intrínseca
innerlicher Beweis

2374. **lack of evidence**
défaut de preuve
falta de pruebas
Mangel an Beweisen

2375. **material, pertinent evidence**
preuve pertinente
prueba pertinente
wesentlicher Beweis

2376. **newly discovered evidence**
preuve récemment trouvée
prueba acabada de descubrir
neues Beweismaterial

2377. **parol evidence**
témoignage verbal
testimonio oral
mündlicher Beweis

2378. **preponderance of evidence**
prépondérance (f) de preuve
preponderancia (f) de la prueba
Überweigen (n) der Beweise

2379. **presumptive evidence**
preuve par déduction
prueba presunta, por indicios
Indizienbeweis

2380. **prima facie evidence**
preuve de prime abord
prueba prima facie
widerlegbarer Beweis

2381. **primary evidence**
preuve de base
prueba primaria
gesetzliches Beweismittel

2382. **probative evidence**
preuve probante
prueba eficiente
bestätigendes Beweismaterial

2383. **production of evidence**
production de preuves
presentación de las pruebas

Vorlage von Beweismaterial

2384. **rebutting evidence**
preuve contraire
contraprueba
Gegenbeweis

2385. **secondary evidence**
preuve indirecte
prueba derivada
indirektes Beweismittel

2386. **State's, King's evidence**
témoin dénonciateur (m) de ses complices (mpl)
testigo (m) de Estado
staatliches Belastungsmaterial

2387. **sufficiency of evidence**
suffisance (f) de preuve
suficiencia (f) de la prueba
Beweiszulänglichkeit (f)

2388. **weight of evidence**
valeur (f) de la preuve
apreciación (f) de la prueba
Beweiskraft (m)

2389. **written evidence**
preuve par écrit
prueba escrita
schriftlicher Beweis

2390. **to adduce evidence**
apporter la preuve
aducir como prueba
Beweis liefern

2391. **to be evidenced by**
être prouvé par
ser probado por
bewiesen sein durch

2392. **to furnish evidence**
apporter, fournir la preuve
suministrar pruebas
beweisen

2393. **to give evidence**
déposer; témoigner
declarar; deponer
aussagen

2394. **to introduce evidence**
avancer, introduire la preuve
presentar pruebas
Beweis antreten

2395. **to offer in evidence**
offrir la preuve; verser au dossier
presentar como prueba
als Beweisstück verlegen

2396. **to put in evidentiary form**
mettre sous la forme de preuve
poner en forma de prueba
in Beweisform bringen

2397. **to weigh evidence**
apprécier les preuves
apreciar las pruebas
Beweis würdigen

2398. **evident**
évident
evidente
offenbar

2399. **exaction**
exaction (f); extorsion (f)
exacción (f); extorsión (f)
Eintreibung (f) einer Forderung (f); Erpressung (f)

2400. **to exact**
exiger
exigir
fordern; erpressen

2401. **examination**
examen (m)
examen (m)
Vernehmung (f)

2402. **direct examination**
interrogatoire (m) par la défense (f)
interrogatorio (m) directo
Vernehmung (f) durch den Verteidiger (m)

2403. **examination-in-chief**
premier interrogatoire du témoin
primer interrogatorio de testigo
erste Zeugenvernehmung

2404. **examiner**
examinateur (m); inspecteur (m)
examinador (m); inspector (m)
Prüfer (m); Revisor (m)

2405. **post-mortem examination**
autopsie (f)
autopsia (f)
Leichenschau (f)

2406. **to examine**
examiner; interroger
examinar; interrogar
untersuchen; vernehmen

2407. **exception**
dérogation (f); exception (f)
excepción (f); objeción (f)
Einwand (m); Einwendung (f)

2408. **to take exception to**
objecter à; soulever une exception
objetar a; oponerse a
Einwand erheben gegen

2409. **excerpt**
extrait (m)
extracto (m)
Exzerpt (n)

2410. **excessive**
excessif
excesivo
übertrieben

2411. **exchange**
échange (m)
cambio (m); canje (m)
Austausch (m)

2412. **commodity, goods exchange**
bourse des marchandises (fpl)
bolsa de comercio (m)
Produktenbörse (f); Warenbörse (f)

2413. **exchange of notes**
échange de notes
intercambio de notas
Notenaustausch

2414. **foreign exchange**
devises (fpl); effets étrangers
divisas (fpl); cambio exterior
Devisen (m)

2415. **rate of exchange**
cours (m), taux (m) du change
tipo (m) de cambio
Wechselkurs (m)

2416. **stock exchange**
bourse (f) des valeurs
bolsa (f) de valores
Börse (f)

2417. **to exchange**
échanger
cambiar; intercambiar
austauschen

2418. **exclusion**
exclusion (f)
exclusión (f)
Ausschluss (m)

2419. **exclusive**
exclusif
exclusivo
ausschliesslich

2420. **to exclude**
exclure
excluir
ausschliessen

2421. **excuse**
excuse (f)
excusa (f)
Entschuldigung (f)

2422. **excusable**
excusable; pardonnable
disculpable; excusable
entschuldbar; verzeihlich

2423. **to excuse**
excuser; pardonner
disculpar; excusar
entschuldigen; rechtfertigen

2424. **to make an excuse**
alléguer; prétexter
excusarse; pretexter
Ausflüchte machen

2425. **execution**
exécution (f)
ejecución (f)
Vollstreckung (f); Hinrichtung (f)

2426. **executory**
exécutoire
ejecutorio
vollstreckbar

2427. **stay of execution**
sursis (m) d'exécution
suspensión (f) temporal de una ejecución
Vollstreckungsaufschub (m)

2428. **to execute**
exécuter
ejecutar
ausführen; vollstrecken; hinrichten

2429. **executioner**
bourreau (m)
verdugo (m)
Scharfrichter (m)

2430. **executive**
exécutif
ejecutivo
exekutiv

2431. **executor of a will**
exécuteur (m) testamentaire
testamentario (m); albacea (m)
Testamentsvollstrecker (m)

2432. **exemption**
exemption (f)
exención (f)
Befreiung (f)

2433. **to exempt**
exempter
exentar
befreien
2434. **exhibit; exhibition**
pièce à conviction (justificative)
documento fehaciente ante tribunales
Beweisstück
2435. **to offer an exhibit**
produire une pièce à conviction
presentar una prueba
ein Beweisstück vorlegen
2436. **exile**
banissement (m); exil (m)
destierro (m); exilio (m)
Exil (n); Verbannung (f)
2437. **to exile**
bannir; exiler
desterrar; exilar
ins Exil senden; verbannen
2438. **existence**
existence (f)
existencia (f)
Existenz (f)
2439. **existing**
actuel; existant
actual; existente
bestehend
2440. **to exist**
être; exister
existir
bestehen
2441. **exoneration**
exonération (f)
exoneración (f)
Entlastung (f)
2442. **to exonerate**
exonérer
exonerar
entlasten
2443. **expansion**
accroissement (m); expansion (f)
aumento (m); expansión (f)
Expansion (f)
2444. **expatriation**
expatriation (f)
expatriación (f)
Ausbürgerung (f)
2445. **to expatriate**
expatrier
expatriar
ausbürgern
2446. **expediency**
convenance (f); opportunité (f)
conveniencia (f); oportunidad (f)
Zweckmässigkeit (f)
2447. **expedient**
expédient; utile
conveniente; oportuno
angemessen; zweckdienlich
2448. **expeditious**
expéditif
expeditivo
beschleunigt
2449. **to expedite**
accélérer; expédier
acelerar; expedir
befördern; beschleunigen
2450. **expendable**
remplaçable
reemplazable
ersetzbar
2451. **expenditure**
dépense (f); débours (m); décaissement (m)
gasto (m); desembolso (m)
Ausgabe (f); Auszahlung (f)
2452. **expenses**
dépenses; frais
costos; gastos
Kosten; Unkosten
2453. **travel expenses**
frais de voyage (m)
gastos de viaje (m)
Reisekosten (pl)
2454. **expert**
expert (m)
experto (m); perito (m)
Experte (m)
2455. **handwriting expert**
expert en écriture
perito caligráfico
Schriftsachverständiger
2456. **expiration; expiry**
échéance (f); expiration (f)
expiración (f); vencimiento (m)
Ablauf (m); Erlöschen (n)
2457. **to expire**
échoir; expirer
expirar; vencer
ablaufen; erlöschen
2458. **explanation**

éclaircissement (m); explication (f)
aclaración (f); explicación (f)
Erklärung (f)

2459. **explanatory**
explicatif
explicativo
erklärend

2460. **to explain**
éclaircir; expliquer
aclarar; explicar
erklären

2461. **exploitation**
exploitation (f)
explotación (f)
Ausbeutung (f)

2462. **to exploit**
exploiter
explotar
ausbeuten

2463. **exportation**
exportation (f)
exportación (f)
Export (m); Ausfuhr (f)

2464. **exports**
articles d'exportation
exportaciones
Ausfuhrwaren

2465. **to export**
exporter
exportar
exportieren; ausführen

2466. **exposition**
exposé (m); exposition (f); interprétation (f)
explicación (f); exposición (f); interpretación (f)
Aufklärung (f); Ausstellung (f); Erklärung (f)

2467. **to expose; to expound**
exposer; interpréter
exponer; revelar
aufklären; auslegen

2468. **exposure (indecent)**
exhibitionnisme (m); outrage (m) public à la pudeur (f)
escándalo (m); ofensa (f) contra el pudor (m)
unsittliches Entblössen (n)

2469. **express**
exprès
expreso
deutlich

2470. **expression**
expression (f)
expresión (f)
Ausdruck (m)

2471. **expropriation**
expropriation (f)
expropiación (f)
Enteignung (f)

2472. **to expropriate**
exproprier
expropiar
enteignen

2473. **expulsion**
expulsion (f)
expulsión (f)
Ausweisung (f)

2474. **to expel**
expulser
expulsar
ausweisen

2475. **expunge, to**
éteindre; purger; rayer
borrar; expurgar; suprimir
auslöschen; ausstreichen; tilgen

2476. **extension**
extension (f); prolongation (f)
extensión (f); prolongación (f)
Ausdehnung (f); Erweiterung (f)

2477. **extensive**
étendu; vaste
extenso; extensivo
ausgedehnt; erweitert

2478. **to extend**
étendre; prolonger
extender; prorrogar
ausdehnen; erweitern

2479. **to get an extension**
obtenir un délai
conseguir una prórroga
eine Fristverlängerung erhalten

2480. **extenuating**
atténuant
atenuante
mildernd

2481. **extermination**
extermination (f)
exterminio (m)
Ausrottung (f)

2482. **to exterminate**
exterminer
exterminar

ausrotten
2483. **exterritoriality; extraterritoriality**
exterritorialité (f)
extraterritorialidad (f)
Exterritorialität (f)
2484. **exterritorial**
exterritorial
extraterritorial
exterritorial
2485. **extinguishment; extinction**
extinction (f)
extinción (f)
Auslöschung (f)
2486. **to extinguish**
éteindre
extinguir
auslöschen
2487. **extinct**
éteint
extinto
erloschen
2488. **extortion**
détournement (m); extorsion (f)
exacción (f); extorsión (f)
Erpressung (f)
2489. **to extort**
extorquer
extorsionar
erpressen
2490. **extract**
extrait (m)
extracto (m)
Auszug (m)
2491. **to extract**
extraire
extraer
einen Auszug anfertigen
2492. **extradition**
extradition (f)
extradición (f)
Auslieferung (f)
2493. **extraditable**
sujet d'extradition
extraditable
auslieferbar
2494. **to extradite**
extrader
entregar por extradición
ausliefern
2495. **extrajudicial**
extrajudiciaire
extrajudicial
aussergerichtlich
2496. **extraneous**
non-essentiel
externo
unwesentlich
2497. **extraordinary**
extraordinaire
extraordinario
ausserordentlich
2498. **extrinsic**
extrinsèque
extrínseco
äusserlich
2499. **eyewitness**
témoin (m) oculaire
testigo (m) ocular
Augenzeuge (m)

F

2500. **face**
aspect (m); visage (m)
aspecto (m); cara (f); faz (f); rostro (m)
Aspekt (m); Gesicht (n)
2501. **facilities**
disponibilités (fpl); moyens (mpl)
servicios (mpl) e instalaciones (fpl); medios (mpl)
Möglichkeiten (fpl); Mittel (n)
2502. **fact**
fait (m)
hecho (m)
Tatsache (f)
2503. **fact of common knowledge**
fait de commune renommée
hecho notorio
allgemein bekannte Tatsache
2504. **facts in issue**
faits litigieux
hechos litigiosos
strittige Tatsachen
2505. **factual**
positif; réel

positivo; real
tatsächlich

2506. **in point of fact**
pour être précis
en realidad
wirklich

2507. **marshalling of facts**
accumulation (f) des faits
acumulación (f) de hechos
Zusammenstellung (f) der Tatsachen

2508. **material fact**
fait essentiel
hecho esencial
wesentliche Tatsache

2509. **recital of facts**
exposé (m) des faits
relación (f) de hechos
Tatsachenwiedergabe (f)

2510. **factor**
agent (m); élément (m); facteur (m)
agente (m); elemento (m); factor (m)
Faktor (m)

2511. **imponderable factors**
les impondérables
factores imponderables
Imponderabilien

2512. **factory**
fabrique (f); usine (f)
fábrica (f)
Fabrik (f)

2513. **faculty**
faculté (f); talent (m); corps (m) enseignant
facultad (f); aptitud (f); cuerpo (m) docente
Befugnis (f); Fähigkeit (f); Fakultät (f)

2514. **failure**
défaillance (f); faillite (f); manquement (m)
falta (f); fracaso (m); quiebra (f)
Bankrott (m); Misserfolg (m); Scheitern (n)

2515. **to fail**
faillir; faire faillite; manquer
faltar; fracasar; quebrar
Bankrott machen; Misserfolg haben; scheitern

2516. **fairness**
équité (f); impartialité (f)
equidad (f); imparcialidad (f)
Billigkeit (f); Unparteilichkeit (f)

2517. **fair**
équitable; impartial; juste
equitativo; justo
billig; unparteiisch

2518. **fair play**
franc-jeu (m)
proceder (m) leal
redliches Verfahren (n); ehrliches Spiel (n)

2519. **fait accompli**
fait accompli
hecho consumado
vollendete Tatsache

2520. **faith**
confiance (f); foi (f)
confianza (f); fe (f)
Glaube (m); Vertrauen (m)

2521. **bad faith**
mauvaise foi
mala fe
wider Treu und Glauben

2522. **faithful**
fidèle
fiel
treu

2523. **good faith**
bonne foi
buena fe
guter Glaube

2524. **to have faith in**
avoir confiance en; croire à
fiarse de; tener fe en
vertrauen auf

2525. **fake**
faux (m); imposteur (m); truque (m)
engaño (m); patraña (f)
Betrug (m); Fälschung (f); Schwindel (m); Betrüger (m)

2526. **fall**
baisse (f); chute (f)
caída (f); descenso (m)
Baisse (f); Sturz (m)

2527. **to fall through**
échouer
no tener éxito
scheitern

2528. **fallacious**
fallacieux; décevant; illusoire

falaz; delusorio; ilusorio
trügerisch
2529. **falsehood**
fausseté (f); mensonge (m)
falsedad (f); mentira (f)
Falschheit (f); Unwahrheit (f)
2530. **false**
faux
falso
falsch
2531. **falsification**
falsification (f)
falsificación (f)
Fälschung (f)
2532. **falsified**
falsifié
falsificado
gefälscht
2533. **to falsify**
falsifier
falsificar
fälschen
2534. **family of nations**
famille des nations
familia de naciones
Staatengemeinschaft
2535. **fault**
faute (f)
falta (f)
Fehler (m)
2536. **federal**
fédéral
federal
Bundes-
2537. **federalism**
fédéralisme (m)
federalismo (m)
Föderalismus (m)
2538. **federation**
fédération (f)
federación (f)
Bundesstaat (m); Staatenbund (f); Vereinigung (f)
2539. **fee**
provision (f); honoraire (m)
derecho (m); honorario (m)
Gebühr (f); Honorar (n)
2540. **contingent fee**
honoraire conditionnel
honorario condicional
Erfolgshonorar
2541. **fee-simple** (see **estate in fee simple**, No. 2321)
2542. **fee tail** (see **estate in fee tail**, No. 2327)
2543. **to grant in fee simple**
céder avec tous droits de jouissance
transmitir en pleno dominio
ins Eigentum übertragen
2544. **felony**
infraction (f) majeure
delito (m) mayor, grave
schweres Verbrechen
2545. **felon**
criminel (m)
criminal (m)
Verbrecher (m)
2546. **felonious**
criminel
criminal
verbrecherisch
2547. **misprision of felony**
non-révélation (f) d'un crime (m)
ocultación (f) de un crimen (m)
Nichtanzeige (m) oder Vertuschung (f) eines Verbrechens (m)
2548. **to compound a felony**
accepter un pot-de-vin pour ne pas poursuivre un coupable
aceptar soborno por no procesar un culpable
gegen Geld die Verfolgung eines Verbrechens unterlassen
2549. **feme covert**
femme mariée
mujer casada
verheiratete Frau
2550. **feme sole**
femme non mariée
mujer soltera
unverheiratete Frau
2551. **feoffment**
saisine (f)
feudo (m)
Belehnung (f)
2552. **fiction**
fiction (f)
ficción (f)
Fiktion (f)

2553. **fictitious**
fictif
ficticio
fiktiv

2554. **fiduciary**
fiduciaire (m)
fiduciario (m)
Betrauter (m)

2555. **fieri facias** (see **writ of fieri facias**, No. 6280)

2556. **file**
dossier (m); fichier (m); archives (fpl)
archivo (m); expediente (m); legajo (m)
Akte (f); Aktenstück (n)

2557. **to file**
classer; déposer
archivar; registrar
ordnen; ablegen; amtlich einreichen

2558. **filibuster (U.S.A.)**
obstruction parlementaire au moyen de discours prolongés
obstrucción parlamentaria mediante largos discursos
parlamentarische Obstruktionspolitik durch lange Reden

2559. **final**
définitif; final
decisivo; final
endgültig

2560. **finance**
finance (f)
finanza (f)
Finanz (f)

2561. **financial**
financier
financiero
finanziell

2562. **financier**
financier (m)
financiero (m)
Finanzier (m)

2563. **financing**
financement (m)
financiamiento (m); financiación (f)
Finanzierung (f)

2564. **to finance**
financer
financiar
finanzieren

2565. **finding**
conclusion sur un point de fait
decisión sobre cuestión de hecho
Gerichtsentscheidung über eine Tatsache

2566. **to find against the accused**
rendre un jugement contre l'accusé
decidir contra el acusado
gegen den Angeklagten entscheiden

2567. **to find for the accused**
rendre un jugement pour l'accusé
decidir en favor del acusado
für den Angeklagten entscheiden

2568. **fine**
amende (f)
multa (f)
Geldstrafe (f)

2569. **to fine**
condamner à une amende
multar
zu einer Geldstrafe verurteilen

2570. **fingerprints**
empreintes (fpl) digitales
huellas (fpl) digitales
Fingerabdrücke (mpl)

2571. **firm**
firme (f); maison (f) de commerce (m); raison (f) sociale
firma (f); casa (f) de comercio (m); razón (f) social
Firma (f)

2572. **fiscal**
fiscal; financier; budgétaire
fiscal
fiskalisch; Steuer-

2573. **fishery**
pêche (f); pêcherie (f)
pesca (f); pesquería (f)
Fischerei (f)

2574. **fixture**
aménagement (m) fixe; immeuble (m) par destination (f)
aditamento (m), accesorio (m) fijo
Zubehörstück (n)

2575. **fluctuation**
fluctuation (f)

fluctuación (f)
Schwankung (f)

2576. **to fluctuate**
flotter
fluctuar
schwanken

2577. **footnote**
note (f) au bas de la page
nota (f) al pie de la página
Fussnote (f)

2578. **footprint**
empreinte (f) de pas
huella (f)
Fusstapfe (f)

2579. **forbearance**
indulgence (f); patience (f)
indulgencia (f); paciencia (f)
Nachsicht (f); Unterlassung (f)

2580. **forbidden**
défendu; interdit
prohibido
verboten

2581. **to forbid**
défendre; interdire
prohibir
verbieten

2582. **force**
force (f); vigueur (f); violence (f)
fuerza (f); vigor (f); violencia (f)
Zwang (m); Kraft (f); Gewalt (f)

2583. **binding force**
caractère obligatoire
capaz de obligar
bindende Kraft

2584. **forceful**
convaincant; vigoureux
enérgico; vigoroso
überzeugend; kräftig

2585. **forcible**
par violence
con violencia
gewaltsam

2586. **to be in force**
être en vigueur
estar en vigor, en vigencia
in Kraft sein

2587. **to come into force**
entrer en vigueur
entrar en vigor, en vigencia
in Kraft treten

2588. **to put in force**
mettre en vigueur
poner en vigor, en vigencia
in Kraft setzen

2589. **force majeure**
force majeure
fuerza mayor
höhere Gewalt

2590. **foreclosure**
forclusion (f)
juicio (m) hipotecario
Zwangsvollstreckung (f)

2591. **to foreclose**
forclore
entablar; excluir
zwangsvollstreckung (f)

2592. **foreign**
étranger
extranjero
auswärtig

2593. **foreign affairs**
affaires étrangères
relaciones exteriores
auswärtige Angelegenheiten

2594. **foreigner**
étranger (m)
extranjero (m)
Ausländer (m)

2595. **foreman**
contre-maître (m)
capataz (m)
Aufseher (m); Werkmeister (m)

2596. **forensic medicine** (see **medical jurisprudence**, No. 3300)

2597. **forfeiture**
déchéance (f); perte (f) de droits (mpl) consécutive à certains faits
decomiso (m); pérdida (f) legal de un derecho por error (m) u omisión (f) o falta (f)
Einziehung (f); Verwirkung (f)

2598. **forfeiture of payment**
suppression (f) de solde (f), de traitement (m)
pérdida (f) legal de pago (m)
Verwirkung (f) der Zahlung (f)

2599. **to forfeit**
perdre
perder
verwirken

2600. **forgery**
faux (m); contrefaçon (f); falsification (f)

falsificación (f)
Fälschung (f)

2601. **forged**
faux; contrefait; falsifié
falsificado
gefälscht

2602. **forger**
faussaire (m)
falsificador (m)
Fälscher (m)

2603. **to forge**
faire un faux
falsificar
fälschen

2604. **form**
forme (f); modèle (m); questionnaire (m)
cuestionario (m); forma (f); modelo (m)
Form (f); Formular (n); Fragebogen (m)

2605. **application form**
formulaire (m) de demande (f)
formulario (m) de solicitud (f)
Antragsformular (n); Bewerbungsschreiben (n)

2606. **in due form**
en bonne forme
en debida forma
formgerecht

2607. **formalities**
formalités (fpl)
formalidades (fpl)
Formalität (fpl)

2608. **formal**
formel; cérémonieux
formal; ceremonioso
förmlich

2609. **formula**
formule (f)
fórmula (f)
Formel ( )

2610. **fornication**
fornication (f)
fornicación (f)
Unzucht (f)

2611. **to fornicate**
forniquer
fornicar
Unzucht treiben

2612. **forthwith**
immédiatement
inmediatamente
sogleich

2613. **fortuitous**
fortuit
fortuito
zufällig

2614. **forum**
forum (m); tribunal (m)
foro (m); tribunal (m)
Gerichtshof (m); Tribunal (n)

2615. **foundation**
base (f); dotation (f); fondation (f)
base (f); dotación (f); fundación (f)
Fundament (n); Anstalt (f); Gründung (f); Stiftung (f)

2616. **to lay the foundation**
poser les fondements
formar la base
die Grundlage schaffen

2617. **foundling**
enfant trouvé
niño expósito
Findelkind

2618. **frame of reference**
contexte (m)
contexto (m)
Aufgabenbereich (n)

2619. **frame-up**
complot (m)
complot (m)
Komplott (n); Intrige (f)

2620. **franchise**
droit de vote; franchise (f)
derecho de votar; franquicia (f)
Wahlrecht (n); Konzession (f)

2621. **frank**
franchise postale
franquicia postal
Portofreiheit

2622. **fratricide**
fratricide (m)
fratricidio (m)
Brudermord (m)

2623. **fraud**
fraude (f)
fraude (m)
Betrug (m)

2624. **fraudulent**
frauduleux
fraudulento

betrügerisch
2625. **to defraud**
frauder
defraudar
betrügen
2626. **free city**
ville (f) libre
ciudad (f) libre
freie Stadt (f)
2627. **freedom**
liberté (f)
libertad (f)
Freiheit (f)
2628. **free**
exempt de; gratuit; libre
exento de; gratuito; libre
frei; kostenlos
2629. **freedom from want**
affranchissement du besoin
sin necesidad
Freiheit von Not
2630. **free on board (F.O.B.)**
franco à bord
franco, libre a bordo
frei an Bord
2631. **freedom of the press**
liberté de la presse
libertad de prensa
Pressefreiheit
2632. **freedom of the seas**
liberté des mers
libertad de los mares
Freiheit der Meere
2633. **freedom of speech**
liberté de la parole
libertad de palabra
Redefreiheit
2634. **freedom with (without) bail**
liberté sous (sans) caution
libertad bajo (sin) fianza
Freiheit gegen (ohne) Kaution
2635. **fundamental freedoms**
libertés fondamentales
libertades fundamentales
Grundfreiheiten
2636. **to curtail freedom**
porter atteinte à la liberté
restringir la libertad
die Freiheit beschränken
2637. **to free, set free**
affranchir; libérer; mettre en liberté
exentar; libertar; librar
freilassen; befreien
2638. **freehold**
franc-fief (m)
dominio (m) absoluto
freier Grundbesitz (m)
2639. **friction**
désaccord (m)
desacuerdo (m)
Reibung (f)
2640. **friend**
ami (m); amie (f)
amigo (m); amiga (f)
Freund (m); Freundin (f)
2641. **next friend**
représentant soutenant un mineur ou un incapable
representante de un menor o de un incapacitado
Beistand eines Minderjährigen oder Recht unfähigen im Prozess
2642. **frustration**
frustration (f)
frustración (f)
Vereitelung (f); Frustration (f)
2643. **to frustrate**
faire échouer; frustrer
frustrar
durchkreuzen; vereiteln; enttäuschen
2644. **fugitive**
réfugié (m); fugitif (m)
fugitivo (m)
Flüchtling (m)
2645. **fulfilment**
accomplissement (m); réalisation (f)
cumplimiento (m); realización (f)
Ausführung (f)
2646. **to fulfil**
accomplir; réaliser
cumplir; realizar
erfüllen
2647. **function**
fonction (f)
función (f)
Funktion (f)
2648. **court functions**
fonctions jurisdictionnelles
funciones jurisdiccionales

gerichtliche Zuständigkeiten

2649. **functionary**
fonctionnaire (m)
funcionario (m)
Beamter (m); Funktionär (m)

2650. **judicial functions**
fonctions judiciaires
funciones judiciales
richterliche Funktionen

2651. **fund**
fonds (m)
fondo (m)
Fonds (m)

2652. **appropriation of funds**
affectation (f) de fonds
asignación (f) de fondos
Geldbewilligung (f)

2653. **funds and properties**
biens meubles et immeubles
bienes muebles y bienes raíces
bewegliches und unbewegliches Vermögen

2654. **misappropriation of funds**
détournement de fonds
malversación de los fondos
unrechtmässige Aneignung von Geld

2655. **public funds**
deniers publics
fondos públicos
öffentliche Gelder

2656. **sinking fund**
fonds d'amortissement
fondo de amortización
Schuldentilgungsfonds

2657. **stabilization fund**
fonds de stabilisation
fondos de estabilización
Stabilisierungsfonds

2658. **trust funds**
fonds en fidéicommis, trust
fondos fiduciarios
Treuhandfonds

2659. **to deposit funds in a bank**
déposer des fonds à la banque
depositar fondos en un banco
Gelder bei einer Bank einlegen

2660. **to earmark funds**
affecter des fonds pour un but spécifique
asignar los fondos para fines específicos
Fonds für einen bestimmten Zweck zurücklegen, reservieren

2661. **fundamental**
fondamental
fundamental
grundlegend

2662. **fungibles**
fongibles (mpl)
bienes (mpl) fungibles
fungible bewegliche Sachen (fpl); Gattungswaren (fpl)

2663. **fusion**
fusion (f)
fusión (f)
Fusion (f)

2664. **future interests**
expectative (f); intérêts à venir
intereses (mpl) futuros
Anwartschaft (f); aufschiebend bedingter Anspruch (m)

2665. **futures**
valeurs (fpl) à terme
futuros (mpl)
Termingeschäfte (npl)

G

2666. **gain**
gain (m); profit (m)
ganancia (f); lucro (m)
Gewinn (m)

2667. **capital gain**
gain (m) en capital; plus-value (f)
ganancia (f) de capital
Wertzuwachs (m); Kapitalgewinn (m)

2668. **net profit, gain**
bénéfice (m) net
utilidad (f) neta
Nettoprofit (m)

2669. **to gain**
gagner; profiter
ganar; lograr
gewinnen

2670. **gambling; gaming; game of chance**
jeu (m) de hasard (m)
juego (m) de azar (m)
Glücksspiel (n)

2671. **gambler**
joueur (m); spéculateur (m)
jugador (m); garitero (m)
Spieler (m)

2672. **to gamble**
jouer
jugar por dinero
spielen

2673. **gang**
bande (f) de malfaiteurs (mpl)
cuadrilla (f); pandilla (f)
Bande (f); Rotte (f)

2674. **gangster**
bandit (m)
pandillero (m)
Bandit (m)

2675. **garnishment**
assignation (f); saisie-arrêt (f)
entredicho (m)
Beschlagnahme (m) einer Forderung (f) des Schuldners (m)

2676. **garnishee**
assigné; tiers-saisi
el que recibe un mandato de entredicho
Drittschuldner

2677. **to garnish**
assigner; saisir
ordenar judicialmente la retención de una cosa
vorladen; mit Beschlag belegen

2678. **gathering**
attroupement (m); réunion (f)
reunión (f)
Ansammlung (f); Versammlung (f)

2679. **to gather**
assembler; réunir
juntar; reunir
versammeln

2680. **gazette; official gazette** (see **official journal**, No. 3252)

2681. **general**
général
general
allgemein

2681a. **generalization**
généralité (f)
generalidad (f)
Verallgemeinerung (f)

2682. **to generalize**
généraliser
generalizar
verallgemeinern

2683. **genocide**
génocide (m)
genocidio (m)
Völkermord (m)

2684. **genuineness**
authenticité (f); véracité (f)
autenticidad (f)
Echtheit (f)

2685. **genuine**
authentique; véritable
auténtico; genuino
authentisch; echt

2686. **germane**
parent; pertinent
pariente; pertinente
entsprechend; passend

2687. **gift**
cadeau (m); don (m); donation (f)
don (m); dádiva (f); donación (f)

Geschenk (n); Schenkung (f)

2688. **gift causa mortis**
don à cause de mort
donación por causa de muerte
Schenkung von Todes wegen

2689. **gift inter vivos**
donation entre vifs
donación entre vivos
Schenkung unter Lebenden

2690. **to give**
donner
dar
geben

2691. **to give up**
céder; renoncer
ceder; renunciar a
aufgeben; verzichten auf

2692. **glossary**
glossaire (m)
glosario (m)
Spezialwörterbuch (n); Glossar (n)

2693. **go-between**
intermédiaire (m)
intermediario (m)
Mittelsperson (f)

2694. **good offices**
bons offices (mpl)
buenos oficios (mpl)
gute Dienste (f)

2695. **good will**
achalandage (m); bienveillance (f)
buen nombre (m); benevolencia (f)
Kundenkreis (m); guter Wille (m)

2696. **goods**
denrées (fpl); marchandises (fpl); produits (mpl)
efectos (mpl); bienes (mpl); mercancías (fpl)
Güte (fpl); Habe (f); Waren (fpl)

2697. **bonded goods**
marchandises entreposées
mercancía afianzada
Waren unter Zollverschluss

2698. **consumer goods**
biens de consommation; denrées
artículos de consumo
Konsumgüter

2699. **goods in transit**
marchandises en transit
mercancías en tránsito
Transitwaren

2700. **goods on approbation, approval**
marchandises à condition
mercancías a condición
Waren zur Ansicht; Ansichtssendung

2701. **manufactured goods**
articles manufacturés
productos manufacturados
Fabrikate (f); Industrieartikel (m)

2702. **perishable goods**
marchandises périssables
bienes perecederos
verderbliche Waren

2703. **receiving stolen goods**
recel d'objets volés
receptar cosas robadas
Hehlerei; Sachhehlerei

2704. **receiver of stolen goods**
receleur (m)
receptador (m)
Hehler (m)

2705. **second hand goods**
marchandises d'occasion
mercancías de ocasión, de segunda mano
gebrauchte Waren

2706. **government**
gouvernement (m)
gobierno (m)
Regierung (f)

2707. **branch of the government**
service du gouvernement
rama de gobierno
Zweigstelle der Regierung

2708. **federal government**
gouvernement fédéral
gobierno federal
Bundesregierung

2709. **military government**
gouvernement militaire
gobierno militar
Militärregierung

2710. **puppet government**
gouvernement fantoche
gobierno títere
Marionettenregierung

2711. **to govern**
gouverner

gobernar
regieren

2712. **grace**
grâce (f)
gracia (f)
Gnade (f)

2713. **days of grace; grace period**
différé (m) d'amortissement
período (m) de gracia
Gnadenfrist (f)

2714. **graft**
corruption (f); pot-de-vin (m)
peculado (m)
Bestechlichkeit (f); Bestechungsgeld (n)

2715. **grant**
concession (f); don (m); octroi (m); subvention (f)
concesión (f); donación (f); permiso (m); privilegio (m)
Bewilligung (f); Schenkung (f); Erteilung (f); Verleihung (f)

2716. **grantee**
bénéficiaire (m); concessionnaire (m)
cesionario (m); concesionario (m)
Begünstigter (m); Zessionär (m)

2717. **grantor**
cédant (m); donateur (m)
cesionista (m); otorgante (m)
Verleiher (m); Zedent (m)

2718. **to grant**
accorder; céder; donner; octroyer
ceder; dar; dispensar; otorgar
bewilligen; gewähren

2719. **gratuity**
gratification (f)
gratificación (f)
Zuwendung (f)

2720. **gratis**
gratuit
gratuito
unentgeltlich

2721. **gravamen**
charge (f) principale
peso (m) del agravio (m)
Beschwerde (f)

2722. **grievance**
grief (m)
agravio (m)
Beschwerde (f); Misstand (m)

2723. **to redress a grievance**
réparer une injustice
reparar une injusticia
einem Übelstand abhelfen

2724. **ground**
motif (m); raison (f)
motivo (m); base (f)
Basis (f); Grund (m); Veranlassung (f)

2724a. **burial ground** (see **cemetery**, No. 1059)

2725. **guaranty**
garantie (f)
garantía (f)
Garantie (f)

2726. **guarantor**
garant (m)
garante (m)
Garant (m)

2727. **to guarantee**
garantir; se porter garant
garantir; ser fiador de
garantieren

2728. **guard**
garde (m); gardien (m); surveillant (m)
guardia (m)
Wache (f); Wächter (m)

2729. **to guard**
garder; surveiller
guardar; vigilar
bewachen; wachen

2730. **guardianship**
tutelle (f)
tutela (f)
Vormundschaft (f)

2731. **guardian**
curateur (m); tuteur (m)
custodio (m); tutor (m); guardián (m)
Hüter (m); Vormund (m)

2732. **guardian ad litem**
tuteur pendant une poursuite
curador *ad litem*
Prozesskurator

2733. **under the care of a guardian**
sous la garde de tuteur
bajo la custodia del tutor
unter Vormundschaft

2734. **guile**
artifice (m); fourberie (f); ruse (f)

engaño (m); malicia (f); picardía (f)
Arglist (f); Betrug (m); Kunstgriff (m)

2735. **guileless**
franc; loyal
sin engaño, malicia
arglos; offen

2736. **guilt**
culpabilité (f)
culpa (f)
Schuld (f)

2737. **guilty**
coupable
culpable
schuldig

2738. **not guilty**
innocent; non-coupable
inocente; no culpable
nicht schuldig

2739. **to be found guilty**
être reconnu coupable
ser declarado culpable
für schuldig befunden werden

2740. **to find guilty**
déclarer coupable
declarar culpable
für schuldig befinden

2741. **to plead guilty**
plaider coupable
declararse culpable
sich schuldig bekennen

H

2742. **habeas corpus** (see **writ of habeas corpus**, No. 6281)

2743. **habit**
coutume (f); habitude (f)
costumbre (f); hábito (m)
Gewohnheit (f)

2744. **habitually**
habituellement
habitualmente
gewohnheitsmässig

2745. **handcuffs**
menottes (fpl)
esposas (fpl)
Handfesseln (fpl)

2746. **handcuffed**
menottes aux mains
esposado
in Handfesseln

2747. **to handcuff**
mettre des menottes
maniatar
fesseln; jdm. Handfesseln anlegen

2748. **handwriting**
écriture (f)
escritura (f)
Handschrift (f)

2749. **handwritten**
écrit à la main
escrito a mano
handgeschrieben

2750. **hanging**
pendaison (f)
ahorcamiento (m)
Tod durch den Strang (m)

2751. **hangman**
bourreau (m)
verdugo (m)
Henker (m)

2752. **to hang**
pendre
ahorcar
hängen; gehenkt werden

2753. **harassment**
harcèlement (m)
hostigamiento (m)
Belästigung (f)

2754. **to harass**
harceler; tourmenter
hostigar; atormentar
belästigen

2755. **harbor, to**
donner asile, refuge à
abrigar; albergar
beherbergen; Unterschlupf gewähren

2756. **harlot**
prostituée (f)
prostituta (f)
Hure (f)

2757. **harm**
dommage (m); préjudice (m)

daño (m); perjuicio (m)
Schaden (m)

2758. **bodily harm**
blessure (f) corporelle
daño (m) corporal
Körperverletzung (f)

2759. **harmful**
dommageable; préjudiciable
dañoso; perjudicial; nocivo
schädlich

2760. **harmless**
inoffensif; pas méchant
inofensivo; inocuo
harmlos; unschädlich

2761. **to harm**
causer un dommage; porter préjudice
dañar; perjudicar
schaden; schädigen

2762. **hazard**
péril (m); risque (m)
peligro (m); riesgo (m)
Gefahr (f); Wagnis (n)

2763. **hazardous**
hasardeux; périlleux
arriesgado; peligroso
gewagt; gefährlich

2764. **to hazard**
hasarder; risquer
arriesgar; poner en peligro
aufs Spiel setzen; wagen

2765. **heading**
en-tête (f); titre (m)
epígrafe (m); título (m)
Titel (m); Überschrift (f)

2766. **headquarters**
siège (m) principal
sede (f) principal
Hauptsitz (m)

2767. **hearing**
audition (f); audience (f); enquête (f)
audiencia (f); examen (m) de testigos (mpl)
Vernehmung (f); Untersuchung (f)

2768. **preliminary hearing**
audience préliminaire; audition préalable
examen preliminar
Voruntersuchung; Vorvernehmung

2769. **public hearing**
audience publique
audiencia pública
öffentliche Sitzung

2770. **hearsay**
ouï-dire (m)
de oídas (fpl)
Hörensagen (n)

2771. **hegemony**
hégémonie (f)
hegemonía (f)
Hegemonie (f)

2772. **heir**
héritier (m)
heredero (m)
Erbe (m)

2773. **heir apparent**
héritier présomptif
heredero forzoso
gesetzlicher Erbe

2774. **presumptive heir**
héritier présomptif
presunto heredero
mutmasslicher Erbe

2775. **rightful heir**
héritier légitime
heredero legítimo
rechtmässiger Erbe

2776. **sole heir**
seul héritier
heredero único
Alleinerbe

2777. **heiress**
héritière (f)
heredera (f)
Erbin (f)

2778. **henchman**
séide (m); supporteur (m)
secuaz (m); seguidor (m)
Gefolgsmann (m); treuer Anhänger (m)

2779. **hereafter**
ci-après; dorénavant
de hoy en adelante; en lo sucesivo
künftig; später

2780. **hereditaments**
biens transmissibles par héritage
todo lo susceptible de ser heredado
Erbgut; vererbliche Gegenstände

2781. **corporeal hereditaments**

biens corporels transmissibles par héritage
bienes tangibles por heredar
im Erbweg übertragbare körperliche Sachen

2782. **incorporeal hereditaments**
biens incorporels transmissibles par héritage
bienes intangibles por heredar
im Erbweg übertragbare nichtkörperliche Vermögenswerte

2783. **hereditary**
héréditaire
hereditario
erblich

2784. **herein**
ci-inclus; ici
incluso en el (la) presente
hierin

2785. **heretofore**
jusqu'ici
anteriormente; hasta ahora
bisher; vorher

2786. **herewith**
ci-joint
con el (la) presente; con este; adjunto
hiermit; beifolgend

2787. **hide-out**
cachette (f)
escondite (m)
Versteck (n)

2788. **high seas**
haute mer (f)
alta mar (f)
hohe See (f)

2789. **highjacking of a plane**
détournement (m) d'avion; piraterie (f) de l'air
secuestro (m) de avión
Luftpiraterie (f)

2790. **highjacker of a plane**
pirate (m) de l'air
secuestrador (m) de avión
Luftpirat (m)

2791. **highjacking of a truck**
détournement de camion (m)
secuestro de camión (m)
Lastkraftwagenpiraterie (f)

2792. **hindrance**
empêchement (m); obstacle (m)
obstáculo (m); estorbo (m)
Hindernis (n); Hinderung (f)

2793. **to hinder**
empêcher; gêner
impedir; obstaculizar; estorbar
hindern; verhindern

2794. **hire**
embauchage (m); louage (m)
alquiler (m); arriendo (m); contratación (f)
Heuer (f); Miete (f)

2795. **to hire**
embaucher; louer
contratar; alquilar; dar, tomar en arriendo
heuern; mieten

2796. **holder**
détenteur (m); titulaire (m)
tenedor (m); titular (m)
Inhaber (m); Titular (m)

2797. **bona fide holder**
détenteur de bonne foi
titular de buena fe
gutgläubiger Inhaber

2798. **holder in due course**
porteur en bonne foi
tenedor de buena fe
legitimierter Inhaber

2799. **holding**
bien (m) possédé
posesión (f) de tierras (fpl); terratenencia (f)
Guthaben (n); Pachtung (f)

2800. **to hold**
avoir; décider; soutenir
poseer; decidir; tener
haben; entscheiden; halten

2801. **holdup** (see **highway robbery**, No. 5203)

2802. **Holy See**
Saint Siège (m)
Santa Sede (f)
Heiliger Stuhl (m)

2803. **homicide**
homicide (m)
homicidio (m)
Totschlag (m); Tötung (f)

2804. **excusable, justifiable homicide**
homicide involontaire, non-punissable
homicidio involuntario, inculpable
nichtstrafbarer Totschlag

2805. **felonious homicide**
assassinat (m); meurtre (m)
asesinato (m)
strafbarer Totschlag (m)

2806. **homicidal attempt**
tentative (f) d'homicide
conato (m), tentativa (f) de homicidio
versuchter Totschlag (m)

2807. **homicide squad; criminal police**
police criminelle
policía criminal
Kriminalpolizei; Mordkommission

2808. **involuntary homicide**
homicide involontaire, par imprudence (f)
asesinato involuntario, por imprudencia (f)
fahrlässiger Totschlag

2809. **voluntary homicide**
homicide volontaire; meurtre
asesinato intencional
versätzlicher Totschlag

2810. **homologation**
homologation (f)
homologación (f)
Anerkennung (f); Billigung (f)

2811. **to homologate**
homologuer
homologar
anerkennen; billigen

2812. **honor**
honneur (m)
honor (m)
Ehre (f); Honorierung (f)

2813. **honor supra protest**
paiement par intervention
pago por intervención
Honorierung nach Protest

2814. **honorable**
honorable
honorable
ehrenvoll

2815. **Your Honor**
Monsieur le Juge, Président
Señor Juez, Presidente; Su Señoría
Herr Präsident, Richter; Hohes Gericht!

2816. **to honor**
honorer
honrar
ehren; honorieren

2817. **honorarium**
honoraires (mpl)
honorarios (mpl)
Honorar (n)

2818. **hostage**
otage (m)
rehén (m)
Geisel (m)

2819. **hostilities**
hostilités (fpl)
hostilidades (fpl)
Feindseligkeiten (fpl)

2820. **hostile**
hostile
hostil
feindlich

2821. **house**
maison (f)
casa (f)
Haus (n)

2822. **disorderly house; house of ill fame**
maison (f) mal famée
burdel (m)
Bordell (n)

2823. **House of Commons (G.B.)**
Chambre (f) des Communes
Cámara (f) de los Comunes
Unterhaus (n)

2824. **House of Lords (G.B.)**
Chambre des Lords
Cámara de los Lores, Pares
Oberhaus

2825. **House of Representatives**
Chambre des Représentants
Cámara de Representantes
Repräsentantenhaus

2826. **lower house**
chambre basse
cámara baja
Unterhaus

2827. **upper house**
chambre haute
alta cámara
Oberhaus

2828. **housebreaking**
effraction (f)
escalamiento (m)
Einbruch (m)

2829. **housebreaker**

voleur (m) avec effraction
ladrón (m) de casas
Einbrecher (m)

2830. **housing**
logement (m)
alojamiento (m); vivienda (f)
Wohngelegenheit (f)

2831. **low-cost housing**
habitations (fpl) à bon marché
vivienda (f) económica
billige Wohnungsbeschaffung (f)

2832. **hue and cry**
cris d'alarme; à cor et à cri
vocería de alarma
Zeter und Mordio

2833. **humanity**
humanité (f)
humanidad (f)
Humanität (f); Menschlichkeit (f)

2834. **human**
humain
humano
menschlich

2835. **human nature**
nature humaine
naturaleza humana
menschliches Wesen

2836. **humane**
humain; compatissant
humanitario
human; menschlich

2837. **humanitarian**
humanitaire
humanitario
Menschenfreund; menschenfreundlich

2838. **humankind**
genre (m) humain
género (m) humano
Menschengeschlecht (n); Menschheit (f)

2839. **husband and wife**
conjoints (mpl); époux (mpl); ménage (m)
marido y mujer; cónyuges (mpl); matrimonio (m)
Mann und Frau; Ehepaar (n)

2840. **hush-money**
prime (f) au silence (m)
dinero (m) acallador
Schweigegeld (n)

2841. **hypothesis**
hypothèse (f)
hipótesis (f)
Hypothese (f)

2842. **hypothetical**
hypothétique; supposé
hipotético
hypothetisch; angenommen

I

2843. **idea**
idée (f)
idea (f)
Idee (f)

2844. **idealism**
idéalisme (m)
idealismo (m)
Idealismus (m)

2845. **ideal**
idéal (m)
ideal (m)
Ideal (n)

2846. **idealist**
idéaliste (m)
idealista (m)
Idealist (m)

2847. **identification**
identification (f)
identificación (f)
Identifizierung (f)

2848. **identification card**
carte (f) d'identité (f)
carnet (m), cédula (f) de identificación (f)
Ausweis (n); Kennkarte (f)

2849. **identification department**
bureau d'identification judiciaire
servicio de identificación
Identifizierungsabteilung

2850. **identification papers**
papiers (mpl) d'identité
documentos (mpl) de identificación

Ausweispapiere (npl)
2851. **to identify**
identifier
identificar
identifizieren
2852. **identity**
identité (f)
identidad (f)
Identität (f)
2853. **mistaken identity**
erreur (f) sur la personne
error (m) en la persona
Irrtum (m) über die Person
2854. **to establish identity**
établir l'identité
identificar
die Identität feststellen
2855. **ideology**
idéologie (f)
ideología (f)
Ideologie (f)
2856. **ideological**
idéologique
ideológico
ideologisch
2857. **ignorance**
ignorance (f)
ignorancia (f)
Unkenntnis (f)
2858. **ignorance of the facts**
ignorance des faits
ignorancia de los hechos
Unkenntnis der Tatsachen
2859. **ignorance of the law**
ignorance du droit
ignorancia de la ley
Unkenntnis des Gesetzes
2860. **to plead ignorance**
alléguer l'ignorance
alegar ignorancia
sich mit Unkenntnis entschuldigen
2861. **illegality**
illégalité (f)
ilegalidad (f)
Gesetzwidrigkeit (f)
2862. **illegal**
illégal
ilegal
gesetzwidrig
2863. **illegally**
illégalement
ilegalmente
gesetzwidrig
2864. **illegitimacy**
illégitimité (f)
ilegitimidad (f)
Unrechtmässigkeit (f); Unehelichkeit (f)
2865. **illegitimate**
illégitime
ilegítimo
widerrechtlich; unehelich
2866. **illicit**
illicite
ilícito
verboten
2867. **illiteracy**
analphabétisme (m)
analfabetismo (m)
Analphabetentum (n)
2868. **illiterate**
analphabète (m)
analfabeto (m)
Analphabet (m)
2869. **ill-treatment**
mauvais traitement (m); sévices (mpl)
maltrato (m)
Misshandlung (f); schlechte Behandlung (f)
2870. **immaterial**
sans importance
sin importancia
unwesentlich
2871. **immediate**
immédiat
inmediato
unmittelbar
2872. **immigration**
immigration (f)
inmigración (f)
Einwanderung (f)
2873. **immigrant**
immigrant (m)
inmigrante (m)
Einwanderer (m)
2874. **to immigrate**
immigrer
inmigrar
einwandern
2875. **immorality**
immoralité (f)
inmoralidad (f)

Unsittlichkeit (f)

2876. **immoral**
immoral
inmoral
unmoralisch

2877. **immovables**
biens immeubles
bienes inmuebles
unbewegliches Eigentum

2878. **immunity**
immunité (f)
inmunidad (f)
Immunität (f)

2879. **impairment**
affaiblissement (m); détérioration (f)
deterioro (m); menoscabo (m)
Beeinträchtigung (f); Verminderung (f)

2880. **to impair**
affaiblir; porter atteinte
deteriorar; menoscabar
schwächen; beeinträchtigen

2881. **impartiality**
impartialité (f)
imparcialidad (f)
Objektivität (f)

2882. **impartial**
impartial
imparcial
unparteiisch

2883. **impeachment (of an official)**
mise en accusation (d'un fonctionnaire)
formulación de cargos (contra un funcionario)
Anklage (gegen einen Beamten)

2884. **impeachable**
récusable
censurable; recusable
anklagbar

2885. **to impeach**
mettre en accusation; récuser (un témoin)
acusar; recusar (un testigo); residenciar
Anklage gegen einen Beamten erheben

2886. **impediment**
empêchement (m); entrave (f)
impedimento (m); obstáculo (m); traba (f)
Hindernis (n)

2887. **to impede**
empêcher; entraver; gêner
obstaculizar; impedir; trabar
behindern; hindern; verhindern

2888. **imperative**
impératif; impérieux; péremptoire
imperativo; imperioso; perentorio
befehlend; gebietend; zwingend

2889. **imperialism**
impérialisme (m)
imperialismo (m)
Imperialismus (m)

2890. **imperialist**
impérialiste (m)
imperialista (m)
Imperialist (m)

2891. **impersonation; personation**
substitution (f) de personne; usurpation (f) de nom ou de fonction
personificación (f); usurpación (f) de nombre ajeno
eine fremde Persönlichkeit (f) vortäuschen

2892. **to impersonate; to personate**
usurper un nom ou une fonction
usurpar nombre, estado legal ajeno
sich für einen anderen ausgeben

2893. **implementation**
mise (f) en oeuvre, en pratique
ejecución (f); realización (f)
Ausführung (f); Erfüllung (f)

2894. **to implement**
mettre en pratique; réaliser; rendre effectif
cumplir; dar efecto; ejecutar
ausführen; erfüllen

2895. **implication**
implication (f); portée (f)
deducción (f); inferencia (f)
selbstverständliche Folgerung (f); Verwicklung (f)

2896. **to implicate**
impliquer
implicar
verwickeln

2897. **implicit**
implicite
implícito
inbegriffen

2898. **implied**
impliqué; sous-entendu
implícito; sobrentendido
miteinbegriffen; stillschweigend gefolgert

2899. **to imply**
impliquer; suggérer
denotar; significar
andeuten; in sich schliessen

2900. **importation**
importation (f)
importación (f)
Einfuhr (f)

2901. **import**
article d'importation; importance; signification
artículo de importación; importancia; significación
eingeführte Ware; Wichtigkeit; Bedeutung; Sinn

2902. **importer**
importateur (m)
importador (m)
Importeur (m)

2903. **to import**
importer
importar
einführen; importieren

2904. **imposition**
imposition (f)
imposición (f)
Auflage (f)

2905. **to impose**
imposer
imponer
auferlegen

2906. **impossibility**
impossibilité (f)
imposibilidad (f)
Unmöglichkeit (f)

2907. **impossible**
impossible
imposible
unmöglich

2908. **imposter**
imposteur (m)
impostor (m)
Betrüger (m)

2909. **impotent**
incapable; impotent; impuissant
incapaz; impotente
unfähig; impotent

2910. **impound, to**
confisquer; saisir; enfermer
incautar
einziehen; in gerichtliche Verwahrung nehmen

2911. **imprisonment**
détention (f); emprisonnement (m)
encarcelación (f); prisión (f)
Gefangehaltung (f); Gefängnisstrafe (f)

2912. **commutation of imprisonment**
commutation (f) de peine (f)
conmutación (f) de pena (f)
Strafumwandlung (f)

2913. **false imprisonment**
arrestation (f); séquestration (f) arbitraire
detención (f) injustificada
Freiheitsberaubung (f)

2914. **imprisonment with hard labor**
peine de travaux forcés
reclusión con trabajo forzado
Zuchthaus mit Zwangsarbeit

2915. **solitary imprisonment**
régime (m) cellulaire
prisión (f) solitaria
Einzelhaft (f)

2916. **to imprison**
écrouer; emprisonner
encarcelar
einsperren; ins Gefängnis stecken

2917. **impropriety**
impropriété (f)
impropiedad (f)
Ungehörigkeit (f)

2918. **improper**
incorrect; malhonnête
impropio; indecente
unangemessen; unpassend

2919. **improvement**
amélioration (f); perfectionnement (m)
mejoramiento (m); perfeccionamiento (m)
Fortschritt (m); Verbesserung (f)

2920. **to improve**

améliorer; perfectionner
mejorar; perfeccionar
Fortschritte machen; verbessern

2921. **improvisation**
improvisation (f)
improvisación (f)
Improvisation (f)

2922. **to improvise**
improviser
improvisar
improvisieren

2923. **impulse**
élan (m); motif (m)
estímulo (m); motivo (m)
Antrieb (m); Impuls (m)

2924. **irresistible impulse**
élan irrésistible
impulso irresistible
unwiderstehlicher Impuls

2925. **impunity**
impunité (f)
impunidad (f)
Straffreiheit (f)

2926. **imputation**
imputation (f)
imputación (f)
Beschuldigung (f)

2927. **to impute**
imputer
imputar
zur Last legen

2928. **inability**
incapacité (f)
incapacidad (f)
Unvermögen (n)

2929. **inadequacy**
insuffisance (f)
insuficiencia (f)
Unzulänglichkeit (f)

2930. **inadequate**
inadéquat
inadecuado
unangemessen

2931. **inadmissibility**
inadmissibilité (f)
inadmisibilidad (f)
Unzulässigkeit (f)

2932. **inadmissible**
inadmissible
inadmisible
unzulässig

2933. **inadvertence**
inadvertance (f)
inadvertencia (f)
Versehen (n)

2934. **inadvertent**
par inadvertance
inadvertido
versehentlich

2935. **inalienable; unalienable**
inaliénable
inalienable
unveräusserlich

2936. **inauguration**
inauguration (f); mise (f) en application (f); installation (f) officielle
inauguración (f); transmisión (f) del mando (m)
Einweihung (f); Amtsantritt (m); Eröffnung (f)

2937. **inaugural**
inaugural
inaugural
Antritts-

2938. **to inaugurate**
inaugurer; commencer; installer
inaugurar; comenzar; transmitir el mando
einweihen; das Amt antreten; eröffnen

2939. **incapacity**
incapacité (f); inhabilité (f)
incapacidad (f); inhabilidad (f)
Unfähigkeit (f); Rechnungsunfähigkeit (f)

2940. **incapable**
incapable
incapaz
unfähig

2941. **legal incapacity**
incapacité légale
incapacidad legal
Handlungsunfähigkeit

2942. **to incapacitate**
rendre incapable
incapacitar
unfähig machen

2943. **incarceration**
incarcération (f); emprisonnement (m)
encarcelación (f); prisión (f)

Einkerkerung (f)

2944. **incendiary**
incendiaire (m)
incendiario (m)
Brandstifter (m)

2945. **incentive**
stimulant (m)
incentivo (m)
Anreiz (m)

2946. **incest**
inceste (m)
incesto (m)
Blutschande (f)

2947. **incestuous**
incestueux
incestuoso
blutschänderisch

2948. **incidence**
incidence (f)
incidencia (f)
Umstand (m); Vorfall (m)

2949. **incidental**
accessoire; fortuit
accesorio; incidental
gelegentlich; zufällig

2950. **incitement; incitation**
incitation (f); instigation (f)
incitación (f); instigación (f)
Anstiftung (f); Verleitung (f)

2951. **to incite**
exciter; inciter à
incitar; instigar
anstiften; verleiten

2952. **inclosure** (see **enclosure**)

2953. **inclusion**
inclusion (f); insertion (f)
inclusión (f)
Einschliessung (f)

2954. **to include**
inclure; insérer
comprender; incluir
(mit) einschliessen

2955. **income**
bénéfice (m); revenu (m)
ingreso (m); renta (f)
Einkommen (n); Einkünfte (fpl)

2956. **gross income**
revenu brut
ingreso bruto
Bruttoeinkommen

2957. **independent income, means**
fortune (f) personnelle
fortuna (f) personal
eigenes Vermögen (n)

2958. **taxable income**
revenue imposable
renta imponible, gravable
steuerpflichtiges Einkommen

2959. **incompatibility**
incompatibilité (f)
incompatibilidad (f)
Unvereinbarkeit (f)

2960. **incompatible**
incompatible
incompatible
unvereinbar

2961. **incompetence**
incompétence (f)
incompetencia (f)
Inkompetenz (f)

2962. **incompetent**
incompétent
incompetente
inkompetent

2963. **inconsistency**
inconséquence (f); contradiction (f)
inconsecuencia (f); contradicción (f)
Folgewidrigkeit (f); innerer Widerspruch (f)

2964. **inconsistent**
contradictoire; inconséquent
contradictorio; incongruente
folgewidrig; widersprechend

2965. **incontestable**
indiscutable
indisputable
unbestreitbar

2966. **incorporation**
incorporation (f)
incorporación (f)
Einverleibung (f)

2967. **articles of incorporation**
statuts (mpl) d'une société (f)
escritura (f) de constitución (f) de una sociedad (f)
Gesellschaftsvertrag (m)

2968. **to incorporate**
constituer en société
constituir una compañía, una sociedad anónima
eine Gesellschaft gründen

2969. **incorporeal**

incorporel
incorpóreo
unkörperlich; immateriell

2970. **increase**
croissance (f); majoration (f)
aumento (m)
Erhöhung (f)

2971. **to increase**
augmenter
aumentar
vergrössern; erhöhen

2972. **increment**
augmentation (f)
aumento (m)
Wertzuwachs (m)

2973. **incrimination**
incrimination (f)
incriminación (f)
Beschuldigung (f)

2974. **to incriminate**
incriminer
incriminar
beschuldigen

2975. **incumbency**
durée (f), étendue (f) d'une fonction (f)
duración (f) de un cargo (m) o empleo (m)
Amtsdauer (f); Amtsperiode (f)

2976. **incumbent**
titulaire (m) d'une fonction
titular (m) de un cargo o empleo
Amtsinhaber (m)

2977. **incumbent upon**
obligatoire
obligatorio
obliegend

2978. **incur, to**
encourir
incurrir
sich aussetzen

2979. **indebtedness**
dette (f); passif (m)
adeudo (m); deuda (f)
Verpflichtung (f); Verschuldung (f)

2980. **indebted**
endetté
adeudado
verpflichtet; verschuldet

2981. **indecency**
indécence (f)
indecencia (f)
Unanständigkeit (f)

2982. **indecent**
indécent
indecente
unanständig

2983. **indefeasible**
inaliénable; irrévocable
irrevocable
unverletzlich; unwiderruflich

2984. **indefinite**
indéfini; imprécis
indefinido
unbestimmt; unverschränkt

2985. **indemnity; indemnification**
dédommagement (m); indemnité (f)
indemnidad (f); indemnización (f)
Abfindung (f); Entschädigung (f)

2986. **to indemnify**
dédommager; indemniser
indemnizar
abfinden; entschädigen

2987. **indenture**
contrat (m) synallagmatique
escritura (f); contrato (m)
förmlicher Vertrag (m)

2988. **to indenture**
lier par contrat; mettre en apprentissage
ligar por contrato (esp. un aprendiz a su maestro)
jdn. vertraglich binden, verpflichten; jdn. durch Lehrvertrag verpflichten

2989. **independence**
indépendance (f)
independencia (f)
Unabhängigkeit (f)

2990. **independent**
indépendant
independiente
unabhängig

2991. **indeterminate**
indéterminé
indeterminado
unbestimmt

2992. **index**
index (m); indice (m)
índice (m); indicio (m)

Inhaltsverzeichnis (n); Index (m)

2993. **to index**
faire l'index
hacer un índice
registrieren

2994. **card index**
fichier (m)
fichero (m)
Kartei (f)

2995. **indicia**
indices (mpl)
indicios (mpl); señales (fpl)
Anzeichen (n); Umstände (mpl)

2996. **indictment**
inculpation (f); mise (f) en accusation (f)
acusación (f); auto (m) de procesamiento (m)
Anklage (f); Anklageschrift (f)

2997. **count of an indictment**
chef (m) d'accusation
motivo (m) de acusación
Anklagepunkt (m)

2998. **to dismiss, quash an indictment**
écarter une accusation
dejar sin efecto un procesamiento
ein Verfahren einstellen

2999. **to indict**
mettre en accusation
acusar ante el juez
anklagen

3000. **to serve an indictment**
signifier un acte d'accusation
notificar una acusación
die Anklageschrift zustellen

3001. **indigent**
indigent
indigente
arm

3002. **indispensable**
indispensable
indispensable
unerlässlich

3003. **individual**
individuel
individual
individuell

3004. **indivisible**
indivisible
indivisible
unteilbar

3005. **indorsement** (see **endorsement**, No. 2247)

3006. **inducement**
cause (f); incitation (f); motif (m); préambule (m)
causa (f); incentivo (m); móvil (m); preámbulo (m) de los alegatos (mpl)
Ursache (f); Anreiz (m); Beweggrund (m); Präambel (f)

3007. **to induce**
causer; influencer; motiver
causar; inducir; influenciar
beeinflussen; bewegen zu

3008. **industry**
industrie (f); assiduité (f)
industria (f); diligencia (f)
Industrie (f); Fleiss (m)

3009. **industrial**
industriel
industrial
industriell

3010. **industrialist**
industriel (m)
industrial (m)
Industrieller (m)

3011. **industrious**
industrieux; travailleur
industrioso; trabajador
arbeitsam; fleissig

3012. **subsidized industry**
industrie (f) primée
industria (f) subvencionada
staatlich subventionierte Industrie (f)

3013. **inebriate**
alcoolique (m, f); ivrogne (m, f)
borracho (m); ebrio (m)
Trunksüchtiger (m)

3014. **ineffective**
inefficace
ineficaz
unwirksam

3015. **ineligible**
inacceptable; inéligible
inaceptable; no elegible
unannehmbar; unwählbar

3016. **inequity**
injustice (f)
falta (f) de equidad (f)
Unbilligkeit (f)

3017. **inequitable**
injuste
injusto
unbillig

3018. **inevitable**
inévitable
inevitable
unvermeidlich

3019. **infallibility**
infaillibilité (f)
infalibilidad (f)
Unfehlbarkeit (f)

3020. **infallible**
infaillible
infalible
unfehlbar

3021. **infamy**
infamie (f)
infamia (f)
Ehrlosigkeit (f)

3022. **infamous**
infâme
infame
ehrlos

3023. **infancy**
minorité (f); première enfance (f)
infancia (f); minoridad (f)
Minderjährigkeit (f)

3024. **infant**
mineur (m); enfant (m) en bas âge
menor (m)
Minderjähriger (m)

3025. **infanticide**
infanticide (m)
infanticidio (m)
Kindesmord (m)

3026. **inference**
inférence (f)
inferencia (f)
Folgerung (f)

3027. **to infer**
inférer
inferir
folgern

3028. **infiltration**
noyautage (m)
infiltración (f)
Infiltrierung (f)

3029. **inflation**
inflation (f); gonflement (m)
inflación (f)
Inflation (f)

3030. **influence**
influence (f)
influencia (f)
Einfluss (m)

3031. **influential**
influent
influyente
einflüssreich

3032. **sphere of influence**
sphère (f) d'influence (f)
esfera (f) de influencia (f)
Einflussphäre (f)

3033. **undue influence**
captation (f) d'influence; intimidation (f)
influencia indebida; intimidación (f)
widerrechtliche Beeinflussung (f)

3034. **to influence**
influencer
influir en, sobre
beeinflussen

3035. **information**
information (f); renseignements (mpl)
información (f); informe (m)
mitteilung (f); Benachrichtigung (f)

3036. **additional information**
complément d'information
información adicional, complementaria
zusätzliche Information

3037. **advance information**
avis (m) préalable
información (f) previa
Benachrichtigung (f) im voraus

3038. **information desk**
bureau (m) d'information
oficina (f) de información
Auskunftsstelle (f)

3039. **informative**
éducatif; instructif
educativo; informativo
lehrreich

3040. **informer**
délateur (m); dénonciateur (m); informateur (m); indicateur (m) de police (f)
delator (m); denunciador (m);

informador (m)
Anzeiger (m); Denunziant (m)
3041. **upon information and belief**
pour autant qu'on sache
según saber y entender
nach besten Wissen und Gewissen
3042. **to inform**
dénoncer; informer
denunciar; informar
denunzieren; informieren; benachrichtigen
3043. **infraction**
infraction (f); violation (f)
infracción (f); violación (f)
Übertretung (f); Verletzung (f)
3044. **to commit an infraction**
commettre une infraction
cometer una infracción
übertreten; verletzen
3045. **infringement**
infraction; violation
infracción
Verletzung
3046. **inhabitant**
habitant (m)
habitante (m)
Bewohner (m)
3047. **to inhabit**
habiter
habitar
bewohnen
3048. **inherent**
inhérent
inherente
innewohnend; inhärent
3049. **inheritance; heritage**
héritage (m); succession (f)
herencia (f); sucesión (f); abolengo (m)
das Erbe (n); Erbschaft (f)
3050. **inheritor**
héritier (m)
heredero (m)
der Erbe (m)
3051. **to inherit**
hériter
heredar
erben
3052. **inhibition**
inhibition (f)
inhibición (f)
Hemmung (f)
3053. **to inhibit**
empêcher; prohiber
inhibir; prohibir
hemmen; hindern
3054. **initials**
initiales (fpl)
iniciales (fpl)
Anfangsbuchstaben (mpl) (eines Vor- und Familiennamens)
3055. **to initial**
apposer ses initiales; parapher
rubricar; poner las iniciales a un documento
paraphieren
3056. **initiative**
initiative (f)
iniciativa (f)
Initiative (f)
3057. **to initiate**
commencer; inaugurer
inaugurar; iniciar
anhängig machen; einführen
3058. **injunction**
injonction (f); ordre (m) d'un tribunal
interdicto (m); mandato (m)
Anordnung (f) des Gerichts; gerichtliche Verfügung (f)
3059. **mandatory injunction**
ordonnance (f) de faire
mandato (m) de ejecución (f)
obligatorische gerichtliche Verfügung (f)
3060. **temporary injunction**
ordre conservatoire
interdicto temporal
einstweilige Verfügung
3061. **to serve an injunction**
prononcer une injonction
notificar un interdicto
eine einstweilige Verfügung erlassen
3062. **injury**
tort (m); préjudice (m); lésion (f); blessure (f)
daño (m); perjuicio (m); lesión (f)
Benachteiligung (f); Schaden (m); Verletzung (f)
3063. **bodily injury**
blessure corporelle

daño, lesión corporal
Körperverletzung

3064. **injurious**
injurieux
perjudicial
schädlich

3065. **occupational injury**
accident (m) du travail (m)
accidente (m) del trabajo (m)
Berufsunfall (m)

3066. **to injure**
faire du tort; léser; porter préjudice
dañar; perjudicar
beschädigen; verletzen

3067. **to sustain injury**
être lésé; subir un préjudice
sufrir daño
Schaden oder Verlust erleiden

3068. **injustice**
injustice (f)
injusticia (f)
Unrecht (n)

3069. **inmate** (of a prison)
prisonnier (m)
prisionero (m)
Sträfling (m)

3070. **innkeeper**
aubergiste (m); hôtclier (m)
hostelero (m); posadero (m); mesonero (m)
Gastwirt (m)

3071. **innocence**
innocence (f)
inocencia (f)
Unschuld (f)

3072. **presumption of innocence**
présomption d'innocence (f)
presunción (f) de inculpabilidad (f)
Vermutung (f) der Schuldlosigkeit (f)

3073. **to be innocent**
être innocent
ser inocente
unschuldig oder schuldlos sein

3074. **innovation**
innovation (f)
innovación (f)
Neuerung (f)

3075. **innuendo; inuendo**
insinuation (f)
insinuación (f)
geheime Andeutung (f)

3076. **inquest**
enquête (f)
investigación (f)
gerichtliche Untersuchung (f)

3077. **to hold an inquest**
faire un examen de cadavre (m)
examinar un cadáver (m)
eine Leichenschau (f) durchführen

3078. **inquiry** (see **enquiry**)

3079. **insanity**
aliénation (f) mentale; démence (f)
demencia (f); locura (f); enajenación (f) mental
Geisteskrankheit (f); Wahnsinn (m)

3080. **to be insane**
être aliéné
estar insano, loco, demente
geisteskrank oder geistesschwach sein

3081. **insertion**
insertion (f)
inserción (f)
Einschaltung (f)

3082. **to insert**
insérer
insertar
einschalten

3083. **insolvency**
faillite (f); insolvabilité (f)
insolvencia (f)
Zahlungsunfähigkeit (f)

3084. **insolvent**
insolvable
insolvente
zahlungsunfähig

3085. **to be insolvent**
être insolvable
ser insolvente
zahlungsunfähig sein

3086. **inspection**
examen (m); inspection (f)
examen (m); inspección (f)
Aufsicht (f); Prüfung (f)

3087. **inspector**
contrôleur (m); vérificateur (m)
examinador (m); inspector (m)
Inspektor (m)

3088. **to inspect**
examiner; inspecter
inspeccionar
prüfen; untersuchen

3089. **installment**
acompte (m); versement (m) partiel
pago (m) a plazos (mpl), por entregas (fpl)
Terminzahlung (f); Rate (f)

3090. **monthly installment**
mensualité (f)
mensualidad (f)
Monatsrate (f)

3091. **to install**
installer
instalar
einsetzen

3092. **to pay by installments**
payer à tempérament
pagar a plazos, por entregas
in Raten zahlen

3093. **instigation**
instigation (f)
instigación (f)
Anstiftung (f)

3094. **instigator**
instigateur (m)
instigador (m)
anstifter (m)

3095. **to instigate**
instiguer
instigar
anstiften

3096. **institute**
institut (m)
instituto (m)
Institut (n)

3097. **Institute of International Law**
Institut de Droit International
Instituto de Derecho Internacional
Institut für Völkerrecht

3098. **to institute**
établir; instituer
establecer; instituir; crear
einführen; gründen

3099. **institution**
établissement (m); institution (f)
establecimiento (m); institución (f)
Anstalt (f); Institution (f)

3100. **charitable, eleemosynary institution**
établissement de bienfaisance (f)
institución de caridad (f)
milde Stiftung (f)

3101. **instructions**
directives (fpl); instructions (fpl)
direcciones (fpl); instrucciones (fpl)
Anweisungen (fpl); Instruktionen (fpl)

3102. **to instruct**
donner des directives, des instructions; instruire
dar órdenes; instruir
anweisen; instruieren

3103. **instrument**
acte (m); instrument (m); titre (m)
documento (m); instrumento (m)
Urkunde (f)

3104. **authentic instrument**
acte authentique
instrumento auténtico
echte Urkunde

3105. **commercial instrument**
effets (mpl) de commerce (m)
instrumento (m) comercial
Handelspapier (n)

3106. **instrumental**
efficace; utile
eficaz; instrumental
wirksam; behilflich

3107. **public instrument**
document officiel; titre authentique
documento, instrumento público
öffentliche Urkunde

3108. **instrumentality**
concours (m); moyen (m)
agencia (f); medio (m)
Mitwirkung (f); Vermittlung (f)

3109. **insubordination**
insubordination (f)
insubordinación (f)
Insubordination (f)

3110. **insubordinate**
insubordonné
insubordinado
unbotmässig

3111. **insufficiency**
insuffisance (f)
insuficiencia (f)
Unzulänglichkeit (f)

3112. **insufficient**
insuffisant
insuficiente
unzulänglich

3113. **insult**
injures (fpl); insulte (f); outrage (m)
insulto (m); ultraje (m)
Beleidigung (f); Ehrenkränkung (f)

3114. **insulting**
injurieux; insultant
insultante
beleidigend

3115. **to insult**
injurier; insulter; outrager
insultar; ultrajar
beleidigen; beschimpfen

3116. **insurance**
assurance (f)
seguro (m)
Versicherung (f)

3117. **accident insurance**
assurance contre accidents
seguro contra accidentes
Unfallversicherung

3118. **automobile insurance**
assurance-auto
seguro de automóviles
Automobilversicherung

3119. **employers' liability insurance**
assurance des patrons contre les accidents de travail
seguro de responsabilidad patronal
Betriebschaftpflichtversicherung

3120. **fire insurance**
assurance-incendie
seguro contra incendios
Feuerversicherung

3121. **insurance policy**
police d'assurance
póliza de seguro
Versicherungspolizze

3122. **insurer**
assureur (m)
asegurador (m)
Versicherer (m)

3123. **liability insurance**
assurance contre les accidents de travail
seguro contra responsabilidad civil
Haftpflichtversicherung

3124. **life insurance**
assurance-vie
seguro de vida
Lebensversicherung

3125. **old-age insurance**
assurance-vieillesse
seguro de vejez
Altersversicherung

3126. **travel insurance**
assurance au voyage
seguro de viaje
Reiseversicherung

3127. **unemployment insurance**
assurance contre le chômage
seguro contra cesantía
Arbeitslosenversicherung

3128. **workmen's compensation insurance**
assurance contre les accidents de travail
seguro de accidentes del trabajo
Betriebsunfallversicherung

3129. **to be insured**
être assuré
estar asegurado
versichert sein

3130. **to insure**
assurer; garantir
asegurar; garantizar
sicherstellen; versichern

3131. **insurgency; insurrection**
émeute (f); insurrection (f)
insurrección (f)
Aufstand (m); Aufruhr (m)

3132. **insurgent**
émeutier (m); insurgé (m)
insurgente (m); insurrecto (m)
Aufständischer (m); Aufrührer (m)

3133. **intangible**
intangible
intangible
immateriell

3134. **integration**
intégration (f)

integración (f)
Integration (f); Ergänzung (f)
3135. **to integrate**
incorporer
integrar
ergänzen
3136. **integrity**
intégrité (f)
integridad (f)
Integrität (f)
3137. **intelligence**
intelligence (f); renseignements (mpl)
inteligencia (f); informes (mpl)
Intelligenz (f); Geheimdienst (m) [Abwehr]
3138. **intelligent**
intelligent
inteligente
intelligent
3139. **intelligentsia**
élite (f) intellectuelle
élite (f) intelectual; intelectualidad (f)
intellektuelle Elite (f)
3140. **intendment**
intention (f); sens (m) véritable
propósito (m); significación (f)
Absicht (f); Zweck (m)
3141. **intendment of law**
esprit (m), sens (m) de la loi (f)
significación (f) correcta de la ley (f)
Sinn (m) des Gesetzes (n)
3142. **intent; intention**
dessein (m); intention (f)
intención (f); propósito (m)
Vorsatz (m); Absicht (f)
3143. **criminal intent**
intention criminelle
intención criminal, dolosa
verbrecherische Absicht, Vorsatz
3144. **fraudulent intent**
intention de frauder
intención de defraudar
Täuschungsabsicht
3145. **intentional**
intentionnel
intencional
absichtlich; vorsätzlich
3146. **malicious intent**
intention malicieuse
intención dolosa
böswilliger Vorsatz
3147. **specific intent**
intention déterminée, préméditée
intención determinada, premeditada
bestimmte Absicht; fester Vorsatz
3148. **intercession**
intercession (f)
intercesión (f)
Vermittlung (f)
3149. **intercessor**
intercesseur (m)
intercesor (m)
Vermittler (m)
3150. **to intercede**
intercéder
interceder
vermitteln
3151. **interdependence**
interdépendance (f)
interdependencia (f)
Wechselseitige Abhängigkeit (f); Verflechtung (f)
3152. **interdiction**
interdiction (f)
interdicto (m)
Verbot (n)
3153. **interest**
intérêt (m)
interés (m)
Interesse (n); Zinsen (mpl)
3154. **accrued interest**
intérêt couru, cumulé
interés acumulado, ganado
aufgelaufene Zinsen
3155. **affected with a public interest**
touchant à l'intérêt public
de interés público
durch öffentliches Interesse beeinflusst, berührt
3156. **back interest**
arrérages (mpl)
interés (m) atrasado
Zinsrückstände (f)
3157. **compound interest**
intérêts composés
interés compuesto
Zinseszins

3158. **controlling interest**
prédominance (f) financière
interés (m) dominante
ausschlaggebender Kapitalanteil (m)

3159. **vested interest**
droit, intérêt acquis, établi
interés creado; derecho adquirido
verbriefte, wohlerworbene Rechte

3160. **vital interests**
intérêts vitaux
intereses vitales
lebenswichtige Interessen

3161. **to bear interest**
produire des intérêts
devengar interés
Zinsen tragen

3162. **interim**
intérim (m); intervalle (m)
ínterin (m); intermedio (m)
Zwischenzeit (f)

3163. **interlocutory**
interlocutoire
interlocutorio
vorläufig

3164. **intermission**
intermission (f)
intermisión (f)
Unterbrechung (f)

3165. **intermittently**
avec intermission
con intermisión
mit Unterbrechungen

3166. **without intermission**
sans relâche (f)
sin interrupción (f)
ohne Unterlass (m)

3167. **internal**
intérieur
interior
inner

3168. **international**
international
internacional
zwischenstaatlich; international

3169. **internment**
internement (m)
internación (f)
Internierung (f)

3170. **to intern**
interner
internar
internieren

3171. **interpleader**
procédure par laquelle un défendeur oblige deux parties ayant les mêmes prétentions contre lui à régler d'abord entre elles leur différend
defensa por la que se exige que dos personas que alegan la propiedad de una cosa en manos de un tercero demandado, litiguen entre sí su disputa
Verfahren, in dem Parteien, die denselben Anspruch erheben, gezwungen werden, die Sache erst unter sich auszutragen

3172. **interpolation**
intercalation (f); interpolation (f)
intercalación (f); interpolación (f)
Einschiebung (f); Interpolation (f)

3173. **to interpolate**
intercaler; interpoler
intercalar; interpolar
einschieben; interpolieren

3174. **interpretation**
interprétation (f)
interpretación (f)
Interpretation (f); Auslegung (f)

3175. **interpreter**
interprète (m)
intérprete (m)
Dolmetscher (m)

3176. **strict interpretation**
interprétation rigide
interpretación rigurosa
enge, restriktive Auslegung

3177. **to interpret**
interpréter
interpretar
interpretieren; auslegen

3178. **interrogation**
interrogation (f); interrogatoire (m)
examen (m); interrogación (f)
Verhör (n)

3179. **interrogator**
interrogateur (m); juge (m) d'instruction (f)

interrogante (m); juez (m) de instrucción (f)
Verhörer (m); Untersuchungsrichter (m)

3180. **interrogatory**
interrogatoire (m)
interrogatorio (m)
Verhör (n)

3181. **to interrogate**
interroger
interrogar
verhören

3182. **interruption**
dérangement (m); interruption (f)
interrupción (f)
Unterbrechung (f)

3183. **to interrupt**
déranger; interrompre
interrumpir
unterbrechen

3184. **intervention**
intervention (f)
intervención (f)
Intervention (f)

3185. **to intervene**
intervenir
intervenir
intervenieren

3186. **interview**
entrevue (f); interview (f)
entrevista (f); conferencia (f)
Befragung (f); Interview (n)

3187. **to interview; to hold an interview**
avoir une entrevue avec
celebrar una entrevista
ein Interview mit jdm. haben

3188. **intestacy**
absence (f) de testament (m)
falta (f) de testamento (m)
Fehlen (n) eines Testaments (n)

3189. **intestate**
intestat
intestado; abintestato
ohne Testament

3190. **intimidation**
intimidation (f)
intimidación (f)
Einschüchterung (f)

3191. **to intimidate**
intimider
intimidar
einschüchtern

3192. **intoxication**
ivresse (f)
embriaguez (f)
Trunkenheit (f)

3193. **intoxicated**
ivre
ebrio
betrunken

3194. **introduction**
introduction (f)
introducción (f)
Einführung (f)

3195. **to introduce**
introduire; présenter
introducir; presentar
einführen

3196. **invalidation**
invalidation (f)
invalidación (f)
Ungültigkeitserklärung (f)

3197. **invalid**
invalide
inválido
ungültig

3198. **to invalidate**
invalider; rendre caduc, inopérant, nul
anular; invalidar
ungültig machen

3199. **invasion**
atteinte (f); invasion (f)
invasión (f)
Einfall (m); Invasion (f)

3200. **to invade**
envahir
invadir
einfallen

3201. **inventory**
état (m) des lieux (mpl); inventaire (m)
inventario (m); existencias (fpl)
Bestandsaufnahme (f); Inventar (n)

3202. **to make an inventory**
faire l'inventaire
hacer un inventario
Inventar aufnehmen

3203. **investigation**
enquête (f); investigation (f)
investigación (f)

Nachforschung (f); Untersuchung (f)

3204. **investigator**
enquêteur (m); investigateur (m)
investigador (m)
mit einer Untersuchung betrauter Beamter (m)

3205. **to make an investigation**
faire une enquête
hacer una investigación
Nachforschung, Untersuchung anstellen

3206. **investment**
investissement (m)
inversión (f)
Investition (f); Anlage (f)

3207. **investor**
investisseur (m)
inversionista (m)
Investor (m); Kapitalanleger (m)

3208. **to invest**
investir
invertir
investieren; anlegen

3209. **inviolability**
inviolabilité (f)
inviolabilidad (f)
Unverletzlichkeit (f)

3210. **inviolable**
inviolable
inviolable
unverletzlich; unverbrüchlich

3211. **invitee**
invité (m); personne (f) ayant affaire dans un lieu
invitado (m); persona (f) con derecho a estar en un lugar
Eingeladener (m)

3212. **invoice**
facture (f)
factura (f)
Faktura (f); Rechnung (f)

3213. **to invoice**
facturer
facturar
in Rechnung stellen

3214. **involuntary**
involontaire
involuntario
unfreiwillig

3215. **involvement**
complication (f); implication (f)
complicación (f); implicación (f)
Schwierigkeit (f); Verwicklung (f)

3216. **involved**
compliqué; embrouillé
complicado; involucrado
verwickelt

3217. **to involve**
impliquer
complicar; involucrar
verwickeln

3218. **iron curtain**
rideau (m) de fer (m)
cortina (f) de hierro (m)
eiserner Vorhang (m)

3219. **irrebuttable**
irréfragable
irrefutable; irrefragable
unwiderleglich

3220. **irregular**
irrégulier
irregular
irregulär; unregelmässig

3221. **irrelevant**
non pertinent; sans lien
irrelevante; fuera de lugar
irrelevant; unwichtig

3222. **irrevocable**
irrévocable
irrevocable
unwiderruflich

3223. **issue**
émission (f); édition (f); conclusion (f) descendance (f); controverse (f); question (f)
emisión (f) de moneda, de valores (mpl) edición (f); resultado (m); prole (f); punto (m) en disputa (f)
Emission (f); Schlussfolgerung (f); Streitfrage (m), Kernfrage (f); Ergebnis (n)

3224. **at, in issue**
en litige
en litigio
strittig; streitig

3225. **collateral issue**
question (f) accessoire
asunto (m) colateral
Nebenfrage (f)

3226. **failure of issue**

faute de descendance; sans postérité (f)
sin prole, sucesión (f)
ohne Nachkommenschaft (f)

3227. **issue of fact**
point de fait
cuestión de hecho
Tatfrage

3228. **issue of law**
point (m) de droit; point juridique
cuestión (f) de derecho, jurídica
Rechtsfrage (f)

3229. **matter in issue**
question en litige
cuestión en disputa
Streitgegenstand

3230. **to die without issue**
mourir sans descendance
morir sin prole, sucesión
ohne Leibesorben, kinderlos sterben

3231. **to issue**
donner; émettre; publier
dictar; emitir; publicar
ausgeben; emittieren; erlassen

3232. **to join issue**
accepter les conclusions de l'adversaire
aceptar las conclusiones de la parte contraria
die Behauptung des Gegners annehmen

3233. **item**
article (m); élément (m); question (f); poste (m) (du budget)
artículo (m); item (m); partida (f)
Einzelheit (f); Punkt (f); Posten (m)

3234. **to itemize**
détailler
detallar
spezifizieren

J

3235. **jail**
prison (f)
cárcel (f)
Gefängnis (n)

3236. **jailbird**
récidiviste (m); repris (m) de justice
presidiario (m)
Rückfälliger (m); Gewohnheitsverbrecher (m)

3237. **jailbreaker**
évadé (m)
fugitivo (m) de la cárcel
Ausbrecher (m)

3238. **jailer**
geôlier (m)
carcelero (m)
Gefängnisaufseher (m)

3239. **jeopardy**
danger (m); péril (m)
peligro (m); riesgo (m)
Gefahr (f)

3240. **double, former, prior jeopardy**
dualité de poursuites pour un même fait
procesamiento por segunda vez por un mismo delito
abermalige Strafverfolgung wegen derselben Straftat

3241. **in jeopardy**
en péril
en peligro
in Gefahr

3242. **to jeopardize**
mettre en péril
arriesgar; exponer
gefährden

3243. **jetsam**
objets (mpl) jetés à la mer
artículos (mpl) echados al mar
Seewurfgut (n); Strandgut (n)

3244. **jettison**
jet (m) à la mer
echazón (f)
Überbordwerfen (n) der Güter

3245. **job**
emploi (m)
empleo (m)

Arbeit (f)

3246. **jobber**
courtier (m); intermédiaire (m)
corredor (m); intermediario (m)
Makler (m)

3247. **joinder of actions**
jonction (f) d'instances (fpl), des procédures (fpl)
unión (f) de acciones (fpl)
Klagenverbindung (f)

3248. **joinder of parties**
jonction des demandeurs ou des défendeurs pour une procédure
unión de codemandantes o codemandados en un pleito
Prozessbeitritt; Streitgenossenschaft

3249. **joint**
commun; conjoint; joint
común; unido
verbunden

3250. **joint and several**
conjoint et solidaire
mancomunado y solidario
gesamtschuldnerisch

3251. **journal**
journal (m)
diario (m)
Zeitschrift (f); Tagebuch (n)

3252. **official journal; gazette**
bulletin (m) des lois; journal officiel
boletín (m), diario (m), gaceta (f) oficial
Amtsblatt (n)

3253. **judge**
juge (m)
juez (m)
Richter (m)

3254. **alternate judge**
juge suppléant
juez suplente
stellvertretender Richter

3255. **associate judge**
assesseur; juge assesseur
juez asociado
beisitzender Richter

3256. **irremovability of judges**
inamovibilité (f) des juges
inamovilidad (f) de los jueces
Unabsetzbarkeit (f) der Richter

3257. **judge advocate**
commissaire (m) du gouvernement (m); procureur (m) militaire
auditor (m) de guerra
Kriegsgerichtsrat (m)

3258. **judge advocate general**
chef de la justice militaire
auditor general de guerra
Chef des Heeresjustizwesens

3259. **judgeship**
magistrature (f) assise
magistratura (f)
Richteramt (n)

3260. **presiding judge**
président (m)
presidente (m)
vorsitzender Richter (m)

3261. **trial judge**
juge de première instance
juez de primera instancia
erstinstanzlicher Richter

3262. **judgment**
décision (f); jugement (m)
fallo (m); sentencia (f)
Urteil (n)

3263. **arrest of judgment**
suspension (f) d'un jugement
suspensión (f) de una sentencia
Vollstreckungsaussetzung (f)

3264. **declaratory judgment**
jugement déclaratoire
sentencia declarativa
Feststellungsurteil

3265. **interim, interlocutory, provisional judgment**
jugement avant dire droit, interlocutoire, provisoire
sentencia interlocutoria, provisional
Zwischenurteil

3266. **judgment creditor**
créancier (m) en vertu d'un jugement
acreedor (m) en virtud de una sentencia
Person (f), die ein vollstreckbares Urteil erwirkt hat

3267. **judgment debtor**
débiteur (m) en vertu d'un jugement
deudor (m) en virtud de una

sentencia
Person (f), gegen die ein vollstreckbares Urteil ergangen ist

3268. **judgment by default**
jugement par contumace, défaut
sentencia en contumacia, rebeldía
Kontumazurteil; Versäumnisurteil

3269. **judgment on the merits**
jugement sur le fond
sentencia relativa al fondo de la demanda
Urteil auf Grund des materiellrechtlichen Tatbestandes

3270. **judgment in personam**
jugement en matière personnelle
sentencia relativa a una obligación personal
Urteil, betr. obligatorische Ansprüche

3271. **judgment in rem**
jugement en matière immobilière, réelle
sentencia relativa a una obligación real
Urteil, betr. dingliche Ansprüche

3272. **reversal of a judgment**
revirement (m) d'un jugement
anulación (f) de una sentencia
Aufhebung (f) eines Urteils

3273. **to arrest judgment**
suspendre l'exécution (f) d'un jugement
suspender la ejecución (f) de una sentencia
das Urteil aussetzen

3274. **to attack, contest a judgment**
attaquer, se pourvoir contre un jugement
atacar una sentencia
gegen ein Urteil ein Rechtsmittel einlegen

3275. **to enter a judgment for**
décider en faveur de
dictar sentencia a favor de
der Klage stattgeben

3276. **to enter judgment**
enregistrer, minuter un jugement
registrar una sentencia
ein Urteil eintragen

3277. **to execute a judgment**
exécuter un jugement
ejecutar una sentencia
ein Urteil vollstrecken

3278. **to judge**
juger
juzgar; sentenciar
richten; urteilen

3279. **to pronounce a judgment**
prononcer un jugement
pronunciar una sentencia
ein Urteil verkünden

3280. **to quash, vacate a judgment**
annuler, casser un jugement
anular, casar una sentencia
ein Urteil annullieren

3281. **to reverse a judgment on appeal**
infirmer un jugement en appel (m)
anular un juicio en la instancia de apelación (f)
das Urteil in der Berufungsinstanz (f) aufheben

3282. **judicature**
judicature (f); magistrature (f)
judicatura (f); magistratura (f)
die höheren Gerichtsbeamten (mpl)

3283. **judicial**
judiciaire
judicial
gerichtlich; richterlich

3284. **judiciary**
pouvoir (m) judiciaire
poder (m) judicial
Richterstand (m)

3285. **juridical**
juridique
jurídico
juristisch

3286. **jurisconsult**
jurisconsulte (m)
jurisconsulto (m)
Rechtsgelehrter (m)

3287. **jurisdiction**
compétence (f); juridiction (f); ressort (m)
competencia (f); jurisdicción (f)

Zuständigkeit (f); Kompetenz (f); Rechtsprechung (f)

3288. **appellate jurisdiction**
compétence, juridiction d'appel
jurisdicción en apelación
Zuständigkeit in höherer Instanz

3289. **compulsory jurisdiction**
compétence, juridiction obligatoire
competencia obligatoria
obligatorische Zuständigkeit

3290. **concurrent jurisdiction**
compétences concurrentes
jurisdicción coexistente, concurrente
gemeinsame, konkurrierende Zuständigkeit

3291. **equity jurisdiction**
juridiction d'équité (f)
jurisdicción de la equidad (f)
Rechtsprechung nach Billigkeitsrecht (n)

3292. **exclusive jurisdiction**
compétence exclusive
jurisdicción exclusiva
ausschliessliche Zuständigkeit

3293. **exercise of jurisdiction**
exercise de la juridiction
ejercicio de la jurisdicción
Ausübung der Gerichtsbarkeit

3294. **lack of jurisdiction**
incompétence (f)
falta (f) de jurisdicción
mangelnde zuständigkeit (f)

3295. **objection to the jurisdiction**
exception (f) d'incompétence
excepción (f) de incompetencia
Einrede (f) der Unzuständigkeit

3296. **original jurisdiction**
compétence propre
jurisdicción original
Zuständigkeit erster Instanz

3297. **summary jurisdiction**
juridiction sommaire
jurisdicción sumaria
Zuständigkeit des Amtsgerichts

3298. **to have jurisdiction over**
avoir juridiction sur
tener jurisdicción sobre
zuständig sein für

3299. **jurisprudence**
jurisprudence (f); science (f) du droit
jurisprudencia (f); ciencia (f) del derecho
Jurisprudenz (f); Rechtswissenschaft (f)

3300. **medical jurisprudence; forensic medicine**
médecine (f) légale
medicina (f) legal
Gerichtsmedizin (f)

3301. **jurist**
juriste (m)
jurista (m)
Jurist (m)

3302. **jury**
jury (m)
jurado (m)
Jury (f); Geschworenengericht (n); Schöffengericht (n)

3303. **coroner's jury**
jury chargé de déterminer la cause d'une mort subite ou violente
jurado de pesquisidor
Geschworenenbank zur Untersuchung verdächtiger Todesursachen

3304. **foreman of a jury**
premier juré (m); chef (m) du jury
presidente (m) del jurado (m)
Obmann (m) der Geschworenen (mpl)

3305. **Gentlemen of the jury**
Messieurs les jurés
Señores del jurado
Meine Herren Geschworenen

3306. **grand jury**
jury d'accusation
jurado de la acusación
Anklagekammer; Anklagejury

3307. **hung jury**
jury indécis
jurado indeciso
Geschworenen, denen die Einstimmigkeit fehlt

3308. **juror; juryman**
juré (m)
jurado (m)
Geschworener (m); Schöffe (m)

3309. **jury box**
banc du jury
tribuna del jurado
Geschworenenbank; Schöffenbank

3310. **jury panel**
liste des jurés
lista de jurados
Geschworenenliste; Schöffenliste

3311. **packing the jury**
sélection frauduleuse de jurés
selección dolosa de jurados
eine Geschworenenbank mit parteiischen Geschworenen besetzen

3312. **petit jury**
jury de jugement
jurado de juicio
Urteilsjury; übliche Geschworenenbank für Straf- und Zivilsachen

3313. **struck jury** (U.S.A.)
jury sélectionné par élimination
jurado escogido por eliminación
durch Eliminierung ernannte Geschworenenbank

3314. **to challenge a juror**
récuser un juré
recusar, tachar a un jurado
einen Geschworenen ablehnen

3315. **to charge a jury**
faire allocation au jury
dar instrucciones al jurado
den Geschworenen Rechtsbelehrung erteilen

3316. **to impanel a jury**
dresser la liste d'un jury
formar la lista de los jurados
Geschworenen aufrufen

3317. **to labor a jury**
influencer un jury
influenciar un jurado
die Geschworenen beeinflussen

3318. **to poll a jury**
demander aux jurés individuellement de confirmer leur verdict
preguntar a los jurados individualmente su conformidad con el veredicto
die Geschworenen hinsichtlich der Entscheidung einzeln befragen

3319. **to serve, sit on a jury**
faire partie du jury
ser miembro de un jurado
Geschworener sein

3320. **justice**
juge (m); justice (f)
juez (m); justicia (f)
Richter (m); Gerechtigkeit (f)

3321. **administration of justice**
administration de la justice
administración de justicia
Rechtsprechung

3322. **associate justice (U.S. Supreme Court)**
juge à la Cour Suprême
juez de la Corte Suprema
beisitzender Richter des Obersten Gerichtshofes

3323. **Chief Justice**
Président de la Cour Suprême
Presidente de la Corte Suprema
Präsident des Obersten Gerichtshofes

3324. **denial of justice**
déni (m) de justice
denegación (f) de justicia
Rechtsverweigerung (f)

3325. **just**
juste
justo
gerecht

3326. **justice of the peace**
juge de paix
juez de paz
Friedensrichter

3327. **justiciable**
justiciable
justiciable
der Gerichtsbarkeit unterworfen

3328. **miscarriage of justice**
erreur (f) judiciaire
perjuicio (m) de derechos
Fehlurteil (n)

3329. **perversion of justice**
simulacre (m) de justice
aplicación (f) dolosa del proceso judicial
Rechtsleugnung (f)

3330. **sense of justice**

sentiment (m) de la justice
sentido (m) de la justicia
Rechtsgefühl (n)

3331. **to administer justice**
rendre la justice
administrar justicia
Recht sprechen

3332. **to bring to justice**
citer en justice
entablar pleito
vor Gericht bringen

3333. **justification**
justification (f)
justificación (f)
Rechtfertigung (f)

3334. **justifiable**
justifiable
justificable
berechtigt

3335. **to justify**
justifier
justificar
rechtfertigen

3336. **juvenile**
juvénile
juvenil
jugendlich

K

3337. **kidnapping**
enlèvement (m); kidnappage (m)
secuestro (m); rapto (m); plagio (m)
Entführung (f); Menschenraub (m)

3337a. **killing**
meurtre (m)
homicidio (m)
Tötung (f)

3338. **mass killings**
massacres (mpl)
masacres (fpl)
Massenmord (mpl)

3339. **mercy killing**
euthanasie (f)
eutanasia (f)
Gnadentod (m)

3340. **to kill**
tuer
matar
töten

3341. **kinship**
parenté (f)
parentesco (m)
Verwandtschaft (f)

3342. **kin**
famille (f); parents (mpl)
familia (f); parientes (mpl)
Familie (f); Blutsverwandte (f)

3343. **kindred**
de la même nature; souche (f)
deudo (m)
gleichartig; verwandt

3344. **next of kin**
le plus proche parent
pariente más cercano
die nächsten Verwandten

3345. **kleptomania**
cleptomanie (f)
cleptomanía (f)
Kleptomanie (f)

3346. **kleptomaniac**
cleptomane (m)
cleptómano (m)
Kleptomane (m)

3347. **know-how**
compétence (f); savoir-faire (m) pratique
competencia (f)
praktische Erfahrung (f)

3348. **knowledge**
connaissance (f)
conocimiento (m)
Kenntnis (f); Wissen (n)

3349. **actual knowledge**
connaissance réelle
conocimiento efectivo, real
tatsächliche Kenntnis

3350. **constructive knowledge**
connaissance dérivée
conocimiento derivado
abgeleitete Kenntnis

3351. **contrary to one's knowledge**
en contradiction avec ce que l'on sait

contrario a su propio saber
wider besseres Wissen

3352. **"Know all men by these presents'**
'Faisons assavoir par ces présentes'
'Sepan todos los que el presente vieren'
'Jedermann zu kund und wissen'

3353. **knowingly**
intentionnellement; sciemment
a sabiendas
wissentlich

3354. **public knowledge**
notoriété (f) publique
conocimiento (m) público
allgemeine Kenntnis (f)

3355. **to the best of my, one's knowledge**
en mon âme et conscience; selon tout ce que l'on sait
según su leal saber y entender
nach bestem Wissen und Gewissen

L

3356. **labor**
main d'oeuvre (f); travail (m)
mano (f) de obra (f); trabajo (m)
Arbeit (f); Arbeitskräfte (fpl); Arbeiterschaft (f)

3357. **compulsory, conscripted, forced, hard labor**
travail obligatoire; travaux forcés
trabajo conscripto, forzado
Arbeitsdienstpflicht; Zwangsarbeit

3358. **labor union**
syndicat (m) ouvrier
sindicato (m) de obreros
Gewerkschaft (m)

3359. **laborer**
ouvrier (m); travailleur (m)
obrero (m); trabajador (m)
Handarbeiter (m)

3360. **manual labor**
travail manuel
trabajo manual
Handarbeit

3361. **migratory labor**
main-d'oeuvre migratoire
mano de obra migratoria
Wanderarbeit

3362. **skilled labor**
main d'oeuvre qualifiée
mano de obra calificada
gelernte Arbeit

3363. **to labor a point**
ressasser
ser prolijo
einen Punkt ausarbeiten

3364. **laches**
carence (f); négligence (f) à agir en temps requis
negligencia (f); tardanza (f) en actuar
Vernachlässigung (f); Versäumnis (f)

3365. **laissez-faire**
laissez-faire (m)
laissez-faire (m)
laissez-faire (m)

3366. **landlord**
propriétaire (m)
terrateniente (m)
Grundeigentümer (m)

3367. **absentee landlord**
propriétaire absent
terrateniente ausentista
abwesender Grundeigentümer

3368. **landmark**
borne (f); limite (f)
marca (f); mojón (m) de lindero (m)
Grenzstein (m); Markstein (m)

3369. **language**
langue (f)
idioma (m)
Sprache (f)

3370. **official language**
langue officielle
idioma oficial

Amtssprache

3371. **lapse**
caducité (f); délai (m)
caducidad (f); lapso (m)
Erlöschen (n); Verfall (m)

3372. **lapse of time**
laps (m), intervalle (m) de temps
caducidad (f) de tiempo
Zeitablauf (m)

3373. **lapsed**
déchu; périmé
prescrito
verfallen; erlöschen

3374. **larceny**
vol (m)
hurto (m); ratería (f)
Diebstahl (m)

3375. **grand larceny**
vol grave, important
robo de cantidades grandes
Diebstahl von Sachen über einer bestimmten Wertgrenze

3376. **petit larceny**
larcin; vol minime, simple
robo de cantidades pequeñas
Diebstahl von Sachen bis zu einer bestimmten Wertgrenze

3377. **latent**
latent; caché
latente; oculto
latent; verborgen

3378. **law**
droit (m); loi (f); jurisprudence (f)
derecho (m); ley (f); jurisprudencia (f)
Recht (n); Gesetz (n); Rechtswissenschaft (f)

3379. **according to law**
conforme à la loi
conforme a derecho
nach geltendem Recht

3380. **adjective law**
droit de procédure
derecho procesal
Prozessrecht; Verfahrensrecht

3381. **administrative law**
droit administratif
derecho administrativo
Verwaltungsrecht

3382. **admiralty law**
droit maritime
derecho marítimo, de almirantazgo
Admiralitätsrecht; Seerecht

3383. **air law**
droit aérien
derecho aéreo
Luftrecht

3384. **alien law**
droit des étrangers
derecho de extranjería
Fremdenrecht

3385. **anti-trust law**
loi contre les monopoles (mpl)
legislación contra los monopolios (mpl)
Anti-Trust-Gesetz (n)

3386. **business, commercial law; law merchant**
droit commercial, des affaires
derecho comercial, mercantil
Handelsrecht

3387. **canon, ecclesiastical law**
droit canonique
derecho canónico
kanonisches Recht; Kirchenrecht

3388. **case law**
droit jurisprudential
derecho jurisprudencial
Rechtsprechung auf Grund von Präzedenzentscheidungen

3389. **civil law**
droit civil
derecho civil
Zivilrecht

3390. **codified law**
droit codifié
derecho codificado
kodifiziertes Recht

3391. **common law**
droit commun, coutumier
derecho común, consuetudinario
gemeines Recht; Gewohnheitsrecht; common law

3392. **comparative law**
droit comparé
derecho comparado
vergleichende Rechtswissenschaft

3393. **conflict of laws** (see **private international law**, No. 3441)

3394. **constitutional law**
droit constitutionnel
derecho constitucional
Verfassungsrecht

3395. **copyright law**
législation sur le droit d'auteur
derecho de propiedad literaria
Urheberrecht

3396. **corporation law**
droit corporatif
derecho corporativo
Gesellschaftsrecht

3397. **criminal, penal law**
droit pénal
derecho penal
Strafrecht

3398. **customary law**
droit coutumier
derecho consuetudinario
Gewohnheitsrecht

3399. **domestic law**
législation interne
legislación interna
innerstaatliches Recht

3400. **due process of law; law of the land**
formes et garanties de procédure
debido procedimiento de ley
ordnungsgemässes Gerichtsverfahren

3401. **enforceable by law**
exécutoire
exigible legalmente
auf dem Rechtsweg erzwingbar

3402. **equal protection of the law**
égalité devant la justice
igual protección de ley
gleicher Rechtsschutz

3403. **family law**
droit de famille
derecho de la familia
Familienrecht

3404. **force of law**
force de loi
fuerza de ley
Gesetzeskraft

3405. **foreign law**
droit étranger
derecho extranjero
ausländisches Recht

3406. **'general principles of law recognized by civilized nations'**
'les principes généraux de droit reconnus par les nations civilisées'
'principios generales de derecho reconocidos por los países civilizados'
'allgemein anerkannte Grundsätze des Völkerrechts'

3407. **infringement of the law**
violation de la loi
violación de la ley
Gesetzesverletzung

3408. **international criminal law**
droit pénal international
derecho criminal internacional
internationales Strafrecht

3409. **international law; law of nations**
droit international; droit des gens
derecho internacional; derecho de gentes
internationales Recht; Völkerrecht

3410. **labor law**
droit du travail; législation ouvrière
derecho del trabajo
Arbeitsrecht

3411. **law-abiding**
respectueux des lois
cumplidor, observante de la ley
gesetzestreu

3412. **lawbreaker**
infracteur (m); transgresseur (m) de la loi
infractor (m); violador (m) de la ley
Gesetzübertreter (m)

3413. **law digest**
recueil (m) de lois
recopilación (f) de leyes
Sammlung (f) von Gesetzen

3414. **law of civil procedure**
droit de la procédure civile
ley de enjuiciamiento civil
Zivilprozessrecht

3415. **law of criminal procedure**
droit de la procédure pénale

ley de enjuiciamiento criminal
Strafprozessrecht

3416. **law of diminishing returns**
loi de rendement décroissant
ley de rendimiento decreciente
Gesetz des abnehmenden Ertrags

3417. **law of neutrality**
droit de la neutralité
derecho de neutralidad
Neutralitätsrecht

3418. **law of outer space**
droit de l'espace
derecho espacial
Weltraumrecht

3419. **law of peace**
droit de la paix
derecho de paz
Friedensrecht

3420. **law of real property**
lois immobilières
derecho inmobiliario
Immobiliarrecht

3421. **law of supply and demand**
loi de l'offre et de la demande
ley de oferta y demanda
Gesetz von Abgebot und Nachfrage

3422. **law of torts**
droit de responsabilité délictuelle
derecho de responsabilidad
Recht der Haftung aus unerlaubten Handlungen

3423. **law report**
recueil de jurisprudence
publicación de los casos y sentencias de los tribunales
Sammlung von Gesetzen, Urteilssprüchen

3424. **law school**
école, faculté de droit
escuela, facultad de derecho
juristische Fakultät

3425. **law of war**
droit de la guerre
derecho bélico
Kriegsrecht; Kriegsgesetz

3426. **lawful** (see **legal**)

3427. **lawless**
illégal; sans loi
desordenado; ilegal
gesetzwidrig; ungesetzlich

3428. **lawmaker**
législateur (m)
legislador (m)
Gesetzgeber (m)

3429. **lawmaking**
législation (f)
legislación (f)
Gesetzgebung (f)

3430. **lawsuit**
action (f) en justice; procès (m)
litigio (m); pleito (m)
Prozess (m); Rechtsstreit (m)

3431. **lawyer**
avocat (m); avoué (m); homme (m) de loi
abogado (m); jurisconsulto (m)
Advokat (m); Anwalt (m); Jurist (m)

3432. **maritime law**
droit maritime
derecho marítimo
Seerecht

3433. **martial law**
loi martiale
ley marcial
Standrecht

3434. **military law**
droit militaire; lois militaires
derecho militar
Militärrecht; Wehrrecht

3435. **municipal law**
droit interne, national; droit municipal
derecho interno, nacional; derecho municipal
innerstaatliches Recht

3436. **natural law; law of nature**
droit naturel
derecho natural
Naturrecht

3437. **parliamentary law**
règlement d'une assemblée
prácticas parlamentarias
parlamentarische Geschäftsordnung

3438. **patent law**
loi sur les brevets d'invention
derecho patentario; ley de patentes
Patentgesetz; Patentrecht

3439. **penal law (see criminal law)**

3440. **point of law**
question de droit
cuestión de derecho
Rechtsfrage

3441. **private international law; conflict of laws**
droit international privé
derecho internacional privado
internationales Privatrecht

3442. **prize law**
droit des prises (fpl)
derecho de presas (fpl) de guerra
Prisenrecht (n)

3443. **public international law**
droit international public
derecho internacional público
öffentliches Völkerrecht

3444. **retroactive law**
loi rétroactive
ley retroactiva
rückwirkendes Gesetz

3445. **Roman law**
droit romain
derecho romano
römisches Recht

3446. **source of law**
source de droit
fuente de derecho
Rechtsquelle

3447. **statutory law**
droit écrit
derecho estatutario
Gesetzesrecht

3448. **substantive law**
droit fondamental, positif
derecho substantivo
materielles Recht

3449. **unwritten law**
droit non écrit; loi morale; droit coutumier
derecho consuetudinario, no escrito
ungeschriebenes Recht; Gewohnheitsrecht

3450. **violation of law**
infraction, violation de la loi
violación de ley
Gesetzesübertretung; Rechtsbruch

3451. **world law**
droit mondial
derecho mundial
Weltrecht

3452. **workmen's compensation law**
loi sur les accidents de travail
ley de accidentes del trabajo
Betriebsunfallgesetz

3453. **to abide by the law**
observer, se conformer à la loi
respetar la ley
das Gesetz befolgen

3454. **to annul, repeal a law**
abroger une loi
abrogar una ley
ein Gesetz annullieren, aufheben

3455. **to be bound by the law**
être soumis à la loi
estar obligado en virtud de una ley
gesetzlich verpflichtet sein

3456. **to enforce a law**
appliquer la loi
aplicar la ley
ein Gesetz durchführen

3457. **to evade the law**
éluder la loi
eludir la ley
das Gesetz umgehen

3458. **to expound a law**
interpréter une loi
explicar, interpretar una ley
ein Gesetz auslegen

3459. **to go to law**
aller en justice; avoir un procès
entablar juicio; demandar
den Rechtsweg beschreiten

3460. **to incorporate into a law**
incorporer à la loi
incorporar en una ley
in ein Gesetz einverleiben

3461. **to pass a law**
adopter, voter une loi
aprobar, votar una ley
ein Gesetz verabschieden

3462. **to practice law**
exercer le droit, une profession juridique
ejercer la abogacía
die Anwaltspraxis ausüben

3463. **to study law**
faire son droit, des études juridiques
estudiar derecho
Rechtswissenschaften studieren

3464. **to violate the law**
violer la loi
violar la ley
das Gesetz verletzen

3465. **lay**
laïque
lego
weltlich; Laien-

3466. **leadership**
conduite (f)
dirección (f)
Führung (f)

3467. **leader**
chef (m); directeur (m)
jefe (m); líder (m)
Führer (m); Leiter (m)

3468. **league**
ligue (f)
liga (f)
Bund (m); Vereinigung (f)

3469. **League of Nations**
Société des Nations
Liga de Naciones
Völkerbund

3470. **lease**
bail (m); louage (m)
arriendo (m); escritura (f) de arrendamiento (m)
Miete (f); Pacht (f)

3471. **lessee**
locataire (m); preneur (m)
arrendatario (m); inquilino (m)
Mieter (m); Pächter (m)

3472. **lessor**
bailleur (m)
arrendador (m)
Vermieter (m); Verpächter (m)

3473. **on a lease**
à bail; en location
en arrendamiento
in Miete, Pacht

3474. **to lease, to let**
donner à bail; louer
arrendar; dar en arriendo
mieten; pachten

3475. **legacy**
disposition (f) testamentaire; legs (m)
legado (m); herencia (f)
Legat (n); Vermächtnis (n)

3476. **general legacy**
legs à titre universel
legado general
allgemeines Vermächtnis

3477. **specific legacy (U.S.A.)**
legs à titre particulier
legado específico
Sondervermächtnis

3478. **universal legacy (U.S.A.)**
legs à titre universel
legado universal
Universalvermächtnis

3479. **legality**
légalité (f)
legalidad (f)
Gesetzmässigkeit (f)

3480. **legal; lawful**
juridique; légal
jurídico; legal
gesetzlich; rechtmässig

3481. **legal advice**
consultation (f) juridique
consejo (m) legal
Rechtsauskunft (f)

3482. **legal adviser**
conseiller (m) juridique
consejero (m), consultor (m), asesor (m) jurídico
Rechtsberater (m)

3483. **legal aid**
assistance (f) judiciaire
asistencia (f) legal voluntaria
unentgeltliche Beratung (f) in Rechtsfragen (fpl)

3484. **legal department, division**
section (f) juridique
departamento (m) legal
Rechtsabteilung (f)

3485. **legal ethics**
règles (fpl) du barreau
ética (f) profesional legal
Standespflichten (fpl) des Juristen

3486. **legal history**
histoire (f) du droit
historia (f) del derecho
Rechtsgeschichte (f)

3487. **legal opinion**
avis (m) juridique
opinión (f) legal
Rechtsgutachten (n)

3488. **legal principle**
principe (m) juridique
principio (m) de derecho
Rechtsgrundsatz (m)

3489. **legal remedy**
instance (f), moyen (m) de droit
recurso (m), remedio (m) legal
Rechtsbehelf (m); Rechtsmittel (n)

3490. **legal status**
état (m), statut (m) juridique
estado (m) legal
Rechtsstellung (f)

3491. **legal validity**
validité (f) en droit; validité juridique
validez (f) legal
Rechtsgültigkeit (f)

3492. **to institute, start, take legal proceedings**
introduire une instance
iniciar procedimiento judicial
einen Prozess anstrengen

3493. **to legalize**
légaliser; rendre légal
legalizar
rechtsgültig machen

3494. **legatee**
légataire (m)
legatario (m)
Legatar (m); Vermächtnisnehmer (m)

3495. **residuary legatee**
légataire universel (après liquidation)
heredero universal (después de liquidación)
Nachvermächtnisnehmer

3496. **legation**
légation (f)
legación (f)
Gesandtschaft (f)

3497. **legislation**
législation (f)
legislación (f)
Gesetzgebung (f)

3498. **emergency legislation**
législation de circonstance exceptionnelle
legislación de emergencia
Notstandsgesetzgebung

3499. **legislative**
législatif
legislativo
legislativ; gesetzgeberisch

3500. **legislator**
législateur (m)
legislador (m)
Gesetzgeber (m)

3501. **legislature**
législature (f)
legislatura (f)
Legislatur (f)

3502. **to legislate**
légiférer
legislar
Gesetze geben

3503. **legitimacy**
légitimité (f)
legitimidad (f)
Legitimität (f)

3504. **legitimate**
légitime
legítimo
legitim; ehelich

3505. **legitimation**
légalisation (f); légitimation (f)
legalización (f); legitimación (f)
Berechtigung (f); Legitimierung (f)

3506. **to legitimate; to legitimize**
légitimer
legitimar
legitimieren

3507. **lend-lease**
prêt-bail (m)
préstamo (m) y arriendo (m)
Pacht- (m) und -Leihe (f)

3508. **lending** (see **loan**, No. 3571)

3509. **leniency**
clémence (f)
clemencia (f); lenidad (f)
Milde (f); Nachsicht (f)

3510. **lenient**
indulgent
indulgente
mild; nachsichtig

3511. **lese, leze majesty**
lèse-majesté (f)

lesa majestad (f)
Majestätsbeleidigung (f)

3512. **letter**
lettre (f)
carta (f); letra (f)
Brief (m); Buchstabe (m)

3513. **letters of administration**
pouvoir donné au liquidateur de succession
auto judicial de designación de albacea
Ernennung einer Nachlassverwaltung

3514. **letters of credence**
lettres de créance
cartas credenciales
Beglaubigungsschreiben

3515. **letters of credit**
lettres de crédit
cartas de crédito
Kreditbriefe

3516. **letters patent**
brevets (mpl); patentes (fpl)
patente (f), título (m) de invención (f), de privilegio (m)
Patentbrief (m); Patenturkunden (fpl)

3517. **letters rogatory**
commissions (fpl) rogatoires
cartas (fpl) rogatorias; exhorto (m)
Rechtshilfeersuchen (n)

3518. **letters testamentary**
pouvoir (m) donné à l'exécuteur (m) testamentaire
auto (m) judicial de autorización (f) de albacea
testamentarische Vollmacht (f)

3519. **levee, levy en masse**
levée (f) en masse (f)
sublevación (f) en masa (f)
Levée en masse (n); Massenaufgebot (n)

3520. **level**
degré (m); niveau (m)
grado (m); nivel (m)
Ebene (f); Niveau (n)

3521. **levy**
imposition (f)
exacción (f); gravamen (m)
Erhebung (f); Auferlegung (f)

3522. **capital levy**
prélèvement (m) sur le capital
impuesto (m) sobre el capital
Kapitalabgabe (f)

3523. **to levy**
imposer; lever; percevoir
imponer; gravar
erheben; auferlegen

3524. **liability**
obligation (f); responsabilité (f)
obligación (f); responsabilidad (f)
Haftung (f); Verantwortlichkeit (f)

3525. **absolute, unlimited liability**
responsabilité absolue, illimitée
responsabilidad absoluta, ilimitada
unbeschränkte Haftung

3526. **basis of liability**
base (f) d'assujettissement (m)
fundamento (m) de la responsabilidad (f)
Grund (m) der Haftung (f)

3527. **criminal liability**
responsabilité criminelle
responsabilidad criminal
strafrechtliche Haftung

3528. **joint liability**
responsabilité conjointe
obligación solidaria
Gesamthaftung

3529. **joint and several liability**
responsabilité conjointe et solidaire
obligación colectiva
Gesamtschuld; Solidarhaftung

3530. **liabilities**
passif (m); engagements (mpl)
pasivo (m); obligaciones (fpl)
Passiva (fpl); Schulden (fpl)

3531. **liable**
responsable; sujet à
obligado; responsable
haftbar; verantwortlich

3532. **limited liability**
responsabilité limitée
responsabilidad limitada
beschränkte Haftung

3533. **not liable**
irresponsable
irresponsable
nicht haftbar

3534. **official liability**
responsabilité publique
responsabilidad oficial
Amtshaftung

3535. **to be unable to meet one's liabilities**
ne pas être à même de faire face à ses obligations
ser incapaz de hacer frente a sus obligaciones
seinen Verpflichtungen nicht nachkommen können

3536. **to incur a liability**
encourir une responsabilité
asumir una responsabilidad
eine Verbindlichkeit eingehen

3537. **to meet one's liabilities**
faire face à ses obligations
honrar una responsabilidad
seinen Verbindlichkeiten nachkommen

3538. **liaison**
liaison (f)
enlace (m)
Verbindung (f); Liaison (f)

3539. **libel**
écrit (m) diffamatoire; libelle (m)
difamación (f) escrita; libelo (m)
Ehrenbeleidigung (f); Verleumdung (f)

3540. **libelous; libellous**
diffamatoire
difamatorio
beleidigend; verleumdend

3541. **to libel**
diffamer par écrit
difamar por escrito
jdn. öffentlich verleumden

3542. **liberation**
libération (f)
liberación (f)
Befreiung (f); Freilassung (f)

3543. **liberated**
libéré
liberado
befreit

3544. **to liberate**
libérer
liberar
befreien

3545. **liberty**
liberté (f)
libertad (f)
Freiheit (f)

3546. **civil liberties**
garanties (fpl) constitutionnelles; libertés (fpl) fondamentales
derechos (mpl) individuales; garantías (fpl) constitucionales
Bürgerrechte (npl); Freiheitsrechte (npl)

3547. **license**
autorisation (f); brevet (m); licence (f); permis (m)
autorización (f); licencia (f); permiso (m)
Erlaubnisschein (m); Konzession (f); Lizenz (f)

3548. **driver's license**
permis (m) de conduire
licencia (f) de manejar; brevete (m)
Führerschein (m)

3549. **import license**
licence d'importation
licencia de importación
Einfuhrerlaubnis (f)

3550. **licensee**
patenté (m)
autorizado (m)
Lizensinhaber (m)

3551. **marriage license**
dispense (f) de bans (mpl)
licencia (f) de matrimonio (m)
Heiratserlaubnis (n)

3552. **lie detector**
machine (f) à déceler les mensonges (mpl)
detector (m) de mentiras (fpl)
Lügendetektor (m)

3553. **lien**
droit (m) de gage (m), de rétention (f); privilège (m)
embargo (m) preventivo; derecho (m) de retención (f)
Pfand (n); Pfandrecht (n)

3554. **mechanic's lien**
droit de rétention de constructeur (m)
embargo de constructor (m)
dinglich gesicherter Anspruch eines Handwerkers (m)

3555. **life expectancy**
l'espérance (f) de vie (f)
esperanza (f) de vida (f) al nacer
mutmassliche Lebensdauer (f)
3556. **limit**
limite (f)
límite (m)
Bereich (m); Grenze (f)
3557. **age limit**
limite d'âge
límite de edad
Altersgrenze
3558. **limited**
limité
limitado
beschränkt
3559 **to limit**
limiter; restreindre
limitar; restringir
begrenzen; beschränken
3560. **limitation**
limitation (f); restriction (f)
limitación (f); restricción (f)
Beschränkung (f); Verjährung (f)
3561. **liquidation**
liquidation (f)
liquidación (f)
Liquidation (f)
3562. **to liquidate**
liquider
liquidar
liquidieren
3563. **list**
liste (f); répertoire (m)
lista (f); nómina (f); planilla (f)
Liste (f); Rolle (f)
3564. **black list**
liste noire
lista negra
schwarze Liste
3565. **list of cases**
rôle (m)
lista (f) de causas (fpl)
Terminkalender (m)
3566. **list of contraband articles**
liste des articles (mpl) de contrebande (f)
lista de artículos (mpl) de contrabando (m)
Konterbandeliste (f)
3567. **litigation**
litige (m); procès (m)
litigio (m); pleito (m)
Prozess (m); Rechtsstreit (m)
3568. **litigant**
plaideur (m)
litigante (m)
Partei (f) im Prozess (m)
3569. **litigious**
litigieux
litigioso
streitig
3570. **to litigate**
plaider
litigar
prozessieren
3571. **loan**
emprunt (m); prêt (m)
empréstito (m); préstamo (m)
Darlehen (n); Anleihe (f)
3572. **lender**
prêteur (m)
prestamista (m); prestador (m)
Kreditgeber (m); Darlehensgeber (m)
3573. **long-term loan**
prêt à long terme (m)
préstamo (m) a largo plazo (m)
langfristiges Darlehen (n); langfristige Anleihe (f)
3574. **unsecured loan**
prêt à fonds (m) perdu
préstamo sin caución (f)
ungedeckter Kredit (f); ungesichertes Darlehen (n)
3575. **usurious loan**
prêt usuraire
préstamo usurero
Darlehen zu Wucherzinsen
3576. **to grant a loan**
consentir un prêt
otorgar un préstamo
ein Darlehen bewilligen
3577. **to lend**
prêter
prestar
Darlehen, Anleihe geben
3578. **to raise a loan**
contracter un emprunt
hacer un empréstito
eine Anleihe aufnehmen
3579. **lobbying**
pratiques destinées à influencer les législateurs

cabildeo; gestión para influenciar legisladores
Beeinflussung von Abgeordneten

3580. **lobbyist**
personne qui cherche à influencer les législateurs
cabildero (m)
Lobbyist (m)

3581. **to lobby**
chercher à influencer une décision législative; faire les couloirs
cabildear
antichambrieren; Abgeordnete beeinflussen

3582. **lockout**
fermeture (f) des ateliers (mpl); grève (f) patronale
cierre (m) de fábrica (f); paro (m) patronal
Aussperrung (f) von Arbeitern (mpl)

3583. **logrolling**
échange (f) de faveurs (fpl) politiques
intercambio (m) de favores (mpl) políticos
gegenseitige politische Unterstützung (f)

3584. **loop-hole**
échappatoire (f); faux-fuyant (m)
escapatoria (f)
Lücke (f) (im Gesetz)

3585. **loot**
butin (m); pillage (m)
botín (m); pillaje (m)
Beute (f); Raubgut (n)

3586. **to loot**
faire du butin; piller
pillar; saquear
Beute machen; plündern

3587. **loss**
perte (f)
pérdida (f)
Schaden (m); Verlust (m)

3588. **to lose**
perdre
perder
verlieren

3589. **lottery**
loterie (f); tirage (m) au sort (m)
lotería (f); rifa (f); sorteo (m)
Lotterie (f); Glücksspiel (n)

3590. **loudspeaker**
haut-parleur (m)
altoparlante (m)
Lautsprecher (m)

3591. **lynch, to**
lyncher; exécuter sommairement
linchar; ejecutar sumariamente
lynchen

M

3592. **machinery**
mécanisme (m); organisation (f)
maquinaria (f); organización (f)
Apparat (m); Mechanismus (m)

3593. **state machinery**
administration (f); rouages (mpl) de l'Etat
administración (f); maquinaria (f) del Estado
Staatsapparat (m)

3594. **madness**
aliénation (f); folie (f); fureur (f); démence (f)
locura (f); rabia (f); demencia (f)
Wahnsinn (m); Verrücktheit (f)

3595. **magistracy**
magistrature (f)
magistratura (f)
höherer Justizbeamter (m)

3596. **magistrate**
magistrat (m)
magistrado (m)
richterlicher Beamter (m)

3597. **maiming**
mutilation (f)
mutilación (f)
Körperverletzung (f); Verstümmelung (f)

3598. **to maim**
mutiler
mutilar

verstümmeln
3599. **maintenance**
entretien (m); maintien (m)
mantenimiento (m); sustento (m)
Unterhalt (m)
3600. **separate maintenance**
pension (f) alimentaire de l'épouse séparée de corps
pensión (f) alimenticia en domicilio separado
Alimente (npl) an die getrennt lebende Frau
3601. **to maintain**
entretenir; maintenir
mantener; sustentar
behaupten; erhalten
3602. **majority**
majorité (f)
mayoría (f)
Majorität (f); Mehrheit (f)
3603. **absolute majority**
majorité absolue
mayoría absoluta
absolute Mehrheit
3604. **bare majority**
faible majorité
escasa mayoría
knappe Mehrheit
3605. **simple majority**
majorité simple
mayoría simple
einfache Mehrheit
3606. **to attain one's majority**
devenir majeur
alcanzar la mayoría de edad
volljährig werden
3607. **malefactor**
malfaiteur (m)
malhechor (m)
Missetäter (m); Übeltäter (m)
3608. **malevolence**
malveillance (f)
malevolencia (f)
böser Wille (m); Bosheit (f)
3609. **malevolent**
malveillant
malévolo
böswillig; vorsätzlich
3610. **malfeasance**
méfait (m)
fechoría (f)
Missetat (f)
3611. **malice**
intention (f) criminelle, frauduleuse
malicia (f)
Arglist (f); Bosheit (f); Vorbedacht (m)
3612. **malice aforethought**
préméditation (f)
premeditación (f)
böser Vorsatz (m)
3613. **malicious**
avec intention de nuire
malicioso
arglistig; böswillig
3614. **malicious mischief**
acte (m) de malveillance
agravio (m) malicioso
vorsätzliche Beschädigung (f) (von Vermögen oder Personen)
3615. **malicious prosecution; vexatious suit**
poursuites (fpl) abusives; dénonciation (f) calomnieuse
acusación (f) maliciosa; demanda (f) de mala fe
böswillige Rechtsverfolgung (f)
3616. **malingering**
simulation (f) de maladie (f)
simulación (f) de enfermedad (f)
Simulation (f); Vortäuschung (f) von Krankheit (f)
3617. **malingerer**
simulateur (m) de maladie
simulador (m) de enfermedad
Simulant (m); Drückeberger (m)
3618. **to malinger**
simuler
simular
Krankheit vortäuschen
3619. **malpractice**
faute (f) professionnelle
error (m) profesional
Amtsvergehen (n); Kunstfehler (m) (in der Ausübung der Heilkunde)
3620. **maltreatment**
mauvais traitement (m)
maltrato (m)
Misshandlung (f); falsche Behandlung (f)

3621. **malversation**
malversation (f)
malversación (f)
Unterschlagung (f) von amtlichen Geldern (npl)
3622. **man of straw; straw man**
homme (m) de paille (f)
testaferro (m)
Strohmann (m)
3623. **manacles**
entraves (fpl); menottes (fpl)
esposas (fpl); manilla (f)
Handfesseln (f)
3624. **management**
administration (f); direction (f); gérance (f)
administración (f); dirección (f); gerencia (f)
Leitung (f); Verwaltung (f)
3625. **manager; managing director**
administrateur (m); directeur (m); gérant (m)
administrador (m); director (m); gerente (m)
Leiter (m); Verwalter (m)
3626. **mandamus** (see **writ of mandamus,** No. 6283)
3627. **mandate**
mandat (m); ordre (m)
mandato (m); orden (f)
Befehl (m); Mandat (n)
3628. **mandatory**
mandataire; obligatoire
mandatorio; obligatorio
obligatorisch; vorgeschrieben
3629. **mandatory power**
puissance (f) mandataire
potencia (f) mandataria
Vollmacht (f)
3630. **manhunt**
chasse (f) à l'homme
perseguimiento (m) de un reo (m)
Menschenjagd (f)
3631. **mania**
manie (f); délire (m)
manía (f); frenesí (f)
Manie (f)
3632. **manifest**
évident; manifeste
evidente; manifiesto
Manifest; öffentliche Erklärung
3633. **manpower**
effectif (m); main d'oeuvre (f)
brazos (mpl); mano de obra (f)
Arbeitskräfte (fpl)
3634. **manslaughter**
homicide (m) par imprudence (f)
homicidio (m) accidental
Tötung (f) ohne Vorsatz (m)
3635. **voluntary manslaughter**
meurtre (m)
homicidio (m) sin premeditación (f)
Totschlag (m)
3636. **manual**
manuel (m)
compendio (m); manual (m)
Handbuch (n)
3637. **manufacture**
fabrication (f)
fabricación (f)
Fabrikation (f)
3638. **manufacturer**
fabricant (m); manufacturier (m)
fabricante (m); industrial (m)
Fabrikant (m)
3639. **to manufacture**
fabriquer; manufacturer
fabricar; manufacturar
erzeugen; verarbeiten
3640. **marauding**
maraudage (m)
merodeo (m); saqueo (m)
Plünderung (f)
3641. **marauding parties**
expéditions (fpl) de maraudage (m)
merodeadores (mpl); saqueadores (mpl)
plündernde Nachzügler (mpl); Plünderer (m)
3642. **maritime**
maritime
marítimo
Meeres-; See-
3643. **maritime belt** (see **marginal sea,** No. 5286)
3644. **mark**
marque (f)
marca (f)
Zeichen (n); Kennzeichen (n)
3645. **to mark**
corriger; marquer; observer

marcar; corregir; notar
korrigieren; bezeichnen; bemerken

3646. **market**
débouché (m); halle (f); marché (m); bourse (f)
mercado (m); plaza (f); bolsa (f)
Markt (m); Absatzgebiet (n)

3647. **black market**
marché noir
mercado negro
schwarzer Markt

3648. **bull market**
marché haussier
mercado alcista
haussierender Markt

3649. **expanding market**
marché en voie d'expansion
mercado en expansión
sich ausweitender Markt

3650. **free market**
marché libre
mercado libre
Freiverkehr

3651. **money market**
marché monétaire
mercado monetario
Geldmarkt

3652. **marketable**
de bon débit; de vente
comerciable; de venta
verkäuflich; marktgängig

3653. **to corner the market**
accaparer le marché
acaparar el mercado
aufkaufen

3654. **marketing**
commercialisation (f); structure (f) des marchés
comercialización (f)
Vertrieb (m); Absatz (m)

3655. **marriage; matrimony**
mariage (m)
matrimonio (m)
Ehe (f); Heirat (f)

3656. **annulment of a marriage**
dissolution (f) d'un mariage
anulación (f) de matrimonio
Aufhebung (f) einer Ehe; Nichtigkeit einer Ehe

3657. **common law marriage**
concubinage (m); union (f) libre
matrimonio (m) consensual
die wilde Ehe (f)

3658. **marital**
marital; matrimonial
marital; matrimonial
ehelich

3659. **marriage bans**
bans (mpl)
amonestaciones (fpl)
Eheaufgebot (n)

3660. **to marry**
épouser
casar
heiraten

3661. **marshal (U.S.A.)**
exécuteur (m) des ordres des tribunaux fédéraux
oficial (m) de justicia
Gerichtsvollzieher (m)

3662. **mass demonstration**
manifestation (f) populaire, en masse (f)
manifestación (f) en masa (f)
Massendemonstration (f)

3663. **mass killings**
tuerie (f); massacre (m); carnage (m); hécatombe (f)
asesinatos (mpl) en masa (f)
Massenmord (m); Massaker (m)

3664. **master**
employeur (m); maître (m); patron (m)
amo (m); dueño (m); patrón (m)
Arbeitgeber (m); Auftraggeber (m); Dienstherr (m)

3665. **master and servant**
employeur et employé
patrón y empleado (m)
Arbeitgeber und Arbeitnehmer (m); Dienstherr und Dienstverpflichterer (m) oder Angestellter (m)

3666. **material**
important; matériel
importante; material
materiell; wesentlich

3667. **classified material**
documents (mpl) secrets
documentos (mpl) secretos
Sache (f) unter Verschluss (m); Geheimmaterial (n)

3668. **raw material**
matière (f) première
materia (f) prima
Rohstoff (m)
3669. **to be material**
être essentiel pour
ser apreciable, significativo
wesentlich sein
3670. **matter**
affaire (f); matière (f); question (f); sujet (m)
cuestión (f); materia (f); sujeto (m)
Angelegenheit (f); Sache (f); Gegenstand (m)
3671. **matter in dispute**
question en litige
asunto en disputa
Streitfrage
3672. **matricide**
matricide (m)
matricidio (m)
Muttermord (m)
3673. **matrimony** (see **marriage**)
3674. **maturity**
échéance (f)
vencimiento (m)
Fälligkeit (f); Verfallszeit (f)
3675. **mature**
arrivé à échéance
vencido
fällig
3676. **to mature**
arriver à échéance
vencer
fällig werden
3677. **maxim**
maxime (f)
máxima (f)
Maxime (f); Grundsatz (m)
3678. **mayhem**
mutilation (f); voie (f) de fait (m)
mutilación (f) criminal de una parte del cuerpo
schwere Körperverletzung (f)
3679. **mayor**
maire (m)
alcalde (m) (municipal)
Bürgermeister (m)
3680. **meaning**
signification (f)
significación (f)
Bedeutung (f); Sinn (m)
3681. **double meaning**
double sens (m)
doble significado (m)
Doppelsinn (m)
3682. **means**
moyens (mpl); ressources (fpl)
medios (mpl); recursos (mpl)
Mittel (f); Vermögen (n)
3683. **means of subsistence**
moyens de subsistance (f)
medios de mantenimiento (m)
Lebensunterhalt (m)
3684. **means of support**
moyens d'existence (f)
medios de sustento (m)
Existenzmittel (fpl)
3685. **without visible means of support**
sans moyens d'existence connus
sin medios aparentes de sustento
ohne bekannte Einkommensquellen
3686. **measures**
mesures (fpl)
medidas (fpl)
Massnahmen (fpl)
3687. **disciplinary measures**
mesures disciplinaires
medidas disciplinarias
Disziplinarmassnahmen
3688. **provisional measures**
mesures provisoires
medidas provisionales
vorläufige Massnahmen
3689. **repressive measures**
mesures répressives
medidas represivas
Massnahmen zur Unterdrückung
3690. **retaliatory measures**
mesures de représailles
medidas de represalia
Wiedervergeltungsmassnahmen
3691. **mediation**
médiation (f)
mediación (f)
Vermittlung (f)
3692. **mediator**
médiateur (m)
mediador (m)

Vermittler (m)
3693. **to mediate**
s'entremettre
mediar
vermitteln
3694. **medium**
moyen (m)
medio (m)
Mittel (n)
3695. **meeting**
assemblée (f); réunion (f); séance (f)
conferencia (f); reunión (f); sesión (f)
Sitzung (f); Versammlung (f)
3696. **board meeting**
réunion du conseil
sesión de la directiva
Verwaltungsratsitzung; Vorstandsitzung
3697. **committee meeting**
réunion de comité
reunión del comité
Ausschussitzung
3698. **executive meeting**
séance du comité de direction
sesión ejecutiva
Exekutivsitzung
3699. **mass meeting**
rassemblement (m) populaire
reunión (f) popular
Massenversammlung (f)
3700. **meeting of the minds**
accord de volontés (fpl)
acuerdo de voluntades (fpl)
Übereinstimmung (f)
3701. **plenary meeting**
séance plénière
sesión plenaria
Vollversammlung
3702. **public meeting**
réunion publique
reunión pública
öffentliche Versammlung
3703. **roundtable meeting**
réunion de la table ronde
reunión de mesa redonda
Rundtischkonferenz
3704. **schedule of meetings**
horaire (m)
horario (m)
Sitzungsplan (m)
3705. **seditious meeting**
réunion séditieuse
reunión sediciosa
aufrührerische Versammlung
3706. **the meeting stands adjourned**
la séance est levée
se levanta la sesión
die Sitzung wird vertagt
3707. **to attend a meeting**
assister à une réunion
asistir a una reunión
an einer Konferenz teilnehmen
3708. **to call a meeting**
convoquer une réunion
convocar a una reunión, sesión
eine Konferenz einberufen
3709. **to call the meeting to order; to open the meeting**
déclarer la séance ouverte
abrir la sesión
die Sitzung eröffnen
3710. **to close the meeting; to adjourn**
lever la séance
levantar la sesión
die Sitzung beenden
3711. **to hold a secret meeting**
siéger à huis clos
celebrar una sesión secreta, a puertas cerradas
eine gehcime Konferenz abhalten
3712. **to hold meetings**
tenir des réunions, séances
celebrar reuniones, sesiones
Konferenzen abhalten
3713. **to resume the meeting**
reprendre séance
reanudar la sesión
die Sitzung wieder aufnehmen
3714. **membership**
les membres (mpl); qualité (f) de membre
calidad de miembro (m), socio (m)
Mitgliedschaft (f)
3715. **alternate member**
membre suppléant
miembro suplente
Ersatzmitglied
3716. **committee membership**
composition (f) du comité (m)
composición (f) del comité (m)

Mitgliedschaft (f) des Ausschusses (m)
3717. **honorary member**
membre honoraire
miembro honorario
Ehrenmitglied
3718. **member**
membre (m)
miembro (m); socio (m)
Mitglied (n)
3719. **to be a member of**
faire partie de
ser miembro de; pertenecer a
teilnehmen an; Mitglied sein von
3720. **memorandum**
mémorandum (m); mémoire (m); note (f)
memorandum (m); apunte (m); nota (f)
Memorandum (n); Denkschrift (f)
3721. **covering memorandum**
note pour prendre acte
memorandum de envío, explicativo
Begleitschreiben
3722. **explanatory memorandum**
exposé (m) des motifs (mpl)
exposición (f) de motivos (mpl)
Erläuterungen (fpl)
3723. **memorial**
mémoire (m)
memorial (m)
Denkschrift (f)
3724. **menace**
menace (f)
amenaza (f)
Drohung (f)
3725. **to menace**
menacer
amenazar
drohen
3726. **mendicant**
mendiant (m)
mendigo (m)
Bettler (m)
3727. **mercantile**
mercantile
mercantil
Handels-; kaufmännisch
3728. **mercenary**
mercenaire (m)
mercenario (m)
Söldner (m)
3729. **mercenary troops**
troupes (fpl) de mercenaires
tropas (fpl) mercenarias
Söldnerheer (n)
3730. **merchandise**
marchandise (f)
mercadería (f); mercancía (f)
Ware (f)
3731. **merchant**
commerçant (m); marchand (m)
comerciante (m); negociante (m); mercader (m)
Geschäftsmann (m); Kaufmann (m)
3732. **merchant marine**
marine (f) marchande
marina (f) mercante
Handelsmarine (f)
3733. **mercy**
clémence (f); grâce (f)
clemencia (f)
Gnade (f)
3734. **to grant mercy**
accorder le pardon
otorgar clemencia
begnadigen
3735. **to petition for mercy**
adresser un recours en grâce
solicitar clemencia
um Gnade ersuchen
3736. **merge**
fusion (f); réunion (f)
fusión (f); unión (f)
Fusion (f); Verbindung (f)
3737. **to merge**
fusionner
fusionar; combinar; unir
fusionieren; verbinden
3738. **merits**
fond (m); substance (f)
fondo (m); mérito (m)
Verdienste (fpl); Vorzüge (fpl)
3739. **on the merits**
sur le fond
sobre el fondo
nach eigentlichem Wert
3740. **message**
message (m); communication (f)
mensaje (m); comunicación (f)

Mitteilung (f)

3741. **method**
méthode (f); moyen (m)
método (m); medio (m)
Methode (f)

3742. **microphone**
microphone (m)
micrófono (m)
Mikrophon (n)

3743. **metropolis**
capitale (f); métropole (f)
metrópoli (f)
Metropole (f); Hauptstadt (f)

3744. **middleman**
intermédiaire (m)
corredor (m); intermediario (m)
Mittelsmann (m)

3745. **might** (see **power**)

3746. **migration**
migration (f)
migración (f)
Wandern (n); Wanderung (f)

3747. **military**
militaire
militar
militärisch

3748. **military government**
gouvernement militaire
gobierno militar
Militärregierung

3749. **military tribunal**
tribunal militaire
tribunal militar
Militärgerichtshof

3750. **mind**
esprit (m); intelligence (f)
espíritu (m); inteligencia (f)
Geist (m)

3751. **of unsound mind**
privé de raison
demente
unzurechnungsfähig

3752. **minimum**
minimum (m)
mínimo (m)
Mindestbetrag (m)

3753. **to minimize**
minimiser; réduire au minimum
reducir al mínimo
auf das kleinste Mass zurückführen

3754. **ministry**
ministère (m)
ministerio (m)
Ministerium (m)

3755. **minister**
ministre (m)
ministro (m)
Minister (m); Gesandter (m)

3756. **minister plenipotentiary**
ministre plénipotentiaire
ministro plenipotenciario
bevollmächtigter Gesandter

3757. **minister without portfolio**
ministre sans portefeuille (m)
ministro sin cartera (f)
Minister ohne Geschäftsbereich (n)

3758. **ministerial responsibility**
responsabilité (f) ministérielle
responsabilidad (f) ministerial
Ministerverantwortlichkeit (f)

3759. **Prime Minister**
Premier Ministre
Primer Ministro
Ministerpräsident; Kanzler; Premierminister

3760. **minor**
mineur(e) (m, f)
menor (m, f)
Minderjährige(r) (f, m)

3761. **minority**
minorité (f)
minoría (f); minoridad (f)
Minderheit (f); Minorität (f); Minderjährigkeit (f)

3762. **mint**
l'hôtel (m) des monnaies (fpl); la monnaie (f)
casa (f) de moneda (f)
Münzanstalt (f); Münzamt (n)

3763. **minutes**
minutes (fpl); procès-verbal (m)
acta (f)
Protokoll (n)

3764. **to take the minutes**
dresser un procès-verbal
levantar acta de
das Protokoll aufnehmen

3765. **misapprehension**
malentendu (m)
error (m); falsa interpretación (f)
Missverständnis (n)

3766. **to misapprehend**

comprendre mal
entender mal
missverstehen

3767. **misappropriation**
détournement (m)
defraudación (f); malversación (f)
unrechtmässige Aneignung (f); Unterschlagung (f)

3768. **miscegenation**
mariage (m), concubinage (m) interracial
matrimonio (m), concubinato (m) interracial
Mischehe (f) oder Beischlaf (m) zwischen Angehörigen (fpl, mpl) verschiedener Rassen (fpl)

3769. **misconduct**
inconduite (f); mauvaise conduite (f)
conducta (f) indebida
schlechtes Betragen (n)

3770. **misconstruction**
contre-sens (m); fausse interprétation (f)
interpretación (f) errónea
falsche Auslegung (f); Missdeutung (f)

3771. **to misconstrue**
mal interpréter
interpretar erróneamente
falsch auslegen; missdeuten

3772. **misdemeanor**
délit (m) contraventionnel
delito (m) menor; fechoría (f)
Vergehen (n); Übertretung (f)

3773. **misfeasance**
abus (m) de l'autorité (f)
abuso (m) de autoridad (f)
Missbrauch (m) der Amtsgewalt (f)

3774. **misinterpretation**
fausse interprétation (f)
falsa interpretación (f)
falsche Auslegung (f); Missdeutung (f)

3775. **to misinterpret**
mal interpréter
interpretar mal
falsch auslegen; missdeuten

3776. **misjudge, to**
mal juger
juzgar erróneamente
falsch beurteilen; verkennen

3777. **misleading**
trompeur
engañoso
irreführend

3778. **to mislead**
tromper
engañar
irreführen

3779. **misnomer**
erreur (f) de nom (m); fausse désignation (f)
nombre (m) equivocado, inapropiado
falsche Bezeichnung (f)

3780. **misrepresentation**
fausse déclaration (f)
falsedad (f)
falsche Darstellung (f); Verdrehung (f)

3781. **fraudulent misrepresentation**
allégation (f) mensongère
falsedad (f) fraudulenta
betrügerische Angabe (f)

3782. **to misrepresent**
dénaturer
falsificar
falsch darstellen

3783. **mistake**
erreur (f)
error (m)
Irrtum (m); Versehen (n)

3784. **mistrial**
jugement (m) entaché d'un vice de procédure (f)
juicio (m) viciado de nulidad (f), nulo por desacuerdo del jurado
fehlerhaftes Gerichtsverfahren (n)

3785. **misunderstanding**
malentendu (m); dissentiment (m)
malentendido (m); mala inteligencia (f); desavenencia (f)
Missverständnis (n); Misshelligkeit (f)

3786. **to misunderstand**
mal entendre
entender mal
missverstehen

3787. **mitigation**
atténuation (f)

atenuación (f)
Milderung (f)

3788. **mitigating**
atténuant
atenuante
mildernd

3789. **to mitigate**
atténuer; adoucir
mitigar; atenuar
mildern; mässigen

3790. **mob**
attroupement (m); foule (f); populace (f)
masa (f); populacho (m)
Pöbel (m); Gesindel (n); Menschenmenge (f)

3791. **mob rule**
loi de la populace
tiranía de las masas
Pöbelherrschaft (f)

3792. **to mob**
s'attrouper; s'ameuter
atropellar tumultuariamente
herfallen über; anfallen (als lärmende Menge)

3793. **mobilization**
mobilisation (f)
movilización (f)
Mobilmachung (f)

3794. **to mobilize**
mobiliser
movilizar
mobilisieren

3795. **modification**
modification (f)
modificación (f)
Modifizierung (f)

3796. **to modify**
modifier
modificar
modifizieren

3797. **money**
argent (m); monnaie (f)
dinero (m); moneda (f)
Geld (n); Zahlungsmittel (n)

3798. **blood money**
prix (m) de la trahison (f) du sang (m)
precio (m) por el derrame (m) de sangre (f)
Blutgeld (n); Sühnegeld (n)

3799. **counterfeit money**
fausse monnaie
dinero falso
Falschgeld

3800. **liquid money**
argent liquide
dinero líquido
flüssiges Geld

3801. **money broker**
agent (m), courtier (m) de change
numulario (m); cambista (m)
Geldwechsler (m)

3802. **money-lender**
prêteur (m); usurier (m)
prestamista (m)
Geldverleiher (m)

3803. **money market**
bourse (f) des valeurs (fpl)
mercado (m) de dinero (m)
Börse (f); Geldmarkt (m)

3804. **money order**
mandat (m) postal; mandat-poste (m)
giro (m) postal; libranza (f) postal
Postanweisung (f); Zahlungsanweisung (f)

3805. **moneys, monies received**
recettes (fpl) effectuées
dinero (m) recibido
Geldeingänge (mpl)

3806. **paper money**
papier-monnaie (m)
papel moneda (m)
Papiergeld (n)

3807. **ready money**
argent comptant, liquide
dinero contante, efectivo
Bargeld; tägliches Geld

3808. **tightness of money**
resserrement (m) de disponibilités (fpl) monétaires
escasez (f) del dinero
Geldverknappung (f); Geldknappheit (f)

3809. **to coin, mint money**
battre monnaie
acuñar moneda
Geld münzen

3810. **to obtain money under false pretences**
escroquer; extorquer de l'argent

sous de faux prétextes
estafar; timar
Geld erschwindeln

3811. **to raise money**
mobiliser des fonds
procurar dinero
Geld aufbringen

3812. **monogamy**
monogamie (f)
monogamia (f)
Monogamie (f)

3813. **monopoly**
monopole (m); accaparement (m)
monopolio (m)
Monopol (n)

3814. **government monopoly**
monopole d'Etat
monopolio del gobierno
Staatsmonopol

3815. **to monopolize**
monopoliser; accaparer
monopolizar
monopolisieren

3816. **morality**
moralité (f)
moralidad (f)
Moralität (f); Sittlichkeit (f)

3817. **moral**
moral
moral
moralisch

3818. **moratorium**
moratorium (m)
moratoria (f)
Moratorium (n); Stundung (f)

3819. **mortality** (see **death rate**)

3820. **mortgage**
hypothèque (f)
hipoteca (f)
Verpfändung (f); Hypothek (f); Pfandrecht (n)

3821. **chattel mortgage**
hypothèque sur biens meubles; nantissement (m) mobilier
hipoteca prendaria
Pfand an beweglichen Sachen und Rechten; Fahrnispfändung (n)

3822. **mortgagee**
créancier (m) hypothécaire
acreedor (m) hipotecario
Hypothekengläubiger (m); Pfandgläubiger (m)

3823. **mortgagor; mortgager**
débiteur (m) hypothécaire
deudor (m) hipotecario
Hypothekenschuldner (m); Pfandschuldner (m)

3824. **to mortgage**
hypothéquer
hipotecar
mit einer Hypothek belasten; verpfänden

3825. **to raise a mortgage**
lever, prendre, purger une hypothèque
obtener una hipoteca
eine Hypothek aufnehmen

3826. **mortmain**
mainmorte (f)
manomuerta (f)
tote Hand (f); unveräusserliches Gut (n)

3837. **mother country** (see **country of origin**)

3828. **motion**
motion (f); demande (f)
moción (f); petición (f)
Antrag (m)

3829. **motion for a directed verdict**
demande pour que le juge dicte le verdict au jury
petición para que el veredicto sea mandado por el juez
Antrag (im Strafprozess) auf Fällung des Urteils durch den Richter

3830. **motion for a new trial**
demande d'un nouveau procès
petición de que se abra de nuevo el juicio
Antrag auf Wiederaufnahme des Verfahrens

3831. **motion for a repleader**
demande d'une reprise de la procédure et des plaidoiries après un verdict
petición para presentar nuevos alegatos
Antrag auf Zulassung neuer Schriftsätze

3832. **motion for a venire facias de novo**

demande d'un nouveau procès devant un autre jury
solicitud de un nuevo juicio ante otro jurado
Antrag auf eine neue Verhandlung vor anderen Geschworenen

3833. **motion to dismiss**
requête en refus
petición para que una demanda sea rechazada
Ablehnungsantrag

3834. **motion to vacate a judgment**
demande d'annulation d'un jugement
recurso de casación de una sentencia
Antrag auf Aufhebung des Urteils (aus triftigen Gründen) [G.B. wegen mangelnder Zuständigkeit]

3835. **the motion is in order**
la motion, proposition est recevable
la moción es aceptable
der Antrag ist zulässig

3836. **to carry a motion**
approuver une motion
aprobar una moción
einen Antrag durchbringen

3837. **to defeat, reject a motion**
écarter, rejeter, repousser, une motion
derrotar una moción
einen Antrag ablehnen

3838. **to file a motion**
déposer des conclusions, une résolution
hacer, presentar una moción
einen schriftlichen Antrag stellen

3839. **to move, make a motion**
faire une pétition; présenter une motion
proponer una moción
beantragen; einen Antrag stellen

3840. **to put a motion to the vote**
mettre une proposition aux voix
someter a votación una moción
über einen Antrag abstimmen

3841. **to second a motion**
appuyer une proposition
apoyar una moción
einen Antrag unterstützen

3842. **to set aside, table (U.S.A.) a motion**
renvoyer une demande
aplazar una moción
einen Antrag vertagen

3843. **to withdraw a motion**
retirer une motion
retirar una moción
einen Antrag vertagen

3844. **motive**
motif (m)
motivo (m)
Motiv (n)

3845. **ulterior motives**
motifs ultérieurs
motivos ulteriores
Hintergedanken

3846. **without motive**
sans motif
sin motivo
grundlos

3847. **movables**
biens (mpl) meubles
bienes (mpl) muebles
bewegliche Sachen (fpl)

3848. **multilateral**
multilatéral
multilateral
mehrseitig; vielseitig

3849. **municipality**
municipalité (f)
municipalidad (f)
Gemeinde (f); Stadt (f) (Mit Selbstverwaltung)

3850. **municipal**
municipal
municipal
städtisch; Landes-

3851. **murder**
meurtre (m); assassinat (m)
asesinato (m); homicidio (m)
Mord (m); Tötung (f)

3852. **first degree murder**
assassinat prémédité
homicidio premeditado
Mord

3853. **murderer**

assassin (m); meurtrier (m)
asesino (m)
Mörder (m)

3854. **second-degree murder**
meurtre non-prémédité
homicidio impremeditado
Totschlag (m)

3855. **to murder**
assassiner
asesinar
morden

3856. **mute**
muet
mudo
stumm

3857. **mutilation**
mutilation (f)
mutilación (f)
Verstümmelung (f)

3858. **to mutilate**
mutiler
mutilar
verstümmeln

3859. **mutiny**
mutinerie (f); rébellion (f); révolte (f)
motín (m); rebeldía (f); rebelión (f)
Aufruhr (f); Meuterei (f)

3860. **mutineer**
mutin (m); rebelle (m)
amotinador (m); rebelde (m)
Meuterer (m); Rebell (m)

3861. **to mutiny**
se mutiner; se révolter
amotinarse; rebelarse
meutern

3862. **mutuality**
mutualité (f)
mutualidad (f)
Gegenseitigkeit (f)

3863. **mutual**
mutuel
mutuo
gegenseitig

N

3864. **name**
nom (m)
nombre (m)
Name (m)

3865. **assumed name**
pseudonyme (m)
(p)seudónimo (m)
Pseudonym (n)

3866. **company, corporate name**
raison (f) sociale
razón (f) social
Firmenname (m)

3867. **family, last name**
nom de famille (f); patronyme (m)
apellido (m); nombre de familia (f)
Familienname (m)

3868. **first name**
prénom (m)
nombre (m) (de pila)
Vorname (m)

3869. **maiden name**
nom de jeune fille
apellido de soltera
Mädchenname

3870. **nameless**
anonyme
anónimo
namenlos

3871. **namesake**
homonyme (m)
homónimo (m); tocayo (m)
Namensvetter (m)

3872. **nickname**
petit nom (m); surnom (m); sobriquet (m)
apodo (m); sobrenombre (m)
Kosename (m); Spitzname (m)

3873. **trade name**
nom commercial
nombre comercial
Firmenname; Handelsname

3874. **to name**
nommer
nombrar
benennen; einen Namen geben

3875. **namely**

c'est-à-dire; à savoir
es decir; a saber
nämlich

3876. **narcotics**
narcotiques (mpl); stupéfiants (mpl); drogues (fpl)
narcóticos (mpl); estupefacientes (mpl); drogas (fpl)
Rauschgifte (fpl)

3877. **illegal sale of narcotics**
vente illégale de drogues
venta ilegal de narcóticos
illegaler Verkauf von Rauschgiften

3878. **nationalization**
étatisation (f); nationalisation (f)
nacionalización (f)
Verstaatlichung (f); Nationalisierung (f)

3879. **to nationalize**
nationaliser
nacionalizar
verstaatlichen; nationalisieren

3880. **native**
indigène (m, f); naturel (m); natif (m)
aborigen (m); nativo (m); originario (m)
Eingeborener (m)

3881. **naturalization**
naturalisation (f)
naturalización (f)
Naturalisierung (f)

3882. **to naturalize**
naturaliser
naturalizar
naturalisieren

3883. **navigation**
navigation (f)
navegación (f)
Seefahrt (f); Schiffsverkehr (m)

3884. **navigable**
navigable
navegable
schiffbar

3885. **navigator**
navigateur (m)
navegante (m)
Schiffer (m); Seefahrer (m)

3886. **to navigate**
naviguer
navegar
lenken; steuern

3887. **ne exeat** (see **writ of ne exeat**)

3888. **necessaries**
dépenses nécessaires; aliments (mpl)
gastos necesarios; alimentos (mpl)
Bedürfnisse (npl)

3889. **necessity**
nécessité (f)
necesidad (f)
Not (f); Notstand (m)

3890. **necessary**
indispensable; nécessaire
indispensable; necesario
notwendig; unvermeidlich

3891. **to necessitate**
rendre nécessaire
necesitar
notwendig machen

3892. **need**
besoin (m)
necesidad (f)
Bedürfnis (n); Not (f)

3893. **negation**
négation (f)
negación (f)
Verneinung (f)

3894. **negative**
négatif
negativo
verneinend; negativ

3895. **neglect**
imprudence (f); négligence (f)
descuido (m); negligencia (f)
Fahrlässigkeit (f); Nachlässigkeit (f)

3896. **neglect of official duty**
négligence dans les devoirs de sa charge
inobservancia de un deber oficial
Amtspflichtverletzung

3897. **neglectful**
imprudent; négligent
descuidado; negligente
fahrlässig; nachlässig

3898. **to neglect**
négliger
descuidar
vernachlässigen

3899. **negligence**

négligence (f)
negligencia (f)
Fahrlässigkeit (f); Verschulden (n)

3900. **comparative negligence**
négligence comparative
negligencia comparativa
verhältnismässige Fahrlässigkeit

3901. **contributory negligence**
faute partagée; négligence contributoire
negligencia contribuyente
Mitverschulden; konkurrierendes fahrlässiges Verschulden

3902. **criminal negligence**
négligence coupable
negligencia criminal
strafbare Fahrlässigkeit

3903. **gross negligence**
négligence grossière
negligencia grave
grobe Fahrlässigkeit

3904. **negligent**
fautif; négligent
negligente
fahrlässig

3905. **negotiability**
commercialité (f); négociabilité (f)
negociabilidad (f)
Übertragbarkeit (f)

3906. **negotiable instrument**
effet de commerce; titre, valeur négociable
instrumento, valor negociable
übertragbares Wertpapier

3907. **negotiation**
négociation (f)
negociación (f)
Verhandlung (f)

3908. **breakdown of negotiations**
insuccès (m) de négociations
paralización (f) de negociaciones
Abbruch der Verhandlungen

3909. **negotiator**
négociateur (m)
negociador (m)
Unterhändler (m)

3909a. **to negotiate**
négocier
negociar
verhandeln

3910. **neutrality**
neutralité (f)
neutralidad (f)
Neutralität (f)

3911. **armed neutrality**
neutralité armée
neutralidad armada
bewaffnete Neutralität

3912. **neutral**
neutre
neutral
neutral

3913. **neutralization**
neutralisation (f)
neutralización (f)
Neutralisierung (f)

3914. **to neutralize**
neutraliser
neutralizar
neutralisieren

3915. **next-of-kin**
parents les plus rapprochés
parientes más cercanos
die nächsten Verwandten

3916. **nomination**
désignation (f); nomination (f); présentation (f) de candidature (f)
designación (f); nombramiento (m); proposición (f) de candidatura (f)
Ernennung (f); Berufung (f); Aufstellung (f), Vorschlag (m) eines Kandidaten (m)

3917. **nominee**
candidat (m) présenté
nombrado (m); candidato (m) propuesto
Vorgeschlagener (m); Ernannter (m)

3918. **to nominate**
nommer; proposer au choix; présenter un candidat
designar; nombrar; proponer una candidatura
ernennen; vorschlagen; zur Wahl aufstellen

3919. **non-combattant**
non-combattant (m)

no combatiente (m)
Nichtkombattant (m); Nichtkämpfer (m)

3920. **noncompliance**
inéxecution (f)
incumplimiento (m); inobservancia (f)
Nichterfüllung (f); Zuwiderhandlung (f)

3921. **nonfeasance**
non-observance (f)
inobservancia (f)
Nichtbefolgung (f)

3922. **nonpayment**
non-paiement (m)
falta (f) de pago (m)
Nichtzahlung (f)

3923. **nonperformance**
non-exécution (f)
incumplimiento (m)
Nichterfüllung (f)

3924. **non-profit-making**
sans but lucratif
sin fines lucrativos
nicht auf Gewinn gerichtet

3925. **nonsuit**
déboutement (m); désistement (m) d'instance (f); non-lieu (m)
caducidad (f) de instancia (f); sobreseimiento (m)
Prozessabweisung (f); Zurücknahme (f)

3926. **to be nonsuited**
bénéficier d'un non-lieu; être débouté
declarar judicialmente de que una acción no ha lugar
mit einer Klage abgewiesen werden

3927. **to nonsuit**
débouter; signer un non-lieu
desechar una instancia
eine Klage abweisen

3928. **nonuser**
non-usage (m)
caducidad (f) de concesión (f), privilegio (m)
Nichtgebrauch (m) (eines Rechts)

3929. **notable; noteworthy**
notable
notable
bemerkenswert

3930. **notary public**
notaire (m) public
notario (m) público; escribano (m)
Notar (m); öffentlicher Urkundsbeamter (m)

3931. **notarial**
notarial
notarial
notariell

3932. **note**
note (f)
nota (f)
Note (f)

3933. **marginal note**
note marginale
nota marginal
Randbemerkung

3934. **promissory note**
billet (m) à ordre
pagaré (m)
Schuldschein (m)

3935. **to take note of**
prendre acte, connaissance; remarquer
tomar nota de
zur Kenntnis nehmen; beachten

3936. **notice**
avertissement (m); avis (m); notification (f); signification (f)
aviso (m); informe (m); nota (f)
Anzeige (f); Bekanntmachung (f); Notiz (f); Warnung (f)

3937. **constructive notice**
avis implicite
notificación sobrentendida
Bekanntmachung, Warnung im Rechtssinn

3938. **official notice**
notification officielle
notificación
amtliche Bekanntmachung

3939. **until further notice**
jusqu'à avis contraire
hasta más aviso
bis auf weiteres

3940. **to give notice**
donner congé; mettre en demeure, en garde; notifier

avisar; despedir; notificar
kündigen; benachrichtigen; ankündigen

3941. **to take judicial notice of**
connaître d'office; prendre acte de
tener conocimiento de oficio
amtliche Kenntnis nehmen von

3942. **notification**
notification (f)
notificación (f)
Ankündigung (f); Bekanntmachung (f)

3943. **to notify**
informer; notifier
notificar
ankündigen; bekanntgeben oder machen

3944. **notoriety**
notoriété (f)
notoriedad (f)
Offenkundigkeit (f)

3945. **notorious**
notoire
notorio
notorisch

3946. **novation**
novation (f)
novación (f)
Novation (f); Schuldumwandlung (f)

3947. **noxious**
nuisible
nocivo
schädlich

3948. **nuisance**
acte (m) dommageable; atteinte (f) aux droits d'autrui
acto (m) perjudicial
Ärgernis (n); Misstand (m); Unfug (m)

3949. **abatement of a nuisance**
suppression d'un abus
eliminación de un acto perjudicial
Abstellen eines Unfugs

3950. **attractive nuisance**
source (f) de danger (m) qui attire les enfants
fuente (f) de peligro (m) atrayente para niños
Gefahrenquelle (f), die Kinder anzieht

3951. **public nuisance**
atteinte (f) au bien public; outrage (m) aux bonnes moeurs (fpl)
desorden (m) público; molestia (f) pública
Gemeinschädlichkeit (f); Verstoss (m) gegen die öffentliche Ordnung (f)

3952. **to commit a public nuisance**
commettre un outrage aux bonnes moeurs
causar molestia pública
öffentliches Ärgernis erregen; gegen die öffentliche Ordnung verstossen

3953. **nullification**
annulation (f)
anulación (f)
Ungültigmachung (f); Nichtigmachung (f)

3954. **to nullify**
annuler
anular
nichtig oder ungültig machen

3955. **nullity**
nullité (f)
nulidad (f)
Nichtigkeit (f)

3956. **null and void**
nul et non avenu
nulo; sin fuerza legal
null und nichtig

3957. **nullity plea**
action en nullité
recurso de nulidad
Nichtigkeitsklage

O

3958. **oath**
serment (m)
juramento (m)
Eid (m)
3959. **false oath**
faux serment; parjure (m)
falso juramento; perjurio (m)
Falscheid (m); Meineid (m)
3960. **oath of allegiance**
serment d'allégeance (f), de fidélité (f)
juramento de fidelidad (f)
Bürgereid (m); Treueid (m)
3961. **on, under oath**
sous serment
bajo juramento
eidlich; unter Eid
3962. **to administer an oath**
assermenter; déférer le serment
administrar, tomar un juramento
einen Eid abnehmen; jemanden beeiden
3963. **to break one's oath**
se parjurer; violer son serment
faltar a un juramento
einen Eid brechen
3964. **to realease, relieve a person from his oath**
délier quelqu'un de son serment
relevar a una persona de su juramento
jdn. von seinem Eid entbinden
3965. **to take an oath; to be sworn in**
être assermenté; prêter serment
jurar; prestar juramento
einen Eid leisten; schwören
3965a. **obedience**
obéissance (f)
obediencia (f)
Gehorsam (m)
3966. **obiter dictum**
obiter dictum; opinion incidente
obiter dictum; opínión accesoria
obiter dictum; beiläufige Bemerkung
3967. **object**
but (m); objet (m)
fin (m); objeto (m)
Objekt (n); Zweck (m)
3968. **objection**
exception (f); objection (f)
objeción (f); réplica (f)
Einwand (m)
3969. **conscientious objector**
objecteur (m) de conscience (f)
objetante (m) de conciencia (f)
Kriegsdienstverweigerer (m)
3970. **to object**
objecter
objetar
einwenden; widersprechen
3971. **to overrule an objection**
passer outre à une objection
hacer caso omiso de una objeción
einem Einwand nicht stattgeben
3972. **to raise an objection**
soulever une objection
formular una objeción
Einspruch erheben
3973. **to sustain an objection**
faire droit à; soutenir une objection
hallar con lugar una objeción
einen Einspruch aufrecht erhalten
3974. **objective**
objectif (m); but (m)
objetivo (m)
Objektiv (m); Ziel (n)
3975. **obligation**
engagement (m); obligation (f)
obligación (f)
Obligation (f); Verbindlichkeit (f)
3976. **obligatory**
obligatoire
obligatorio
obligatorisch; rechts-verbindlich
3977. **to be under obligation**
être astreint, obligé à
estar obligado, bajo una obligación
verpflichtet sein
3978. **to oblige**

astreindre; obliger
obligar
verpflichten

3979. **obnoxious**
insupportable; odieux
odioso; detestable
anstössig

3980. **obscene**
obscène
obsceno
obszön; unzüchtig

3981. **obscure**
obscure
o(b)scuro
unbekannt; unklar

3982. **observation**
observation (f)
observación (f)
Befolgung (f); Beobachtung (f); Bemerkung (f)

3983. **observer**
observateur (m)
observador (m)
Beobachter (m)

3984. **observing**
attentif; observant
observante
aufmerksam; beobachtend

3985. **to observe**
noter; observer
observar; velar
befolgen; beobachten; bemerken

3986. **obsolete**
hors d'usage; périmé; suranné; désuet
obsoleto; anticuado; caducado
ausser Gebrauch; überholt; veraltet

3987. **obstacle; obstruction**
empêchement (m)
obstáculo (m)
Hindernis (n)

3988. **obtain, to**
obtenir
obtener
erhalten; erlangen; bekommen

3989. **obvious**
apparent; évident
obvio
augenscheinlich; deutlich

3990. **occupancy**
possession (f); prise (f) de possession
ocupación (f)
Besitz (m); Innehabung (f)

3991. **occupation**
emploi (m); métier (m); occupation (f); profession (f)
empleo (m); ocupación (f); profesión (f)
Beschäftigung (f); Beruf (m); Besetzung (f); Okkupation (f)

3992. **occupational illness**
maladie (f) professionnelle
enfermedad (f) del trabajo, profesional
Berufskrankheit (f)

3993. **to occupy**
occuper
ocupar
besetzen; okkupieren

3994. **occurrence**
événement (m)
hecho (m); suceso (m)
Ereignis (n); Vorfall (m)

3995. **to occur**
arriver; se produire
ocurrir; suceder
sich ereignen; vorkommen

3996. **offense**
infraction (f); offense (f); outrage (m)
infracción (f); ofensa (f); violación (f)
Beleidigung (f); strafbare Handlung (f); Verstoss (m)

3997. **capital offense**
crime (m) capital
crimen (m) capital
Kapitalverbechen (n)

3998. **first offense**
première infraction (f)
primera infracción (f)
erstmalige Straffälligkeit (f)

3999. **grave, serious offense**
faute (f) grave; flagrant délit (m)
delito (m) grave
schwere Straftat (f)

4000. **habitual offender**
repris (m) de justice (f)
infractor (m) habitual
Berufsverbrecher (m)

4001. **indictable offense**

acte (m) délictueux
ofensa (f) encausable
strafrechtlich verfolgbares Verbrechen (n) oder Vergehen (n)

4002. **military offense**
délit militaire
delito militar
Militärvergehen

4003. **minor offense**
contravention (f)
contravención (f)
Übertretung (f)

4004. **offender**
délinquant (m); malfaiteur (m)
malhechor (m); transgresor (m)
Missetäter (m); Schuldiger (m)

4005. **offensive**
injurieux
ofensivo
beleidigend; anstössig

4006. **petty offender**
contrevenant (m)
infractor (m)
Übertreter (m)

4007. **second or subsequent offender** (see **recidivist**)

4008. **to offend, give offense**
commettre une faute; offenser
ofender; violar
Anstoss erregen; beleidigen

4009. **offer**
offre (f)
oferta (f)
Offerte (f); Angebot (n)

4010. **cash offer**
offre réelle
oferta de dinero efectivo
Realofferte; Realangebot

4011. **to offer**
offrir
ofrecer
offerieren; anbieten

4012. **office**
bureau (m); office (m); service (m)
oficina (f); despacho (m); cargo (m)
Büro (n); Amt (n); Stelle (f)

4013. **branch office**
succursale (f)
sucursal (f)
Filiale (f); Nebenstelle (f)

4014. **clearing office**
bureau, office de compensation (f)
cámara, oficina de compensación (f)
Verrechnungsamt (n)

4015. **foreign exchange office**
office des changes
oficina de cambios
Devisenstelle

4016. **foreign office**
Ministère des Affaires étrangères
Ministerio de Relaciones Exteriores
Ministerium des Äussern

4017. **head office**
siège (m) principal
oficina (f) central; sede (f)
Zentralamt (n)

4018. **office-seeker**
candidat (m)
candidato (m)
Kandidat (m)

4019. **patent office**
bureau (m) des brevets (mpl) d'inventions (fpl)
dirección (f) de patentes (fpl)
Patentamt (n)

4020. **public office**
service (m) public
cargo (m) público
öffentliches Amt (n)

4021. **record office**
greffe (m)
archivo (m)
Geschäftsstelle (f); Gerichtkanzlei (f)

4022. **rotation in office**
roulement (m)
rotación (f) en el cargo (m)
Turnus (m) in der Amtsbesetzung (f)

4023. **term of office**
durée (f) du mandat
mandato (m)
Amtszeit (f)

4024. **to hold office**
exercer, remplir une fonction
desempeñar un cargo
ein Amt innehaben

4025. **to leave office**
quitter ses fonctions
abandonar un cargo

ein Amt niederlegen
4026. **to remain in office**
demeurer en fonction
continuar en sus functiones
im Amt bleiben
4027. **to take office**
entrer en fonctions; prendre le pouvoir
tomar posesión de un cargo
ein Amt antreten
4028. **officer**
fonctionnaire (m); officier (m)
funcionario (m); oficial (m)
Beamter (m); Offizier (m)
4029. **customs officer**
douanier (m)
aduanero (m)
Zollbeamter (m)
4030. **liaison officer**
officier (m) de liaison (f)
oficial (m) de enlace (m)
Verbindungsoffizier (m)
4031. **official**
fonctionnaire (m)
funcionario (m)
Beamter (m)
4031a. **official (adj.)**
officiel
oficial
offiziell
4032. **offset; set-off**
compensation (f) judiciaire; reconvention (f)
compensación (f) judicial; reconvención (f)
Aufrechnung (f); Gegenforderung (f)
4033. **offspring**
descendance (f); descendant (m)
descendencia (f); prole (f)
Nachkomme (m); Nachkommenschaft (f)
4034. **oligarchy**
oligarchie (f)
oligarquía (f)
Oligarchie (f)
4035. **omission**
omission (f)
omisión (f)
Unterlassung (f)
4036. **to omit**
manquer à
omitir
unterlassen
4037. **on or about**
approximativement
aproximadamente
ungefähr am
4038. **opening**
débouché (m); ouverture (f)
abertura (f); oportunidad (f) de empleo (m)
freie Stelle (f); Öffnung (f)
4039. **formal opening**
inauguration (f)
inauguración (f)
feierliche Eröffnung (f)
4040. **to open**
ouvrir
abrir
öffnen; eröffnen
4041. **operation**
action (f); fonctionnement (m); opération (f)
operación (f); transacción (f)
Betrieb (m); Verfahren (n); Wirksamkeit (f)
4042. **operative**
valide
válido
wirksam
4043. **to be in operation**
fonctionner
funcionar
in Kraft oder wirksam sein
4044. **to come into operation**
entrer en vigeur
entrar en vigor, en vigencia
in Kraft treten; wirksam werden
4045. **to operate**
diriger; gérer
hacer funcionar; operar
betreiben; wirken
4046. **opinion**
avis (m); opinion (f)
opinión (f)
Ansicht (f); Meinung (f)
4047. **advisory opinion**
avis consultatif
opinión consultiva
Gutachten (n); Ratschlag (m)
4048. **divergence of opinion**
divergence (f) de vues (fpl)

divergencia (f) de opiniones (fpl)
Meinungsverschiedenheit (f)

4049. **expert opinion**
avis d'expert
dictamen pericial
Sachverständigengutachten

4050. **legal opinion**
consultation (f) juridique
opinión (f) legal
Rechtsgutachten (n)

4051. **prevailing opinion**
opinion dominante
opinión dominante
herrschende Meinung

4052. **public opinion**
opinion publique
opinión pública
öffentliche Meinung

4053. **opportunity**
occasion (f)
ocasión (f)
Gelegenheit (f)

4054. **opposition**
opposition (f)
oposición (f)
Opposition (f); Widerspruch (m)

4055. **opponent**
adversaire (m)
adversario (m)
Opponent (m)

4056. **to oppose**
faire opposition; s'opposer
oponerse
sich einer Sache widersetzen; opponieren

4057. **oppression**
oppression (f)
opresión (f)
Unterdrückung (f)

4058. **oppressive**
oppressif
opresivo
bedrückend; tyrannisch

4059. **to oppress**
opprimer
oprimir
unterdrücken

4060. **option**
option (f)
opción (f)
Option (f); Wahl (f); Wahlmöglichkeit (f)

4061. **optional**
facultatif
facultativo; opcional
fakultativ; freistehend

4062. **oral**
oral
oral
mündlich

4063. **order**
arrêté (m); ordre (m)
orden (f)
Anordnung (f); Befehl (m)

4064. **by order of**
par ordre; sur ordre de
por orden de
im Auftrag

4065. **call to order**
rappel à l'ordre
llamar al orden
Ordnungsruf

4066. **executive order**
ordre exécutif (du Président)
orden ejecutiva (del Ejecutivo)
Dienstanweisung (f); Verfügung (f) des Präsidenten

4067. **interim order**
ordre provisoire
orden provisional
einstweilige Anordnung

4068. **maintenance of order**
maintien (m) de l'ordre (m)
mantenimiento (m) del orden (m)
Aufrechterhaltung (f) oder Ordnung (f)

4069. **order for enforcement**
formule (f) exécutoire
orden (f) ejecutiva
Vollstreckungsbefehl (m)

4070. **order in Council**
ordre de cabinet
orden del gabinete
Kabinettserlass (m) ohne Parlamentsgenehmigung (f)

4071. **order nisi**
ordre conditionnel
orden condicional
bedingter Gerichtsbeschluss

4072. **order of arrest**

ordre d'arrêt
orden de arresto
Arrestbefehl

4073. **order of business**
plan (m) de travail (m)
temario (m)
Tagesordnung (f); Geschäftsordnung (f)

4074. **order of confinement**
ordre d'écrou, de détention
orden de detención, prisión
Haftbefehl

4075. **order of precedence, of priority, of seating**
ordre de préséance, de priorité
orden de prioridad, de comparecer
Vorrangliste

4076. **order of release**
ordre de levée, d'écrou
orden de liberación, de poner en libertad
Entlassungsbefehl; Freilassungsbefehl oder -beschluss

4077. **order of the day**
ordre du jour
orden del día
Tagesordnung

4077a. **order to show cause** (see **rule nisi,** No. 5221)

4078. **orderly**
méthodique
metódico; ordenado
systematisch

4079. **point of order**
motion d'ordre
cuestión de orden
Anfrage zur Geschäftsordnung

4080. **public order**
ordre public
orden público
öffentliche Ordnung

4081. **restraining, stay order**
interdiction (f); ordonnance (f) de ne pas faire
interdicto (m); prohibición (f)
gerichtliches Verbot (n); Unterlassungsbefehl (m)

4082. **standing order**
ordre permanent
orden permanente
Dauerauftrag

4083. **superior order**
ordre supérieur
orden, mandamiento superior
höherer Befehl

4084. **out of order**
déréglé
desarreglado; descompuesto
in Unordnung; im Widerspruch zur Geschäftsordnung

4085. **to call to order**
rappeler à l'ordre
llamar al orden
zur Ordnung rufen

4086. **to countermand an order**
révoquer une commande
revocar un mandamiento
einen Auftrag widerrufen

4087. **to order**
ordonner
mandar; ordenar
anordnen; befehlen

4088. **to raise a point of order**
soulever une question de procédure
presentar una cuestión de procedimiento
gegen eine Verfahrensfrage Einspruch erheben

4089. **to rule on a point of order**
statuer sur une question d'ordre
fallar sobre una cuestión de orden
über eine Verfahrensfrage entscheiden

4090. **ordinance**
ordonnance (f)
ordenanza (f)
Verordnung (f)

4091. **municipal ordinance**
ordonnance municipale
ordenanza munipal
städtische Verordnung

4092. **organ**
organe (m)
órgano (m)
Organ (n)

4093. **organization**
organisation (f)
organización (f)
Organisation (f)

4094. **to organize**
organiser

organizar
organisieren

4095. **origin**
origine (f)
origen (m)
Herkunft (f); Ursprung (m)

4096. **originality**
originalité (f)
originalidad (f)
Originalität (f); Ursprünglichkeit (f); Eigenheit (f)

4097. **original**
original
original
originell; original; ursprünglich

4098. **to originate**
faire naître; provenir
originar
herstammen; abstammen

4099. **orphanage**
orphelinat (m)
orfanato (m)
Waisenhaus (n)

4100. **orphan**
orphelin (m)
huérfano (m)
Waise (m)

4101. **ostensible**
prétendu; soi-disant
ostensible
angeblich; scheinbar

4102. **ouster**
dépossession (f) illégale; éviction (f)
desplazamiento (m); desposeimiento (m)
Vertreibung (f) aus dem Besitz (m)

4103. **to oust**
déposséder illégalement; évincer
desalojar; desposeer
entfernen; verdrängen

4104. **outbreak**
début (m); soulèvement (m)
brote (m)
Ausbruch (m)

4105. **outbreak of war**
ouverture (f) des hostilités (fpl)
estallido (m) de una guerra (f)
Kriegsausbruch (m)

4106. **outcome**
conséquence (f); résultat (m)
consecuencia (f); resultado (m)
Ergebnis (n); Folge (f)

4107. **outlaw**
hors la loi (m); proscrit (m)
proscrito (m)
Geächteter (m)

4108. **to outlaw**
mettre hors la loi
declarar fuera de la ley
ächten

4109. **outlawry of war**
mise de la guerre hors la loi
proscripción de la guerra
die ächtung des Krieges

4110. **outlet**
débouché (m)
salida (f)
Markt (m); Absatzmöglichkeit (f)

4111. **outline**
aperçu (m); schéma (m)
bosquejo (m); esquema (m)
Skizze (f); Umriss (m)

4112. **to outline**
donner un aperçu
delinear; dar una idea de
skizzieren; umreissen

4113. **outlook**
perspectives (fpl)
perspectiva (f)
Aussicht (f)

4114. **output**
production (f)
producción (f)
Produktion (f); Arbeitsleistung (f)

4115. **outstanding**
éminent; arriéré
destacado; pendiente
hervorragend; ausstehend

4116. **overdue**
échu
vencido
überfällig

4117. **overlap, to**
chevaucher; recouvrir
superponer; traslapar
sich überschneiden; übergreifen

4118. **overpopulation**
population excédentaire
exceso de población
Übervölkerung

4119. **overrule, to**
décider contre; rejeter

denegar; rechazar
anders entscheiden; verwerfen

4120. **to be overruled**
être rejeté
quedar rechazado
abgelehnt werden

4121. **oversight**
inadvertance (f); oubli (m)
descuido (m); inadvertencia (f)
Übersehen (n); Versehen (n)

4122. **overt act**
acte qui atteste intention criminelle
acción que revela la intención del que la ejecuta
offenkundige Tat

4123. **overthrow**
renversement (m); coup (m) d'Etat
derrocamiento (m); golpe (m) de Estado
Staatsstreich (n); Sturz (m)

4124. **to overthrow**
renverser
derrocar
stürzen

4125. **overtime**
heures (fpl) supplémentaires
horas (fpl) extraordinarias
Überstunden (fpl)

4126. **owing**
dû
debido
schuldig

4127. **owing to**
en raison de
debido a
infolge von

4128. **to owe**
devoir; être redevable de
deber; estar endeudado
schuldig sein; verdanken

4129. **ownership**
possession (f); propriété (f)
posesión (f); propiedad (f)
Eigentum (n); Eigentumsrecht (n)

4130. **adjacent owner**
propriétaire (m) limitrophe
proprietario (m) adyacente, contiguo
Nachbareigentümer (m)

4131. **legal owner**
propriétaire légal
dueño en derecho
rechtmässiger Eigentümer

4132. **owner**
possesseur (m); propriétaire (m)
dueño (m); propietario (m)
Eigentümer (m)

4133. **part-owner**
copropriétaire (m)
condueño (m); copropietario (m)
Miteigentümer (m); Mitbesitzer (m); Teilhaber (m)

4134. **reputed owner**
propriétaire apparent
dueño aparente
anscheinender oder vermutlicher Eigentümer

4135. **rightful owner**
ayant droit
legítimo propietario
rechtmässiger Eigentümer

4136. **sole owner**
seul propriétaire
único propietario
Alleineigentümer

4137. **to own**
posséder
poseer
besitzen; eingestehen; bekennen

P

4138. **packing**
emballage (m)
embalaje (m)
Verpackung (f)

4139. **pact**
convention (f); pacte (m)
convenio (m); pacto (m)
Pakt (m); Vertrag (m)

4140. **pamphlet**
brochure (f)
folleto (m)
Broschüre (f)

4141. **Pandects**
Pandectes (fpl)
Pandectas (fpl)
Pandekten (fpl)

4142. **pander; panderer**
entremetteur (m)
alcahuete (m)
Kuppler (m)

4143. **to pander**
servir d'entremetteur à
alcahuetear
kuppeln

4144. **panel**
liste (f); groupe (m)
lista (f); grupo (m)
Liste (f); Gruppe (f)

4145. **to impanel**
dresser la liste
formar la lista
in eine Liste eintragen

4146. **paper**
étude (f); journal (m); papier (m)
artículo (m); periódico (m); papel (m)
Abhandlung (f); Zeitung (f); Papier (n)

4147. **accommodation paper**
effet (m) de complaisance (f)
letra (f) de favor (m)
Gefälligkeitswechsel (m)

4148. **papers**
documents (mpl)
documentos (mpl)
Dokumente (npl); Papiere (npl)

4149. **working paper**
document de travail
documento de trabajo
Arbeitsunterlage

4150. **par**
égalité (f); pair (m)
paridad (f)
pari; Parikurs (m)

4151. **above par**
au-dessus du pair
por encima del valor nominal
über Pari

4152. **at par**
au pair
a la par
auf Pari

4153. **below par**
en-dessous du pair
por debajo del valor nominal
unter Pari

4154. **paragraph**
paragraphe (m)
párrafo (m)
Absatz (m); Paragraph (m)

4155. **sub-paragraph**
sous-paragraphe
subpárrafo
Unterabsatz; Unterabschnitt

4156. **parcel of land**
parcelle (f) de terrain (m)
lote (m) de terreno (m)
Landparzelle (f)

4157. **parcener**
cohéritier (m)
coheredero (m)
Miterbe (m)

4158. **pardon**
grâce (f); pardon (m)
gracia (f); perdón (m)
Begnadigung (f); Straferlass (m)

4159. **to pardon**
gracier
perdonar
begnadigen

4160. **to receive a pardon, be pardoned**
être gracié
recibir un indulto
begnadigt werden

4161. **parents**
parents (mpl)
padres (mpl)

Eltern (mpl)
4162. **parity**
parité (f)
paridad (f)
Gleichheit (f); Parität (f)
4163. **parley**
conférence (f)
conferencia (f)
Verhandlung (f)
4164. **Parliament**
Parlement (m)
Parlamento (m)
Parlament (n)
4165. **parliamentary**
parlementaire
parlamentario
parlamentarisch
4166. **parliamentary system**
régime parlementaire
sistema parlamentario
Parlamentssystem
4167. **parole**
libération (f) conditionnelle
liberación (f) condicional
bedingte Haftentlassung (f)
4168. **to be put on parole**
être placé en liberté conditionnelle
ser puesto en libertad condicional
Bewährungsfrist erhalten
4169. **to parole**
libérer sous condition
liberar bajo condición
bedingt aus der Haft entlassen
4170. **parricide**
parricide (m)
parricida (m)
Elternmord (m); Vatermörder (m); Muttermörder (m)
4171. **part**
partie (f)
parte (f)
Teil (m)
4172. **partial**
partial; partiel
parcial
partiell; einseitig; parteiisch
4173. **participation**
participation (f)
participación (f)
Beteiligung (f) an; Teilnahme (f) an
4174. **to participate**
participer
participar
teilhaben an; teilnehmen an
4175. **particulars**
circonstances (fpl); détails (mpl)
circunstancias (fpl); detalles (mpl)
Einzelheiten (fpl); Angaben (fpl)
4176. **partition**
cloison (f); partage (m)
partición (f); reparto (m)
Aufteilung (f); Teilung (f)
4177. **partnership**
société de personnes en nom collectif
sociedad colectiva
Teilhaberschaft
4178. **dormant, silent, sleeping, partner**
bailleur (m) de fonds (mpl); commanditaire (m) (non-divulgué)
socio (m) secreto
stiller Teilhaber (m)
4179. **general partner**
associé commanditaire
socio general
Kommanditist
4180. **limited partnership**
société en commandite simple, en nom collectif
sociedad en comandita, limitada
Kommanditgesellschaft
4181. **partner**
associé (m)
socio (m)
Gesellschafter (m); Teilhaber (m)
4182. **senior partner**
associé principal
socio principal
älterer Teilhaber
4183. **party**
parti (m); partie (f)
partido (m); parte (f)
Partei (f)
4184. **accomodation party**
avaliseur (m)

parte (f) por acomodación (f)
Wechselbürge (m)

4185. **aggrieved, offended party**
la partie lésée
parte dañada
beleidigter Teil

4186. **charter party**
charte-partie (f); contrat (m) d'affrètement (m)
contrato (m) de fletamento (m)
Charterpartie (f)

4187. **coalition parties**
partis de la coalition (f)
coalición (f) de partidos
Koalitionsparteien (fpl)

4188. **communist party**
le parti communiste
el partido comunista
die kommunistische Partei

4189. **democratic party**
le parti démocratique
el partido demócrata
die demokratische Partei

4190. **guilty party**
le coupable (m)
el culpable (m)
der Schuldige (m)

4191. **High Contracting Parties**
Hautes Parties Contractantes
Altas Partes Contratantes
Hohe Vertragschliessender Parteien

4192. **injured party**
l'offensé (m); la partie (f) lésée
el ofendido (m)
Beschädigter (m); Verletzter (m)

4193. **labor party**
le parti travailliste
el partido laboral
die Arbeiterpartei

4194. **majority party**
le parti de la majorité
el partido de la mayoría
die Mehrheitspartei

4195. **minority parties**
les partis de la minorité
los partidos de la minoría
die Minderheitsparteien

4196. **misjoinder of parties**
constitution irrégulière des parties
acumulación indebida de partes
unzulässiger Prozessbeitritt

4197. **multiple party system**
système des partis multiples
sistema político de varios partidos
Vielparteiensystem

4198. **opposition party**
le parti de l'opposition
el partido de la oposición
die Oppositionspartei

4199. **party entitled**
ayant droit (m)
parte (f) con derecho (m) a
Berechtigter (m)

4200. **party in default**
partie défaillante
parte en rebeldía
säumige Partei

4201. **party in power**
parti gouvernant
partido gobernante
Regierungspartei

4202. **party of the first part**
partie de première part
parte de la primera parte
zuerst erwähnte Partei

4203. **party ticket**
programme (m) du parti
programa (m) del partido
Parteiprogramm (n)

4202. **party to an action at law**
partie au procès
parte en un proceso
Prozesspartei

4205. **party platform, program**
programme du parti, électoral
programa político de un partido
Parteiprogramm

4206. **party wall**
mur (m) mitoyen
pared (f) medianera; medianería (f)
Scheidewand (f); gemeinsame Mauer (f)

4207. **republican party**
le parti républicain
el partido republicano
die republikanische Partei

4208. **rescue party**
équipe (f) de secours (m)

grupo (m) de salvamento (m)
Rettungsmannschaft (f)

4209. **socialist party**
le parti socialiste
el partido socialista
die sozialistische Partei

4210. **signatory parties** (see **signatories**)

4211. **third party**
tiers (m); tierce personne (f)
tercera persona (f)
dritte Partei (f)

4212. **two-party system**
système bipartite
sistema político de dos partidos
Zweiparteiensystem

4213. **working party**
groupe (m) de travail
grupo (f) de trabajo
Arbeitsgruppe (f)

4214. **pass**
laissez-passer (m)
pase (m); permiso (m)
Ausweis (m); Passierschein (m)

4215. **to pass**
passer
pasar
vorübergehen; vorbeigehen

4216. **passage**
passage (m)
pasaje (m)
Durchgang (m); Durchfahrt (f)

4217. **innocent passage**
passage innocent, inoffensif
pasaje inocente
friedliche Durchfahrt

4218. **patent**
brevet (m) d'invention (f)
patente (f)
Patent (n)

4219. **assignment of patent**
concession (f) de brevet
concesión (f) de patente
Übertragung (f) eines Patents

4220. **infringement of a patent**
contrefaçon (f) d'un brevet
violación (f) de una patente
Patentverletzung (f)

4221. **patent applied for**
brevet sollicité
patente solicitada
Patentgesuch eingereicht

4222. **patent office**
bureau (m) de brevets
oficina (f) de patentes
Patentamt (n)

4223. **patent pending**
marque (f) déposée
patente (f) pendiente
Patent (n) angemeldet

4224. **patent rights**
droits attachés au brevet
derechos de patente
Patentrechts

4425. **patentable**
brevetable
patentable
patentierbar; patentfähig

4226. **to apply for a patent**
solliciter un brevet d'invention
solicitar una patente
einen Patentantrag einreichen

4227. **to patent**
breveter
patentar
patentieren

4228. **paternity**
paternité (f)
paternidad (f)
Vaterschaft (f)

4229. **acknowledgement of paternity**
reconnaissance (f) de paternité
reconocimiento (m) de la paternidad
Anerkennung (f) der Vaterschaft

4230. **paternal**
paternel
paternal
väterlich

4231. **patronage**
patronage (m)
patrocinio (m)
Protektion (f)

4232. **pauperism**
indigence (f); paupérisme (m)
indigencia (f); pauperismo (m)
Armut (f); allgemeine Verarmung (f)

4233. **pauper**
indigent (m)
indigente (m,f); pobre (m)
Armer (m); Bedürftiger (m)

4234. **pawnbroker**

prêteur (m) sur gages
prestamista (m)
Pfandleiher (m)

4235. **pawnshop**
Mont de Piété (m)
casa (f) de préstamos (mpl); monte (m) de piedad (f)
Pfandleihanstalt (f)

4236. **to pawn**
mettre en gage
empeñar
verpfänden

4237. **pay**
paye (f); solde (f)
paga (f); sueldo (m)
Bezahlung (f); Lohn (m)

4238. **extra pay**
paiement (m) additionnel
pago (m) adicional
Zulage (f)

4239. **half pay**
demi-solde (f)
mitad (f) de pago (m)
Wartegeld (n)

4240. **payroll**
bordereau (m) des salaires (mpl)
planilla (f) de pago (m); nómina (f)
Lohnliste (f)

4241. **payment**
paiement (m)
pago (m)
Zahlung (f)

4242. **advance payment**
paiement, versement (m) anticipé
anticipo (m); pago adelantado
Vorauszahlung (f)

4243. **balance of payments**
balance (f) des paiements
balanza (f) de pagos
Zahlungsbilanz (f)

4244. **cash payment**
paiement comptant, en espèces (fpl)
pago al contado (m)
Barzahlung (f)

4245. **deferred payment**
paiement par versements échelonnés
pago pospuesto
Ratenzahlung; hinausgeschobene Zahlung

4246. **down payment**
acompte (m)
primer plazo (m)
Anzahlung (f)

4247. **final payment**
paiement (m) libératoire
último pago
Abschlusszahlung (f)

4248. **in full and final payment**
pour solde de tout compte
en pago definitivo
zur endgültigen Abfindung

4249. **part-payment; partial payment**
paiement partiel
pago parcial
Teilzahlung

4250. **monthly payments**
mensualités (fpl)
mensualidades (fpl)
monatliche Zahlungen (fpl)

4251. **payable at sight**
payable à vue
pagadero a la vista
zahlbar bei Sicht

4252. **payable on demand**
payable sur demande
pagadero a presentación
zahlbar auf Anforderung

4253. **payable to bearer**
payable au porteur
pagadero al portador
zahlbar an den Überbringer

4254. **payable to order**
payable à ordre
pagadero a la orden
zahlbar an Order

4255. **payee of a bill**
preneur (m) d'une traite (f)
portador (m) de una letra (f)
Nehmer (m) einer Tratte (f)

4256. **payment by check**
versement par chèque
pago por cheque
Zahlung durch Scheck

4257. **payment in arrears**
paiement arriéré
pago en mora
Zahlungsrückstand

4258. **payment in due course**
paiement aux dates fixées
pago a su debido tiempo

rechtzeitige Erfüllung einer Zahlungsverpflichtung; Zahlung zu einer bestimmten Zeit

4259. **payment on delivery**
livraison contre espèce, remboursement
pago contra entrega
Lieferung gegen bar oder Nachnahme

4260. **payment supra protest**
paiement sous protêt
pago bajo protesta
Protestzahlung

4261. **periodical payments**
paiements périodiques
pagos periódicos, regulares
wiederkehrende Zahlungen

4262. **terms of payment**
conditions de paiement
condiciones de pago
Zahlungsbedingungen

4263. **to make a payment**
faire un paiement
efectuar un pago
eine Zahlung leisten

4264. **to pay**
payer
pagar
zahlen

4265. **to stop payments**
suspendre les paiements
suspender pago
Zahlungen einstellen

4266. **peace**
paix (f)
paz (f)
Frieden (m)

4267. **breach of the peace**
attentat contre l'ordre public
perturbación del orden público
Friedensbruch

4268. **peace society**
association pour la paix
sociedad de paz
Friedenvereinigung

4269. **peace terms**
conditions de paix
condiciones de paz
Friedensbedingungen

4270. **peaceful**
pacifique
pacífico
friedlich

4271. **perpetual peace**
paix perpétuelle
paz perpetua
ewiger Friede

4272. **peculation**
péculat (m)
peculado (m)
Veruntreuung (f)

4273. **pecuniary**
pécuniaire
pecuniario
pekuniär

4274. **peddling**
colportage (m)
buhonería (f)
Hausieren (n)

4275. **narcotics peddler**
trafiquant (m) de stupéfiants (mpl)
vendedor (m) ambulante de narcóticos (mpl), estupefacientes (mpl)
Rauschgifthändler (m)

4276. **peddler; pedlar**
camelot (m); colporteur (m)
buhonero (m); vendedor (m) ambulante
Hausierer (m)

4277. **pedigree**
arbre (m) généalogique; généalogie (f)
genealogía (f); linaje (m)
Abstammung (f); Herkunft (f)

4278. **penalty**
peine (f); pénalité (f)
pena (f); penalidad (f)
Bestrafung (f); Strafe (f)

4279. **death penalty**
peine (f) de mort (f)
pena (f) capital, de muerte (f)
Todesstrafe (f)

4280. **heavy penalty**
peine lourde
pena grave
schwere Strafe

4281. **light penalty**
peine légère
pena ligera
leichte Strafe

4282. **maximum penalty**

maximum de la peine
pena máxima
Höchststrafe

4283. **minimum penalty**
minimum de la peine
pena mínima
Mindeststrafe

4284. **penal**
pénal
penal
strafrechtlich

4285. **to carry, to entail a penalty**
entraîner une peine
traer aparejada una pena
Bestrafung nach sich ziehen

4286. **pending**
pendant
durante; pendiente
anhängig; schwebend

4287. **penitentiary**
établissement (m) pénitentiaire
penitenciaría (f); presidio (m)
Zuchthaus (n); Gefängnis (n)

4288. **penology**
pénologie (f)
criminología (f)
Kriminalwissenschaft (f)

4289. **pension**
pension (f); pension (f) de retraite (f)
pensión (f); retiro (m); jubilación (f)
Pension (f); Rente (f)

4290. **to pension**
pensionner
pensionar; jubilar
pensionieren

4291. **percentage**
pourcentage (m)
porcentaje (m)
Prozentsatz (m)

4292. **per cent**
pour-cent (m)
por ciento (m)
Prozent (n)

4293. **peremptory**
péremptoire
perentorio
bestimmt; entscheiden

4294. **perfidy**
perfidie (f)
perfidia (f)
Perfidie (f); Treulosigkeit (f)

4295. **perfidious**
perfide
pérfido
falsch; heimtückisch

4296. **performance**
accomplissement (m); exécution (f)
cumplimiento (m); ejecución (f)
Leistung (f); Erfüllung (f)

4297. **part performance**
exécution partielle
ejecución parcial
Teilleistung

4298. **specific performance**
exécution précise (d'un contrat)
cumplimiento preciso (de un contrato)
genaue Ausführung (eines Vertrags)

4299. **to perform**
accomplir; exécuter
cumplir; ejecutar
erfüllen; leisten

4300. **period**
époque (f); période (f); temps (m)
época (f); período (m); tiempo (m)
Periode (f); Zeit (f)

4301. **period of appointment**
durée (f) des fonctions (fpl)
duración (f) de las funciones (fpl)
Amtsdauer (f)

4302. **perjury**
faux serment (m); parjure (m)
juramento (m) falso; perjurio (m)
Meineid (m)

4303. **perjurer**
parjure (m)
perjuro (m)
Meineidiger (m)

4304. **subornation of perjury**
incitation à faire un faux serment; subornation
soborno de otro para que jure en falso
Verleitung zum Meineid

4305. **to commit perjury**
faire un faux serment; se parjurer
jurar en falso; perjurar
Meineid begehen oder leisten

4306. **permission**
autorisation (f); permission (f)
licencia (f); permiso (m)
Erlaubnis (f)

4307. **permissible**
permis
permisible
erlaubt

4308. **permit**
permis (m)
pase (m); permiso (m)
Erlaubnisschein (m); Passierschein (m)

4309. **to grant permission**
accorder une autorisation
conceder, otorgar permiso
erlauben; Erlaubnis erteilen

4310. **to permit**
autoriser; permettre
autorizar; permitir
erlauben; zulassen

4311. **perpetration**
perpétration (f)
perpetración (f)
Verübung (f); Begehung (f)

4312. **perpetrator**
auteur (m)
perpetrador (m)
Missetäter (m); Täter (m)

4313. **to perpetrate**
perpétrer
perpetrar
verüben; begehen

4314. **perpetual**
perpétuel
perpetuo
dauernd; unkündbar

4315. **in perpetuity**
à perpétuité
en perpetuidad
für immer

4316. **to perpetuate**
perpétuer
perpetuar
fortsetzen; verewigen

4317. **perquisites**
profit (m) éventuel; émoluments (mpl); revenant-bons (mpl)
gaje (m) eventual; emolumentos (mpl); obvención (f); adehala (f)
Nebeneinkünfte (fpl); Nebenerwerb (m)

4318. **persecution**
persécution (f)
persecución (f)
Verfolgung (f)

4319. **to persecute**
persécuter
perseguir
verfolgen

4320. **person**
individu (m); personne (f)
persona (f)
Person (f)

4321. **artificial, juristic, legal, person**
personne morale
persona moral, jurídica
juristische Person

4322. **banished person**
banni; expulsé
desterrado; proscrito
Ausgewiesener; Verbannter

4323. **displaced persons**
réfugiés (mpl) et déportés (mpl)
personas (fpl) desplazadas
Flüchtlinge (mpl) und Vertriebene (mpl)

4324. **person of unsound mind**
aliéné (m)
persona (f) demente
Geistekranker (m)

4325. **personal**
personnel
personal
persönlich

4326. **personality**
individualité (f); personnalité (f)
individualidad (f); personalidad (f)
Wesen (n); Persönlichkeit (f)

4327. **juridical, legal personality**
personnalité juridique
personalidad jurídica
Rechtspersönlichkeit

4328. **personalty; personal property**
biens (mpl) meubles, mobiliers
bienes (mpl) muebles
bewegliches oder persönliches Vermögen (n)

4329. **personation** (see **impersonation**)
4330. **personnel**
personnel (m)
personal (m)
Personal (n)
4331. **perspective**
perspective (f)
perspectiva (f)
Perspektive (f)
4332. **persuasion**
persuasion (f)
persuasión (f)
Überzeugung (f)
4333. **to persuade**
persuader
persuadir
überzeugen
4334. **pertinent**
à propos; pertinent
pertinente
einschlägig; passend
4335. **petition**
demande (f); pétition (f); requête (f)
demanda (f); petición (f) súplica (f)
Antrag (m); Bittschrift (f); Gesuch (n)
4336. **petitioner**
pétitionnaire (m); requérant (m)
demandante (m); peticionario (m)
Antragsteller (m); Bittsteller (m)
4337. **to petition**
présenter une requête
dirigir un memorial; suplicar
eine Bittschrift oder ein Gesuch einreichen
4338. **photostat** (see **photostatic copy**)
4339. **picket; picketing**
piquet (m) de grève (f)
piquete (m) de huelguistas (mpl)
Streikposten (m)
4340. **to picket**
placer un piquet de grève
estacionar piquetes de huelguistas
Streikposten stehen oder stellen
4341. **pickpocket**
voleur (m) à la tire (f)
carterista (m)
Taschendieb (m)
4342. **piecework**
travail (m) à la tâche (f)
trabajo (m) pagado por pieza (f)
Stückarbeit (f)
4343. **pilferage; pilfering**
larcin (m); chapardage (m)
ratería (f); sisa (f)
Diebstahl (m) von geringwertigen Sachen (fpl); Entwendung (f)
4344. **to pilfer**
commettre un larcin; chaparder
hurtar; ratear
entwenden
4345. **pillage**
pillage (m)
pillaje (m)
Plünderung (f)
4346. **to pillage**
piller
pillar
plündern
4347. **pimp**
entremetteur (m)
alcahuete (m)
Kuppler (m)
4348. **piracy**
piraterie (f)
piratería (f)
Piraterie (f)
4349. **pirate**
pirata (m)
pirata (m)
Pirat (m)
4350. **plagiarism**
plagiat (m)
plagio (m)
Plagiat (n)
4351. **plagiarist**
plagiaire (m)
plagiario (m)
Plagiator (m)
4352. **to plagiarize**
plagier
plagiar
plagiieren
4353. **plaintiff**
demandeur (m); plaignant (m)
demandante (m)
Kläger (m)

4354. **to find for the plaintiff**
adjuger au demandeur
fallar a favor del demandante
zugunsten des Klägers entscheiden

4355. **plan**
plan (m); projet (m)
plan (m); proyecto (m)
Plan (m); Projekt (n)

4356. **on the instalment plan**
par abonnement (m)
por cuotas (fpl)
in Ratenzahlung (f); Abzahlung (f)

4357. **to plan**
projeter
planear
planen; entwerfen

4358. **platform**
programme (m)
programa (m)
Programm (n)

4359. **play**
jeu (m)
juego (m)
Spiel (n)

4360. **fair play**
franc jeu (m)
proceder (m) leal
ehrliches Spiel (n)

4361. **foul play**
jeu déloyal
proceder desleal
unredliches Spiel

4362. **plea**
demande (f); allégations (fpl) par une partie
contestación (f); defensa (f)
Einrede (f); Einwendung (f); Verteidigung (f)

4363. **dilatory plea**
exception (f) dilatoire
excepción (f) dilatoria
aufschiebende Einrede (f)

4364. **plea in abatement**
demande (f) en nullité (f)
instancia (f) de nulidad (f)
Antrag (m) auf Einstellung (f) des Verfahrens (n)

4365. **plea in bar**
fin de non-recevoir (f)
excepción (f) perentoria
prozesshindernde Einrede (f)

4366. **plea in confession and avoidance**
admission des faits tout en contestant la responsabilité
alegación admitiendo hechos pero negando responsabilidad
Einrede ohne Leugnung des Klagevorbringens

4367. **plea in mitigation of damages**
demande en réduction de dommages-intérêts
pedido de rebaja de daños y perjuicios
Gesuch um Herabsetzung des Schadenersatzes

4368. **plea in suspension**
demande en sursis pénal
pedido de suspensión de la pena
Einrede zur Aussetzung des Verfahrens

4369. **plea puis darrein continuance**
introduction *a posteriori* de faits nouveaux
introducción *a posteriori* de nuevos hechos
Einrede gegen Ereignisse, die nach dem ursprünglichen Prozess eingetreten sind

4370. **plea to the jurisdiction**
exception d'incompétence
declinatoria; defensa
Einrede der Unzuständigkeit

4371. **pleadings**
plaidoirie (f); débats (mpl)
alegatos (mpl)
Vortrag (m) des Rechtsanwalts (m)

4372. **capable of pleading**
capable d'ester
capaz de litigar
verhandlungsfähig

4373. **contents of the pleadings**
contenu (m) des plaidoires (fpl)
contenido (m) de los alegatos (mpl)
Prozesstoff (m)

4374. **refusal to plead**
refus de plaider
denegación de defender

Weigerung zu verhandeln
4375. **unable to plead**
incapable d'agir en justice
incapaz de litigar
verhandlungsunfähig
4376. **to plead; to put in a plea**
alléguer; se défendre; plaider
defender una causa; alegar
einwenden; plädieren
4377. **to plead guilty**
plaider coupable; se reconnaître coupable
declararse culpable
seine Schuld eingestehen; sich schuldig bekennen
4378. **to plead not guilty**
plaider non coupable
declararse inocente
sich für unschuldig erklären
4379. **plebiscite**
plébiscite (m)
plebiscito (m)
Volksabstimmung (f)
4380. **pledge**
engagement (m); nantissement (m); promesse (f)
prenda (f); promesa (f)
Bürgschaft (f); Pfand (m)
4381. **to pledge**
engager; promettre; nantir
dar en prenda; prometer
sich verpflichten; etw. verpfanden
4382. **plenipotentiary**
plénipotentiaire (m)
plenipotenciario (m)
Bevollmächtigter (m)
4383. **plot**
complot (m); parcelle (f) de terre (f)
complot (m); parcela (f) de terreno (m)
Verschwörung (f); Grundstück (n)
4384. **to plot**
comploter; dresser un plan
conspirar; hacer el plano de
intrigieren; sich verschwören; Pläne schmieden
4385. **plunder**
pillage; butin
pillaje; saqueo
Plünderung; Beute
4386. **to plunder**
piller
pillar
plündern
4387. **plurality**
majorité (f) relative; pluralité (f)
mayoría (f); pluralidad (f)
Mehrheit (f); relative Stimmenmehrheit (f)
4388. **poaching**
braconnage (m)
caza (f) o pesca (f) en vedado
Wilddieberei (f)
4389. **point**
point (m); question (f)
punto (m); cuestión (f)
Punkt (m); Gegenstand (m)
4390. **crucial point**
point décisif
punto decisivo
Kernfrage
4391. **point of view; viewpoint**
point de vue
punto de vista
Standpunkt
4392. **point raised**
question soulcvée
cuestión planteada
aufgeworfene Frage
4393. **poisoning**
empoisonnement (m)
envenenamiento (m)
Vergiftung (f)
4394. **poison**
poison (m)
veneno (m)
Gift (n)
4395. **to poison**
empoisonner
envenenar
vergiften
4396. **to take poison**
s'empoisonner
envenenarse
Gift nehmen
4397. **police**
police (f)
policía (f)
Polizei (f)
4398. **border, frontier police**
police frontière

policía de frontera
Grenzpolizei

4399. **chief of police**
chef (m), commissaire (m), préfet (m) de police
jefe (m) de policía
Polizeichef (m); Polizeipräsident (m)

4400. **criminal police** (see **homicide squad**)

4401. **military police**
police militaire
policía militar
Militärpolizei

4402. **mounted police**
police à cheval
policía a caballo
berittene Polizei

4403. **plain-clothes police**
agent (m) de la sûreté (f)
agente (m) de policía (f) secreta
Detektiv (m)

4404. **police beat**
ronde (f) de police
ronda (f) de policía
Runde (f) eines Polizisten

4405. **police court** (see **courts, police court**)

4406. **police dog**
chien (m) policier
perro (m) policía
Polizeihund (m)

4407. **police headquarters**
commissariat (m), préfecture (f) de police
cuartel (m) general, jefatura (f) de la policía
Polizeipräsidium (n)

4408. **police inspector**
officier (m) de paix (f)
comisario (m) de policía
Polizeiinspektor (m)

4409. **police intervention**
intervention (f) de la police
intervención (f) de la policía
Einschreiten (n) der Polizei

4410. **police station**
commissariat (m), poste (m) de police
estación (f) de policía
Polizeistation (f)

4411. **policeman**
agent (m) de police; gardien (m) de la paix
agente (m) de policía
Polizist (m); Schutzmann (m)

4412. **resisting the police**
résistance (f) à la police
oposición (f) a la policía
Widerstand (m) gegen die Polizei

4413. **security police**
police de sûreté (f)
policía (f) secreta
Sicherheitspolizei (f)

4414. **superintendent of police**
commissaire de police
superintendente de policía
Polizeikommissar

4415. **traffic police**
agent de la circulation
agente de tráfico
Verkehrspolizist

4416. **to police**
maintenir l'ordre
mantener el orden
Ordnung aufrecht erhalten

4417. **policy**
politique (f)
política (f)
Politik (f)

4418. **foreign policy**
politique étrangère
política extranjera
Aussenpolitik

4419. **good neighbor policy**
politique de bon voisinage (m)
política del buen vecino (m)
Politik der guten Nachbarschaft (f)

4420. **open door policy**
politique de la porte ouverte
política de la puerta abierta
Politik der offenen Tür

4421. **policy-holder**
assuré (m)
asegurado (m)
Policeeinhaber (m)

4422. **public policy**
l'intérêt (m), l'ordre (m) public
orden (m) público
öffentliche Ordnung (f); gute Sitten (fpl)

4423. **politics**
la politique
política
Politik

4424. **party politics**
politique de parti
política del partido
Parteipolitik

4425. **political**
politique
político
politisch

4426. **politician**
homme (m) politique; politicien (m)
político (m)
Politiker (m)

4427. **poll**
liste (f) électorale; scrutin (m); vote (m); sondage (m)
lista (f) electoral; votación (f); encuesta (f)
Wählerliste (f); Abstimmung (f); Stimmenzahl (f); Meinungsforschung (f)

4428. **second poll**
scrutin de ballotage (m)
segunda votación; segundo escrutinio (m)
zweite Abstimmung oder Wahl (f)

4429. **to go to the polls**
aller au scrutin, aux urnes (fpl)
ir a las urnas (fpl) electorales
zur Wahl (f) gehen

4430. **pollution**
impuretés (fpl); pollution (f)
contaminación (f)
Verunreinigung (f); Verschmutzung (f)

4431. **to pollute**
polluer
contaminar
verunreigigen; verschmutzen

4432. **polyandry**
polyandrie (f)
poliandría (f)
Vielmännerei (f)

4433. **polygamy**
polygamie (f)
poligamia (f)
Polygamie (f)

4434. **polygamist**
polygame (m)
polígamo (m)
Polygamist (m)

4435. **poorhouse**
asile (m) des indigents (mpl)
asilo (m) de indigentes (mpl)
Armenhaus (n)

4436. **pornography**
pornographie (f)
pornografía (f)
Pornographie (f)

4437. **pornographic**
pornographique
pornográfico
pornographisch

4438. **position**
emploi (m); état (m)
empleo (m); situación (f)
Stand (m); Stellung (f)

4439. **key position**
position, situation clef
posición clave
Schlüsselstellung

4440. **to apply for a position**
solliciter un emploi
solicitar un empleo
sich um eine Anstellung bewerben

4441. **possession**
possession (f)
posesión (f)
Besitz (m)

4442. **actual possession**
possession effective
posesión efectiva
tatsächlicher Besitz

4443. **adverse possession**
possesión contestée; prescription (f)
prescripción (f) adquisitiva
rechtswidriger Besitz (m)

4444. **to possess**
posséder
poseer
besitzen

4445. **post**
emploi (m); position (f)
empleo (m); cargo (m)
Amt (n)

4446. **poster**
affiche (f); annonce (f); placard (m)
aviso (m); cartel (m)
Anschlagzettel (m); Plakat (n)

4447. **to post**
afficher
avisar; fijar, pegar carteles
anschlagen

4448. **posterity**
postérité (f)
posteridad (f)
Nachwelt (f)

4449. **postliminium; postliminy**
postliminie (f)
postliminio (m)
Postliminium (n)

4450. **postponement**
ajournement (m); remise (f); renvoi (m)
aplazamiento (m); posposición (f); postergación (f)
Aufschub (m); Verschiebung (f); Vertagung (f)

4451. **to postpone**
ajourner; remettre; renvoyer
aplazar; posponer; postergar
aufschieben; verschieben; vertagen

4452. **postulate**
postulat (m)
postulado (m)
Postulat (n)

4453. **potent**
puissant
potente
mächtig; stark

4454. **potential**
potentiel
potencial
potentiell

4455. **poverty**
indigence (f); pauvreté (f)
indigencia (f); pobreza (f)
Armut (f)

4456. **power; might**
pouvoir (m); puissance (f)
poder (m); potencia (f)
Macht (f); Gewalt (f)

4457. **abuse, misuse of power**
détournement (m) de pouvoir
abuso (m) de poder
Missbrauch der Macht

4458. **Axis Powers**
Puissances de l'Axe
Potencias del Eje
Achsenmächte

4459. **balance of power**
l'équilibre (m) des puissances
equilibrio (m) entre las grandes potencias
Gleichgewicht (n) der Mächte

4460. **concurrent powers**
compétence concurrente; pouvoirs concurrents
poderes concurrentes
konkurrierende Vollmacht

4461. **delegation of powers**
délégation de pouvoirs
delegación de poderes
Übertragung von Vollmachten

4462. **disciplinary powers**
pouvoirs disciplinaires
poderes disciplinarios
Disziplinargewalt

4463. **discretionary powers**
pouvoirs discrétionnaires
poderes discrecionales
freies Ermessen

4464. **executive power**
pouvoir exécutif
poder ejecutivo
ausführende oder vollziehende Gewalt

4465. **foreign power**
puissance étrangère
potencia extranjera
ausländische Macht

4466. **full, plenary powers**
pleins pouvoirs
plenos poderes
diplomatische Vollmacht

4467. **judicial power**
pouvoir judiciaire
poder judicial
richterliche Gewalt

4468. **legislative power**
pouvoir législatif
poder legislativo
gesetzgebende Gewalt

4469. **maritime power**
puissance maritime
potencia marítima
Seemacht

4470. **police power**
pouvoir de police
fuerza pública; facultad policial
Polizeigewalt

4471. **power to appoint**
pouvoir de nomination
facultad de nombrar
Ernennungsrecht

4472. **power of attorney**
mandat (m); procuration (f)
poder (m); procuración (f)
Prozessvollmacht (f)

4473. **purchasing power**
pouvoir (m) d'achat (m)
poder (m) adquisitivo
Kaufkraft (f)

4474. **signatory powers**
puissances signataires
potencias signatarias
Signatarmächte

4475. **sovereign powers**
états souverains
estados soberanos
souveräne Mächte

4476. **The Allied and Associated Powers**
Les Puissances alliées et associées
Las Potencias aliadas y asociadas
Die Alliierten und Assoziierten Mächte

4477. **The Great Powers**
Les Grandes Puissances
Las Grandes Potencias
Die Grossmächte

4478. **to exceed one's powers**
outrepasser ses pouvoirs
abusar de sus poderes
seine Befugnisse überschreiten

4479. **practique**
pratique (f); usage (m)
práctica (f); uso (m)
Übung (f); Usus (m)

4480. **corrupt practices**
brigue (f); corruption (f)
costumbres (fpl) corruptas
Bestechungsmanöver (n)

4481. **sharp practique**
procédés (mpl) peu honnêtes; filouterie (f)
estafa (f)
unlautere Machenschaften (fpl)

4482. **to practice**
exercer; pratiquer
ejercer; practicar
ausführen; praktizieren

4483. **prayer**
demande (f); requête (f)
demanda (f); solicitación (f)
Antrag (m); Gesuch (n)

4484. **to pray**
demander
solicitar
beantragen

4485. **preamble**
préambule (m)
preámbulo (m)
Präambel (n)

4486. **precedent**
préséance (f); priorité (f);
precedencia (f)
Vortritt (m); Vorrang (m);

4487. **precedent**
précédent (m); décision (f) faisant jurisprudence
precedente (m); decisión (f) que hace jurisprudencia
Präzedenzurteil (n); Präzedenzfall (m)

4488. **precedents**
jurisprudence (f)
precedentes (mpl)
Präzedenzfälle (mpl); Rechtsprechung (f)

4489. **without precedent**
sans précédent
sin precedente
ohne Präzedenzfall

4490. **to create a precedent**
créer un précédent
crear un precedente
einen Präzedensfall schaffen

4491. **precept**
précepte (m)
precepto (m)
Vorschrift (f)

4492. **precinct**
circonscription (f) électorale; division (f) administrative
distrito (m); división (f) administrativa
Stadbezirk (m); Wahlbezirk (m)

4493. **predecessor**
prédécesseur (m)
predecesor (m)
Vorgänger (m)

4494. **predicament**
embarras (m); situation (f) difficile
dificultad (f); apuro (m)
schwierige Lage (f)

4495. **predicated**
appuyé; fondé
fundado
gestützt auf; begründet durch

4496. **pre-emption**
préemption (f)
derecho (m) de preferencia (f)
Vorkaufsrecht (n)

4497. **preference**
préférence (f)
preferencia (f)
Vorrecht (n); Vorzug (m)

4498. **preferential**
de préférence; privilégié
preferencial
bevorrechtet; bevorzugt

4499. **preferential treatment**
traitement préférentiel
trato preferencial
Vorzugsbehandlung

4500. **to prefer**
préférer
dar preferencia
vorziehen

4501. **prejudice**
détriment (m); préjudice (m)
detrimento (m); perjuicio (m); prejuicio (m)
Schaden (m); Voreingenommenheit (f)

4502. **prejudiced**
de parti pris; influencé
con prejuicio; parcial
befangen; voreingenommen

4503. **prejudicial**
préjudiciel
prejudicial
nachteilig

4504. **without prejudice**
sans préjudice
sin prejuicio
ohne Präjudiz

4505. **to prejudice**
influencer
predisponer
beeinflussen; schädigen

4506. **premature**
prématuré
prematuro
verfrüht

4507. **premeditation**
préméditation (f)
premeditación (f)
Überlegung (f); Vorbedacht (m)

4508. **premise**
prémisse (f)
premisa (f)
Prämisse (f); Voraussetzung (f)

4509. **premises**
lieux (mpl); locaux (mpl)
local (m); propiedad (f)
Gebäude (n); Grundstück (n)

4510. **on the premises**
sur les lieux
en el lugar del caso
an Ort und Stelle

4511. **to vacate the premises**
vider les lieux
evacuar, desocupar, el local
die Lokalitäten räumen

4512. **premium**
prime (f)
prima (f)
Prämie (f)

4513. **to be at a premium**
faire prime
estar a premio, sobre la par
über Pari stehen

4514. **preparation**
préparation (f)
preparación (f)
Vorbereitung (f)

4515. **to prepare**
préparer
preparar
vorbereiten

4516. **prepayment**
paiement (m) d'avance
pago (m) adelantado
Vorauszahlung (f)

4517. **to prepay**
payer d'avance
pagar adelantado

vorausbezahlen
4518. **prerequisite**
condition (f) préliminaire, requise, sine qua non
requisito (m) previo
Vorbedingung (f)
4519. **prerogative**
prérogative (f)
prerrogativa (f)
Prärogative (f)
4520. **prescription**
prescription (f)
prescripción (f)
Verjährung (f)
4521. **presentation**
présentation (f)
presentación (f)
Präsentation (f)
4522. **to present**
présenter
presentar
präsentieren; schenken
4523. **presentment**
déclaration (f) émanant d'un jury (m)
declaración (f) por un jurado (m)
Bericht (m) der Geschworenen (mpl)
4524. **presents, by these**
par les présentes
conste por las presentes
hierdurch; hiermit
4525. **presidency**
présidence (f)
presidencia (f)
Präsidentschaft (f)
4526. **president**
président (m)
presidente (m)
Präzident (m); Vorsitzender (m)
4527. **retiring president**
président sortant
presidente saliente
ausscheidender Präsident
4528. **to preside**
présider
presidir
den Vorsitz führen
4529. **press, the**
la presse
la prensa
die Presse
4530. **freedom of the press**
liberté de la presse
libertad de imprenta
Pressefreiheit
4531. **pressure**
pression (f)
presión (f)
Druck (m)
4532. **to exert pressure**
exercer une pression
ejercer presión
einen Druck ausüben
4533. **presumption**
présomption (f)
presunción (f)
Vermutung (f)
4534. **irrebuttable presumption**
présomption absolue, irréfragable
presunción irrefutable
unwiderlegbare Vermutung
4535. **presumption of death**
présomption de décès
presunción de muerte
Todesvermutung
4536. **presumptive**
présomptif
presunto
präsumptiv
4537. **rebuttable presumption**
présomption discutable, simple
presunción refutable
widerlegbare Vermutung
4538. **to raise a presumption**
motiver une présomption
causar presunción
eine Vermutung begründen
4539. **pretense**
faux semblant (m); prétexte (m)
pretensión (f); pretexto (m)
Vorwand (m)
4540. **under false pretenses**
sous de faux prétextes; par moyens frauduleux
bajo falsas apariencias; con dolo
unter Vorspiegelung falscher Tatsachen
4541. **pretext**
prétexte
pretexto

Vorwand
4542. **prevalence**
prédominance (f)
predominio (m)
Vorherrschen (n)
4543. **prevailing**
dominant; général
dominante; general
herrschend; massgebend
4544. **prevalent**
prédominant
predominante
vorherrschend
4545. **to prevail**
prédominer
predominar
vorherrschen; gewinnen
4546. **prevention**
empêchement (m)
prevención (f)
Verhinderung (f)
4547. **to prevent**
empêcher; éviter
evitar; impedir
verhindern
4548. **price**
prix (m)
precio (m)
Preis (m)
4549. **agreed price**
prix convenu
precio convenido
vereinbarter Preis
4550. **at a greatly reduced price**
au grand rabais (m)
con gran rebaja (f)
mit grossem Rabatt (m)
4551. **at any price**
à tout prix
a toda costa
um jeden Preis
4552. **bargain prices**
prix exceptionnels
precios de ganga
Spottpreise oder Ausverkaufspreise
4553. **ceiling price**
prix plafond
precio tope
Höchstpreis
4554. **extortionate price**
prix exorbitant
precio exorbitante
Wucherpreis
4555. **fair price**
prix juste
precio justo
angemessener Preis
4556. **fixed price**
prix fixe, forfaitaire
precio fijo
fester Preis
4557. **half price**
demi-tarif (m)
a mitad (f) de precio (m)
halber Preis (m)
4558. **high price**
prix élevé
precio elevado
hoher Preis
4559. **increase, rise in price**
hausse (f) de prix
alza (f) de precios
Preissteigerung (f)
4560. **market price**
prix courant, marchand
precio corriente, de mercado
Marktpreis
4561. **net price**
prix net
precio neto
Nettopreis
4562. **price-control**
contrôle des prix
control de precios
Preisüberwachung
4563. **price-fixing**
fixation (f) des prix
fijación (f) de precios
Preisfixierung (f); Preisvereinbarung (f)
4564. **price freeze**
blocage (m) des prix
congelación (f) de precios
Preisstopp (m)
4565. **price-level**
niveau des prix
nivel de precios
Preisniveau
4566. **prohibitive price**
prix inabordable
precio prohibitivo
unerschwinglicher Preis
4567. **purchase, purchasing price**

prix d'achat
precio de compra
Kaufpreis

4568. **quoted price**
cote des prix
precio cotizado
notierter Preis

4569. **reasonable price**
prix modéré
precio justo
angemessener Preis

4570. **reduced price**
prix réduit
precio rebajado
herabgesetzter Preis

4571. **retail price**
prix de détail
precio (al) por menor
Einzelhandelspreis

4572. **selling price**
prix de vente
precio de venta
Verkaufspreis

4573. **stabilization of prices**
stabilisation (f) des prix
estabilización (f) de precios
Preisstabilisierung (f)

4574. **wholesale price**
prix de gros
precio (al) por mayor
Grosshandelspreis

4575. **to quote a price**
donner un prix
cotizar precio
einen Preis nennen

4576. **primary**
primaire; primordial
primario; principal
hauptsächlich; ursprünglich

4577. **primaries**
élections préliminaires
elecciones preliminares
Vorwahlen

4578. **primogeniture**
primogéniture (f)
primogenitura (f)
Erstgeburtsrecht (n)

4579. **right of primogeniture**
droit d'aînesse
derecho de primogenitura
Erstgeburtsrecht

4580. **principal**
principal
principal
hauptsächlich

4581. **principal in the first degree**
auteur (m) principal
culpable (m) principal
Hauptschuldiger (m)

4582. **principal in the second degree**
complice (m)
cómplice (m)
Mitschuldiger (m)

4583. **undisclosed principal**
mandant (m) non révélé
mandante (m) encubierto
nicht genannter Auftraggeber (m)

4584. **principle**
principe (m)
principio (m)
Grundsatz (m); Prinzip (m)

4585. **basic principles**
principes de base
principios fundamentales
Grundprinzipien

4586. **print**
impression (f); imprimé (m)
impresión (f); impreso (m)
Druck (m)

4587. **print shop**
imprimerie (f)
imprenta (f)
Druckerei (f)

4588. **printed**
imprimé
impreso; imprimido
gedruckt

4589. **printed matter**
imprimé (m)
impresos (mpl)
Drucksache (f)

4590. **to print**
imprimer
imprimir
drucken

4591. **priority**
priorité (f)
prioridad (f)
Priorität (f); Vorrang (m)

4592. **prison**
prison (f)
cárcel (f); prisión (f)
Gefängnis (n); Kerker (m)

4593. **order of commitment to prison**
mandat (m) de dépôt (m)
orden (f) de encarcelar
Befehl (m) zur Einlieferung (f) ins Gefängnis

4594. **prisoner**
détenu (m); prisonnier (m)
preso (m); prisionero (m)
Gefangener (m)

4595. **prisoner of war**
prisonnier de guerre
prisionero de guerra
Kriegsgefangener

4596. **to serve one's prison term, time**
faire son temps; purger une peine
cumplir la pena, sentencia
eine Gefängnisstrafe abbüssen, absitzen

4597. **privacy**
retraite (f)
retiro (m)
Privatleben (n)

4598. **private**
personnel
personal
Privat-; persönlich

4599. **privateering**
course (f)
corso (f)
Kaperei (f); Seeräuberei (f); Freibeuterei (f)

4600. **privateer**
corsaire (m)
corsario (m)
Kaper (m); Freibeuter (m)

4601. **privilege**
privilège (m)
privilegio (m)
Privileg (n); Vorrecht (n)

4602. **privileged**
privilégié
privilegiado
bevorrechtet; privilegiert

4603. **privity**
lien (m) de droit
relación (f) de partes
Rechtsverhältnis (n); Rechtsbeziehung (f)

4604. **privity of contract**
obligation contractuelle; rapport contractuel
relación especial de las partes contratantes
Rechtsbeziehung zwischen den unmittelbarren Vertragsparteien

4605. **privy council**
conseil privé du souverain
consejo privado del soberano
geheimer Rat; Staatsrat; Kronrat

4606. **prize**
prise (f); prix (m)
presa (f); premio (m)
Prise (f)

4607. **probate of a will**
homologation (f) d'un testament (m)
verificación (f) judicial de un testamento (m)
gerichtliche Bestätigung (f) eines Testaments (n)

4608. **probation**
épreuve (f); stage (m); sursis (m)
libertad (f) condicional; probación (f)
bedingte Verurteilung (f); bedingter Straferlass (m)

4609. **probationary period**
période de sursis
período de libertad vigilada
Bewährungsfrist

4610. **probation officer**
délégué d'épreuve
agente de vigilancia
Justizbeamter; Bewährungshelfer

4611. **probationer**
personne mise à l'épreuve; délinquant en liberté surveillée
persona a prueba; delincuente bajo libertad vigilada
Angestellter auf Probe; bedingt freigelassener Sträfling

4612. **problem**
problème (m); question (f)
problema (m); cuestión (f)
Problem (n); Aufgabe (f)

4613. **procedure**
procédure (f)
procedimiento (m)
Prozessführung (f); Verfahren (n)

4614. **civil procedure**
procédure civile
procedimiento civil
Zivilverfahren

4615. **criminal procedure**
procédure pénale
procedimiento criminal
Strafverfahren

4616. **rules of procedure**
règlement (m) intérieur
reglas (fpl) de procedimiento
Geschäftsordnung (f)

4617. **summary procedure**
procédure sommaire
procedimiento sumario
summarisches Verfahren

4618. **to proceed**
procéder; continuer
proceder
fortfahren; vorgehen

4619. **proceedings**
débats (mpl); poursuites (fpl)
actuaciones (fpl); actos (mpl)
Verhandlung (f); Verfahren (n)

4620. **adversary proceeding**
procès contentieux
juicio adversario
Streitverfahren

4621. **ancillary proceeding**
procès ancillaire
proceso auxiliar, secundario
Nebenintervention

4622. **bar to proceedings**
fin de non-recevoir
obstrucción a los procedimientos; excepción dilatoria
Ausschluss oder Präklusion des Rechtswegs

4623. **conduct of proceedings**
direction (f) des débats
dirección (f) del proceso
Verhandlungsführung (f)

4624. **judicial proceedings**
débats judiciaires; procès (m)
proceso judicial; diligencia (f)
Gerichtsverfahren (n)

4625. **preliminary proceedings**
mesures provisoires; poursuites préliminaires
actuaciones preliminares
Vorverfahren

4626. **stay of proceedings**
suspension d'instance
suspensión de la instancia
Aussetzung des Verfahrens

4627. **to initiate, to institute proceedings**
intenter des poursuites
iniciar una causa; incoar un proceso
ein Verfahren einleiten

4628. **to take proceedings**
intenter un procès, une action; recourir à la justice
proceder judicialmente contra
ein Verfahren anstrengen, einleiten

4629. **proceeds**
bénéfices (mpl); gains (mpl); montant (m)
frutos (mpl); productos (mpl); réditos (mpl)
Ertrag (m); Gewinn (m); Erlöss (m)

4630. **process**
procès (m); méthode (f)
proceso (m); método (m)
Prozess (m); Methode (f)

4631. **judicial process**
procédure judiciaire
procedimiento judicial
gerichtliches Verfahren

4632. **process server**
huissier (m) exploitant
portador (m) de citaciones (fpl) o notificaciones (fpl)
Zusteller (m); Gerichtsvollzieher (m)

4633. **proclamation**
proclamation (f)
proclamación (f)
Bekanntmachung (f); Proklamation (f)

4634. **to proclaim**
proclamer
proclamar
bekanntmachen

4635. **production**
production (f)
producción (f)
Produktion (f); Herstellung (f); Erzeugung (f)

4636. **cost of production**
coût de production

costo de producción
Herstellungskosten

4637. **product**
produit (m)
producto (m)
Erzeugnis (n); Produkt (n)

4638. **productive**
productif
productivo
produktiv

4639. **to produce**
présenter; produire
presentar; producir
einführen; herstellen; erzeugen

4640. **profession**
déclaration (f); profession (f)
declaración (f); profesión (f)
Bekenntnis (n); Beruf (m)

4641. **legal profession**
profession (f) d'avocat (m)
abogacía (f)
Anwaltsberuf (m)

4642. **professional**
professionnel
profesional
berufsmässig

4643. **proffer**
offre (f)
oferta (f)
Angebot (n); Anerbieten (n)

4644. **to proffer**
faire une offre
ofrecer; proponer
anbieten; Angebot machen

4645. **profit**
bénéfice (m); profit (m)
utilidad (f); beneficio (m); ganancia (f)
Gewinn (m); Profit (m)

4646. **gross profit**
bénéfice net; profit brut
utilidades brutas
Bruttogewinn

4647. **net profit**
profit net
utilidad neta
Nettogewinn; Reingewinn

4648. **profit and loss**
profits et pertes (fpl)
ganancias y pérdidas (fpl)
Gewinn und Verlust (m)

4649. **profitable**
avantageux; profitable
provechoso; ventajoso
nützlich; einträglich

4650. **profit-sharing**
participation (f) au gain (m)
participación (f) en las utilidades (fpl)
Gewinnbeteiligung (f)

4651. **to make a profit on**
faire un bénéfice de
obtener una ganancia en
einen Gewinn erzielen aus

4652. **to profit by**
tirer profit de
sacar provecho de
profitieren

4653. **profiteering**
mercantilisme (m)
usura (f)
Wuchergeschäfte (npl); Preistreiberei (f)

4654. **to profiteer**
faire des bénéfices excessifs; exploiter
usurear; explotar
Wuchergeschäfte betreiben

4655. **profit à prendre**
profit à prendre
usufructo
Ususfructus; Fruchtgenuss (m) (-recht) (n)

4656. **profligate**
libertin (m); prodigue (m)
libertino (m); pródigo (m)
liederlicher Mensch (m)

4657. **progenitor**
aïeul (m); ancêtre (m)
progenitor (m)
Ahne (m); Vorfahre (m)

4658. **program**
programme (m)
programa (m)
Programm (n)

4659. **austerity program**
programme d'austérité
plan de austeridad
auf Konsumbeschränkung abgestelltes Sanierungsprogramm

4660. **progress**
progrès (m)
desarrollo (m); progreso (m)

Fortschritt (m)

4661. **prohibition** (see also **writ of prohibition**)
défense (f); prohibition (f)
prohibición (f)
Verfügung (f) eines Verbots (n); Verbot (n)

4662. **prohibited**
interdit
prohibido
verboten

4663. **to prohibit**
défendre; prohiber
prohibir
untersagen; verbieten

4664. **project**
projet (m)
proyecto (m)
Projekt (n)

4665. **prolixity**
prolixité (f)
prolijidad (f)
Weitschweifigkeit (f)

4666. **promise**
espérance (f); promesse (f)
promesa (f)
Versprechen (n); Zusage (f)

4667. **to promise**
promettre
prometer
versprechen; zusagen

4668. **promotion**
avancement (m); promotion (f)
ascenso (m); promoción (f)
Beförderung (f); Förderung (f)

4669. **to promote**
avancer; promouvoir
ascender; promover; fomentar
befördern; unterstützen

4670. **promulgation**
promulgation (f)
promulgación (f)
Verkündung (f) (des Gesetzes); Bekanntmachung (f)

4671. **to promulgate**
promulguer
promulgar
verkünden; bekanntmachen

4672. **proof**
preuve (f)
prueba (f); probanza (f)
Beweis (m)

4673. **adequate proof**
preuve satisfaisante
prueba adecuada
hinreichender Beweis

4674. **bullet proof**
à l'épreuve des balles
a prueba de bala
kugelsicher; Panzer-

4675. **burden of proof; onus probandi**
charge (f), fardeau (m) de la preuve
peso (m) de la prueba
Beweislast (f)

4676. **fire-proof**
incombustible
incombustible
feuerfest

4677. **galley proof**
épreuves (fpl) en placard (m)
pruebas (fpl) de imprenta (f)
Fahnenabzug (m); Fahnenkorrekturen (fpl)

4678. **proof-reader**
correcteur (m)
corrector (m)
Korrektor (m)

4679. **proof-reading**
correction (f) des éprcuves
corrección (f) de pruebas
Korrekturlesen (n)

4680. **written proof**
preuve par écrit
prueba escrita
schriftlicher Beweis

4681. **to furnish proof**
produire des preuves
producir pruebas
den Beweis erbringen

4682. **to prove**
démontrer; prouver
demo(n)strar; probar
beweisen

4683. **propaganda**
propagande (f)
propaganda (f)
Propaganda (f)

4684. **proper**
convenable; exact; juste; propre
adecuado; apropiado; exacto; justo
eigen; geeignet; genau; richtig

4685. **property**

biens (mpl); effets (mpl); propriété (f)
bienes (mpl); propiedad (f)
Besitztum (n); Eigentum (n); Hab und Gut (n)

4686. **community property**
communauté (f) de biens
comunidad (f) de bienes
Gütergemeinschaft (f); Gemeinschaftsgeld (n)

4687. **industrial property**
propriété industrielle
propiedad industrial
gewerbliches Eigentum

4688. **incorporeal, intagible property**
biens incorporels
bienes incorporales
Rechte und Forderungen

4689. **intellectual property**
propriété intellectuelle
propiedad intelectual
geistiges Eigentum

4690. **landed property**
biens fonciers
bienes raíces
Grundbesitz

4691. **landed proprietor; landowner**
propriétaire (m) terrien
terrateniente (m)
Grundbesitzer (m)

4692. **literary property**
propriété littéraire
derechos de autor
literarisches Eigentum

4693. **personal property** (see **personalty**)

4694. **property rights**
droits de propriété
derechos de propiedad
Eigentumsrechte

4695. **public property** (see **public domain**)

4696. **real property**
bien immobilier
bienes inmuebles
Grundeigentum

4697. **wilful damage to property**
dommage intentionnel, matériel
daño premeditado a la propiedad
vorsätzliche Sachbeschädigung

4698. **proposal; proposition**
proposition (f)
proposición (f)
Vorschlag (m)

4699. **alternate, counter proposal**
contre-projet (m)
contraproyecto (m)
Gegenvorschlag (m)

4700. **to accept a proposal**
accepter une proposition
aceptar una proposición
einen Vorschlag annehmen

4701. **to propose**
proposer
proponer
beantragen; vorschlagen

4702. **to submit a proposal**
soumettre une proposition
presentar una proposición
einen Vorschlag unterbreiten

4703. **to support a proposal**
soutenir une proposition
apoyar una proposición
einen Antrag unterstützen

4704. **prorogation**
prorogation (f)
prórroga (f); prorrogación (f)
Aufschub (m); Prorogation (f); Vertagung (f)

4705. **to prorogue**
proroger
prorrogar
prorogieren

4706. **pros and cons**
le pour et le contre
a favor y en contra
das Für und Wider

4707. **proscription**
interdiction (f); proscription (f)
prohibición (f); proscripción (f)
Untersagung (f); Verbot (n)

4708. **prosecution**
accusation (f); poursuites (fpl)
acusación (f)
Anklage (f); gerichtliche Verfolgung (f)

4709. **office of the prosecution**
parquet (m)
oficina (f) del fiscal (m)
Staatsanwaltschaft (f); Anklagebehörde (f)

4710. **public prosecutor**

Ministère (m) Public; procureur (m)
fiscal (m); acusador (m) público
Staatsanwalt (m); öffentlicher Ankläger (m)

4711. **'The prosecution rests'**
'Plaise au tribunal d'accepter mes conclusions'
'El fiscal eleva a definitiva sus conclusiones'
'Die Staatsanwaltschaft schliesst ihr Plädoyer'

4712. **to prosecute**
diriger les poursuites; poursuivre
acusar; perseguir ante los tribunales
anklagen; verfolgen

4713. **prostitution**
prostitution (f)
prostitución (f)
Prostitution (f)

4714. **prostitute**
fille (f) publique; prostituée (f)
prostituta (f)
Prostituierte (f)

4715. **protectorate**
protectorat (m)
protectorado (m)
Protektorat (n)

4716. **protest**
protestation (f); protêt (m)
protesta (f)
Protest (m); Verwahrung (f)

4717. **under protest**
sous réserve
bajo protesta
unter Protest

4718. **to protest**
protester
protestar
protestieren

4719. **protocol**
protocole (m)
protocolo (m)
Protokoll (n)

4720. **additional protocol**
protocole additionnel
protocolo adicional
Zusatzprotokoll

4721. **chief of protocol**
chef (m) du protocole
jefe (m) de protocolo
Chef (m) des Protokolls

4722. **provision**
article (m); disposition (f); stipulation (f)
artículo (m); disposición (f); estipulación (f)
Bestimmung (f); Verfügung (f)

4723. **provided that**
attendu que
a condición que
vorausgesetzt dass

4724. **provisional**
provisoire
provisional
vorläufig; provisorisch

4725. **to provide**
prévoir; stipuler
estipular; disponer; proveer
bestimmen; verordnen

4726. **proviso**
clause conditionnelle; condition
condición; estipulación
(Bedingungs)Klausel; Vorbehalt

4727. **provocation**
provocation (f)
provocación (f)
Provokation (f); Herausforderung (f)

4728. **provocative**
provocateur
provocativo
herausforderend

4729. **to provoke**
provoquer
provocar
provozieren; herausfordern

4730. **provost marshal**
grand prévôt (m)
capitán (m) preboste
Generalprofos (m)

4731. **proxy**
procuration (f)
poder (m); procuración (f)
Stellvertretung (f); Vollmacht (f)

4732. **proxy holder**
fondé (m) de pouvoir; mandataire (m)
apoderado (m); delegado (m);

mandatario (m)
Bevollmächtigter (m); Stellvertreter (m)

4733. **psychiatry**
psychiatrie (f)
(p)siquiatría (f)
Psychiatrie (f)

4734. **psychiatric**
psychiatrique
(p)siquiátrico
psychiatrisch

4735. **psychiatrist**
psychiatre (m)
(p)siquiatra (m)
Psychiater (m)

4736. **psychology**
psychologie (f)
(p)sicología (f)
Psychologie (f)

4737. **psychological**
psychologique
(p)sicológico
psychologisch

4738. **psychologist**
psychologue (m)
(p)sicólogo (m)
Psychologe (m)

4739. **puberty**
puberté (f)
pubertad (f)
Pubertät (f)

4740. **public**
le public (m)
el público (m)
Öffentlichkeit (f); Publikum (n)

4740a. **public**
public
público
öffentlich

4741. **public health**
hygiène (f) publique
sanidad (f) pública
Volksgesundheit (f); öffentlicher Gesundheitsdienst (m)

4742. **public land register**
cadastre (m) du domaine public
catastro (m); registro (m) de tierras
Grundbruch (n)

4743. **public official**
fonctionnaire (m)
funcionario (m)
Beamter (m); Funktionär (m)

4744. **public prosecutors (body of)**
magistrature (f) debout; Ministère (m) Public; parquet (m)
cuerpo (m) de acusadores (mpl) públicos
Staatsanwaltschaft (f)

4745. **public utilities**
entreprises (fpl) d'intérêt (m) public
servicio (m) público
gemeinnützige Betriebe (mpl); öffentliche Versorgungsbetriebe (mpl)

4746. **public works**
travaux (mpl) publics
obras (fpl) públicas
öffentliche Arbeiten (fpl)

4747. **publication**
publication (f)
publicación (f)
Veröffentlichung (f)

4748. **publisher**
éditeur (m)
editor (m)
Verleger (m)

4749. **publishing company**
société (f) d'éditions (fpl)
casa (f) editorial
Verlag (m)

4750. **to publish**
publier
publicar
veröffentlichen

4751. **publicity**
publicité (f)
publicidad (f)
Öffentlichkeit (f); Reklame (f)

4752. **punishment**
peine (f); punition (f)
castigo (m)
Bestrafung (f); Strafe (f)

4753. **capital punishment**
peine capitale; peine de mort
pena capital, de muerte
Todesstrafe

4754. **corporal punishment**
peine corporelle
pena corporal
körperliche Züchtigung; Prügelstrafe

4755. **cruel and unusual punishment**

punition cruelle et inaccoutumée
castigo cruel y desacostumbrado
grausame und ungewöhnliche Strafe

4756. **maximum punishment**
maximum de la peine
pena máxima
Höchststrafe

4757. **punishable; punitive**
passible d'une peine; punissable
punible
strafbar

4758. **to punish**
punir
castigar
bestrafen

4759. **purchase**
achat (m)
compra (f)
Kauf (m)

4760. **purchaser**
acheteur (m)
comprador (m)
Käufer (m)

4761. **to acquire by purchase**
acquérir à titre onéreux
adquirir por compra
käuflich erwerben

4762. **to purchase**
acheter
comprar
kaufen

4763. **purge**
épuration (f)
depuración (f)
Säuberung (f)

4764. **to purge**
épurer; purger
limpiar; purgar
reinigen; säubern

4765. **purport**
sens (m); signification (f)
sentido (m); significado (m)
Sinn (m); Bedeutung (f)

4766. **purported**
prétendu
presunto
angeblich

4767. **purpose**
but (m); intention (f)
intención (f); propósito (m); objeto (m)
Ziel (n); Zweck (m)

4768. **on purpose**
exprès
a propósito; adrede
absichtlich

4769. **pursuant to; in pursuance of**
conformément à
de acuerdo con
zufolge

4770. **pursuit**
poursuite (f)
persecución (f); perseguimiento (m)
Verfolgung (f)

4771. **hot pursuit**
poursuite extraterritoriale
perseguimiento extraterritorial
extraterritoriale Verfolgung

Q

4772. **qualification**
capacité (f); qualification (f); restriction (f)
capacidad (f); habilitación (f); restricción (f)
Befähigung (f); Einschränkung (f); Qualifikation (f)

4773. **qualified**
capable; propre à; restreint
capacitado; habilitado; limitado
befähigt; qualifiziert; eingeschränkt

4774. **qualifying**
qualifiant; restreignant
calificado; condicional
qualifizierend; einschränkend

4775. **to qualify**
qualifier; restreindre
condicionar; llenar los requisitos

qualifizieren; einschränken

4776. **quality**
qualité (f)
calidad (f)
Qualität (f)

4777. **quantity**
quantité (f)
cantidad (f)
Quantität (f)

4778. **quarantine**
quarantaine (f)
cuarentena (f)
Quarantäne (f)

4779. **quarrel**
dispute (f); querelle (f)
riña (f); querella (f)
Hader (m); Streit (m)

4780. **to quarrel**
disputer
reñir
streiten

4781. **quasi**
quasi
cuasi
Quasi-; ähnlich

4782. **question**
question (f)
cuestión (f); pregunta (f)
Frage (f)

4783. **a fair question**
une question légitime
une pregunta legítima
eine legitime Frage

4784. **catch question**
question captieuse, insidieuse
pregunta capciosa
eine verfängliche oder heikle frage

4785. **controversial question**
question controversable
asunto controvertible
strittige Frage

4786. **hypothetical question**
question hypothétique
pregunta hipotética
eine hypothetische Frage

4787. **interlocutory question**
question interlocutoire
cuestión incidental
Zwischenfrage

4788. **leading question**
question suggérant la réponse
pregunta que insinúa la respuesta
Suggestivfrage

4789. **legal question**
question juridique
cuestión jurídica
Rechtsfrage

4790. **mixed question of law and fact**
question mélangée de droit et de fait
materia que comparte cuestiones de derecho y de hecho
eine Frage sowohl der Tatsachen als auch des Rechts

4791. **preliminary question**
question préalable
cuestión previa
Vorfrage

4792. **question of fact**
question de fait
cuestión de hecho
Tatfrage

4793. **question of law**
question de droit
cuestion de derécho
Rechtsfrage

4794. **questionable**
contestable; douteux; suspect
discutible; dudoso; sospechoso
fraglich; zweifelhaft; bedenklich

4795. **without question**
sans aucun doute
sin duda alguna
ohne Frage; zweifellos

4796. **to propound, to raise a question**
poser, soumettre une question
plantear, presentar una cuestión
eine Frage stellen oder unterbreiten

4797. **to put the question to a vote**
mettre la question aux voix
proceder a votar
die Frage zur Abstimmung bringen

4798. **to question**
interroger
interrogar; preguntar
befragen; verhören

4799. **questioning**

interrogatoire (m)
interrogatorio (m)
Vernehmung (f)

4800. **questionnaire**
questionnaire (m)
cuestionario (m)
Fragebogen (m)

4801. **quitclaim**
renonciation (f) à un droit
renuncia (f)
Verzichtleistung (f)

4802. **quittance**
quittance (f); reçu (m)
quitanza (f); descargo (m)
Quittung (f); Bezahlung (f)

4803. **quorum**
quorum (m)
quorum (m)
Quorum (n)

4804. **to constitute a quorum**
constituer un quorum
constituir, reunir un quorum
beschlussfähig sein oder Beschlussfähigkeit haben

4805. **quota**
contingent (m); quota (m); quote-part (f)
cuota (f); prorrata (f); cupo (m); contingente (m)
Anteil (m); Quote (f); Teilbetrag (m)

4806. **quotation**
citation (f); cote (f)
cita (f); citación (f); cotización (f)
Zitat (n); Preisnotierung (f)

4807. **market quotation**
prix du marché
precio del mercado
Kursnotierung; Marktpreis

4808. **to quote**
citer; coter
citar; cotizar
zitieren; ein Preisangebot machen

R

4809. **race**
race (f)
raza (f)
Rasse (f)

4810. **racial**
racial
de raza
rassisch

4811. **racketeering**
manoeuvres (fpl) d'extorsion (f)
extorsión (f) por intimidación (f)
erpresserische oder betrügerische Machenschaften (fpl)

4812. **racket**
extorsion organisée
extorsión sistematizada
organisierter Gelderwerb mit Gangstermethoden

4813. **racketeer**
extorqueur (m)
extorsionista (m)
Betrüger (m); Erpresser (m)

4814. **raffle**
loterie (f)
rifa (f)
Lotterie (f); Auslosung (f)

4815. **raid**
expédition (f); rafle (f)
correría (f); incursión (f) de policía (f)
Razzia (f); Überfall (m)

4816. **to raid**
opérer une rafle
incurrir (por la policía)
eine Razzia veranstalten auf; überfallen

4817. **ramification**
ramification (f)
ramificación (f)
Verzweigung (f)

4818. **rank**
grade (m); rang (m)
grado (m); rango (m)
Rang (m); Stand (m)

4819. **ransom**
rançon (f)
rescate (m)
Lösegeld (n); Loskauf (m)

4820. **to ransom**
rançonner
rescatar
auslösen; loskaufen

4821. **rape**
rapt (m); viol (m)
estupro (m); violación (f)
Notzucht (f); Schändung (f); Vergewaltigung (f)

4822. **to rape**
violer
estuprar; violar
Notzucht begehen; schänden

4823. **rapporteur**
rapporteur (m)
relator (m)
Berichterstatter (m)

4824. **rate**
tarif (m); taux (m)
tarifa (f); tasa (f)
Kurs (m); Satz (m)

4825. **birth rate**
taux de natalité
tasa, índice de natalidad
Geburtenziffer

4826. **death rate**
taux de mortalité
tasa, índice de mortalidad
Sterblichkeitsziffer

4827. **going rate**
taux (de change) en cours
tipo de cambio vigente
gegenwärtiger Kurs; Tageskurs

4828. **local rates** (G.B.)
taxes locales
tarifa local; impuesto local
Gemeindesteuern

4829. **rate of interest**
taux d'intérêt
tasa de interés
Zinssatz; Zinsfuss

4830. **ratification**
confirmation (f); ratification (f)
confirmación (f); ratificación (f)
Bestätigung (f); Ratifizierung (f)

4831. **exchange of ratifications**
échange (m) de ratifications
intercambio (m) de ratificaciones
Austausch (m) von Ratifikationsurkunden

4832. **to ratify**
confirmer; ratifier
confirmar; ratificar
bestätigen; ratifizieren

4833. **rating**
classement (m); évaluation (f)
clasificación (f); rango (m)
Bewertung (f)

4834. **rational**
rationnel
racional
rationell

4835. **reality**
réalité (f)
realidad (f)
Realität (f); Wirklichkeit (f)

4836. **real**
réel
real
wirklich

4837. **realist**
réaliste (m)
realista (m)
Realist (m)

4838. **realistic**
réaliste
realista
realistisch

4839. **realization**
réalisation (f)
realización (f)
Verwirklichung (f); Verwertung (f)

4840. **to realize**
réaliser; se rendre compte de
realizar; darse cuenta
verwerten; verwirklichen; sich vorstellen

4841. **realty; real estate**
biens (mpl) fonciers, immobiliers
bienes (mpl) raíces
Grundbesitz (m)

4842. **real estate agency**
agence (f) de vente immobilière
agencia (f) de bienes inmuebles
Liegenschaftsagentur (f)

4843. **real estate agent**
agent (m) de biens immeubles
agente (m) de bienes inmuebles
Grundstücksmakler (m)

4844. **reason**
motif (m); raison (f)

motivo (m); razón (f)
Grund (m); Ursache (f)

4845. **reasonable**
raisonnable
razonable
vernünftig

4846. **rebate**
escompte (m); rabais (m)
descuento (m); rebaja (f)
Rabatt (m)

4847. **rebellion**
rébellion (f)
rebelión (f)
Rebellion (f); Aufruhr (m)

4848. **rebel**
rebelle (m)
rebelde (m)
Rebell (m); Aufrührer (m)

4849. **to rebel**
entrer en rébellion; se rebeller
rebelarse; sublevarse
rebellieren; aufständisch werden

4850. **rebuttal**
réfutation (f)
refutación (f)
Widerlegung (f)

4851. **rebuttable**
réfutable
refutable
widerlegbar

4852. **to rebut**
réfuter
refutar
widerlegen

4853. **rebutter**
réplique (f) à la triplique
contrarréplica (f) a la tríplica
Quadruplik (f)

4854. **recall**
rappel (m); révocation (f)
retiro (m); revocación (f)
Abberufung (f); Rückberufung (f)

4855. **to recall**
rappeler; révoquer
retirar; revocar
abberufen; kündigen

4856. **receipt**
quittance (f); récépissé (m); reçu (m)
recibo (m)
Empfang (m); Quittung (f)

4857. **acknowledgement of receipt**
accusé (m) de réception (f)
acuse (m) de recibo (m)
Empfangsbestätigung (f)

4858. **gross receipts**
recettes (fpl) brutes
ingreso (m) bruto
Bruttoeinnahmen (fpl)

4859. **receivership**
administration (f) judiciaire; séquestre (m)
sindicatura (f); receptoría (f)
Geschäftsaufsicht (f); Zwangsverwaltung (f); Konkursverwaltung (f)

4860. **receiver**
administrateur (m) judiciaire; séquestre (m)
síndico (m)
Konkursverwalter (m)

4861. **recess**
ajournement (m)
receso (m)
Vertagung (f)

4862. **to take a recess**
ajourner; remettre
disponer un receso
Pause machen; sich vertagen

4863. **recession**
récession (f)
recesión (f)
Rezession (f) oder wirtschaftlicher Rückgang (m)

4864. **recidivist**
récidiviste (m)
criminal (m) reincidente
Rückfälliger (m)

4865. **recipient**
bénéficiaire (m)
beneficiario (m)
Empfänger (m); Bezugsberechtigter (m)

4866. **reciprocity**
réciprocité (f)
reciprocidad (f)
Gegenseitigkeit (f)

4867. **reciprocal**
réciproque
recíproco

gegenseitig

4868. **to reciprocate**
répondre à
reciprocar
erwidern; vergelten

4869. **recklessness**
imprudence (f); témérité (f)
imprudencia (f); temeridad (f)
Rücksichtslosigkeit (f); Verwegenheit (f)

4870. **reckless**
imprudent; téméraire
imprudente; temerario
rücksichtslos; fahrlässig

4871. **recklessly**
avec témérité
temerariamente
mit bewusster Fahrlässigkeit

4872. **to be reckless**
commettre une imprudence
ser imprudente, temerario
leichtsinnig oder rücksichtslos sein

4873. **reckoning**
calcul (m); compte (m)
cálculo (m); cuenta (f)
Abrechnung (f); Rechnen (n)

4874. **recognition**
reconnaissance (f)
reconocimiento (m)
Anerkennung (f)

4875. **to recognize**
reconnaître; donner la parole à
reconocer; conceder la palabra
anerkennen; das Wort erteilen

4876. **recognizance**
engagement pris devant un tribunal
obligación inscrita ante un tribunal
schriftliche Verpflichtung (vor Gericht übernommen)

4877. **recommendation**
recommandation (f)
recomendación (f)
Empfehlung (f)

4878. **to recommend**
recommander
recomendar
empfehlen

4879. **recompense**
dédommagement (m); récompense (f)
recompensa (f)
Entschädigung (f); Ersatz (m)

4880. **to recompense**
dédommager; récompenser
recompensar
entschädigen; ersetzen

4881. **reconcilement; reconciliation**
rapprochement (m); réconciliation (f)
reconciliación (f)
Beilegung (f); Versöhnung (f)

4882. **to reconcile**
réconcilier
reconciliar
beilegen; versöhnen

4883. **reconstruction**
reconstruction (f)
reconstrucción (f)
Wiederaufbau (m)

4884. **to reconstruct**
reconstruire
reconstruir
wiederaufbauen

4885. **record**
compte-rendu (m); minute (f); procès-verbal (m); registre (m)
acta (f); informe (m);· memorial (m)
Aufzeichnung (f); Protokoll (n); Register (n); Urkunde (f)

4886. **criminal, police record**
casier (m) judiciaire; sommiers (mpl) judiciaires
antecedentes (mpl) penales
Vorstrafen (fpl)

4887. **judicial record**
casier judiciaire
protocolo judicial
Gerichtsprotokoll

4888. **long criminal record**
casier judiciaire bien rempli
antecedentes penales numerosos
oft vorbestraft

4889. **no criminal record**
casier judiciaire vierge
sin antecedentes penales
nicht vorbestraft

4890. **of record**

enregistré aux procès-verbaux
inscrito; registrado
aktenkundig; registriert

4891. **off the record**
hors de procès-verbal
fuera de actas
nicht für die Öffentlichkeit; nicht protokolliert; inoffiziell

4892. **past record**
antécédents
antecedentes
Vorleben

4893. **record of the proceedings**
acte; procès-verbal d'audience
autos de una causa; protocolo
Protokolle der Gerichtssitzungen

4894. **recorder**
greffier (m)
registrador (m)
Protokollführer (m); Urkundsbeamter (m) (der Geschäftsstelle)

4895. **stenographic, verbatim record**
compte-rendu, procès-verbal sténographique
transcripción estenográfica, taquigráfica
stenographisches Protokoll

4896. **to enter a document into the record**
verser une pièce au dossier
protocolizar
ein Dokument zu den Prozessakten nehmen

4897. **to read into the record; place on record**
inscrire au procès-verbal
hacer constar en acta
zur Aufnahme in das Protokoll verlesen

4898. **to record**
enregistrer; dresser le procès-verbal
inscribir; registrar
eintragen; protokollieren

4899. **to strike from the record**
rayer du procès-verbal
borrar del acta
aus dem Protokoll streichen

4900. **records**
archives (fpl)
archivos (mpl)
Archiv (n); Geschäftsbücher (npl); Aufzeichnungen (fpl)

4901. **public records**
archives publiques
archivos, registros públicos
öffentliche Archieve oder Register

4902. **recoupment**
compensation (f) judiciaire; défalcation (f)
reembolso (m); resarcimiento (m)
Aufrechnung (f); Zurückbehaltung (f)

4903. **to recoup**
récupérer; défalquer
resarcir; recobrar
zurückbehalten

4904. **recourse**
recours (m)
recurso (m)
Rechtsmittel (n)

4905. **without recourse**
sans recours
sin recurso
ohne Rechtsmittel oder Berufungsmöglichkeit

4906. **recovery**
recouvrement (m); reprise (f)
recuperación (f)
Eintreibung (f); Wiedererlangung (f)

4907. **to recover**
reprendre; revendiquer
obtener; recuperar
eintreiben; wiedererlangen

4908. **recrimination**
récrimination (f)
recriminación (f)
Gegenbeschuldigung (f)

4909. **recurrence**
répétition (f)
repetición (f)
Wiederkehr (f); Wiederholung (f)

4910. **recurrent**
périodique
periódico
wiederkehrend

4911. **recusation**
récusation (f)
recusación (f)

Ablehnung (f)
4912. **Red Cross**
Croix Rouge
Cruz Roja
Rotes Kreuz
4913. **red tape**
bureaucratie (f); paperasserie (f) administrative
papeleo (m); rutina (f) oficinesca; burocratismo (m)
Bürokratie (f); Amtsschimmel (m)
4914. **redemption**
amortissement (m); purge (f); rachat (m)
amortización (f); redención (f); rescate (m)
Amortisation (f); Einlösung (f); Rückkauf (m); Tilgung (f)
4915. **right of redemption**
droit de rachat
derecho de redención, de retracto
Rückkaufsrecht
4916. **to redeem**
amortir; purger; racheter
amortizar; redimir; rescatar
amortisieren; einlösen; tilgen; abzahlen
4917. **redress**
réparation (f)
reparación (f)
Abhilfe (f); Wiedergutmachung (f)
4918. **to give redress**
accorder réparation
reparar
entschädigen; wiedergutmachen
4919. **to obtain redress**
obtenir justice; réparation
obtener justicia, reparación
Entschädigung (f) oder Ersatz (m) erhalten
4920. **reduction**
réduction (f)
reducción (f)
Herabsetzung (f)
4921. **to reduce**
réduire
reducir
herabsetzen
4922. **re-eligible**
rééligible
reelegible
wiederwählbar
4923. **reexamination**
nouvel interrogatoire (m)
reexaminación (f)
Nachprüfung (f); Wiedervernehmung (f)
4924. **to reexamine**
interroger à nouveau
reexaminar
nochmals prüfen oder verhören
4925. **referee**
arbitre (m)
árbitro (m)
Schiedsrichter (m)
4926. **reference**
référence (f)
referencia (f)
Referenz (f); Verweisung (f)
4927. **cross-reference**
renvoi (m)
remisión (f)
Kreuzverweis (m)
4928. **to refer to**
faire allusion à
aludir a
verweisen auf
4919. **references**
bibliographie (f); références
bibliografía (f); referencias
Bibliographie (f); Referenzen (fpl)
4930. **referendum**
référendum (m)
referendum (m)
Volksentscheid (m)
4931. **reformatory**
maison (f) de correction (f)
reformatorio (m)
Besserungsanstalt (f)
4932. **refuge**
asile (m); refuge (m)
refugio (m); asilo (m)
Zuflucht (f); Asyl (n)
4933. **to seek, to take refuge**
se réfugier
refugiarse
Zuflucht suchen oder nehmen
4934. **refugee**
réfugié (m); asilé (m)
refugiado (m); asilado (m)

Asylberechtigter (n); Flüchtling (m); Vertriebener (m)

4935. **refund**
restitution (f); ristourne (f)
reembolso (m)
Rückzahlung (f); Rückvergütung (f)

4936. **to refund**
rembourser; rendre
reembolsar
zurückzahlen; rückvergüten; ersetzen

4937. **refusal**
déni (m); refus (m)
denegación (f); rechazo (m)
Ablehnung (f); Verweigerung (f)

4938. **to refuse**
dénier; refuser
denegar; rechazar
ablehnen; verweigern

4939. **refutation**
réfutation (f)
refutación (f)
Widerlegung (f)

4940. **refutable**
réfutable
refutable
widerlegbar

4941. **to refute**
réfuter
refutar
widerlegen

4942. **regency**
régence (f)
regencia (f)
Regentschaft (f)

4943. **regent**
régent (m)
regente (m)
Regent (m)

4944. **registration**
immatriculation (f)
matrícula (f)
Registrierung (f); Eintragung (f)

4945. **registered**
enregistré; immatriculé
matriculado; registrado
eingeschrieben

4946. **registrar**
greffier (m)
registrador (m)
Registraturbeamter (m); Standesbeamter (m)

4947. **to register**
enregistrer; recenser; s'inscrire
inscribirse; matricular; registrar
eintragen; registrieren; einschreiben

4948. **register**
enregistrement (m); greffe (m); registre (m)
matrícula (f); registro (m)
Register (n); Registratur (f)

4949. **penal register**
casier (m) judiciaire
registro (m) de antecedentes (mpl) penales
Strafregister (n)

4950. **registry of property**
cadastre (m)
catastro (m)
Grundbuch (n)

4951. **regular**
régulier
normal; regular
gewöhnlich; regulär; regelmässig

4952. **regulations**
règlements (mpl); prescriptions (fpl)
reglamentos (mpl); regulaciones (fpl)
Bestimmungen (fpl); Vorschriften (fpl)

4953. **to regulate**
régler
regular
regulieren

4954. **rehabilitation**
réhabilitation (f); redressement (m)
rehabilitación (f)
Rehabilitierung (f); Wiedereinsetzung (f)

4955. **to rehabilitate**
réhabiliter
rehabilitar
rehabilitieren; wiedereinsetzen

4956. **rehearing**
nouvelle audition
nueva audiencia
erneute Verhandlung

4957. **reimbursement**

remboursement (m)
reembolso (m)
Wiedererstatung (f); Rückzahlung (f)

4958. **to reimburse**
rembourser
reembolsar
wiedererstatten; zurückzahlen

4959. **reinstatement**
réintégration (f); rétablissement (m)
rehabilitación (f); restablecimiento (m)
Wiedereinsetzung (f)

4960. **to reinstate**
réintégrer; rétablir
rehabilitar; restablecer
widereinsetzen

4961. **rejection**
refus (m); rejet (m)
rechazo (m); rehuso (m)
Ablehnung (f); Zurückweisung (f)

4962. **to reject**
refuser; rejeter
rechazar; rehusar
ablehnen; zurückweisen

4963. **rejoinder**
duplique (f)
dúplica (f)
Erwiderung (f); Duplik (f)

4964. **relations**
parent (m); rapports (mpl)
parientes (fpl); relaciones (fpl)
Verwandte (f,m); Beziehungen (fpl)

4965. **blood relations**
parents par le sang
parientes consanguíneos
Blutsverwandte

4966. **commercial relations**
relations commerciales
relaciones commerciales
Handelsbeziehungen

4967. **relationship**
parenté (f); rapport (m)
parentesco (m)
Verwandtschaft (f); Beziehung (f); Verhältnis (n)

4968. **related in the direct line**
apparenté en ligne directe
pariente en línea directa
in gerader Linie verwandt

4969. **related to**
apparenté; ayant trait à
emparentado; conexo à
verwandt mit; mit bezug auf

4970. **relative**
relatif
relativo
relativ; bezüglich

4971. **relatives by marriage**
parents par alliance
parientes políticos
Verschwägerte

4972. **release**
décharge (f); levée (f) d'écrou (m); mise (f) en liberté (f)
exoneración (f); liberación (f); quita (f)
Entlassung (f); Freigebe (f); Verzichtleistung (f)

4973. **to release**
décharger; mettre en liberté
exonerar; liberar; poner en libertad
entlassen; freigeben; verzichten auf

4974. **relentless**
implacable; inflexible
implacable; inexorable
unbarmherzig; unnachsichtig; unelastisch

4975. **relevance; relevancy**
applicabilité (f); pertinence (f)
pertinencia (f)
Erheblichkeit (f)

4976. **relevant**
applicable; pertinent
pertinente
erheblich

4977. **reliability**
crédibilité (f); sûreté (f)
confiabilidad (f)
Verlässlichkeit (f); Glaubwürdigkeit (f); Kreditwürdigkeit (f)

4978. **reliable**
digne de confiance
fidedigno; seguro
verlässlich; glaubwürdig; kreditwürdig

4979. **reliance**
confiance (f)
confianza (f)

Vertrauen (n)

4980. **to rely on**
avoir confiance en; compter sur
contar con; tener confianza en
sich verlassen auf; bauen auf

4981. **relief**
assistance (f); redressement (m); secours (m)
alivio (m); desagravio (m); satisfacción (f)
Beistand (m); Abhilfe (f); Unterstützung (f)

4982. **prayer for relief**
action en réparation
demanda de satisfacción
Antrag auf Rechtshilfe (equity); Gesuch um gerichtliche Hilfe (Schadenersatz); Klage auf Schadenersatz

4983. **to apply for relief**
demander justice
solicitar justicia
Rechtshilfe beantragen

4984. **to grant relief**
redresser; réparer
exonerar; reparar
Rechtshilfe oder Schadenersatz gewähren

4985. **relinquishment**
abandon (m); renonciation (f)
abandono (m); renuncia (f)
Aufgabe (f); Verzicht (m); Verzichtleistung (f)

4986. **to relinquish**
renoncer; se désister
abandonar; renunciar
abtreten; Verzicht leisten auf

4987. **relocation**
relogement (m)
reasentamiento (m)
Wohnsitzverlegung (f); Geschäftsverlegung (f); Erneuerung (f) des Pachtvertrags

4988. **remainder**
reversion (f); reste (m)
reversión (f); resto (n)
Anfallsrecht (n); Nacherbenrecht (n); Rest (m) (-bestand)

4989. **contingent remainder**
substitution sous condition suspensive
legado bajo condición, que puede efectuarse o no
bedingte Anwartschaft

4990. **vested remainder**
substitution immédiate
legado que se efectúa al expirar el derecho de propiedad anterior
unentziehbare Anwartschaft

4991. **remand, to**
renvoyer (la cause) à une autre audience; renvoyer (en prison)
reenviar; reencarcelar
zurücksenden; in die Haft zurücksenden

4992. **remedy**
réparation (f); voie (f) de recours (m)
recurso (m)
Abhilfe (f); Rechtsmittel (n)

4993. **election of remedies**
choix (m) des moyens de droit
elección (f) de recursos
Wahl (f) der Rechtsmittel

4994. **exhaustion of local remedies**
épuisement (m) des recours légaux internes
agotamiento (m) de recursos legales internos
Erschöpfung (f) der innerstaatlichen Rechtsmittel

4995. **extraordinary legal remedies**
recours légaux exceptionnels
recursos legales excepcionales
ausserordentliche gerichtliche Messnahmen

4996. **to resort to a remedy**
avoir recours aux moyens de droit
interponer recurso
ein Rechtsmittel ergreifen

4997. **remission**
pardon (m)
perdón (m); remisión (f)
Begnadigung (f); Erlass (m)

4998. **remissness**
négligence (f)
negligencia (f)
Nachlässigkeit (f)

4999. **remittance**
envoi (m); remise (f)
envío (m); remesa (f)

Überweisung (f); Zahlung (f)
5000. **to remit**
remettre; renvoyer
remitir
erlassen; zurückverweisen; überweisen
5001. **remnant**
reste (m); reliquat (m)
residuo (m); resto (m)
Überrest (m)
5002. **removability**
amovibilité (f)
amovilidad (f)
Versetzbarkeit (f)
5003. **removable**
amovible
amovible
versetzbar
5004. **removal**
éloignement (m); révocation (f); suppression (f)
remoción (f); traslado (m)
Beseitigung (f); Amtsenthebung (f); Entlassung (f)
5005. **to remove**
éloigner; révoquer
mudar; trasladar
beseitigen; des Amtes entheben; entlassen
5006. **remuneration**
rémunération (f)
remuneración (f)
Entlohnung (f); Vergütung (f)
5007. **to remunerate**
rémunérer
remunerar
entlohnen; vergüten
5008. **rendition**
interprétation (f); reddition (f)
versión (f); rendición (f)
Auslieferung (f); Übergabe (f); Auslegung (f); Wiedergabe (f)
5009. **to rçnder**
interpréter; rendre; traduire
rendir; traducir; verter
auslegen; wiedergeben; übersetzen
5010. **renewal**
prorogation (f); reconduction (f); renouvellement (m)
prórroga (f); reanudación (f); renovación (f)
Verlängerung (f); Erneuerung (f)
5011. **tacit renewal**
reconduction tacite
reconducción tácita
stillschweigende Verlängerung oder Erneuerung
5012. **to renew**
proroger; reconduire
reanudar; renovar
verlängern; erneuern
5013. **rent; rental**
loyer (m); redevance (f)
alquiler (m); arrendamiento (m)
Miete (f); Pacht (f); Zins (m)
5014. **assessed rental**
valeur locative
alquiler amillarado
steuerlicher Mietwert
5015. **to rent**
louer
alquilar; arrendar
mieten; pachten
5016. **renouncement; renunciation**
renonciation (f)
renuncia (f); renunciación (f)
Verzichtleistung (f)
5017. **to renounce**
renoncer
renunciar
verzichten auf
5018. **renvoi**
renvoi (m)
reenvío (m)
Rückverweisung (f)
5019. **reparations**
réparations (fpl)
reparaciones (fpl)
Reparationen (fpl)
5020. **repatriation**
repatriement (m)
repatriación (f)
Repatriierung (f)
5021. **to repatriate**
repatrier
repatriar
repatriieren
5022. **repayment**
remboursement (m)
reembolso (m)
Rückzahlung (f)
5023. **to repay**
rembourser

reembolsar
zurückzahlen

5024. **repeal**
abrogation (f); rappel (m); révocation (f)
derogación (f); revocación (f)
Aufhebung (f); Widerruf (m) (Testament); Ausserkraftsetzung (f) (Gesetz); Widerrufung (f) (Vollmacht)

5025. **to repeal**
abroger; rappeler; révoquer
derogar; revocar
aufheben; widerrufen

5026. **replevin** (see **action of replevin**)

5027. **replication**
réplique (f)
réplica (f)
Replik (f)

5028. **reply**
réplique (f); réponse (f)
contestación (f); respuesta (f)
Antwort (f)

5029. **to reply**
répliquer; répondre
contestar; responder
antworten auf; erwidern

5030. **report**
compte-rendu (m); rapport (m)
informe (m); relato (m)
Bericht (m)

5031. **interim report**
rapport intérimaire
informe provisional
Zwischenbericht

5032. **preliminary report**
rapport préliminaire
informe preliminar
Vorbericht

5033. **progress report**
rapport sur l'état des travaux
informe sobre la marcha de los trabajos
Bericht über den Stand der Arbeiten

5034. **verbatim report**
compte-rendu sténographique
informe al pie de la letra
wörtlicher Bericht; Wortprotokoll

5035. **to bring a report up to date**
mettre à jour un rapport
poner al día un informe
einen Bericht auf den jeweiligen Stand bringen

5036. **to report**
faire un rapport
informar; relatar
berichten; melden

5037. **to table a report**
déposer un rapport (U.K.); renvoyer l'examen d'un rapport (U.S.A.)
presentar un informe (U.K.); postergar la presentación de un informe (U.S.A.)
einen Antrag vorlegen (U.K.); einen Antrag zurückztellen (U.S.A.)

5038. **reprehensible**
répréhensible
reprensible
tadelnswert

5039. **representation**
représentation (f)
representación (f)
Vertretung (f)

5040. **legal representative**
avocat (m); avoué (m)
abogado (m)
Anwalt (m)

5041. **proportional representation**
représentation proportionnelle
representación proporcional
proportionelle Vertretung

5042. **representative**
délégué (m); représentant (m); député (m)
delegado (m); representante (m); diputado (m)
Delegierter (m); Vertreter (m)

5043. **to make false representations**
déguiser la vérité
prestar declaraciones falsas
falsche Tatsachen vorspiegeln

5044. **to represent**
représenter
representar
repräsentieren; vertreten

5045. **reprieve**
sursis à l'exécution d'une sentence
suspensión temporal de una sentencia

Strafaufschub
5046. **to reprieve**
surseoir
suspender la ejecución
Aufschub gewähren
5047. **reprimand**
blâme (m); réprimande (f)
reprimenda (f)
Tadel (m); Verweis (m)
5048. **to reprimand**
réprimander
reprender
tadeln; rügen
5049. **reprint**
réimpression (f)
reimpresión)f)
Neudruck (m)
5050. **reprinted**
réimprimé
reimpreso
neu gedruckt
5051. **to reprint**
réimprimer
reimprimir
wieder abdrucken
5052. **reprisal**
représaille (f)
represalia (f)
Repressalie (f)
5053. **republic**
république (f)
república (f)
Republik (f)
5054. **repudiation**
répudiation (f)
repudio (m)
Verwerfung (f)
5055. **to repudiate**
répudier
repudiar
verwerfen
5056. **repugnancy**
contrariété (f); répugnance (f)
repugnancia (f)
Unvereinbarkeit (f); Widerspruch (m); Widerwille (m)
5057. **repugnant**
répugnant
repugnante
unvereinbar mit; anstössig
5058. **repurchase**
rachat (m); réméré (m)
recompra (f)
Wiederkauf (m)
5059. **to repurchase**
racheter
recomprar
wiederkaufen
5060. **reputation; repute**
renommée (f); réputation (f); renom (m)
fama (f); reputación (f)
Ansehen (n); Ruf (m); Leumund (m)
5061. **common repute**
commune renommée
reputación conocida
allgemeiner Ruf
5062. **reputable**
estimé
estimable
angesehen; achtbar
5063. **request**
demande (f); requête (f)
demanda (f); petición (f)
Ersuchen (n); Gesuch (n)
5064. **to grant a request**
accéder à une demande
acceder a una demanda
ein Gesuch bewilligen
5065. **to request**
présenter une requête
pedir; rogar
ein Gesuch einreichen; ersuchen; ansuchen
5066. **requirement**
besoin (m); exigence (f)
exigencia (f); requisitò (m)
Forderung (f); Erfordernis (n)
5067. **to require**
exiger
exigir
erfordern
5068. **requisite**
nécessaire; requis; chose nécessaire
necesario; requisito
erforderlich
5069. **requisition**
réquisition (f)
requisición (f)
Beschlagnahme (f); Requisition (f) (mil.)
5070. **to requisition**

réquisitionner
requisar
beschlagnahmen; mit Beschlag belegen; requirieren (mil.)

5071. **resale**
revente (f)
reventa (f)
Wiederverkauf (m)

5072. **rescission**
annulation (f); recision (f)
anulación (f); rescisión (f)
Annullierung (f); Nichtigkeitserklärung (f); Aufhebung (f)

5073. **to rescind**
annuler; rescinder
anular; rescindir
annulieren für nichtig oder ungültig erklären; aufheben

5074. **research**
recherche (f)
investigación (f)
Forschung (f)

5075. **director of research**
administrateur (m); directeur (m) de recherche
administrador (m); director (m) de investigación
Forschungsdirektor (m)

5076. **reservation**
réserve (f)
reserva (f); reservación (f)
Vorbehalt (m); Reservation (f)

5077. **mental reservation**
arrière-pensée (f)
reserva (f) mental
Mentalreservation (f)

5078. **to reserve; to make reservations**
faire des réserves
hacer salvedades; reservar
Vorbehalte machen; reservieren

5079. **residence**
domicile (m); résidence (f)
domicilio (m)
Wohnsitz (m)

5080. **resident**
domicilié (m); résident (m)
domiciliado (m); vecino (m)
Einwohner (m); Bewohner (m)

5081. **resignation**
démission (f); résignation (f)
dimisión (f); renuncia (f)
Demission (f); Niederlegung (f) eines Amtes (n); Rücktritt (m)

5082. **to resign; to tender resignation**
démissionner; donner sa démission
dimitir; renunciar
demissionieren; ein Amt niederlegen

5083. **resistance**
résistance (f)
resistencia (f)
Widerstand (m)

5084. armed resistance
résistance armée
resistencia armada
bewaffneter Widerstand

5085. **to offer resistance**
opposer de la résistance
ofrecer resistencia
Widerstand leisten

5086. **to resist**
résister
resistir
Widerstand leisten; sich widersetzen

5087. **resolution**
résolution (f)
resolución (f)
Beschluss (m); Resolution (f)

5088. **to adopt a resolution**
adopter une résolution
aprobar una resolución
einen Beschluss fassen

5089. **to resolve**
décider
decidir
beschliessen

5090. **resort**
recours (m); ressort (m)
recurso (m)
Instanz (f)

5091. **last resort**
dernier ressort
último recurso
höchste Instanz

5092. **resources**
ressources (fpl)
medios (mpl); recursos (mpl)
Hilfsquellen (fpl); Hilfsmittel (npl)

5093. **to pool resources**

mettre en commun des ressources
reunir recursos
Mittel zusammenlegen

5094. **respondent**
défendeur (m) (dans un procès en équité)
demandado (m) (en equidad)
Beklagter (m)

5095. **response**
réponse (f)
respuesta (f)
Klagebeantwortung (f)

5096. **responsibility**
responsabilité (f)
responsabilidad (f)
Verantwortung (f)

5097. **responsible**
responsable
responsable
verantwortlich

5098. **restatement**
mise au point (f)
nueva exposición (f)
Neuformulierung (f)

5099. **restitution**
restitution (f)
restitución (f)
Rückerstattung (f); Widerherstellung

5100. **restoration**
restauration (f); rétablissement (m)
restauración (f); restablecimiento (m)
Rückgabe (f); Wiedereinsetzung (f)

5101. **to restore**
restaurer; rétablir
restaurar; restablecer
rückerstatten; wieder einsetzen

5102. **restraint**
contrainte (f); restriction (f)
represión (f); restricción (f)
Beschränkung (f); Zwang (m)

5103. **restraint of trade**
atteinte à la liberté de commerce
restricción de la libertad de comercio
Handelsbeschränkung; Wettbewerbsbeschränkung

5104. **to restrain**
contraindre; restreindre
limitar; reprimir
beschränken; abhalten

5105. **restriction**
restriction (f)
restricción (f)
Beschränkung (f)

5106. **to restrict**
limiter; restreindre
limitar; restringir
beschränken; einschränken

5107. **result**
résultat (m)
resultado (m)
Resultat (n); Folge (f)

5108. **resumption**
reprise (f)
reanudación (f); reasunción (f)
Wiederaufnahme (f)

5109. **to resume**
reprendre; recommencer
reanudar; reasumir
wieder aufnehmen

5110. **retail**
vente au détail
venta al detalle; al por menor
Einzelhandel; Kleinhandel

5111. **retailer**
détaillant (m)
comerciante (m) al por menor; detallista (m); minorista (m)
Einzelhändler (m)

5112. **retainer**
avance (f) sur les honoraires (mpl)
anticipo (m) sobre los honorarios (mpl)
Honorarvorschuss (m)

5113. **retaliation**
représailles (fpl); revanche (f)
desquite (m); represalia (f)
Wiedervergeltung (f)

5114. **to retaliate**
exercer des représailles; rendre la pareille
desquitarse; talionar; usar de represalias
wiedervergelten

5115. **retirement**
retraite (f)
jubilación (f)
Pensionierung (f)

5116. **retired**
en retraite; retraité
jubilado
pensioniert; im Ruhestand

5117. **in retirement**
en retraite
en jubilación
ausser Dienst; im Ruhestand

5118. **to retire**
prendre sa retraite
jubilarse
in den Ruhestand treten; sich pensionieren lassen

5119. **retorsion**
rétorsion (f)
retorsión (f)
Retorsion (f)

5120. **retrenchment**
retranchement (m)
cercenamiento (m)
Kürzung (f); Abbau (m)

5121. **policy of retrenchment**
politique d'austérité
política de austeridad
Abbaupolitik

5122. **retrial**
opposition (f); procès (m) en révision (f)
revisión (f) de un proceso (m)
neue Verhandlung (f); Wiederaufnahmeverfahren (n)

5123. **to demand a retrial**
demander la révision d'un procès
pedir la revisión de un proceso
Wiederaufnahmeverfahren beantragen

5124. **retribution**
récompense (f); rétribution (f)
recompensa (f); retribución (f)
Strafe (f); Vergeltung (f)

5125. **retroactive**
rétroactif
retroactivo
rückwirkend

5126. **retrospective**
rétrospectif
retrospectivo
rückwirkend

5127. **return**
retour (m); revenu (m)
regreso (m); rendimiento (m)
Rückkehr (f); Rückerstattung (f); Ertrag (m)

5128. **income tax return**
déclaration (f) de revenu
declaración (f) de renta (fiscal)
Einkommensteuererklärung (f)

5129. **revenue**
revenu (m)
ingresos (mpl) (del erario (m)); recaudación (f)
Einkommen (n); Einkünfte (f)

5130. **collector of internal revenue**
percepteur (m)
recaudador (m) de impuestos (mpl)
Steuereinzieher (m)

5131. **reversal**
infirmation (f)
revocación (f)
Aufhebung (f)

5132. **reversible**
annulable; révocable
revocable
aufhebbar; umstossbar

5133. **to reverse**
annuler; infirmer
anular; revocar
aufheben; umstossen

5134. **reversion**
réversion (f)
reversión (f)
Heimfall (m); Rückfall (m)

5135. **to revert to**
faire retour à; revenir
volver a
heimfallen; zurückfallen

5136. **review**
révision (f)
examen (m); revisión (f)
nochmalige Prüfung (f); Revision (f)

5137. **judicial review**
contrôle judiciaire de la validité des actes législatifs
revisión judicial
Nachprüfung der Verfassungsmässigkeit

5138. **to be subject to review**
être sujet à revision
estar sujeto a revisión
einer Revision unterliegen; der Normenkontrolle unterliegen

5139. **to review**
réexaminer; réviser
revisar
nochmals prüfen; revidieren; einer Revision oder Normenkontrolle; unterziehen

5140. **revision**
correction (f)
corrección (f)
Revision (f)

5141. **to revise**
corriger
corregir
verbessern; überprüfen; revidieren

5142. **revival**
remise (f) en vigueur
renovación (f)
Wiedererweckung (f); Wiederinkraftsetzung (f)

5143. **to revive**
remettre en vigueur; reprendre
reanimar; revivir
wieder in Kraft setzen

5144. **revocation**
révocation (f)
revocación (f)
Widerruf (m); Rücknahme (f)

5145. **to revoke**
révoquer
revocar
widerrufen; zurücknehmen

5146. **revolt**
révolte (f)
rebelión (f)
Aufstand (m); Erhebung (f)

5147. **to revolt**
se révolter; se soulever
levantarse; rebelarse
sich erheben; revoltieren

5148. **revolution**
révolution (f)
revolución (f)
Revolution (f)

5149. **reward**
récompense (f)
premio (m); recompensa (f)
Belohnung (f); Lohn (m)

5150. **to reward**
récompenser
premiar; recompensar
belohnen

5151. **rider**
avenant (m); clause (f) additionnelle
añadidura (f); cláusula (f) adicional
Nachtrag (m); Zusatzklausel (f)

5152. **right**
droit (m)
derecho (m)
Recht (n); Berechtigung (f)

5153. **abandonment of a right**
abandon (m) d'un droit
abandono (m) de un derecho
Rechtsverzicht (m)

5154. **constitutional right**
droit constitutionnel
derecho constitutionnel
Grundrecht

5155. **enjoyment of a right**
jouissance (f) d'un droit
disfrute (m) de un derecho
Genuss (m) eines Rechtes

5156. **inchoate right**
droit non parfait
derecho en expectativa
noch in der Entstehung begriffenes Recht

5157. **inherent right**
droit inhérent
derecho inherente
natürliches, angeborenes Recht

5158. **prescriptive right**
droit consacré par un long usage
derecho adquirido por costumbre
ein durch Ersitzung erworbenes Recht

5159. **right of action**
droit d'ester en justice
derecho a una acción
Klagerecht

5160. **right of appeal**
droit de recours
derecho de apelar, recurrir
Berufungsrecht

5161. **right of assembly**
droit de réunion, de s'assembler
derecho de reunión
Versammlungsrecht

5162. **right of asylum**
droit d'asile

derecho de asilo
Asylrecht

5163. **right of enjoyment**
droit de jouissance
derecho de disfrute
Nutzniessungsrecht

5164. **right of entry**
droit d'accès à un immeuble
derecho de entrada
Besitzergreifungsrecht; Eintrittsbefugnis

5165. **right of inheritance, succession**
droit de succession
derecho de sucesión
Erbrecht

5166. **right of inspection**
droit à l'inspection
derecho de inspección
Recht der Einsicht

5167. **right of passage**
droit de passage
derecho de pasaje
Durchfahrsrecht

5168. **right of pre-emption**
droit de préemption
derecho de prioridad
Vorkaufsrecht

5169. **right of redemption**
droit de rachat
derecho a redimir una propiedad
Rückkaufsrecht: Loskaufsrecht

5170. **right of self-determination of peoples**
droit des peuples à disposer d'eux-mêmes
derecho de libre determinación
Selbstbestimmungsrecht der Völker

5171. **right of visit and search**
droit de visite et de perquisition
derecho de visita y pesquisa
Recht der Hausdurchsuchung

5172. **right of way**
droit de passage, de priorité
servidumbre de paso
Wegerecht; Vorfahrtsrecht

5173. **right to bear arms**
droit de porter des armes
derecho a portar armas
das Recht, Waffen zu tragen

5174. **right to speak**
droit d'avoir la parole
derecho de uso de la palabra
das Recht, das Wort zu erhalten

5175. **to be in the right**
être dans son droit
tener razón
im Recht sein

5176. **to right a wrong**
redresser un tort
corregir un abuso
ein Unrecht gutmachen

5177. **rights**
droits (mpl)
derechos (mpl)
Rechte (npl)

5178. **all rights reserved**
tous droits réservés
reservados todos los derechos
alle Rechte vorbehalten

5179. **citizenship rights**
droit de cité, de citoyenneté
derechos de ciudadanía
Staatsangehörigkeitsrechte

5180. **civil rights**
droits civils, civiques
derechos civiles, individuales
Bürgerrechte

5181. **deprivation of civil rights**
déchéance des droits civiques
privación de derechos civiles
Entziehung der Bürgerrechte

5182. **fundamental rights**
droits fondamentaux
derechos fundamentales
Grundrechte

5183. **human rights**
droits humains
derechos humanos
Menschenrechte

5184. **infringement of rights**
violation des droits
infracción, violación de derechos
Beeinträchtigung oder Verletzung der Rechte

5185. **loss of civil rights**
perte des droits civiques
pérdida de derechos civiles
Verlust der bürgerlichen Rechte

5186. **precarious rights**
droits précaires
derechos precarios
unsichere Rechte

5187. **proprietary rights**
droits de propriété
derechos de propiedad
Eingentumsrechte

5188. **riparian rights**
droits des riverains
derechos ribereños
Uferrechte

5189. **state's rights (U.S.A.)**
le droit particulier de chaque Etat de l'Union
los derechos particulares de los Estados de la Unión
die den Einzelstaaten vorbehaltenen Rechte

5190. **vested rights**
droits acquis
derechos adquiridos
wohlerworbene Rechte

5191. **to assert one's rights**
revendiquer des droits
reivindicar su derecho
sein Recht geltend machen

5192. **to waive one's rights**
abdiquer son droit
abdicar su derecho
sein Recht aufgeben; auf ein Recht verzichten

5193. **ringleader**
chef (m) de bande (f)
cabecilla (m)
Rädelsführer (m)

5194. **riot**
attentat (m) à l'ordre (m) public; émeute (f)
motín (m); tumulto (m)
Aufruhr (f); Ausschreitung (f); Strassenkrawall (m)

5195. **rise**
augmentation (f); enchérissement (m); hausse (f)
alza (f); crecimiento (m)
Erhöhung (f); Steigerung (f); Hausse (f)

5196. **rise in prices**
hausse des prix
alza de precios
Preiserhöhung; Preissteigerung

5197. **rise in wages**
hausse sur les salaires (mpl)
alza de salarios (mpl)
Ansteigen der Löhne (mpl)

5198. **risk**
risque (m)
riesgo (m)
Risiko (n)

5199. **calculated risk**
risque bien calculé
riesgo calculado
wohlerwogenes Risiko

5200. **to risk**
risquer
arriesgar
wagen; riskieren

5201. **to run a risk**
courir le risque
correr un peligro, riesgo
Gefahr laufen

5202. **robbery**
vol (m) qualifié
robo (m)
Raub (m)

5203. **highway robbery, holdup**
brigandage (m)
salteo (m)
Strassenraub (m)

5204. **robber**
voleur (m)
ladrón (m)
Räuber (m)

5205. **to rob**
voler
robar
rauben

5206. **Roe, Richard** (see **Doe, John**)

5207. **roll call**
appel (m) nominatif
acto (m) de pasar lista
Namensaufruf (m)

5208. **rolling stock**
matériel (m) roulant
material (m) rodante
Rollmaterial (n)

5209. **root**
racine (f)
raíz (f)
Wurzel (f); Grund (m)

5210. **roster**
liste (f); tableau (m)
lista (f); registro (m)

Dienstliste (f); Namensliste (f)
5211. **rostrum**
tribune (f)
tribuna (f)
Rednertribüne (f)
5212. **rout**
défaite (f) complète; attroupement (m); foule (f) tumultueuse
derrota (f); fuga (f) desordenada; tumulto (m)
wilde Flucht (f); Aufruhr (m); Tumult (m)
5213. **royalty of an author**
montant (m) des droits (mpl) d'auteur (m)
regalía (f) del autor (m)
Verfassertantieme (f)
5214. **rubric**
rubrique (f)
rúbrica (f)
Rubrik (f)
5215. **rule**
gouvernement (m); règle (f)
gobierno (m); regla (f)
Herrschaft (f); Regel (f)
5216. **hard and fast, inflexible rule**
règle rigoureuse
regla rígida
feste, strenge Regel
5217. **home rule**
autonomie (f)
autonomía (f)
Selbstregierung (f)
5218. **majority rule**
principe majoritaire
por mayoría de votos
Majoritätsherrschaft
5219. **mob rule**
voyoucratie (f)
gobierno (m) de la muchedumbre (f)
Herrschaft (f) der Massen (fpl)
5220. **rule of law**
principe de droit
principio de derecho
Rechtsnorm; Rechtsstaatsprinzip
5221. **rule nisi; order to show cause**
ordonnance provisoire
fallo condicional
vorläufige Verfügung
5222. **rule of the road**
code de la route
reglamento del tráfico
Strassenordnung
5223. **rules and regulations**
règles et règlements
reglamento y regulaciones
Vorschriften und Verordnungen
5224. **rules of procedure**
règles de procédure
reglas de procedimiento
Verfahrensvorschriften
5225. **to adopt rules**
établir des règlements
establecer el reglamento
Vorschriften adoptieren
5226. **to overrule**
passer outre; rejeter
denegar
anders entschieden; ausser Kraft setzen; zurückweisen
5227. **to rule**
dominer; réglementer; régner; statuer
dominar; reinar; reglamentar
herrschen; verordnen; entscheiden
5228. **to rule out**
écarter; ne pas retenir
desechar; descartar
ausschliessen; ablehnen
5229. **ruling**
décision (f); ordonnance (f) de juge (m)
decisión (f); fallo (m)
Gerichtsentscheid (m) über eine Rechtsfrage (f)
5230. **ruse**
ruse (f)
artimaña (f)
List (f)

S

5231. **sabotage**
sabotage (m)
sabotaje (m)
Sabotage (f)
5232. **economic sabotage**
sabotage économique
sabotaje económico
Wirtschaftssabotage
5233. **to sabotage**
saboter
sabotear
sabotieren
5234. **safety**
sûreté (f)
seguridad (f)
Sicherheit (f)
5235. **public safety**
sécurité publique
seguridad pública
öffentliche Sicherheit
5236. **safe**
coffre-fort (m)
caja (f) de seguro (m); caja de caudales (mpl); caja-fuerte (f)
Geldschrank (m)
5237. **safe-conduct**
sauf-conduit (m)
salvoconducto (m)
freies oder sicheres Geleit (n)
5238. **safe-cracker**
cambrioleur (m) de coffre-fort
ladrón (m) de caja-fuerte
Geldschrankknacker (m)
5239. **salary**
traitement (m)
sueldo (m)
Gehalt (n)
5240. **sale**
vente (f)
venta (f)
Verkauf (m)
5241. **clearance sale**
liquidation (f) totale
liquidación (f)
Liquidationsverkauf (m); Saison-ausverkauf (m)
5242. **conditional sale**
vente résolutoire, suspensive
venta condicional
Verkauf unter Eigentumsvorbehalt
5243. **for, on sale**
à vendre; en vente
en venta
zu verkaufen
5244. **judicial sale**
vente judiciaire
venta judicial
gerichtlicher Verkauf
5245. **public sale**
vente aux enchères publiques
subasta, venta pública
Auktion; öffentliche Versteigerung
5246. **sale by auction**
adjudication (f); vente aux enchères (fpl)
remate (m); venta (f) en subasta (f)
Verkauf (m) durch Versteigerung (f)
5247. **sale of joint property**
vente par licitation
venta de propiedad indivisa
Verkauf (m) von gemeinsamen Eigentum (n)
5248. **sale by private contract**
vente à l'amiable
venta por contrato privado
privatrechtlicher Verkauf
5249. **sale on approval**
vente à l'essai
venta sujeta a aprobación
Verkauf auf Probe
5250. **seller**
vendeur (m)
vendedor (m)
Verkäufer (m)
5251. **to sell**
vendre
vender
verkaufen
5252. **to sell at a sacrifice**
vendre à perte
vender con pérdida
verschleudern
5253. **salesman**
vendeur (m)

vendedor (m)
Verkäufer (m)

5254. **travelling salesman**
commis-voyageur (m)
agente (m) viajero
Handlungsreisender (m); Vertreter (m)

5255. **salvage**
sauvetage (m); objets (mpl) sauvés
salvamento (m)
Bergung (f)

5256. **sample**
échantillon (m)
muestra (f)
Muster (n)

5257. **sanction**
sanction (f)
sanción (f)
Sanktion (f); Strafmassnahme (f)

5258. **to sanction**
sanctionner
sancionar
sanktionieren

5259. **sanctuary**
asile (m); immunité (f)
refugio (m); sanctuario (m)
Asyl (n); Zufluchtsort (m)

5260. **right of sanctuary**
droit d'asile
derecho de asilo
Asylrecht

5261. **to take sanctuary**
chercher asile; se réfugier
acogerse a sagrado
Asyl nehmen

5262. **satellite**
Etat (m) satellite
Estado (m) satélite
Satellitenstaat (m)

5263. **satisfaction**
paiement (m); satisfaction (f)
pago (m); satisfacción (f)
Zahlung (f); Erfüllung (f)

5264. **satisfactory**
satisfaisant
satisfactorio
befriedigend

5265. **to satisfy**
payer; satisfaire
pagar; satisfacer
bezahlen; erfüllen

5266. **scab** (see **strike-breaker**)

5267. **scaffold**
échafaud (m)
cadalso (m)
Schafott (n)

5268. **scale**
barème (m); échelle (f)
balanza (f); escale (f)
Massstab (m); Skala (f)

5269. **sliding scale**
barème, échelle mobile
escala móvil, variable
gleitende Skala

5270. **to scale down**
abaisser
reducir según escala
herabsetzen; reduzieren

5271. **scalper**
revendeur (m)
revendedor (m) de acciones (fpl) o billetes (mpl)
Wiederverkäufer (m) von Aktien (fpl) oder Eintrittskarten (fpl)

5272. **scandal**
scandale (m)
escándalo (m)
Skandal (m)

5273. **scandalous**
scandaleux; honteux
escandaloso; vergonzoso
anstossig; skandalös

5274. **to scandalize**
scandaliser
escandalizar
Anstoss erregen

5275. **scapegoat**
souffre-douleur (m); bouc (m) émissaire
víctima (f) propiciatoria; cabeza (f) de turco (m)
Sündenbock (m)

5276. **scarcity**
pénurie (f); rareté (f)
escasez (f); rareza (f)
Knappheit (f)

5277. **schedule**
liste (f); tableau (m); programme (m)
lista (f); cuadro (m); programa (m)
Liste (f); Tabelle (f)

5278. **according to, on schedule**
suivant l'horaire prévu
de acuerdo con el horario
planmässig; pünktlich

5279. **to schedule**
fixer la date; inscrire au rôle
incluir en una lista; programar
auf die Terminliste setzen; planen

5280. **scintilla**
fragment (m)
chispa (f)
kleinste Spur (f)

5281. **scope**
étendue (f)
alcance (m); extensión (f)
Bereich (m); Umfang (m)

5282. **scoundrel**
gredin (m)
pícaro (m)
Schurke (m)

5283. **scroll**
rôle (m); rouleau (m)
lista (f); rollo (m)
Liste (f); Rolle (f)

5284. **sea**
mer (f)
mar (m)
See (f); Meer (n)

5285. **high, open seas**
haute mer
alta mar
hohe See

5286. **marginal sea; maritime belt; territorial waters**
eaux territoriales
aguas jurisdiccionales, territoriales
Küstenmeer

5287. **seal**
cachet (m); sceau (m); scellés (mpl)
sello (m); sigilo (m)
Siegel (n)

5288. **under my hand and seal**
signé et scellé de ma main
bajo mi firma y sello
unter Brief und Siegel; von mir unterzeichnet und versiegelt

5289. **under private seal**
sous sceau, seing privé
bajo sello privado
mit privatem Siegel versehen

5290. **to affix the seals**
apposer les scellés
fijar sellos
besiegeln; Siegel anbringen

5291. **to remove the seals**
lever les scellés
levantar sellos
die Siegel entfernen

5292. **to seal**
sceller
sellar
siegeln

5293. **search**
perquisition (f); recherche (f)
busca (f); investigación (f)
Durchsuchung (f); Untersuchung (f); Suche (f)

5294. **to search**
chercher; perquisitionner
buscar; investigar
durchsuchen

5295. **seasonal**
saisonnier
estacional
saisonbedingt

5296. **seat**
siège (m)
sede (f)
Sitz (m)

5297. **seconded by**
appuyé par
apoyado por
unterstützt von

5298. **secrecy**
secret (m); discrétion (f)
secreto (m)
Geheimhaltung (f)

5299. **professional secrecy**
secret professionnel
secreto profesional
Berufsverschwiegenheit

5300. **secret**
secret (m)
secreto (m)
Geheimnis (n)

5301. **top secret**
secret absolu (d'Etat)
estrictamente secreto
Staatsgeheimnis; ganz geheim

5302. **trade secret**
secret commercial (de fabrication)
secreto comercial (de fábrica)
Geschäftsgeheimnis; Fabrikationsgeheimnis

5303. **to impose secrecy**
exiger le secret
exigir el secreto
Schweigepflicht auferlegen

5304. **secretariat**
secrétariat (m)
secretaría (m)
Sekretariat (n)

5305. **secretary**
secrétaire (m)
secretario (m)
Sekretär (m)

5306. **secretary general**
secrétaire général
secretario general
Generalsekretär

5307. **section**
section (f)
sección (f)
Sektion (f)

5308. **securities**
actions (fpl) et obligations (fpl); valeurs (fpl)
valores (mpl)
Wertpapiere (npl)

5309. **gilt-edged securities**
valeurs de premier ordre
valores de primera clase
mündelsichere Wertpapiere

5310. **security**
garantie (f); sécurité (f)
seguridad (f)
Sicherheit (f)

5311. **collateral security**
caution (f); nantissement (m)
garantía (f) subsidiaria
zusätzliche Sicherheit (f)

5312. **secure**
sûr
seguro
sicher

5313. **social security**
sécurité sociale
seguro social
Sozialversicherung

5314. **to secure**
cautionner; garantir
asegurar; obtener
sichern; verschaffen

5315. **sedition**
sédition (f)
sedición (f)
Aufstand (m)

5316. **seditious**
séditieux
sedicioso
aufrührerisch

5317. **seduction**
séduction (f)
seducción (f)
Verführung (f)

5318. **to seduce**
séduire
seducir
verführen

5319. **segregation**
ségrégation (f)
segregación (f)
Trennung (f); Absonderung (f)

5320. **racial segretation**
ségrégation raciale
segregación racial
Rassentrennung

5321. **to segregate**
séparer
segregar
trennen; absondern

5322. **seizin; seisin**
prise (f) de possession (f)
posesión (f)
Besitzergreifung (f)

5323. **livery of seizin**
saisine (f)
entrega (f)
Besitzeinweisung (f)

5324. **seizure**
mainmise (f); prise (f) de possession (f); saisie (f)
captura (f); embargo (m); secuestro (m)
Beschlagnahme (f); Pfändung (f); Verhaftung (f)

5325. **immune from seizure**
insaisissable
exento de embargo
der Beschlagnahme nicht unterwerfen

5326. **to seize**

saisir
embargar
in Beschlag nehmen

5327. **selection**
choix (m); sélection (f)
selección (f)
Auswahl (f); Wahl (f)

5328. **to select**
choisir; désigner
escoger; seleccionar
auswahlen

5329. **self-defense**
légitime défense (f)
defensa (f) propia
Notwehr (f); Selbstverteidigung (f)

5330. **self-determination**
autodétermination (f); droit (m) des peuples (mpl) à disposer d'eux-mêmes
derecho (m) de libre determinación (f); libre albedrío (m)
Selbstbestimmungsrecht (n)

5331. **self-employed**
indépendant; non-salarié
independiente; no-asalariado
selbständig

5332. **self-executing**
immédiatement exécutoire
efectivo inmediatamente
unmittelbar anwendbar; Ausführungsbestimmungen enthaltend

5333. **self-government**
autonomie (f)
autonomía (f)
Selbstregierung (f)

5334. **self-help**
efforts personnels
auto-ayuda
Selbsthilfe

5335. **self-incrimination**
auto-accusation (f); incrimination (f) de soi-même
auto-incriminación (f)
Selbstbeschuldigung (f)

5336. **self-interest**
intérêt (m) personnel
propio interés (m)
Eigennutz (m)

5337. **self-preservation**
conservation (f) de soi-même
propia conservación (f)
Selbsterhaltung (f)

5338. **self-sufficient**
suffisant à soi-même
autosuficiente
selbstgenügsam

5339. **senility**
sénilité (f)
senilidad (f)
Altersschwäche (f)

5340. **seniority**
ancienneté (f)
antigüedad (f)
höheres Dienstalter (n)

5341. **sentence**
condamnation (f); sentence (f)
condena (f); sentencia (f)
Strafzumessung (f); Urteil (n)

5342. **commutation of sentence**
commutation (f) de peine (f)
conmutación (f) de la sentencia (f)
Strafumwandlung (f)

5343. **concurrent sentences**
peines simultanées
condenas simultáneas
gleichzeitige Verbüssung zweier Freiheitsstrafen

5344. **cumulative sentences**
cumul (m) des peines
condenas (fpl) acumuladas
Strafenhäufung (f)

5345. **death sentence**
condamnation (f) à mort; sentence, arrêt (m) de mort
sentencia (f) de muerte
Todesstrafe (f)

5346. **execution of sentence**
exécution (f) d'une peine
ejecución (f) de una sentencia
Vollstreckung (f) eines Strafurteils

5347. **heavy sentence**
peine stricte
condena grave
schwere Strafe

5348. **indeterminate sentence**
peine indéterminée
sentencia indeterminada
Verurteilung auf unbestimmte Dauer

5349. **life sentence**
condamnation à perpétuité

sentencia de prisión perpetua
lebenslängliche Zuchthausstrafe

5350. **maximum sentence**
peine maxima
máxima sentencia
Höchststrafe

5351. **minimum sentence**
peine minimum
mínima sentencia
Mindeststrafe

5352. **mitigation of sentence**
atténuation de peine
atenuación de la sentencia
Strafmilderung

5353. **prison sentence**
peine de prison
sentencia de prisión
Gefängnisstrafe

5354. **suspended sentence**
condamnation avec sursis
sentencia suspendida
Urteil mit Strafaufschub

5355. **suspension of sentence**
sursis; suspension de sentence
suspensión de la sentencia
Strafaufschub

5356. **to commute a sentence**
commuer une peine
conmutar una sentencia
ein Strafurteil umwandeln

5357. **to give a suspended sentence**
condamner avec sursis
dictar una sentencia condicional
Strafaufschub gewähren

5358. **to sentence; to pronounce a sentence**
condamner; prononcer une condamnation
dictar sentencia; sentenciar
das Urteil verkünden

5359. **to serve one's sentence**
purger sa peine
cumplir una condena
seine Strafe absitzen

5360. **to reduce the sentence**
réduire la peine
rebajar la pena, sentencia
die Strafe herabsetzen

5361. **separation**
séparation (f)
separación (f)
Trennung (f)

5362. **judicial separation**
séparation de corps
separación de cuerpos
Aufhebung der ehelichen Gemeinschaft

5363. **separation a mensa et thoro, from bed and board**
séparation de corps et de biens
separación de cuerpos y bienes
Trennung von Tisch und Bett

5364. **separation of powers**
séparation des pouvoirs
separación de poderes
Trennung der Gewalten

5365. **to separate**
séparer
separar
trennen

5366. **sequestration**
séquestration (f)
embargo (m); secuestro (m)
Sequestration (f); Zwangsverwaltung (f)

5367. **to sequestrate, sequester**
séquestrer
secuestrar
zwangsverwalten

5368. **servant**
employé (m); serviteur (m)
empleado (m); servidor (m)
Angestellter (m); Diener (m)

5369. **fellow servant**
camarade (m) de travail (m)
compañero (m) de trabajo (m)
Mitangestellter (m)

5370. **service**
notification (f); service (m)
notificación (f); servicio (m)
Zustellung (f) (einer Anklage); Dienst (m)

5371. **compulsory service**
service obligatoire
servicio obligatorio
Dienstpflicht

5372. **consular service**
service consulaire
servicio consular
Konsulardienst

5373. **diplomatic service**
service diplomatique
servicio diplomático

diplomatischer Dienst

5374. **foreign service**
service au dehors, diplomatique
servicio exterior
diplomatischer Dienst; Aussendienst

5375. **return of service**
procès-verbal (m) de signification (f)
auto (m) de significación (f)
Protokollzustellungsnachweis (m)

5376. **secret service**
le service (m) secret
policía (f) secreta
Geheimdienst (m)

5377. **to serve**
notifier; servir
notificar; servir
zustellen; dienen

5378. **servitude**
servitude (f)
servidumbre (f)
Servitut (f); Dienstbarkeit (f)

5379. **penal servitude for life**
travaux forcés à perpétuité
pena perpetua aflictiva
lebenslängliche Zwangsarbeit

5380. **penal servitude for time**
travaux forcés à temps
pena temporal aflictiva
zeitliche Zwangsarbeit

5381. **session**
audience (f); séance (f); session (f)
sesión (f)
Sitzung (f); Tagung (f)

5382. **between sessions**
entre les sessions
entre sesiones
zwischen den Sitzungsperioden

5383. **in closed session**
à huis clos
a puertas cerradas
in geheimer Sitzung

5384. **opening session**
séance inaugurale
sesión inaugural
Eröffnungssitzung

5385. **plenary session**
séance plénière
sesión plenaria
Vollsitzung

5386. **regular session**
session ordinaire
sesión ordinaria
ordentliche Tagung

5387. **special session**
session extraordinaire
sesión extraordinaria
ausserordentliche Tagung

5388. **working session**
séance de travail
sesión de trabajo
Arbeitssitzung

5389. **to adjourn a session**
lever la séance
levantar la sesión
ein Sitzung vertagen

5390. **to be in session**
être en session; siéger
celebrar sesión; sesionar
eine Sitzung abhalten; tagen

5391. **to call a session**
convoquer, tenir une audience
convocar a una sesión
eine Sitzung einberufen

5392. **to close the session**
clôturer la session
clausurar la sesión
die Tagung schliessen

5393. **to declare a court in session**
déclarer l'audience ouverte
declarar la sesión abierta
eine Sitzung eröffnen

5394. **to exclude from a session**
exclure de la salle d'audience
excluir de una sesión
von der Sitzung ausschliessen

5395. **to hold a session**
tenir une session
celebrar una sesión
eine Sitzung oder Tagung abhalten

5396. **set-off** (see **offset**)

5397. **settlement**
accord (m); liquidation (f); règlement (m)
ajuste (m); arreglo (m); liquidación (f)
Abkommen (n); Bezahlung (f); Begleichung (f); Beilegung (f); Vergleich (m)

5398. **amicable settlement**

réglementation à l'amiable
transacción amigable
gütliche Beilegung

5399. **arbitral settlement**
règlement arbitral
arreglo arbitral
schiedsgerichtliche Beilegung

5400. **judicial settlement**
règlement judiciaire
arreglo judicial
gerichtlicher Vergleich

5401. **out-of-court settlement**
règlement extrajudiciaire
arreglo extrajudicial
aussergerichtlicher Vergleich

5402. **pacific settlement**
règlement pacifique
arreglo pacífico
friedliche Beilegung

5403. **to settle disputes**
régler les différends
arreglar disputas
Streitigkeiten beilegen oder schlichten

5404. **severance**
disjonction (f); séparation (f)
partición (f); separación (f)
Abbruch (m); Trennung (f)

5405. **shadow, to**
prendre en filature
espiar; seguir secretamente
(unbemerkt) überwachen

5406. **share**
action (f); part (f); portion (f)
acción (f); interés (m); participación (f)
Aktie (f); Anteil (m)

5407. **shareholder**
actionnaire (m)
accionista (m)
Aktionär (m)

5408. **to share**
partager; participer
compartir; repartir
teilen; teilnehmen

5409. **sheriff**
chef (m) de police d'un comté (m)
jefe (m) de policía de un condado (m)
Polizeichef (m) eines Bezirks (m) oder einer Gemeinde (f)

5410. **shipping**
expédition (f); navigation (f)
expedición (f); navegación (f)
Verladung (f); Schiffahrt (f)

5411. **ship**
navire (m); bateau (m)
nave (f); navío (m); barco (m)
Schiff (n)

5412. **shipment**
envoi (m); expédition (f)
embarque (m); envío (m)
Verladung (f); Verschiffung (f)

5413. **shipper**
expéditeur (m)
cargador (m); embarcador (m)
Verlader (m); Verschiffer (m)

5414. **shipwreck**
naufrage (m)
naufragio (m)
Schiffbruch (m)

5415. **to ship**
envoyer; transporter
despachar; expedir
verladen; verschiffen

5416. **shop**
boutique (f); magasin (m); atelier (m)
almacén (m); tienda (f); taller (m)
Geschäft (n); Laden (m); Betrieb (m); Werkstatt (f)

5417. **bucket shop**
officine (f) de paris (mpl) clandestins
oficina (f) clandestina de especulación (f) y apuestas (fpl)
Winkelbankgeschäft (n), wo Wetten (fpl) usw. abgeschlossen werden

5418. **closed shop**
monopole syndical
monopolio gremial
gewerkschaftsgebundener Betrieb

5419. **open shop**
entreprise ouverte à tous les travailleurs
empresa asequible a todos los trabajadores
gewerkschaftsfreier Betrieb

5420. **shoplifting**
vol (m) à l'étalage (m)
ratería (f) en las tiendas (fpl)

Ladendiebstahl (m)
5421. **shopkeeper**
boutiquier (m); commerçant (m)
almacenero (m); tendero (m)
Geschäftsinhaber (m); Ladeninhaber (m)
5422. **sweat shop**
atelier où les salaires sont insuffisants par rapport au travail
taller donde los pagos son insuficientes en relación con el trabajo
Ausbeutebetrieb
5423. **union shop**
entreprise qui n'embauche que des travailleurs qui s'engagent à adhérer au syndicat
empresa cuyo contrato colectivo exige la afiliación del contratado en el sindicato
Betrieb, der nur Arbeiter anstellt, die sich verpflichten, der Gewerkschaft beizutreten
5424. **shortage**
deficit (m); crise (f); pénurie (f)
deficit (m); falta (f); escasez (f)
Mangel (m); Knappheit (f)
5425. **housing shortage**
crise (f) de logement (m)
falta (f) de viviendas (fpl)
Wohnungsknappheit (f)
5426. **shot**
coup (m) de feu (m)
disparo (m); tiro (m)
Schuss (m)
5427. **to be shot**
être fusillé; recevoir une balle
ser fusilado; recibir un balazo
erschossen werden; eine Schusswunde erhalten
5428. **to shoot**
tirer
disparar
erschiessen
5429. **signatories; signatory parties**
signataires (mpl)
signatarios (mpl)
Unterzeichner (mpl)
5430. **signature**
signature (f)
firma (f)
Unterschrift (f)
5431. **signature in blank**
signature en blanc
firma en blanco
Blanko Unterschrift (f)
5432. **to sign**
signer
firmar
unterschreiben
5433. **similarity**
ressemblance (f)
semejanza (f); similitud (f)
ähnlichkeit (f)
5434. **similar**
pareil; semblable; similaire
similar; semejante
ähnlich; gleichartig
5435. **simple**
simple
simple
einfach
5436. **situation**
emploi (m); situation (f)
empleo (m); situación (f)
Stellung (f); Lage (f)
5437. **skyjacking** (see **highjacking**)
5438. **slacker**
tire-au-flanc (m)
haragán (m); gandul (m)
Drückeberger (m)
5439. **slander**
diffamation (f) verbale; injure (f) publique
calumnia (f) oral
mündliche Verleumdung (f); üble Nachrede (f)
5440. **slanderer**
diffamateur (m)
calumniador (m)
Verleumder (m)
5441. **slanderous**
diffamatoire; injurieux
calumnioso
verleumderisch
5442. **to slander**
diffamer; injurier
calumniar
verleumden
5443. **slavery**
esclavage (m)
esclavitud (f)
Sklaverei (f)

5444. **slave**
esclave (m)
esclavo (m)
Sklave (m)
5445. **white slavery**
traite des blanches (fpl)
trata (f) de blancas (fpl)
Mädchenhandel (m)
5446. **slayer**
meurtrier (m)
asesino (m)
Mörder (m)
5447. **sleuth**
détective (m); limier (m)
detective (m); sabueso (m)
Detektiv (m); Geheimpolizist (m)
5448. **slot machine**
appareil (m) à jetons (mpl)
máquina (f) traga-monedas
Spielautomat (m)
5449. **smuggling**
contrebande (f)
contrabando (m)
Schmuggel (m)
5450. **smuggler**
contrebandier (m)
contrabandista (m)
Schmuggler (m)
5451. **to smuggle**
passer en contrebande, en fraude
hacer, pasar de contrebando; pasar en fraude
schmuggeln
5452. **sneak-thief**
chapardeur (m)
ratero (m)
Gelegenheitsdieb (m)
5453. **socialist**
socialiste
socialista
Sozialist; sozialistisch
5454. **society**
société (f)
sociedad (f)
Gesellschaft (f)
5455. **sodomy** (see **bestiality**)
5456. **solicitation**
sollicitation (f)
solicitación (f)
Anliegen (n); Verleitung (f)
5457. **solicitor**
avoué (m) avec fonctions de notaire
procurador (m)
nichtplädierender Anwalt (m)
5458. **solicitor general**
conseiller (m) juridique (du Ministre de la Justice, U.S.A.); (de la Couronne, U.K.)
asesor (m) jurídico (del Ministro de Justicia, U.S.A.); de la Corona, U.K.)
Rechtsberater (m) im Justizministerium (U.S.A.), Kronanwalt (U.K.)
5459. **solvency**
solvabilité (f)
solvencia (f)
Zahlungsfähigkeit (f)
5460. **solvent**
solvable
solvente
zahlungsfähig
5461. **source**
source (f)
fuente (f); origen (m)
Quelle (f)
5462. **sovereignty**
souveraineté
soberanía (f)
Souveränität (f)
5463. **sovereign**
souverain (m)
soberano (m)
Souverän (n)
5464. **space**
espace (m)
espacio (m)
Raum (m)
5465. **outer space**
milieu (m) spatial
espacio (m) sideral
Weltraum (m)
5466. **speaker**
orateur (m)
orador (m)
Sprecher (m)
5467. **keynote speaker**
orateur principal
orador principal
Hauptredner
5468. **Speaker of the House** (U.S.A.)
Président de la Chambre

Presidente de la Cámara
Präsident des Unterhauses
5469. **to recognize (the speaker)**
donner la parole
dar la palabra
das Wort erteilen
5470. **specialty**
spécialité (f)
especialidad (f)
Spezialität (f)
5471. **special**
spécial
especial
speziell
5472. **specialist**
spécialiste (m)
especialista (m)
Fachmann (m); Spezialist (m)
5473. **specialization**
spécialisation (f)
especialización (f)
Spezialisierung (f)
5474. **to specialize**
spécialiser
especializar
spezialisieren
5475. **specie**
numéraire (m)
numerario (m)
Hartgeld (n)
5476. **specification**
spécification (f)
especificación (f)
Spezifikation (f)
5477. **specific**
spécifique
específico
spezifisch
5478. **to specify**
spécifier; préciser
especificar
bezeichnen; zur Bedingung machen
5479. **speculation**
spéculation (f)
especulación (f)
Spekulation (f)
5480. **speculator**
spéculateur (m)
especulador (m)
Spekulant (m)
5481. **to speculate**
spéculer
especular
spekulieren
5482. **speech**
discours (m)
discurso (m)
Rede (f)
5483. **after-dinner speech**
discours de table (f)
discurso de sobremesa (f)
Tischrede (f)
5484. **closing speech**
discours de clôture (f)
discurso de clausura (f)
Schlussansprache (f)
5485. **free speech** (see **freedom of speech**)
5486. **maiden speech**
discours de début (m)
primer discurso (m)
Antrittsrede (f)
5487. **opening speech**
discours inaugural
discurso inaugural
Eröffnungsrede
5488. **to deliver, to make a speech**
prononcer un discours
pronunciar un discurso
eine Rede halten
5489. **to speak**
parler
hablar
sprechen
5490. **spendthrift**
prodigue
pródigo
verschwenderisch
5491. **spirit**
élan (m); esprit (m); vigueur (f)
ánimo (m); energía (f); espíritu (m)
Geist (m)
5492. **spoliation**
spoliation (f)
espoliación (f)
Plünderung (f); unberechtigte Abänderung (f) einer Urkunde (f)
5493. **sponsorship**
patronage (m)

patrocinio (m)
Patronat (n); Förderung (f); Schirmherrschaft (f)

5494. **sponsor**
parrain (m); garant (m)
patrocinador (m); padrino (m)
Schirmherr (m); Förderer (m)

5495. **to sponsor**
patronner; se porter garant
patrocinar; apadrinar
fördern

5496. **spouse**
épouse (f); époux (m)
esposa (f); esposo (m)
Ehegattin (f); Ehegatte (m)

5497. **spurious**
contrefait; falsifié; faux
adulterado; espurio; no genuino
unecht; gefälscht

5498. **spy**
espion (m)
espía (m)
Spion (m)

5499. **to spy**
espionner
espiar
spionieren

5500. **staff**
état-major (m); personnel (m)
estado (m) mayor; personal (m)
Stab (m); Personal (n)

5501. **standard**
mesure (f); modèle (m); standard (m)
criterio (m); norma (f); medida (f)
Massstab (m); Richtschnur (f); Standard (m)

5502. **gold standard**
étalon-or (m)
patrón (m) de oro (m)
Goldstandard (m)

5503. **standard of living**
niveau (m) de vie (f)
nivel (m) de vida (f)
Lebensstandard (m)

5504. **standardization**
standardisation (f)
normalización (f)
Normung (f); Standardisierung (f)

5505. **standing**
importance (f); rang (m); situation (f)
crédito (m); posición (f); reputación (f)
Rang (m); Stellung (f)

5506. **state**
Etat (m); état (m)
Estado (m); condición (f)
Staat (m); Zustand (m)

5507. **buffer state**
Etat tampon
Estado entre dos países rivales
Pufferstaat

5508. **confederate state** (see **confederation**)

5509. **federal state**
Etat fédéral
Estado federal
Bundesstaat

5510. **head of state**
chef d'Etat
jefe del Estado
Staatsoberhaupt

5511. **police state**
Etat de police
Estado de policía
Polizeistaat

5512. **riparian state**
Etat riverain
Estado ribereño
Uferstaat

5513. **sovereign state**
Etat souverain
Estado soberano
souveräner Staat

5514. **state machinery**
administration (f); rouages (mpl) de l'Etat
administración (f); maquinaria (f) del Estado
Staatsapparat (n); Staatsverwaltung (f)

5515. **state of mind**
disposition (f), état (m) d'esprit (m)
estado (m) de ánimo (m)
Geisteszustand (m)

5516. **state of origin**
Etat, pays d'origine
Estado, país de nacimiento, origen
Heimatstaat

5517. **statement**
constatation (f); déclaration (f); exposé (m); rapport (m)
constatación (f); declaración (f); informe (m); reporte (m)
Angabe (f); Feststellung (f); Behauptung (f); Bericht (m)

5518. **audited statement**
bilan (m) vérifié
cuenta (f) certificada
geprüfte Rechnung

5519. **bank statement**
état de compte (m)
extracto de cuenta (f)
Bankausweis (m)

5520. **closing, final statement**
déclaration finale; conclusions
declaración final; conclusiones
Schlussplaidoyer

5521. **false statement**
faux rapport
estado falsificado
falsche Angabe

5522. **opening statement**
exposé introductif
declaración inaugural
Eröffnungsansprache

5523. **statement of the defense**
exposé des moyens de la défense; plaidoirie
declaración de la defensa
Vorbringen der Verteidigung

5524. **statement of the prosecution**
exposé des moyens de l'accusation; requisitoire
declaración de la acusación
Vorbringen der Anklage

5525. **sworn statement**
déclaration sous serment
declaración jurada
eidliche Erklärung

5526. **to prove the truth of one's statement**
prouver la vérité d'une déclaration
demostrar la verdad de una declaración
den Wahrheitsbeweis antreten

5527. **to state**
affirmer; constater; dire
constatar; declarar; informar
feststellen; darlegen; erklären

5528. **statistics**
statistique (f)
estadística (f)
Statistik (f)

5529. **vital statistics**
statistiques de l'état civil
estadísticas del estado civil
Bevölkerungsstatistik

5530. **status**
état (m); rang (m); statut (m)
estado (m); posición (f)
Stand (m); Status (m); Zustand (m)

5531. **civil status**
état civil
registro civil
Personenstand

5532. **legal status**
statut légal, juridique
estado legal
Rechtslage

5533. **official status**
titre officiel
estado oficial
offizieller Status

5534. **statute**
statut (m)
estatuto (m)
Statut (n); Gesetz (n)

5535. **disabling statute**
statut qui restreint l'exercice d'un droit
ley que restringe el ejercicio de un derecho
Gesetz, das die Ausübung eines bestimmten Rechtes reguliert

5536. **Statute of Frauds**
Statut contre Fraudes
Ley contra Fraudes
Gesetz zur Vermeidung von Arglist und Betrag

5537. **Statute of Limitations**
Loi de Prescription
Ley de Prescripción
Verjährungsgesetz; Verjährungsfrist

5538. **Statutes at Large (U.S.A.)**
Recueil annuel d'Actes du Congrès
Compilación de Leyes del Congreso
Bundesgesetzblatt

5539. **statutory**
statutaire
estatutario
gesetzlich
5540. **to come under the Statute of Limitations**
être forclos
estar sujeto a la Ley de Prescripción
verjähren
5541. **steal, to**
voler
robar
stehlen
5542. **step**
démarche (f)
gestión (f)
Schritt (m)
5543. **steps**
mesures (fpl)
medios (mpl)
Massnahmen (fpl)
5544. **appropriate steps**
mesures utiles
medidas útiles
geeignete Massnahmen
5545. **to take steps**
faire des démarches
hacer gestiones
Massnahmen ergreifen oder treffen
5546. **stigmatization**
flétrissure (f); mise (f) à l'index (m)
estigmatización (f)
Brandmarkung (f)
5547. **to stigmatize**
flétrir; stigmatiser
estigmatizar
brandmarken; stigmatisieren
5548. **stipulation**
stipulation (f)
estipulación (f)
Bedingung (f); Übereinkommen (n)
5549. **stipulated**
spécifié; stipulé
específico; estipulado
vereinbart
5550. **to stipulate**
stipuler
estipular
Übereinkommen; stipulieren; ausbedingen
5551. **stock**
actions (fpl); fonds (m)
acción (f); fuente (f)
Aktien (fpl)
5552. **common stock**
actions ordinaires
acción común, ordinaria
Stammaktien
5553. **preferred stock**
actions de préférence, privilégiées
acción preferente
Vorzugsaktien
5554. **stock exchange**
bourse (f) d'effets (mpl), des valeurs (fpl)
bolsa (f) de valores (mpl)
Börse (f)
5555. **stockbroker**
agent (m) de change; courtier (m) en valeurs
corredor (m) de bolsa
Börsenmakler (m)
5556. **stockholder**
actionnaire (m)
accionista (m)
Aktionär (m)
5557. **watered stock**
capital dilué
capital diluido
verwässertes Kapital
5558. **stool pigeon**
délateur (m); indicateur (m) de police (f); mouchard (m)
soplón (m); espía (m) de la policía (f)
Spitzel (m)
5559. **stoppage in transitu**
arrêt de marchandises en cours de transit
embargo de mercancías durante su transporte
Aufhalten verschiffter Waren auf dem Transport
5560. **stowage**
arrimage (m); magasinage (m)
arrumaje (m); estiba (f)
Verstauung (f); Stauerlohn (m)
5561. **stratagem**
stratagème (m)

estratagema (m)
List (f); Kriegslist (f)

5562. **straw man** (see **man of straw**)

5563. **street walker**
fille (f) publique
prostituta (f) de calle (f)
Strassendirne (f); Prostituierte (f)

5564. **stress**
emphase (f); importance (f); tension (f)
énfasis (m); importancia (f); tensión (f)
Betonung (f); Nachdruck (m)

5565. **to stress**
souligner
subrayar; hacer hincapié en
betonen; unterstreichen; hervorheben

5566. **strike**
grève (f)
huelga (f)
Streik (m); Ausstand (m)

5567. **right to strike**
droit de grève
derecho a la huelga
Streikrecht

5568. **strike-breaker**
renard; jaune
esquirol
Streikbrecher

5569. **general strike**
grève générale
huelga general
Generalstreik

5570. **sit-down strike**
grève des bras croisés; grève sur le tas
huelga de brazos caídos
Sitzstreik

5571. **slow-down strike**
grève perlée
huelga de trabajo lento
Arbeitsverlangsamung

5572. **strikers**
grévistes (mpl)
huelguistas (mpl)
Streiker (mpl)

5573. **wildcat strike**
grève non contrôlée
huelga no oficial
wilder Streik

5574. **to call a strike**
décréter la grève
declarar una huelga
einen Streik ausrufen

5575. **to go on strike; to strike**
faire la grève; se mettre en grève
declararse en huelga
streiken

5576. **to strike off, out**
biffer; rayer
suprimir
ausstreichen

5577. **subheading; subhead**
sous-titre (m)
subtítulo (m)
Untertitel (m)

5578. **subject**
sujet (m)
sujeto (m)
Gegenstand (m)

5579. **subject matter**
contenu (m)
asunto (m)
Inhalt (m); Thema (n)

5580. **subjugation**
subjugation (f)
subyugación (f)
Unterwerfung (f)

5581. **to subjugate**
subjuguer
subyugar
unterwerfen

5582. **subletting**
sous-location (f)
subarrendamiento (m)
Untervermietung (f)

5583. **to sublet**
sous-louer
subarrendar
untervermieten

5584. **submission**
soumission (f)
sometimiento (m)
Unterwerfung (f)

5585. **to submit**
soumettre; présenter
someter; presentar
vorlegen; beantragen

5586. **to submit to**
soumettre à
someter a
gehorchen; sich fügen

5587. **subordination**
subordination (f)
subordinación (f)
Unterstellung (f); Unterordnung (f)

5588. **subordinate**
subalterne; subordonné
subordinado
Untergebener; untergeordnet

5589. **to subordinate**
subordonner
subordinar
unterordnen

5589a. **subpoena**
avertissement (m)
apercibimiento (m)
Gerichtsvorladung (f) unter Strafandrohung (f)

5590. **subrogation**
subrogation (f)
subrogación (f)
Subrogation (f); Forderungsübergang (m)

5591. **to subrogate**
subroger
subrogar
ersetzen

5592. **subsequent**
subséquent
subsecuente
folgend; nachträglich

5593. **subsequently**
subséquemment
posteriormente; subsiguientemente
später; nachher

5594. **subsidiary**
subsidiaire
subsidiario
Hilfs-

5595. **subsidy**
subside (m); subvention (f)
subsidio (m); subvención (f)
staatliche Beihilfe (f); Subvention (f)

5596. **to subsidize**
subventionner
subvencionar
subventionieren

5597. **subsistence**
subsistance (f)
subsistencia (f)
Existenzmittel (npl)

5598. **substantial**
considérable; important; réel; substantiel
apreciable; considerable; importante; sustancial
ansehnlich; wesentlich; wirklich

5599. **substantiate, to**
conformer; établir; prouver
confirmar; establecer; probar
begründen; dartun; substantiieren

5600. **substantive**
de fond; réel
real; substantivo
wesentlich

5601. **substitution**
remplacement (m); substitution (f)
su(b)stitución (f); reemplazo (m)
Substituierung (f); Ersetzung (f)

5602. **substitute**
remplaçant (m); substitut (m); suppléant (m)
su(b)stituto (m); suplente (m)
Stellvertreter (m); Substitut (m)

5603. **to substitute**
substituer; suppléer
su(b)stituir; reemplazar
substituieren; ersetzen

5604. **subvention**
subvention (f)
subvención (f)
Subvention (f); Unterstützung (f)

5605. **subversion**
subversion (f)
subversión (f)
Umsturz (m); Subversion (f)

5606. **subversive**
subversif
subversivo
umstürzerisch; subversiv

5607. **to subvert**
subvertir
subvertir
umstürzen

5608. **succession**
héritage (m); succession (f)
herencia (f); sucesión (f)
Erbschaft (f); Nachfolge (f)

5609. **state succession**
succession d'Etat

sucesión estatal
Staatensukzession

5610. **successor**
successeur (m)
sucesor (m)
Nachfolger (m)

5611. **to succeed**
succéder
heredar; suceder
nachfolgen

5612. **sufferance**
consentement (m); tolérance (f)
consentimiento (m); tolerancia (f)
Einwilligung (f); Duldung (f)

5613. **suffrage**
suffrage (m)
sufragio (m)
Wahlrecht (n)

5614. **suggestion**
proposition (f); suggestion (f)
proposición (f); sugestión (f)
Anregung (f); Vorschlag (m)

5615. **to suggest**
proposer; suggérer
proponer; sugerir
anregen; vorschlagen

5616. **suicide**
suicide (m)
suicidio (m)
Selbstmord (m)

5617. **attempt to commit suicide**
tentative de suicide
tentativa de suicidarse
Selbstmordversuch

5618. **suit**
action (f); procès (m); poursuite (f)
acción (f); litigio (m); pleito (m); proceso (m)
Klage (f); Prozess (m); Rechtssache (f)

5619. **immunity from suit**
exception (f) de juridiction (f)
excepción (f) de jurisdicción (f)
zivilrechtliche Immunität (f)

5620. **libel suit**
action en diffamation
proceso por difamación
Ehrenbeleidigungsklage; Verleumdungsklage

5621. **multiplicity of suits**
multiplicité des poursuites
multiplicidad de acciones judiciales
mehrere Klagen, die in rechtlichem oder tatsächlichem Zusammenhang stehen

5622. **vexatious suit** (see **malicious prosecution**)

5623. **to bring suit**
intenter des poursuites
entablar pleito
gerichtlich belangen

5624. **to sue**
intenter une action; ester, poursuivre en justice
entablar juicio contra; pedir en juicio; demandar
gerichtlich belangen; klagen

5625. **sum**
somme (f)
suma (f)
Summe (f)

5626. **lump sum**
somme globale, forfaitaire
suma global
runde Summe

5627. **total sum; sum total**
montant global
cifra; suma total
Gesamtsumme

5628. **summary**
abrégé (m); résumé (m); sommaire (m)
resumen (m); sumario (m)
kurze Übersicht (f); Zusammenfassung (f)

5629. **to summarize**
résumer
resumir
zusammenfassen

5630. **summation**
résumé (m) des charges (fpl)
escrito (m) de conclusiones (fpl)
Schlussrede (f) des Anklägers (m); Resumé (n)

5631. **summing up**
récapitulation (f); résumé des débats
recapitulación (f)
Zusammenfassung (f) der Ergebnisse (npl) der Verhandlung (f)

5632. **to sum up**
résumer
resumir
zusammenfassen; resümieren
5633. **summons** (see **writ of summons**)
5634. **to serve a summons**
remettre une citation
entregar una citación
eine Ladung zustellen
5635. **to summon**
assigner; citer
citar; notificar
laden; vorladen
5636. **supersedeas** (see **writ of supersedeas**)
5637. **supersede, to**
annuler; remplacer
invalidar; reemplazar; sobreseer
abschaffen; ersetzen
5638. **supervision**
supervision (f); surveillance (f)
superintendencia (f); supervisión (f)
Aufsicht (f); Überwachung (f)
5639. **supervisor**
surveillant (m)
supervisor (m)
Aufseher (m)
5640. **supervisory**
de surveillance
relativo a superintendencia
Aufsichts-
5641. **to supervise**
superviser; surveiller
intervenir; superentender
beaufsichtigen
5642. **supplement**
addition; supplément
suplemento
Nachtrag
5643. **supplemental**
supplémentaire
suplementario
ergänzend
5644. **to supplement**
amplifier; compléter
completar; suplementar
vervollständigen; ergänzen
5645. **supplies**
approvisionnements; fournitures; ravitaillement
abasto; existencias; provisiones; pertrechos
Lieferungen; Materalien; Nachschub; Vorräte
5646. **to supply**
approvisionner; fournir; ravitailler
abastecer; proveer; suministrar
liefern; versehen mit
5647. **support**
appui (m); soutien (m); support (m)
apoyo (m)
Beistand (m); Unterhalt (m); Unterstützung (f)
5648. **in support of**
à l'appui de; en aide à; en faveur de
en apoyo, favor de
zur Bekräftigung oder Unterstützung; zu Gunsten
5649. **to support**
soutenir
apoyar; sostener
unterstützen
5650. **suppression**
suppression (f)
supresión (f)
Unterdrückung (f)
5651. **to suppress**
supprimer
suprimir
unterdrücken
5652. **supremacy**
suprématie (f)
supremacía (f)
höchste Gewalt (f); die Herrschaft (f) über
5653. **supreme**
suprême
supremo
höchst; oberst
5654. **surcharge**
supplément (m); surcharge (f)
recargo (m); sobretasa (f)
Aufgeld (n); Zuschlag (m)
5655. **suretyship**
cautionnement (m)
seguridad (f)
Bürgschaft (f)
5656. **surety**

caution (f); garant (m); porte-fort (m); sûreté (f)
caución (f); fiador (m); fianza (f); garantía (f)
Kaution (f); Bürge (m); Bürgerschaft (f); Sicherheit (f)

5657. **surplus**
excédents (mpl); surcroît (m); surplus (m)
excedentes (mpl); demasía (f); sobrante (m)
Überschuss (m)

5658. **surplusage**
allégations (fpl) superflues
alegaciones (fpl) superfluas o impertinentes
unwesentlicher Umstand (m)

5659. **surrebutter**
réponse (f) à la réplique à la triplique
respuesta (f) a la contrarréplica a la tríplica
Quintuplik (f)

5660. **surrejoinder**
triplique (f)
tríplica (f)
Triplik (f); Gegenerwiderung (f)

5661. **surrender**
abandon (m); dessaisissement (m); reddition (f); remise (f)
capitulación (f); cesión (f); rendición (f); sumisión (f)
Aufgabe (f); Abtretung (f); Übergabe (f)

5662. **unconditional surrender**
reddition sans condition
rendición incondicional
bedingungslose Übergabe

5663. **to surrender**
abandonner; remettre; se rendre
capitular; ceder; rendirse
sich ergeben oder stellen; (sich) übergeben

5664. **surtax**
surtaxe (f)
recargo (m)
Steuerzuschlag (m)

5665. **survey**
enquête (f); examen (m); inspection (f)
estudio (m); examen (m); inspección (f)
Erhebung (f); Uberprüfung (f); Übersicht (f)

5666. **to make a survey**
examiner
hacer una inspección
eine Erhebung anstellen; eine Übersicht geben

5667. **survivorship**
survie (f)
supervivencia (f)
Überleben (n)

5668. **survivor**
survivant (m)
superviviente (m, f)
Überlebender (m)

5669. **suspension**
levée (f); suspension (f)
suspensión (f)
Aufschub (m); Aussetzung (f)

5670. **to suspend**
suspendre
suspender
aufschieben; aussetzen

5671. **suspicion**
soupçon (m); suspicion (f)
sospecha (f)
Argwohn (m); Verdacht (m)

5672. **reasonable grounds for suspicion**
raisons justifiées de suspicion
motivos fundados de sospecha
hinreichende Verdachtsgründe

5673. **suspect**
suspect (m)
sospechoso (m)
Verdächtigter (m)

5674. **to suspect**
suspecter; soupçonner
sospechar
verdächtigen

5675. **sustain, to**
soutenir
sostener
unterhalten

5676. **suzerainty**
suzeraineté (f)
soberanía (f)
Oberherrschaft (f); Suzeränität (f)

5677. **suzerain**
suzerain (m)
soberano (m)
Suzerän (m)

5678. **swindling**
escroquerie (f); fraude (f)
estafa (f); timo (m)
Betrügerei (f); Schwindelei (f)

5679. **swindler**
escroc (m); filou (m)
estafador (m); timador (m)
Betrüger (m); Schwindler (m)

5680. **to swindle**
escroquer
estafar; timar
betrügen; schwindeln

5681. **symposium**
colloque (m); conférence (f)
simposio (m); conferencia (f)
Symposium (n); Konferenz (f)

5682. **syndicate**
syndicat (m)
sindicato (m)
Syndikat (n)

5683. **synonymous**
synonyme
sinónimo
synonym; sinnverwandt

5684. **system**
système (m)
sistema (m)
System (n)

5685. **bicameral system**
système bicaméral
sistema bicameral
Zweikammersystem

5686. **case system**
enseignement de droit par l'étude de précédents
enseñanza de derecho mediante el estudio de precedentes
juristische Lehrmethode durch Studium von Präzedenzfällen

5687. **electoral system**
système électoral
sistema electoral
Wahlsystem

5688. **legal system**
régime (m) juridique
régimen (m) jurídico
Rechtssystem (n)

5689. **monetary system**
système monétaire
sistema monetario
Wahrungssystem

5690. **quota system**
contingentement (m)
sistema (m) de cuotas (fpl)
Kontingentierungssystem (n)

5691. **system of government**
système de gouvernement
sistema de gobierno
Regierungsform

T

5692. **table**
tableau (m)
cuadro (m)
Tafel (f)

5693. **conference table**
table de la conférence
mesa de conferencia
Konferenztisch

5694. **tacit**
tacite
tácito
stillschweigend

5695. **taint**
corruption (f)
corrupción (f)
Makel (m)

5696. **talesman**
juré (m) suppléant
jurado (m) suplente
Ersatzgeschworener (m)

5697. **tangible**
tangible
tangible
materiell

5698. **tantamount**
équivalent
equivalente
gleichwertig; gleichbedeutend mit

5698a. **tape**

ruban (m); bande (f) magnétique
cinta (f) magnetofónica
Tonband (n)

5699. **tariff**
tarif (m); tarif douanier
derecho (m) aduanero; arancel (m)
Zolltarif (m)

5700. **preferential tariff**
tarif préférentiel
aranceles preferenciales
Präferenzzoll; Vorzugszoll

5701. **protective tariff**
tarif protecteur
arancel proteccionista
Schutzzoll

5702. **tax**
impôt (m); contribution (f); taxe (f)
impuesto (m); contribución (f)
Steuer (f); Abgabe (f)

5703. **corporation tax**
impôt sur les sociétés
impuesto a las sociedades de capital
Körperschaftssteuer

5704. **direct tax**
impôt direct; contribution directe
impuesto directo
direkte Steuer

5705. **estate tax**
impôt successoral, sur les successions
impuesto de sucesión
Nachlassteuer

5706. **excess profits tax**
impôt sur les bénéfices exceptionnels
impuesto sobre ganancias excesivas
Mehrgewinnsteuer

5707. **excise tax**
impôt indirect; droits d'accise
impuesto al consumo
Verbrauchssteuer

5708. **exemption from tax; tax exemption**
exemption fiscale; franchise de taxe
exención tributaria
Steuerfreiheit

5709. **income tax**
impôt sur le revenu
impuesto sobre la renta
Einkommensteuer

5710. **indirect tax**
impôt indirect; contributions indirectes
impuesto indirecto
indirekte Steuer

5711. **inheritance tax**
droits de succession; impôt sur les successions
impuesto de sucesión, sobre la herencia
Erbschaftssteuer

5712. **land tax**
impôt foncier
contribución territorial; impuesto a los precios
Grundsteuer

5713. **luxury tax**
taxe de luxe
impuesto suntuario
Luxussteuer

5714. **poll tax; head tax**
capitation (f)
capitación (f)
Kopfsteuer (f)

5715. **progressive tax**
impôt progressif
impuesto progresivo
Progressivsteuer

5716. **sales tax**
impôt sur les ventes, sur le chiffre d'affaires
impuesto sobre la venta
Umsatzsteuer

5717. **tax bracket**
tranche (f) du barême fiscal
grupo (m) impositivo
Steuergruppe (f)

5718. **tax collector**
percepteur (m); receveur (m) des contributions
recaudador (m) de impuestos
Steuereinnehmer (m)

5719. **taxable**
imposable
imponible; gravable
steuerpflichtig

5720. **taxpayer**
contribuable (m)

contribuyente (m)
Steuerzahler (m)

5721. **to collect a tax**
percevoir un impôt
cobrar, recaudar un impuesto
Steuern eintreiben

5722. **to levy taxes**
lever des taxes
gravar impuestos
Steuern erheben

5723. **to pay taxes**
payer des impôts
pagar impuestos
Steuern zahlen

5724. **to tax**
frapper d'une taxe
imponer contribuciones; tasar
besteuern

5725. **taxation**
charge (f) fiscale; imposition (f); taxation (f); prélèvement (m)
fijación (f) de impuestos
Besteuerung (f)

5726. **double taxation**
double imposition
doble imposición, tributación
Doppelbesteuerung

5727. **technicality**
formalité; technicité (f)
formalidad (f); tecnicismo (m)
Formalität (f); technische Eigentümlichkeit (f)

5728. **technical**
technique
técnico
technisch

5729. **teller (of votes)**
scrutateur (m)
escrutador (m)
Stimmenzähler (m)

5730. **paying teller**
caissier (m) payeur
cajero (m) pagador
Auszahlungskassier (m)

5731. **receiving teller**
caissier (m) encaisseur
cajero (m) cobrador
Einzahlungskassier (m)

5732. **temporary**
temporaire
temporal
einstweilig; zeitlich

5733. **tenable**
soutenable; tenable
defendible; sostenible
haltbar

5734. **tenancy**
[durée (f) du] bail (m); location (f)
[tiempo (m) de] arrendamiento (m)
Miete (f) [-zeit] (f); Pacht (f) [-zeit (f)]

5735. **joint tenancy**
co-propriété (f)
condominio (m)
gemeinsamer Besitz, Miteigentum

5736. **sub-tenant**
sous-locataire (m)
sub-inquilino (m)
Untermieter (m); Unterpächter (m)

5737. **tenancy at will**
location résiliable à volonté
arrendamiento cancelable en cualquier momento
jederzeit kündbare Miete oder Pacht

5738. **tenancy by the entirety**
co-propriété des époux
condominio de matrimonio
Gemeinschaftsbesitz der Ehegatten

5739. **tenancy in common**
propriété indivise
tenencia en común
Gemeinschaftsbesitz

5740. **tenant**
locataire (m)
arrendatario (m); inquilino (m)
Mieter (m); Pächter (m)

5741. **tender**
offre (f); soumission (f)
oferta (f); ofrecimiento (m)
Angebot (n); Zahlungsangebot (n)

5742. **legal tender**
monnaie (f) légale
moneda (f) de curso (m) legal
gesetzliches Zahlungsmittel (n)

5743. **to tender**
faire une offre; soumettre
ofrecer; presentar

als Erfüllung anbieten
5744. **tenement**
immeuble (m) locatif; fonds (m) de terre
casa (f) de vecindad (f); heredamiento (m)
Miethaus (n); Grundstück (n)
5745. **dominant tenement**
fonds dominant
predio dominante
herrschendes, berechtigtes Grundstück
5746. **servient tenement**
fonds servant
predio sirviente
dienendes Grundstück
5747. **tenet**
doctrine (f); dogme (m); principe (m)
credo (m); dogma (m); principio (m)
Grundsatz (m); Dogma (n)
5748. **tenor**
contenu (m); portée (f); teneur (f)
contenido (m); tenor (m)
Tenor (m); Wesen (n)
5749. **tension**
tension (f)
tensión (f)
Spannung (f)
5750. **tentative**
provisoire; tentatif
tentativo
vorläufig; versuchsweise
5751. **tenure**
durée (f) du mandat (m); tenure (f)
duración (f) del mandato (m); tenencia (f)
Besitzdauer (f); Amtsdauer (f); Pachtdauer (f)
5752. **land tenure**
régime (m) foncier
terratenencia (f)
Pacht (f)
5753. **term**
terme (m)
término (m)
Amtsperiode (f); Frist (f)
5754. **for a long term**
à longue échéance; à long terme
a largo plazo
langfristig
5755. **for a short term**
à courte échéance; à court terme
a corto plazo
kurzfristig
5756. **term of office**
durée des fonctions (fpl)
período del cargo (m)
Amtszeit (f)
5757. **terms of a treaty**
texte (m) d'un traité (m)
texto (m) de un tratado (m)
Bestimmungen (fpl), Text (m) eines Vertrags (m)
5758. **terms of reference**
stipulations (fpl) d'un mandat (m); délimitation (f) du sujet (m) d'une enquête (f)
instrucciones (fpl) de un mandato (m)
Leitsätze (mpl); Bestimmung (f) des Gegenstandes (m) einer Untersuchung (f); Aufgabenkreis (m)
5759. **unexpired term of office**
mandat non expiré
mandato inconcluso
noch nicht abgelaufene Amtzeit
5760. **termination**
cessation (f); extinction (f); fin (f)
expiración (f); fin (m); terminación (f)
Ende (n); Erlöschen (n)
5761. **to terminate**
mettre fin
terminar; poner término
aufhören; beenden
5762. **terminology**
terminologie (f)
terminología (f)
Terminologie (f)
5763. **legal terminology**
terminologie juridique
terminología jurídica
Rechtssprache (f)

5764. **territorial waters** (see **marginal sea**)
5765. **territory**
domaine (m); territoire (m)
región (f); territorio (m)
Gebiet (n)
5766. **occupied territory**
territoire occupé; zone occupée
territorio ocupado; zona ocupada
besetztes Gebiet
5767. **trust territory**
territoire sous tutelle
territorio bajo fideicomiso
Treuhandgebiet
5768. **test**
épreuve (f)
ensayo (m); prueba (f)
Probe (f); Versuch (m)
5769. **to test**
mettre à l'épreuve
ensayar; probar
prüfen
5770. **testament**
testament (m)
testamento (m)
letztwillige Verfügung (f); Testament (n)
5771. **testamentary**
testamentaire
testamentario
letztwillig; testamentarisch
5772. **testate**
succession (f) avec testament
testado
unter Hinterlassung einer letztwilligen Verfügung, eines Testaments
5773. **testator**
testateur (m)
testador (m)
Erblasser (m)
5774. **testimony**
témoignage (m)
testimonio (m)
Zeugnis (n); Zeugenaussage (f); Aussage (f)
5775. **expert testimony**
témoignage d'expert (m)
dictamen pericial de experto (m)
Aussage eines Sachverständigen (m)
5776. **false testimony**
faux témoignage
falso testimonio
falsches Zeugnis
5777. **testimony for the defense**
témoignage à décharge (f)
testimonio de la defensa (f)
Aussage der Entlastungszeugen (mpl)
5778. **testimony for the prosecution**
témoignage à charge (f)
testimonio de la acusación (f)
Aussage der Belastungszeugen (mpl)
5779. **testimony of witnesses**
déposition (f) des témoins (mpl)
declaración (f) de testigos (mpl)
Zeugenaussage (f)
5780. **to testify**
témoigner
testificar
Zeugnis ablegen; aussagen
5781. **text**
texte (m)
texto (m)
Text (m); Wortlaut (m)
5782. **annotated text**
texte avec commentaire, commenté
texto comentado
Text mit Anmerkungen
5783. **original text**
version originale
texto original
Originalfassung
5784. **theft**
vol (m)
robo (m)
Diebstahl (m)
5785. **thief**
voleur (m)
ladrón (m)
Dieb (m)
5786. **theme**
sujet (m); thème (m)
asunto (m); tema (m)
Gegenstand (m); Thema (n)
5787. **theory**
théorie (f)
teoría (f)

Theorie (f)

5788. **theory of the case**
base (f) juridique d'un procès (m)
base (f) jurídica del caso (m)
Rechtsgrundlage (f)

5789. **third degree**
interrogatoire (m) sous torture (f)
interrogatorio (m) bajo tortura (f)
Zwangsmassnahmen (fpl), um einen Beschuldigten zum Geständnis (n) zu bringen

5790. **threat**
menace (f)
amenaza (f)
Drohung (f)

5791. **threatening letter**
lettre (f) de menaces
carta (f) amenazadora
Drohbrief (m)

5792. **to threaten**
menacer
amenazar
drohen

5793. **thumbprint**
empreinte (f) du pouce (m)
impresión (f) del pulgar (m)
Daumenabdruck (m)

5794. **ticket**
avis (m) de contravention (f); billet (m); liste (f) électoral
multa (f); billete (m); entrada (f); lista (f) electoral
Straf; Einlasskarte (f); Fahrkarte (f); Wahl (f); Kandidatenliste (f)

5795. **time**
période (f); temps (m)
período (m); tiempo (m); vez (f)
Frist (f); Zeit (f)

5796. **extension of time**
prorogation (f) de délai (m)
prórroga (f) del plazo (m), término (m)
Fristverlängerung (f)

5797. **lapse of time**
intervalle (m), laps (m) de temps
transcurso (m) del tiempo
Zeitablauf (m)

5798. **time-limit**
délai (m)
demora (f)
Frist (f)

5799. **tithe**
dime (f)
diezmo (m)
Zehnt (m)

5800. **title**
titre (m)
título (m)
Titel (m)

5801. **abstract of title**
extrait d'un titre de propriété
copia de título de propiedad
Auszug aus den Besitztitelurkunden

5802. **bad title**
titre défectueux, sans valeur
título defectuoso, imperfecto
mangelhafter Rechtsanspruch

5803. **chain of title**
succession de titres
títulos sucesivos
vollkommener Eigentumsnachweis auf Grund von Dokumenten

5804. **clear, good title**
titre incontestable
título seguro, inobjetable
einwandfreier Rechtstitel

5805. **cloud on title**
réclamation (f) affectant le titre d'un bien
imperfección (f) del título
Rechtsmangel (m), welcher das volle Eigentum an Grundbesitz in Frage stellt oder einschränkt.

5806. **honorary title**
titre honoraire
título honorífico
Ehrentitel

5807. **inchoate title**
titre non parfait
título en trámite
potentieller oder in Entstehung begriffener Rechtsanspruch

5808. **transfer of title**
transfert (m) de la propriété
traslación (f) de dominio
Übertragung (f) eines Rechtes

5809. **toleration**
tolérance (f)

tolerancia (f)
Duldung (f)

5810. **to tolerate**
supporter; tolérer
tolerar
dulden

5811. **toll**
péage (m)
peaje (m)
Strassen oder Brückenbenutzungsabgabe (f); Maut (f)

5812. **topic**
question (f); sujet (m)
asunto (m); materia (f); tópico (m)
Thema (n); Gegenstand (m)

5813. **tort**
préjudice (m); tort (m); dommage (m) extra-contractuel; délit (m)
agravio (m); daño (m) legal extracontractual; delito (m)
unerlaubte Handlung (f); Delikt (n)

5814. **quasi tort**
quasi-délit
cuasidelito
Quasidelikt

5815. **tortfeasor**
délinquant (m)
delincuente (m)
rechtswidrig Handelnder (m)

5816. **tortious**
préjudiciable
agravioso; dañino
rechtswidrig

5817. **to commit a tort**
commettre un dommage; porter préjudice
cometer un daño legal
eine unerlaubte Handlung begehen

5818. **torture**
torture (f)
tortura (f)
Folter (f)

5819. **to torture**
torturer
torturar
foltern; martern

5820. **Town Hall**
Hôtel (m) de ville; mairie (f)
Palacio (m) Municipal
Rathaus (n)

5821. **trade**
commerce (m); métier (m)
comercio (m); ocupación (f)
Handel (m); Gewerbe (n)

5822. **adverse, unfavorable balance of trade**
balance commercial défavorable
balanza de pagos deficitaria
passive Handelsbilanz

5823. **domestic trade**
commerce intérieur
comercio interior
Binnenhandel

5824. **favorable balance of trade**
balance commerciale favorable
balanza de pagos superavitaria
aktive Handelsbilanz

5825. **foreign trade**
commerce extérieur
comercio exterior
Aussenhandel

5826. **free trade**
libre-échange (m)
libre comercio (m), intercambio (m)
Freihandel (m)

5827. **retail trade**
commerce de détail
comercio al por menor
Einzel oder Detailhandel

5828. **trademark**
marque (f) de commerce (m), de fabrique (f)
marca (f) de fábrica (f)
Warenzeichen (n)

5829. **trade union**
syndicat (m)
sindicato (m)
Gewerkschaft (f)

5830. **trading**
commerce (m)
comercio (m)
Handel (m)

5831. **wholesale trade**
commerce de gros
comercio al por mayor, mayorista
Grosshandel

5932. **world trade**

commerce international
comercio internacional
Welthandel

5833. **to trade**
faire du commerce
comerciar; intercambiar
Handel treiben; handeln

5834. **tradition**
tradition (f)
tradición (f)
Tradition (f)

5835. **traffic**
commerce (m); négoce (m); trafic (m)
comercio (m); tráfico (m); tránsito (m)
Handelsverkehr (m); Verkehr (m); Strassenverkehr (m)

5836. **traffic regulations**
code (m) de route (f); règlements (mpl) sur la circulation (f)
reglamento (m) de tránsito (m)
Verkehrsordnung (f)

5837. **traitor**
traître (m)
traidor (m)
Verräter (m)

5838. **tramp**
vagabond (m)
vagabundo (m)
Vagabund (m)

5839. **transaction**
affaire (f); opération (f); transaction (f)
operación (f); transacción (f)
Geschäft (n); Durchführung (f); Abmachung (f)

5840. **commercial transaction**
transaction commerciale
operación comercial
Handelsgeschäft

5841. **transcript**
compte rendu (m); copie (f) conforme
copia (f); transcripción (f)
Verhandlungsprotokoll (n); Abschrift (f)

5842. **transfer**
transfert (m); virement (m)
cesión (f); traspaso (m)
Abtretung (f); Übertragung (f)

5843. **to transfer**
transférer
transferir
abtreten; übertragen

5844. **transit**
transit (m)
tránsito (m)
Durchfuhr (f)

5845. **transitory**
transitoire
transitorio
transitorisch

5846. **translation**
traduction (f)
traducción (f)
Übersetzung (f)

5847. **translator**
traducteur (m)
traductor (m)
Übersetzer (m)

5848. **to translate**
traduire
traducir
übersetzen

5849. **transnational**
transnational
transnacional
überstaatlich

5850. **transportation**
transport (m)
transporte (m)
Transport (m); Beförderung (f)

5851. **to transport**
transporter
transportar
transportieren; befördern

5852. **traverse**
dénégation (f) de faits (mpl)
contradicción (f); denegación (f) de hechos (mpl)
Einrede (f); Leugnung (f); Ableugnung (f)

5853. **treachery**
perfidie (f); trahison (f)
perfidia (f); traición (f)
Treulosigkeit (f); Verrat (m)

5854. **treacherous**
perfide
pérfido
treulos; verräterisch

5855. **treason**

trahison (f)
traición (f)
Verrat (m)

5856. **high treason**
haute-trahison
alta traición
Hochverrat

5857. **misprision of treason**
non-révélation (f) de trahison
ocultación (f) de traición
pflichtwidrige Nichtanzeige (f) eines hochverräterischen Unternehmens

5858. **Treasury (U.S.A.)**
Ministère (m) des Finances (fpl)
Ministerio (m) de Hacienda (f)
Finanzministerium (n)

5859. **treasurer**
trésorier (m); Ministre (m) des Finances (fpl)
tesorero (m); Ministro (m) de Hacienda (f)
Schatzmeister (m); Finanzminister (m)

5860. **treaty**
traité (m)
tratado (m)
Vertrag (m)

5861. **bilateral treaty**
traité bilatéral
tratado bilateral
zweiseitiger oder bilateraler Vertrag

5862. **multilateral treaty**
traité multilatéral, plurilatéral
tratado multilateral
vielseitiger oder multilateraler Vertrag

5863. **non-proliferation treaty**
traité de non-prolifération (f)
tratado sobre no proliferacion (f)
Atomsperrvertrag (m)

5864. **registration of treaties**
enregistrement (m) de traités
registro (m) de tratados
Registrierung (f) von Verträgen

5865. **inviolability of treaties**
inviolabilité (f) de traîtés
inviolabilidad (f) de tratados
Unverletzlichkeit (f) der Verträge

5866. **termination of a treaty**
extinction (f) d'un traité
expiración (f) de un tratado
Ablauf (m) oder Erlöschen (n) eines Vertrags

5867. **treaty of arbitration and conciliation**
traité d'arbitrage et de conciliation
tratado de arbitraje y conciliación
Schieds- und Schlichtungsvertrag

5868. **treaty of commerce**
traité de commerce
tratado de comercio
Handelsvertrag

5869. **treaty of extradition**
traité d'extradition
tratado de extradición
Auslieferungsvertrag

5870. **treaty of friendship and alliance**
traité d'amitié et d'alliance
tratado de amistad y de alianza
Freundschafts- und Bündesvertrag

5871. **treaty of mutual guarantee**
traité de garantie mutuelle
tratado de garantías mutuas
gegenseitiger Garantievertrag

5872. **treaty of non-aggression**
traité de non-agression
tratado de no agresión
Nichtangriffspakt

5873. **treaty of peace**
traité de paix
tratado de paz
Friedensvertrag

5874. **to conclude a treaty**
conclure un traité
hacer un pacto
einen Vertrag abschliessen

5875. **to denounce a treaty**
dénoncer un traité
denunciar un tratado
einen Vertrag kündigen

5876. **trespass** (see also **action of trespass**)
transgression (f); violation (f)
transgresión (f); violación (f)
Besitzstörung (f); Hausfriedensbruch (m)

5877. **trespasser**
intrus (m); personne (f) violant la propriété d'autrui
transgresor (m); violador (m)
Besitzstörer (m); Hausfriedensbrecher (m)

5878. **to trespass**
transgresser; violer
traspasar; violar
widerrechtlich betreten; jds. Rechte verletzen oder beeinträchtigen; übertreten

5879. **trial**
cause (f); procès (m)
causa (f); juicio (m); proceso (m)
Gerichtsverfahren (n); Verhandlung (f); Prozess (m)

5880. **at the trial of**
lors du procès intenté contre
durante el juicio de
in der Verhandlung gegen

5881. **civil trial**
procès civil
juicio civil
Zivilverfahren

5882. **criminal trial**
procès criminel
juicio criminal
Strafverfahren

5883. **former trial**
procès antérieur
juicio anterior
fruheres Verfahren

5884. **new trial**
nouveau procès; nouvelle procédure
nuevo juicio
neues Verfahren

5885. **re-opening of the trial**
reprise du procès
reanudación del juicio
Wiederaufnahme des Verfahrens

5886. **trial by injury**
procès devant le jury
juicio ante jurado
Verhandlung vor dem Geschworenengericht

5887. **trial and punishment**
le jugement (m) et le châtiment (m)
juicio (m) y castigo (m)
Prozess (m) und Strafe (f)

5888. **to assign a day for trial**
fixer le jour d'audience
señalar día para el juicio
einen Termin (für die Verhandlung) festsetzen

5889. **to be brought up for trial**
être mis en jugement
ser sometido a juicio
vor Gericht gebracht werden

5890. **to try a case**
juger une cause
defender un pleito
einen Fall verhandeln

5891. **tribunal**
tribunal (m)
tribunal (m)
Gerichtshof (m); Tribunal (m)

5892. **appearance before a tribunal**
comparution devant le tribunal
comparecencia ante un tribunal
vor Gericht auftreten

5893. **by order of the tribunal**
par ordre du tribunal
por orden del tribunal
auf Anordnung des Gerichts

5894. **International Military Tribunal**
Tribunal Militaire International
Tribunal Militar Internacional
InternationalerMilitär-Gerichtshof

5895. **may it please the tribunal**
Plaise au Tribunal; Messieurs les Juges
con la venia del Tribunal; Señores Jueces
das Gericht wolle erkennen

5896. **mixed tribunals**
tribunaux mixtes
tribunales mixtos
gemischte Gerichtshöfe

5897. **to lodge with the tribunal**
porter devant un tribunal; remettre en justice
someter al tribunal
bei Gericht einreichen; vor Gericht vorbringen

5898. **trover** (see **action of trover**)

5899. **truce**
trêve (f)
tregua (f)
Waffenstillstand (m)

5900. **flag of truce**
drapeau (m) parlementaire
bandera (f) de parlamento
Parlamentärflagge (f)

5901. **trust**
cartel (m); confiance (f); trust (m); fidéicommis (m)
cartel (m); confianza (f); fideicomiso (m)
Kartell (n); Trust (m); Treuhandverhältnis (n); Vertrauen (n)

5902. **brain trust**
conseillers (mpl) intellectuels
asesores (mpl) intelectuales
Beraterstab (m)

5903. **cestui que trust**
le bénéficiaire (m) d'un trust (m)
beneficiario (m) de un fideicomiso (m)
Bedachter (m); Begünstigter (m); Nutzniesser (m)

5904. **charitable trust**
fondation (f) de charité
fideicomiso (m) caritativo
milde Stiftung (f)

5905. **constructive trust**
obligation d'un possesseur de restituer
fideicomiso impuesto por la ley
von Gesetz auferlegtes Fideikomiss

5906. **resulting trust**
fidéicommis résultant de l'interprétation de la loi
fideicomiso presuntivo
fingiertes Treuhandverhältnis

5907. **spendthrift trust**
fidéicommis protégeant les prodigues
fideicomiso en protección de los pródigos
Verschwendertrust

5908. **to create a trust**
créer un trust, un fidéicommis
crear un fideicomiso
einen Treuhänder bestellen

5909. **trusteeship**
administration (f); tutelle (f)
cargo (m) de fiduciario (m), fideicomisario (m)
Treuhandschaft (f)

5910. **trustee**
administateur (m); fidéicommissaire (m)
fiduciario (m); síndico (m)
Vermögensverwalter (m); Treuhänder (m)

5911. **truth**
vérité (f)
verdad (f)
Wahrheit (f); Richtigkeit (f)

5912. **turnover**
chiffre (m) d'affaires (fpl)
movimiento (m) de mercancías (fpl), de capital
Umsatz (m)

5913. **turpitude**
turpitude (f)
infamia (f)
Verworfenheit (f)

5914. **moral turpitude**
turpitude (f) morale
torpeza (f) moral
Unsittlichkeit (f)

5915. **tyranny**
tyrannie (f)
tiranía (f)
Tyrannei (f)

U

5916. **ulterior**
ultérieur
ulterior
anderweitig
5917. **ultimate**
final; ultimate
final; último
endlich; Schluss-
5918. **ultimatum**
ultimatum (m)
ultimátum (m)
Ultimatum (n)
5919. **umpire**
arbitre (m)
árbitro (m)
Schiedsrichter (m)
5920. **unable**
incapable; incompétent
incapaz; impotente
unfähig
5921. **unacceptable**
inacceptable
inaceptable
unannehmbar
5922. **unalienable** (see **inalienable**)
5923. **unalterable**
inaltérable; immuable
inalterable; invariable
unveränderlich
5924. **unaltered**
inaltéré; inchangé; tel quel
inalterado; no modificado
unverändert
5925. **unanimity**
unanimité (f)
unanimidad (f)
Einstimmigkeit (f)
5926. **unanimous**
unanime
unánime
einstimmig
5937. **unanimously**
à l'unanimité; par acclamations
por unanimidad; por aclamación
einstimmig
5928. **unanswerable**
irréfutable
indisputable
unwiderlegbar
5929. **unascertainable**
indéterminable
indeterminable
nicht feststellbar
5930. **unassailable**
irréfutable
irrefutable
unangreifbar
5931. **unauthenticated**
non-légalisé
no legalizado
unbeglaubigt
5932. **unauthorized**
non-autorisé
no autorizado; desautorizado
unbefugt
5933. **unavailable**
indisponible
indisponible
nicht verfügbar
5934. **unavoidable**
inévitable
inevitable
unvermeidlich
5935. **unbiassed**
impartial
imparcial
unparteiisch
5936. **uncertainty**
incertitude (f)
incertidumbre (f)
Ungewissheit (f)
5937. **uncertain**
incertain
incierto
ungewiss
5938. **uncommon**
rare
raro
ungewöhnlich
5939. **uncompromising**
intransigeant
intransigente
unbeugsam; unnachgiebig
5940. **unconditional**
inconditionnel
incondicional
unbedingt

5941. **unconstitutionality**
inconstitutionnalité (f)
inconstitucionalidad (f)
Verfassungswidrigkeit (f)
5942. **unconstitutional**
inconstitutionnel
inconstitucional
verfassungwidrig
5943. **uncontested**
incontesté
no disputado
unbestritten
5944. **unconvinced**
sceptique
escéptico
nicht überzeugt
5945. **unconvincing**
peu convaincant
no convincente
nicht überzeugend
5946. **undamaged**
indemne; en bon état; intact
indemne; intacto; ileso
unbeschädigt
5947. **underdeveloped; undeveloped**
sous-développé
subdesarrollado
unterentwickelt; Entwicklungs-
5948. **underestimate, to**
sous-évaluer
subestimar
unterschätzen
5949. **undergo, to**
subir
sufrir
durchmachen
5950. **Underground, The**
la Résistance (f)
la Resistencia (f)
Widerstandsbewegung (f)
5951. **to go underground**
entrer dans la clandestinité
actuar clandestinamente
in der Widerstandsbewegung arbeiten, sein
5952. **undermine, to**
détruire; miner; saper
socavar; minar
untergraben
5953. **undersigned, the**
le soussigné (m)
el infrascrito (m)
der Unterzeichnete (m)
5954. **understanding**
compréhension (f); entendement (m)
comprensión (f); entendimiento (m)
Einverständnis (n); Übereinkunft (f)
5955. **tacit understanding**
accord tacite
acuerdo tácito
stillschweigende Übereinkunft
5956. **understood**
compris; entendu
entendido
wohl verstanden
5957. **to come to an understanding**
s'accorder; s'entendre
comprender; entender
sich verständigen mit; ein Einverständnis mit jdm. erreichen
5958. **undertaking**
engagement (m); entreprise (f)
compromiso (m); empresa (f)
Unterfangen (n); Unternehmen (n)
5959. **underworld**
le milieu (m)
mundo (m) del hampa (f)
Unterwelt (f)
5960. **underwritten**
souscrit
su(b)scrito
versichert
5961. **underwriter**
assureur (m)
asegurador (m)
Versicherer (m)
5962. **to underwrite**
assurer
asegurar
versichern
5963. **unduly**
indûment; illégalement
indebidamente; ilícitamente
ungehörigerweise; unbesetzlicherweise
5964. **unemployment**
chômage (m)
desempleo (m); desocupación (f)
Arbeitslosigkeit (f)
5965. **seasonal unemployment**

chômage saisonnier
desempleo estacional
saisonbedingte Arbeitslosigkeit

5966. **unemployed**
en chômage
desocupado; desempleado
arbeitslos

5967. **unemployment benefit, compensation**
allocation (f) de chômage
seguro (m) de desempleo
Arbeitslosenunterstützung (f)

5968. **war on unemployment**
lutte contre le chômage
lucha contra el desempleo
Kampf gegen die Arbeitslosigkeit

5969. **to be unemployed**
être en chômage
estar desocupado, sin empleo, sin trabajo
arbeitslos sein

5970. **unencumbered**
libre; non grevé
libre de gravamen
schuldenfrei; unbelastet; unbehindert

5971. **unenforceable**
non exécutoire
no ejecutorio
nicht klagbar

5972. **unequivocal**
clair; net; sans équivoque
inequívoco
eindeutig; unzweideutig

5973. **unexpired**
non-échu; non-expiré
no vencido
noch nicht abgelaufen

5974. **unfit**
incapable
incompetente
untauglich

5975. **unforeseen**
imprévu
imprevisto
unvermutet

5976. **unfounded**
sans fondement
sin motivo
unbegründet; gegenstandslos

5977. **unfulfilled**
inachevé
incumplido
unerfüllt

5978. **unicameral**
unicaméral
unicameral
Einkammer-

5979. **unification**
unification (f)
unificación (f)
Vereinheitlichung (f); Einigung (f)

5980. **to unify**
unifier
unir
verinheitlichen; einigen

5981. **uniformity**
uniformité (f)
uniformidad (f)
Gleichförmigkeit (f)

5982. **uniform**
uniforme
uniforme
gleichförmig

5983. **unilateral**
unilatéral
unilateral
einseitig

5984. **unimpaired**
intact
inalterado
unvermindert

5985. **uninpeachable**
incontestable; irréprochable
irrecusable; irreprensible
unanfechtbar; tadellos

5986. **union**
union (f)
unión (f)
Bund (m); Union (f)

5987. **personal union**
union personnelle
unión personal
Personalunion

5988. **real union**
union réelle
unión real
Realunion

5989. **United Nations** (see Appendix IV)

5990. **unity**
unité (f)

unidad (f)
Einheit (f)

5991. **united**
uni
unido
vereinigt; vereint

5992. **universal**
universel
universal
universell; allgemein

5993. **unjust**
injuste
injusto
ungerecht; unbillig

5994. **unjustifiable**
injustifiable
injustificable
unverantwortlich

5995. **unjustified**
injustifié
injustificado
ungerechtfertigt

5996. **unknown**
inconnu
desconocido
unbekannt

5997. **unlawful**
illégal; illicite
ilegal; ilícito
rechtswidrig; unrechtmässig

5998. **unlimited**
illimité
ilimitado
unbeschränkt

5999. **unliquidated**
non-liquidé
no liquidado
nicht liquidiert

6000. **unnecessary**
inutile; superflu
inútil; superfluo
unnötig

6001. **unofficial**
officieux
oficioso
nichtamtlich; inoffiziell

6002. **unpaid**
non-affranchi
no pagado
unbezahlt

6003. **unpredictable**
incertain
incierto
ungewiss

6004. **unprejudiced**
impartial
imparcial
unparteiisch

6005. **unpremeditated**
non-prémédité
impremeditado
unbeabsichtigt

6006. **unprofessional**
non-professionnel
no profesional; contrario a las reglas de una profesión
unfachmännisch

6007. **unprofitable**
inutile; peu lucratif
inproductivo, inútil
uneinträglich

6008. **unpublished**
inédit
inédito
unveröffentlicht

6009. **unqualified**
incompétent; inhabile
incompetente
unberechtigt; ungceignet

6010. **unrealistic**
chimérique
quimérico
nicht realistisch

6011. **unreasonable**
déraisonnable
irrazonable
unvernünftig

6012. **unrecorded**
non-enregistré
no registrado
unverzeichnet

6013. **unreliable**
douteux
indigno de confianza; inseguro
unzuverlässig

6014. **unsecured**
sans garantie
sin garantía
ungesichert

6015. **unsettled**
indécis; troublé
inestable; vago
unbeständig; unruhig

6016. **unsound**

défectueux
defectuoso
nicht stichhaltig; unbegründet

6017. **unsubstantiated**
non-prouvé
no probado
unbewiesen

6018. **unsuccessful**
infructueux; sans succès
sin éxito
fruchtlos

6019. **untenable**
insoutenable
insostenible
unhaltbar

6020. **untrue**
dénué de vérité; faux; inexact; infidèle
falso; mendaz; pérfido
unwahr; falsch; ungenau; unrichtig

6021. **unwarranted**
injustifié; sans autorité
incierto; inexcusable
unberechtigt; unbefugt

6022. **upgrading**
reclassement (m)
calificación (f) a nivel (m) superior
Beförderung (f) (auf eine höhere Stellung)

6023. **uphold, to**
soutenir; supporter
sostener
aufrechterhalten; stützen

6024. **uprising**
insurrection (f)
levantamiento (m)
Aufstand (m); Erhebung (f)

6025. **urgency**
urgence (f)
urgencia (f)
Dringlichkeit (f)

6026. **urgent**
urgent
urgente
dringend

6027. **to urge**
exhorter; pousser à
solicitar; urgir
drängen; dringend bitten

6028. **usage**
coutume (f); habitude (f); usage (m)
costumbre (f); uso (m)
Gewohnheit (f); Brauch (m); Gebrauch (m)

6029. **common usage**
usage courant
uso común
weit verbreiteter Gebrauch

6030. **established usage**
usage établi
uso establecido
bestehende Gewohnheit

6031. **use**
usage (m); jouissance (f) (d'un bien, droit)
uso (m)
Gebrauch (m); Ausübung (f) eines Rechts (n)

6031a. **cestrui que use**
usufruitier (m)
usufructuario (m)
Niessbraucher (m); Niessbrauchberechtighter (m); Nutzniesser (m)

6032. **for official use only**
réservé au service officiel
solamente para uso oficial
nur zum amtlichen Gebrauch

6033. **useful**
utile
útil
nützlich; brauchbar

6034. **useless**
inutile
inútil
unbrauchbar

6035. **to use**
employer; se servir de
usar
anwenden; gebrauchen

6036. **usher**
huissier (m)
ujier (m)
Gerichtsdiener (m)

6037. **usual**
habituel; ordinaire; usuel
habitual; ordinario; usual
gewöhnlich; üblich

6038. **usufruct**
usufruit (m)
usufructo (m)

Niessbrauch (m)
6039. **usurpation**
usurpation (f)
usurpación (f)
widerrechtliche Aneignung (f)
6040. **usurper**
usurpateur (m)
usurpador (m)
unrechtmässiger Besitzer (m)
6041. **usury**
usure (f)
usura (f)
Wucher (m)
6042. **usurer**
usurier (m)
usurero (m)
Wucherer (m)
6043. **usurious**
usuraire
usurario
wucherisch
6044. **utility**
utilité (f)
utilidad (f)
Nützlichkeit (f)
6045. **utilization**
utilisation (f)
utilización (f)
Nutzbarmachung (f); Nutzung (f)
6046. **to utilize**
utiliser
utilizar
benutzen
6047. **utopia**
utopie (f)
utopía (f); utopia (f)
Utopie (f)
6048. **utter, to**
exprimer; mettre en circulation
expresar; poner en circulación
äussern; in Umlauf setzen (Falschgeld)

V

6049. **vacancy**
vacance (f)
vacancia (f); vacante (f)
offene Stelle (f)
6050. **vacant**
vacant
vacante
unbesetzt
6051. **to fill a vacancy**
remplir un poste vacant
proveer una vacante
eine offene Stelle besetzen
6052. **to vacate**
annuler; quitter; vider
anular; evacuar; revocar
annullieren; aufheben; räumen
6053. **vacuum**
vide (m)
vacío (m)
Vakuum (n); Lücke (f)
6054. **vagabond**
errant; vagabond
errante; vagabundo
Landstreicher; Vagabund
6055. **vagrancy**
vagabondage (m)
vagancia (f)
Landstreicherei (f); Vagabundieren (n)
6056. **validity**
validité (f); justesse (f)
validez (f); vigencia (f)
Rechtsgültigkeit (f); Triftigkeit (f) (der Gründe)
6057. **valid**
valide; en vigueur
válido; vigente
rechtsgültig; bindend; stichhaltig
6058. **to validate**
valider
validar
rechtskräftig erklären
6059. **value**
valeur (f)
valor (m)
Wert (m)
6060. **cash surrender value**
valeur de rachat
valor de rescate
Rückkaufswert (einer Lebensversicherungspolice)
6061. **decrease in value**

moins-value (f)
disminución (f) de valor (m)
Wertminderung (f)

6062. **face value**
valeur nominale
valor nominal
Nominalwert

6063. **fair market value**
valeur marchande normale
valor normal
angemessener Marktpreis

6064. **for value received**
valeur reçue
por valor recibido
Wert erhalten

6065. **increase in value**
plus-value (f)
aumento (m) de valor (m)
Mehrwert (m)

6066. **market value**
valeur marchande
valor de mercado
Marktpreis

6067. **nominal value**
valeur nominale
valor nominal
Nennwert

6068. **par value**
parité (f); pair (m); valeur (f) nominale
paridad (f); valor (m) a la par; valor (m) nominal
Parität (f) pari (adv)

6069. **probative value**
force probante
valor probatorio
Beweiswert

6070. **purchase value**
valeur d'achat
precio de compra
Anschaffungswert

6071. **sentimental value**
valeur affective
valor afectivo
Affektionswert; Liebhaberwert

6072. **valuable**
précieux
valioso
wertvoll

6073. **value received**
valeur reçue
valor recibido
Wert empfangen; betrag erhalten

6074. **to value**
estimer; évaluer
apreciar; valorar
veranschlagen; schätzen

6075. **valuables**
objets (mpl) de valeur
objetos (mpl) de valor
Wertsachen (fpl)

6076. **variance**
contradiction (f); désaccord (m); divergence (f)
discordia (f); oposición (f); variación (f)
Widerspruch (m); Uneinigkeit (f); Meinungsverschiedenheit (f)

6077. **at variance with**
en désaccord avec
reñido con
abweichend von; im Gegensatz zu . . .

6078. **variety**
diversité (f)
diversidad (f)
Verschiedenheit (f)

6079. **vassal**
vassal (m)
vasallo (m)
Vasall (m)

6080. **venality**
vénalité (f)
venalidad (f)
Käuflichkeit (f)

6081. **venal**
vénal
venal
käuflich

6082. **vendee**
acheteur (m)
comprador (m)
Käufer (m)

6083. **vendor**
vendeur (m)
vendedor (m)
Verkäufer (m)

6084. **venireman (U.S.A.)**
citoyen convoqué pour faire partie d'un jury
persona convocada para jurado
berufener Geschworener

6085. **venture**

entreprise (f); risque (m); tentative (f)
especulación (f); riesgo (m)
Spekulation (f); Risiko (n)

6086. **venue**
lieu (m) de jugement; lieu où le tribunal (m) est saisi
jurisdicción (f) del caso (m)
Verhandlungsort (m)

6087. **change of venue**
renvoi à un autre tribunal
traslado de jurisdicción
Verweisung an ein anderes Gericht

6088. **verbatim**
mot pour mot
al pie de la letra
Wort für Wort; wörtlich

6089. **verdict**
verdict (m)
veredicto (m)
Urteilspruch (m); Entscheidung (f); Wahrspruch (m)

6090. **directed verdict**
verdict dicté par le juge au jury
veredicto instruido por el juez
Spruch der Geschworenen auf Grund eines richterlichen Auftrags

6091. **general verdict**
réponse du jury pour ou contre le demandeur
veredicto general
Schuldspruch; Freispruch

6092. **partial verdict**
verdict en partie
sentencia en parte
Teilurteil

6093. **special verdict**
réponse du jury sur une question spéciale
veredicto sobre los hechos solamente
Tatentscheidung ohne Bestimmung des Schuldigen

6094. **suspended verdict**
verdict renvoyé
sentencia suspendida
Urteil mit Strafaufschub

6095. **verdict of acquittal, of not guilty**
acquittement (m); décharge (f)
absolución (f); exculpación (f)
Freispruch (m)

6096. **to return a verdict of guilty**
rapporter un verdict de culpabilité
pronunciar veredicto de culpabilidad
der Angeklagten für schuldig erklären

6097. **to return a verdict of not guilty**
rapporter un verdict de non-culpabilité
pronunciar veredicto de inculpabilidad
den Angeklagten für unschuldig erklären

6098. **verification**
confirmation (f); vérification (f)
comprobación (f); verificación (f)
Bestätigung (f) der Richtigkeit (f); Überprüfung (f)

6099. **verified**
confirmé; vérifié
jurado; verificado
bestätigt; überprüft

6100. **to verify**
confirmer; vérifier
jurar; verificar
bestätigen; überprüfen

6101. **version**
version (f)
versión (f)
Fassung (f)

6102. **versus; vs.**
contre
contra
gegen; wider

6103. **vestige**
vestige (m)
vestigio (m)
Spur (f)

6104. **veto**
veto (m)
veto (m)
Veto (m)

6105. **to veto**
mettre le veto à
vetar
Einspruch oder ein Veto einlegen

6106. **vicarious**
délégué; substitué

vicario
stellvertretend

6107. **vice**
débauche (f)
vicio (m)
Laster (n)

6108. **victim**
victime (f)
víctima (f)
Opfer (n)

6109. **to be a victim**
être victime
ser víctima
jdm. zum Opfer fallen; ein Opfer sein

6110. **to victimize a person**
faire de quelqu'un sa victime
hacer una persona víctima
jemanden zum Opfer machen; opfern

6111. **view**
opinion (f); vue (f)
opinión (f); vista (f)
Ansicht (f); Meinung (f); Aussicht (f)

6112. **viewpoint** (see **point of view**)

6113. **vindication**
justification (f); défense (f)
vindicación (f)
Rechtsfertigung (f); Verteidigung (f)

6114. **to vindicate**
défendre; justifier
vindicar
rechtfertigen; verteidigen

6115. **vindictive**
vindicatif; vengeur
vengativo; vindicativo
nachtragend; nachträgerisch; rachesüchtig

6116. **violation**
infraction (f); violation (f)
infracción (f); violación (f)
Verstoss gegen; Verletzung

6117. **to violate**
violer
violar
verstossen gegen; verletzen; übertreten

6118. **violence**
violence (f)
violencia (f)
Gewalttätigkeit (f)

6119. **visa**
visa (m)
visa (f)
Visum (n)

6120. **visit and search, the right to**
droit de visite
derecho de visita
Durchsuchungsrecht

6121. **visual aids**
aides visuelles
ayuda visual
optische oder visuelle Hilfsmittel

6122. **vitiate, to**
vicier
viciar
ungültig machen

6123. **vocational guidance**
orientation (f) professionnelle
orientación (f) profesional
Berufsberatung (f)

6124. **void**
non avenu; nul
nulo
nichtig; ungültig

6125. **void ab initio**
nul dès le commencement
nulo desde el principio
von Anfang an nichtig

6126. **voidable**
annulable
anulable
anfechtbar

6127. **to void**
annuler; résilier; résoudre
anular; invalidar
annullieren; kraftlos oder ungültig machen

6128. **voir dire**
examen préliminaire d'un témoin ou d'un juré
examen preliminar de calificación de testigo o miembro del jurado
Untersuchung eines Zeugen oder Geschworenen, um seine Qualifizierung zu prüfen

6129. **volume**
quantité (f); tome (m)
suma (f); volumen (m)
Quantität (f); Band (m); Buch (n)

6130. **voluntary**

gratuit; volontaire
gratuito; voluntario
freiwillig; spontan

6131. **volunteer**
volontaire (m)
voluntario (m)
Freiwilliger (m)

6132. **vote**
élection (f); voix (f); vote (m)
sufragio (m); voto (m)
Wahlrecht (n); Wahlgang (m); Wahlstimme (f)

6133. **abstention from voting**
abstention de vote
abstención de votar
Stimmenthaltung

6134. **casting vote**
voix décisive; prépondérante
voto de calidad, decisivo
entscheidende Stimme

6135. **counting of votes**
dépouillement du scrutin
escrutinio
Stimmenzählung

6136. **majority vote**
vote à la majorité
voto de pluralidad
Stimmenmehrheit

6137. **oral vote**
vote par scrutin public
votación oral
mündliche Abstimmung

6138. **plurality vote**
pluralité des voix
mayoría relativa de votos
relative Stimmenmehrheit

6139. **standing vote**
vote par debout
voto que se efectúa poniéndose de pie
Abstimmung durch Aufstehen

6140. **straw vote**
vote d'essai
voto extraoficial
inoffizielle Probeabstimmung

6141. **tie vote**
vote égal
empate
Stimmengleichheit

6142. **unanimous vote**
unanimité; vote unanime
unanimidad; votación unánime
Einstimmigkeit; einstimmiger Beschluss

6143. **vote by acclamation**
vote par acclamation
voto por aclamación
Wahl oder Abstimmung durch Zuruf

6144. **vote by ballot**
vote par scrutin secret
votación mediante balotas
geheime Abstimmung oder Wahl

6145. **vote by proxy**
vote par procuration
voto por poder
Stimmrechtsausübung durch Vertreter

6146. **vote by roll call**
vote par appel nominal
voto nominal
Abstimmung durch Namensaufruf

6147. **vote by show of hands**
vote à mains levées
votación a mano alzada
Abstimmen durch Erheben der Hände

6148. **vote of confidence**
vote de confiance
voto de confianza
Vertrauensvotum

6149. **vote of lack of confidence**
vote de méfiance
moción de desconfianza
Misstrauensvotum

6150. **vote of thanks**
remerciements de la session
voto de gracias
Dankesvotum

6151. **voter**
électeur; votant
elector; votante
Wähler; Stimmberechtigter

6152. **voting**
action de voter; vote
votación; comicios
Abstimmung; Wahlen

6153. **to be eligible to vote**
avoir le droit de voter
tener el derecho al voto
stimmberechtigt sein

6154. **to cast a vote; to vote**

voter
votar
eine Stimme abgeben
6155. **to have the right to vote**
avoir le droit de suffrage
tener derecho a sufragio
Stimmrecht besitzen
6156. **to put to a vote**
aller, mettre aux voix
someter a votación
zur Abstimmung bringen
6157. **to vote against**
voter contre
votar contra
stimmen gegen
6158. **vouch for, to**
affirmer; appuyer; soutenir
certificar; garantizar
einstehen oder zeugen für; garantieren
6159. **voucher**
pièce (f) comptable
comprobante (m); recibo (m)
Beweisurkunde (f); Bescheinigung (f)

W

6160. **wage**
salaire (m); gages (mpl); paie (f); paye (f)
salario (m); paga (f)
Arbeitslohn (m); Lohn (m)
6161. **minimum wage**
salaire minimum
salario mínimo
Mindestlohn
6162. **nominal wage**
salaire nominal
salario nominal
Nominallohn
6163. **wage-earner**
salarié (m)
asalariado (m)
Lohnempfänger (m)
6164. **wage-scale**
barème (m) des salaires
escala (f), tarifa (f) de salarios
Lohntarif (m)
6165. **wager**
pari (m)
apuesta (f)
Wette (f)
6166. **to wager**
parier
apostar
wetten
6167. **waiver**
abandon (m); désistement (m)
renuncia (f); repudio (m)
Aufgabe (f); Verzicht (m) auf
6168. **to waive**
abandonner; se désister
desistir de; renunciar a
aufgeben; verzichten auf
6169. **walkout**
grève (f) d'ouvriers (mpl)
huelga (f) de obreros (mpl)
Streik (m)
6170. **want**
détresse (f); misère (f)
falta (f); privación (f)
Mangel (m) an; Armut (f)
6171. **wanton**
avec une malice consommée; licencieux
desenfrenado; licencioso
mutwillig; böswillig; zügellos
6172. **war**
guerre (f)
guerra (f)
Krieg (m)
6173. **atomic war**
guerre atomique
guerra atómica
Atomkrieg
6174. **civil war**
guerre civile
guerra civil
Bürgerkrieg
6175. **cold war**
guerre froide
guerra fría
kalter Krieg
6176. **declaration of war**
déclaration de guerre

declaración de guerra
Kriegserklärung

6177. **defensive war**
guerre défensive
guerra defensiva
Verteidigungskrieg

6178. **internecine war**
guerre d'extermination réciproque
guerra de exterminación recíproca
gegenseitiger Vernichtungskrieg

6179. **state of war**
état de guerre
estado de guerra
Kriegszustand

6180. **theater of war**
théâtre (m) de la guerre
teatro (m) de guerra
Kriegsschauplatz (m)

6181. **undeclared war**
guerre non-déclarée
guerra no declarada
Krieg ohne vorherige Kriegserklärung

6182. **war crimes**
crimes (mpl) de guerre
crímenes (mpl) de guerra
Kriegsverbrechen (n)

6183. **war-monger**
agitateur (m) de guerre
agitador (m) de guerra
Kriegshetzer (m)

6184. **war of aggression**
guerre d'agression
guerra de agresión
Angriffskrieg

6185. **to declare war**
déclarer la guerre
declarar la guerra
Krieg erklären

6186. **to wage war**
faire la guerre
hacer la guerra
Krieg führen

6187. **ward**
arrondissement (m) (d'une ville); pupille (m); salle (f) (d'hôpital)
barrio (m) (de ciudad); menor (m) o huérfano (m) bajo tutela; pupilo (m); sala (f) (de hospital)
Stadtbezirk (m); Mündel (n); Krankensaal (m)

6188. **electoral ward**
circonscription (f)
circunscripción (f)
Wahlbezirk (m)

6189. **warden**
directeur (m) de prison (f); gardien (m); surveillant (m)
director (m) de cárcel (f); custodio (m); guardián (m)
Gefängniswärter (m); Gefängnisbeamter (m); Aufseher (m)

6190. **warehouse**
entrepôt (m); magasin (m)
almacén (m); depósito (m)
Lagerhaus (n); Speicher (m)

6191. **bonded warehouse**
entrepôt de douane
almacén afianzado
Zollspeicher; Zollager

6192. **warehouseman**
entreposeur (m)
almacenero (m)
Lagerverwalter (m)

6193. **warfare**
guerre (f)
guerra (f)
Kriegsführung (f)

6194. **bacteriological warfare**
guerre bactériologique
guerra bacteriológica
Bakterienkrieg

6195. **chemical warfare**
guerre chimique
guerra química
chemischer Krieg

6196. **economic warfare**
guerre économique
guerra económica
Wirtschaftskrieg

6197. **guerrilla warfare**
guerre de maquis
guerra de guerrillas
Partisanenkrieg

6198. **psychological warfare**
guerre psychologique
guerra (p)sicológica
psychologische Kriegsführung

6199. **warning**
avertissement (m); notification (f)

advertencia (f); aviso (m)
Warnung (f); Ermahnung (f)

6200. **to warn**
donner un avertissement
advertir; prevenir
warnen; ermahnen

6201. **warrant**
autorisation (f); mandat (m); ordre (m)
autorización (f); mandato (m); orden (f)
Vollmacht (f); Ausweis (m); Gewährleistung (f); Garantie (f); Vollziehungsbefehl (m)

6202. **bench warrant**
mandat d'arrêt
auto de juez
richterlicher Haftbefehl

6203. **death warrant**
ordre d'exécution
orden de ejecución
Hinrichtungsbefehl

6204. **search warrant**
mandat de perquisition (f)
orden judicial de entrada (f) y registro (m)
Hausdurchsuchungsbefehl (m)

6205. **warrant for, of arrest**
mandat d'amener, d'arrêt
orden de arresto, prisión
Haftbefehl

6206. **to issue a warrant**
lancer un mandat d'arrêt
dictar una orden de prisión
einen Haftbefehl gegen jdn. erlassen

6207. **warranty**
garantie (f)
garantía (f)
Garantie (f); Verbürgung (f)

6208. **to warrant**
certifier; garantir
garantir; garantizar
garantieren; verbürgen

6209. **waste**
dégât (m); dégradation (f); gaspillage (m)
desperdicio (m); destrozo (m); destrucción (f)
Verschwendung (f); Abfall (m); Vernachlässigung (f)

6210. **to waste**
gaspiller; perdre; se consumer
desperdiciar; destrozar; destruir
verschwenden; vernachlässigen; brachliegen lassen

6211. **way**
chemin (m); manière (f); moyen (m)
vía (f); manera (f); medio (m)
Weg (m); Art (f) und Weise (f); Mittel (n)

6212. **in any way**
de toute façon
de cualquier manera; de todos modos
auf jede Art; auf jede Weise

6213. **wealth**
richesse (f)
riqueza (f)
Reichtum (m); Vermögen (n)

6214. **national wealth**
patrimoine national; richesse nationale
riqueza nacional
Volksvermögen; Nationalvermögen

6215. **weapon**
arme (f)
arma (f)
Waffe (f)

6216. **concealed weapon**
arme dissimulée
arma disimulada
verborgenes Tragen von Waffen

6217. **whereas**
attendu que; vue que
considerando; por cuanto
in Anbetracht der Tatsache

6218. **whereas clauses**
les attendus
considerandos; por cuantos
einleitender Teil einer Urkunde

6219. **wholesale**
en gros; vente en gros
al por mayor
en gros; Grosshandel

6220. **wholesaler**
grossiste (m)
mayorista (m)
Grosshändler (m)

6221. **whore**
prostituée (f); putain (f)
prostituta (f); puta (f)

Prostituierte (f); Hure (f)
6222. **widow**
veuve (f)
viuda (f)
Witwe (f)
6223. **widower**
veuf (m)
viudo (m)
Witwer (m)
6224. **will**
testament (m)
testamento (m)
Testament (n); letzter Wille (m)
6225. **executor of a will**
exécuteur (m) testamentaire
albacea (m); testamentario (m)
Testamentsvollstrecker (m)
6226. **holographic will**
testament olographe
testamento ológrafo
eigenhändig geschriebenes Testament
6227. **last will and testament**
dernier testament
último testamento
letzter Wille
6228. **nuncupative will**
testament nuncupatif
testamento nuncupativo
mündliches Testament von Zeugen
6229. **to break a will**
annuler un testament
quebrantar un testamento
ein Testament aufheben
6230. **to contest a will**
contester un testament
impugnar un testamento
ein Testament anfechten
6231. **to make a will**
faire un testament
hacer testamento
ein Testament errichten
6232. **to probate a will**
homologuer
probar judicialmente un testamento
ein Testament gerichtlich bestätigen
6233. **to take by will**
recevoir par testament
suceder por testamento
testamentarisch erben
6234. **willful**
intentionnel; volontaire
premeditado; voluntario
absichtlich; wissentlich
6235. **wire-tapping**
interception (f) de messages (mpl) téléphoniques ou télégraphiques
intercepción (f) de mensajes (mpl) telefónicos o telegráficos
Abhören (n) von Telefongesprächen (npl); Abfangen (n) von Telegrammen (npl)
6236. **wit, to**
à savoir
a saber
das heisst; nämlich
6237. **witchcraft**
sorcellerie (f)
sortilegio (m)
Hexerei (f)
6238. **withdrawal**
désistement (m); rejet (m); retrait (m)
retirada (f); retiro (m)
Aufgabe (f); Zurückziehung (f); Kündigung (f); Abhebung (f)
6239. **to withdraw**
retirer
retirar; retractar
aufgeben; zurückziehen; kündigen; abheben
6240. **witness**
témoin (m)
testigo (m)
Zeuge (m)
6241. **attendance of witnesses**
comparution des témoins
comparecencia de testigos
Erscheinen der Zeugen vor Gericht
6242. **attesting witness**
témoin instrumentaire
testigo declarante
Beglaubigungszeuge
6243. **character witness**
témoin de moralité
testigo de conducta y carácter
Leumundszeuge
6244. **chief witness**
témoin principal
testigo principal
Hauptzeuge; Kronzeuge

6245. **coercion of witnesses**
pression exercée sur les témoins
coacción de testigos
Zwangsausübung auf Zeugen

6246. **corruption of a witness**
subornation d'un témoin
soborno de un testigo
Zeugenbestechung

6247. **credible witness**
témoin digne de foi
testigo digno de crédito
glaubwürdiger Zeuge

6248. **deposition by a witness**
déposition écrite d'un témoin
deposición de un testigo
schriftliche Zeugenaussage

6249. **examination of a witness**
interrogatoire d'un témoin
examen de un testigo
Zeugenvernehmung

6250. **expert witness**
expert appelé comme témoin
perito; testigo experto
sachverständiger Zeuge

6251. **eyewitness**
témoin oculaire
testigo de vista, ocular
Augenzeuge

6252. **friendly witness**
témoin bienveillant
testigo favorable
wohlwollender Zeuge

6253. **hostile witness**
témoin hostile
testigo desfavorable
gegnerischer Zeuge

6254. **in witness whereof**
en foi de quoi
en vista de lo cual
zur Urkund dessen

6255. **swearing of a witness**
prestation (f) de serment (m) par un témoin (m)
juramento (m) de un testigo (m)
Zeugenvereidigung (f)

6256. **witness box**
banc (m), barre (f) des témoins
banquillo (m) de los testigos
Zeugenstand (m)

6257. **witness fee**
indemnité (f) des témoins
dietas (fpl) de testigo
Zeugengebühr (f)

6258. **witness for the defense**
témoin à décharge
testigo de descargo, de la defensa
Entlastungszeuge

6259. **witness for the prosecution**
témoin à charge
testigo de cargo, de la parte actora
Belastungszeuge

6260. **to call a person as a witness**
citer quelqu'un comme témoin
presentar a una persona como testigo
jdn. als Zeugen nennen

6261. **to confront a witness**
confronter un témoin
confrontar un testigo
einen Zeugen konfrontieren

6262. **to swear a witness**
faire prêter serment à un témoin
tomar juramento a un testigo
einen Zeugen vereidigen

6263. **to take the witness stand**
venir à la barre
dirigirse al estrado
auf den Zeugenstand gehen

6264. **to witness**
être témoin; porter témoignage
atestar; dar testimonio
Zeugnis ablegen; Zeuge sein von ...

6265. **wording**
expression (f); style (m)
expresión (f); redacción (f)
Fassung (f); Wortlaut (m)

6266. **work**
travail (m); ouvrage (m)
obra (f); trabajo (m)
Arbeit (f)

6267. **seasonal work**
travail saisonnier
trabajo estacional
Saisonarbeit

6268. **social work**
assistance (f) sociale
asistencia (f) social
Sozialarbeit (f)

6269. **workman; worker**
ouvrier (m); travailleur (m)
obrero (m); trabajador (m)
Arbeiter (m)

6270. **worth**
valeur (f)
valor (f)
Wert (m)

6271. **wound**
blessure (f)
herida (f)
Wunde (f); Verletzung (f)

6272. **wounded**
blessé
herido
verwundet; verletzt

6273. **to wound**
blesser
herir
verwunden; verletzen

6274. **writ**
assignation (f); mandat (m); ordre (m)
auto (m); mandamiento (m)
gerichtliches Verfügen (n); Gerichtsbefehl (m)

6275. **writ of attachment**
saisie-arrêt
mandamiento de embargo
Pfändungsbeschluss

6276. **writ of capias**
mandat d'amener ou de saisie
orden judicial de embargo de bienes o de prisión
Haft- oder Vollstreckungsbefehl

6277. **writ of certiorari**
ordonnance d'un tribunal supérieur à un tribunal inférieur pour réexamen du dossier
auto de avocación
Anweisung eines höheren an sein niedrigeres Gericht zur Übersendung der Prozessakten zum Zweck der Entscheidung eines Revisionantrags

6278. **writ of detainer**
ordre autorisant détention
orden judicial de arresto
Haftbestätigungsbefehl

6279. **writ of error**
recours pour vice de forme et violation de la loi
recurso de casación
Rechtsmittel wegen Verletzung des Verfahrens oder des Gesetzes

6280. **writ of fieri facias**
requête du créancier à fin de saisie
orden de ejecución relativa a bienes muebles o inmuebles
Pfändungsantrag des Gläubigers

6281. **writ of habeas corpus**
droit de tout prisonier de comparaître pour vérifier la légalité de son emprisonnement
orden judicial para evitar que una persona sea detenida ilegalmente
Recht eines Gefangenen vor Gericht zu erscheinen um die Gesetzmässigkeit seiner Verhaftung zu verifizieren

6282. **writ of injunction**
injonction de s'abstenir ou de ne pas faire
orden judicial por la cual se dispone una conminación
Gerichtsbefehl, der Personen auffordert, sich gewisser Handlungen zu enthalten

6283. **writ of mandamus**
injonction à une personne physique d'exécuter un acte de fonction publique
orden de un tribunal superior para obligar el cumplimiento de un deber oficial
Gerichtsbefehl (einer höheren Instanz), um die Ausführung einer öffentlichen Funktion zu erzwingen

6284. **writ of ne exeat**
ordonnance interdisant quelqu'un de sortir du territoire
prohibición judicial al acusado de abandonar el lugar de la jurisdicción del tribunal
Mandat, den Gerichtsbezirk nicht zu verlassen

6285. **writ of prohibition**
défense de statuer dictée par un tribunal supérieur à un tribunal inférieur
inhibitoria
bindende Anweisung einer höheren Instanz

6286. **writ of quo warranto**
recours exceptionnel en vue de déterminer par quelle autorité une personne a été investie de certaines fonctions

recurso excepcional encaminado a determinar en virtud de qué autoridad una persona se halla investida de ciertas funciones
Verfahren, in dem jemand gezwungen wird, seine Berechtigung zur Ausübung eines Amtes usw. nachzuweisen

6287. **writ of scire facias**
ordonnance d'un tribunal demandant qu'une partie justifie les raisons pour lesquelles une décision ne doit pas être exécutée ou annulée
orden judicial que exige a una parte que pruebe por que motivo la decisión no deberá ser ejecutada, anulada o abrogada
Gerichtsbefehl, der eine Partei auffordert, Gründe anzugeben, warum eine Entscheidung nicht vollstreckt oder annulliert werden soll

6288. **writ of summons**
mandat de comparution
citación
Vorladung

6289. **writ of supersedeas**
acte suspensif d'instance
sobreseimiento
Gerichtsverfügung zur Einstellung des Verfahrens

6290. **wrong**
dommage (m); faute (f); préjudice (m)
agravio (m); error (m)
Unrecht (n)

6291. **wrongfully**
à tort; injustement
erróneo; injustamente
ungerechterweise; zu Unrecht; ungesetzlich

X

6292. **xenophobia**
xénophobie (f)
xenofobia (f)
Fremdenhass (m)

Y

6293. **yearbook**
annuaire (m)
anuario (m)
Jahrbuch (n)

6294. **yield**
produit (m); rendement (m)
producto (m); rendimiento (m)
Ertrag (m); Ausbeute (f); Nachgeben (n)

6295. **to yield**
produire; céder; consentir
producir; ceder; rendir
hervorbringen; tragen; nachgeben

Z

6296. **zeal**
zèle (m)
afán (m); celo (m)
Eifer (m)

6297. **zealous**
zélé; ardent
afanoso; celoso
eifrig

6298. **zone**
zone (f)
zona (f)
Zone (f); Gebiet (n); Bezirk (m)

6299. **buffer zone**
zone-tampon
zona intermediaria
Pufferzone

6300. **occupied zone**
zone d'occupation
zona de ocupación
Besatzungszone

French Index

A

B

C

D

E

F

G

H

I

J

K

L

M

N

O

P

Q

R

S

T

U

V

X

Z

Spanish Index

* las palabras que empiezan con la letra *Ch* se hallan bajo la letra *C*
* words starting with *Ch* in Spanish are found under letter *C*
* Les mots commençant par *Ch* en espagnol sont insérés à la lettre *C*
* Die spanische Worte die mit *Ch* anfangen, sind mit den Worten der Buchstabe *C* zu finden

A

B

C

* Page/Paginá/Seite 346.

D

E

F

G

H

I

J

L

M

N

O

P

Q

R

S

T

U

V

X

Z

German Index

A

B

C

D

E

F

G

H

I

J

K

L

M

N

O

P

Q

R

S

T

U

V

W

Z

Appendix I
Some Useful Meanings of Selected Terms

(Especially as an aid to interpreters and translators without legal training)

A

abatement decrease; diminution; mitigation; extinction
abetment assistance; cooperation, encouragement, especially in committing a crime
ab intestato from an intestate; in the case of intestacy
abrogation annulment; repeal (of a law)
absconder one who hides himself from or avoids legal proceedings
acceptance assent to or compliance with terms of an offer
acceptor for honor one who accepts a bill of exchange for the honor of an involved party
constructive ~ implied acceptance
accessory
~ after the fact person who, knowing a crime has been committed, aids an offender or conceals the crime
~ before the fact person who assists, entices or commands another to commit a crime without being present at the crime
accord and satisfaction an executed agreement in satisfaction of a claim or a contact
accretion growth by external accumulation; gradual or imperceptible addition to riparian land
accrual accumulation, as of interest on money invested, vesting of a right or liability
acquittal freeing a prisoner as the result of a jury verdict or a court judgment; discharge; release, finding of not guilty
acquittance release from debt or other liability
act
~ of God exclusively natural accident or happening, such as a flood or hurricane
~ of state act done by sovereign power
authentic ~ act legally attested and rendered public by appropriate authority
enabling ~ act conferring power or removing disability
overt ~ open act to carry out an intent
action (at law) formal demand brought in account of a person's rights; judicial proceedings
~ in rem action to determine the right in specific property
~ in personam a remedy in which the proceedings are against the person
~ of assumpsit one to recover damages for nonperformance of a promise or breach of contract
~ of covenant one which lies for damages for breach of a contract under seal
~ of debt one which lies for a specific sum of money
~ of detinue one which lies for recovery of personal chattels taken lawfully, wrongfully detained and for damages for their detention
~ of ejectment action brought to test title to possession of land by parties making claims and to recover property adversely held

~ **of replevin** one for recovery of personal chattels unlawfully taken and for damages for their detention
~ **of trespass** one which lies for the recovery of damages for injury to a person or to property in his possession, or to a relative right
~ **of trover** one which lies for converting plaintiff's personalty
~ **on the case** one to recover damages for a tort or the tortious breach of duty
ademption revocation or taking away by action, as of a legacy
adhesion acceptance by a state of an existing treaty between other states or specified provisions thereof
ad hoc for this case or purpose
ad interim in the meantime
adjournment sine die adjournment without setting a time for another meeting
administration
~ **cum testamento anexo** administration with will annexed
administrator de bonis non administrator appointed to act in case of a vacancy in the office or executor or administrator
advocate one who pleads causes in court
affiant person who makes an affidavit
affidavit affirmed or sworn statement before an officer with authority to administer oaths
affreightment contract of hire for a vessel or its use
age of discretion age at which the law imputes responsibility for criminal acts and the ability to consent to matters affecting the person
agent
accredited ~ authorized representative
del credere ~ agent who stands surety for a purchaser's solvency
aggrieved suffering from denial of rights sufficient to sue for legal redress; injured; oppressed
agreement
executive ~ agreement made between the United States and a foreign state without Senate participation
gentleman's ~ agreement binding only as a matter of honor
standstill ~ agreement to draw a halt to something at its present state
working ~ agreement adopted to facilitate further discussion
aider and abettor one who advises or encourages commission of a crime
alderman senior judicial or administrative municipal officer
alibi defense showing defendant at another place when crime was committed
alien
~ **enemy** alien who owes allegiance to a hostile belligerent
~ **property custodian** person who takes charge of the property of alien enemies in wartime
alienation estrangement; insanity; transfer of property rights
alimony legally enforced right of maintenance allowance granted to wife from former husband after separation
allegation assertion of fact, usually unproved; a party's statement of what he intends to prove
allonge paper added to a bill of exchange for additional indorsements
alluvion (alluvium) gradual or imperceptible addition of matter to river banks by flow of water
alternat procedure by which precedence of diplomats of the same rank is determined
ambassador-at-large ambassador whose mission is not limited to a given post

amicus curiae (friend of the court), advisor of the court on a relevant point of law
amortization (amortisement) payment of indebtness by installments or by a sinking fund
ancient lights right to unobstructed light through windows
ancient writings (documents) writings 30 years old or more
angary belligerent's right to seize and control neutral property
animo furandi with intent to steal
appearance
special ~ appearance for the sole purpose of objecting to the court's jurisdiction
apportionment division, as of rights of liabilities; division of legislative delegates of an elected body
appurtenance adjunct; something, like a right of way, belonging to a more important thing
a priori by analogy; by the former reason
arbitration settlement of disputes by arbitrators rather than by judicial tribunal
arraignment procedure of calling accused before a court to answer indictment charges
array jury panel; orderly arrangement
arson malicious burning of a house or other property of another
asportation carrying away of goods feloniously ~ an element of larceny and robbery
assassination murder committed for hire; murder by stealth
assault
aggravated ~ assault with intent to commit another crime; serious assault
~ and battery injurious attack on another's person ~ the doing of the harm constitutes the battery
assets
frozen ~ assets that cannot be readily utilized without loss
liquid ~ assets that are easily converting into cash
real ~ assets in real estate in the hands of an heir
tangible ~ corporeal assets which may be valued
assignment transfer of property or interests to another; task assigned the assignment of errors is the list of specific errors on which appelant relies
assigns persons to whom an assignment is made
assumpsit (see **action of assumpsit**)
attachment (see writ **of attachment**)
attack
collateral ~ proceeding which challenges the integrity of a judgement
attainder (see **bill of attainder**)
attempt, criminal overt effort to commit a crime ~ it is punishable as a crime itself
attestation authentication of an act or document by a witness or official;
attorney
state's ~ legal officer who represents the state in the courts
attornment acceptance by a tenant of one person as a landlord in the place of another
authentication verification; establishment of the validity of a document for legal purposes
authority
apparent ~ authority which, though not actually granted by the principal, is permitted by him to the agent

autrefois acquit formerly acquitted
aval guaranty of bill of exchange
averment positive factual allegation
avulsion sudden re-channelling of a water course boundary
award decision of arbitrators; grant

B

bail surety to procure a person's release from legal custody or his appearance in court and to assure that he will appear when and where directed by the court
bailment delivery to another of personal property in trust, the property to be returned later to the bailor
banktruptcy legal process for relief of debt by paying such debts as are possible and absolving the rest; also the equitable marshalling of assets among creditors to be paid
  receiver (referee, trustee) in bankruptcy a commissioner or aide of a court of bankruptcy with extensive judicial powers but subject to court control to collect and dispose of assets
  voluntary bankrupt one who declares bankruptcy by his own petition
bargain and sale transfer of property in consideration of an agreed price
bargaining
  collective ~ union-management negotiation
barratry (barretry) exciting frequent quarrels or lawsuits
barrister advocate, counsel who pleads at the bar
battery unlawful touching or beating of a person
bill draft of a proposed law; written account of things to be paid for; paper money
  accommodation ~ bill endorsed without consideration and as a favor
  appropriation ~ proposed measure to regulate disbursement of public funds
  ~ in equity formal written complaint to a court of equity
  ~ of attainder legislative act pronouncing a person guilty and inflicting a punishment without trial
  ~ of exceptions formal written statement of exceptions taken to a judge's rulings or decisions
  ~ of health physician's statement certifying a person's good condition of health; official statement certifying a ship's healthful condition
  ~ of indictment document stating a criminal charge before it is considered by the grand jury
  ~ of particulars detailed statement of a claim or counterclaim at law
  ~ of peace bill to secure relief from repeated and vexatious litigation
  ~ quia timet bill in equity to seek protection against an anticipated injury
  deficiency ~ appropriation bill for items not sufficiently covered previously
  due ~ written acknowledgement of indebtness
  true ~ grand jury's endorsement upon a bill of indictment
bona fide genuine; in good faith; sincere
breaking and entering housebreaking; forcible intrusion into a private property
bribery giving or receiving of anything of value to influence someone in a position of trust
brief counsel's written summary in support of a client's case
burglary breaking and entering the house or other structure of another with felonious intent

C

capias (see **writ of capias**)
capitulations regime by which foreigners in certain eastern countries were not subject to local jurisdiction
capital offense one for which the death penalty may be inflicted
cartel written agreement to regulate intercourse between enemy states; agreement between procedures or companies to restrict trade
case
moot ~ case to determine a hypothetical question
causa mortis in anticipation of death
cause
probable ~ reasonable ground for supposing that a cause of action is valid; most likely cause; direct, immediate cause
proximate ~ primary or dominating cause ~ an element of tort liability
to show ~ to demonstrate why an order, decree, etc. should not take effect
caveat emptor let the buyer beware
certiorari (see **writ of certiorari**)
challenge
~ for cause challenge to a juror for an alleged reason
~ to the array motion to strike the whole jury panel
~ to the polls motion to eliminate an individual juryman
peremptory ~ challenge to a juror limited by statute and granted without need to state cause
champerty maintenance by a third person of a lawsuit for profit from the matter in dispute
chance
last clear ~ doctrine declaring the party liable who has the last clear chance to avoid injury to another
chartering hiring of means of transportation for exclusive use; granting of rights or franchises from the sovereign
charter-party contract of affreightment
chattels movable or immovable goods or property, except land
incorporeal ~ incorporeal rights derived from personal things
real ~ interests derived from real estate
chose in action personal right not in possession but upon which an action may be obtained
claims
multifariousness of ~ misjoinder of causes or parties delaying settlement of a case
clause
arbitration ~ clause providing for compulsory arbitration in case of dispute
attestation ~ clause formally authenticating an act or instrument by witnesses
enacting ~ the part of a statute declaring its enactment
escape ~ clause in a contract relieving a promissor from liability if future developments make performance impossible
most-favored-nation ~ treaty clause providing equal treatment between contracting states
saving ~ clause in a statute providing an exception, restriction or exemption from operation of law
clearing reciprocal exchange of checks by banks
cloture procedure for closing legislative debate

cognizance judicial knowledge; notice
collective bargaining negotiation seeking a fair agreement between employers and unions
color of office pretence of a right to do an act by an official who does not have that right
combine agreement tending to create a monopoly or to constitute a restraint on trade
comity courtesy, especially recognition given by one court to decisions of another court which are not legally binding
company
joint stock ~ company possessing capital divided into transferable shares
limited liability ~ company in which the liability of the shareholder is limited to the amount of shares he has taken
winding up of a ~ liquidation of a company
competition
unfair ~ act by a seller to deceive the public with intent to acquire a larger share of the market
complicity involvement in an unlawful act
composition compromise agreement by which creditors accept partial payment to satisfy a debt
compromis agreement to arbitrate, stipulating arbitrators, procedures, etc.
concordat compact between the Pope and a temporal state
condition condition which must be fulfilled before the estate or
condition precedent obligation begins or the bequest becomes effective condition which takes effect only subsequent to the vesting
condition subsequent of an estate or bequest or the beginning of an obligation confirm or release from obligation
condominium joint sovereignty by several states over a territory
condonation forgiveness of a matrimonial offense with an implied condition that it shall not be repeated
confession and avoidance plea admitting the truth of facts set out in the declaration and alleging obstacles tending to show that defendant is not liable
connivance secret cooperation with corrupt intent
consideration inducement to conclude a contract by benefit offered or detriment sustained
valuable ~ consideration on which a promise is founded to enforce an obligation
consortium international business combination; the rights and duties of husband and wife resulting from marriage
conspiracy combinations of persons for an unlawful purpose or, by unlawful means, for a purpose not unlawful
~ in restraint of trade agreement to benefit by restricting or monopolizing trade
constabulary armed but non-military police body; civilian police
contempt of court any act which impedes the court in administering justice or affronts its dignity
continental shelf the land mass under sea water contiguous to a continent
continuous voyage voyage though interrupted, considered continuous because of its purpose
contra bonos mores in violation of good morals
contract
nude ~ (nudum pactum) void contract or agreement

specific performance of a ~ court judgment requiring performance according to the precise terms agreed upon

third party beneficiary ~ contract made for the benefit of a party not privy to it

contumacy willful disobedience of a court order; refusal of a person to appear when cited by a court; default

conversion unauthorized assumption or use of another's property; appropriation transformation; exchange

equitable ~ the change of property from personal to real or from real into personal, not actually taking place but by intendment of equity; to put into effect the provisions of a contract or will

conveyance deed transferring title or land

coparcenary estate held by joint inheritance, two or more persons forming one heir

co-respondent person charged in a divorce suit, usually with adultery, and proceeded against jointly with the respondent

coroner's inquest examination of the circumstances of any violent or suspicious death by a coroner with, at times, the aid of a jury

corpus delicti fundamental fact or essence of a crime

counterclaim defendant's claim presented in opposition to that of the plaintiff as a species of set-off or recoupment

courts

~ of record court whose acts are recorded, with power to fine or imprison for contempt

court

~ of record court whose acts are recorded, with power to fine or imprison for contempt

nisi prius ~ court exercising general original jurisdiction in civil cases; trial court

surrogate ~ state court with jurisdiction relating to probate matters

covenant (see also action of covenant) solemn agreement; written pledge, signed and sealed

~ running with the land one that transfers the burden when the estate is transferred, and which cannot be separated from the land

restrictive ~ agreement restricting the free use of land

coverture, under legal disability of a woman arising from the conjugal relation

curtesy common law right of a husband in the deceased wife's property

cy-pres doctrine equity doctrine in accordance with which written instruments are construed as nearly as possible to the intention of the parties when impossible or illegal to give them legal effect

D

damages

compensatory ~ damages which will merely make good the loss sustained

exemplary ~ damages awarded in excess of the loss sustained as solace to plaintiff or punishment for defendant

damnum abque injuria loss without legally redressable injury

de bene esse provisionally

debenture certificate of indebtedness

debt (see action of debt)

active debt ~ debt bearing interest

floating ~ claims against a corporation for which there is no money specifically provided

funded ~ debt for the payment of which a sufficient sum is appropriated
debtor
judgment ~ one whose obligation to pay a debt is evidenced by a judgment of a court of law but remains unfulfilled
declaration statement made out of court; plaintiff's first pleading; unsworn statement of an interested party used as evidence; announcement; proclamation
dying ~ declaration of a person given in anticipation of impending death, with reference to the immediate cause of his death
decree judgement of a court of equity or admiralty; authoritive decision; often used as a synonym of judgment
~ nisi preliminary or provisional judgment
interlocutory ~ provisional decree pronounced to allow further proceedings preparatory to a final decree
~ law an executive decree with the provisional force of law
deed instrument of conveyance or contract
~ of trust instrument transferring legal title to real property to a trustee as security
quitclaim ~ deed of conveyance which gives no warranty of validity of the title
defamation harming another's reputation by false and malicious statements ~ it includes libel and slander
defeasance clause in a deed or collateral deed containing conditions whose performance defeats the force of the deed or of the collateral deed; nullifying limitation
delict minor offense; failure to fulfill an obligation
demurrer allegation of insufficiency of a plea
denial disavowal; traverse of an allegation pleaded by opposing party; deprivation; rejection
deposition oral or written testimony of a witness taken under oath out of court
detainer (see **writ of detainer**)
detention on demand; preventive detention detention of a persistent offender to protect the public
detinue (see **action of detinue**)
devise disposition of land by will
direction court's instruction to a jury; order
discontinuance technical interruption of proceedings of irregularity in pleading; termination of an action
discovery legal means prescribed in a court or criminal action to find something previously unknown; disclosure of facts or things in the exclusive knowledge or possession of the other party
dishonor refusal to accept or pay a bill of exchange
dismissal final removal of a case from court without trial; discharge; release from employment
disseisin dispossession of one who has an ownership right
distraint seizure of goods for payment of debts
distress seizure of personal property to pay a debt
distribution apportionment of an intestate's estate; allotment; division; marketing; merchandising
diversity plea of a prisoner alleging that he is not the person attainted
divorce
~ a mensa et thoro legal separation; limited divorce
~ a vinculo matrimonii absolute divorce dissolving the bonds of matrimony
dock for prisoners space occupied by a prisoner in a criminal court

docket brief, formal record of court proceedings; calendar of causes to be tried
Doe, John fictitious name sometimes used in court cases
domain absolute right of ownership of land; legislature's sovereign control of private property for public use
drawback allowance on customs duties made for re-exportation; refund; hindrance selling in bulk regardless of low price; selling in another country at a price below that charged at home
duplicity in pleading, the uniting of two or more causes of action in one court; double-dealing; fraud

E

easement a right to use the land of another, usually a neighbor, for a special purpose
  affirmative ~ one involving active use of the land, for example a right of way
  negative ~ one not involving active use of the land, such as the easement of light
edict law ordained publicly by a sovereign
eleemosynary charitable; philanthropic
embargo detention of goods and ships by a state in time of war or hostility; restriction imposed upon commerce; prohibition
emblements annual cultivated produce; right of outgoing tenant to crops left growing on the land
embracery attempted corruption of a juror
eminent domain sovereign's right to appropriate private property for public use upon payment of reasonable compensation
encroachment gradual intrusion into the rights or property of another
encumbrance (incumbrance) claim or liability attached to property; burden; impediment
enjoyment, quiet ~ a covenant assuring a lessee disturbance of his possession for leased land
enrichment doctrine that a person shall not enrich himself inequitably at another's expense
entailment limited inheritance
entrapment inducing a person to commit a crime which he had not intended to commit, in order to prosecute him
equity system of jurisprudence which decides conflicting claims for which no legal remedy at law exists; money value of property or ownership right in property
  ~ of redemption right of a mortgagor to redeem a legally forfeited estate
escheat reversion to the state of the property of an intestate without lawful heirs
escrow deed, instrument on money deposited with a third party to be delivered to a grantee upon fulfillment of a condition
estate all forms of interest in property
  contingent ~ estate dependent upon a future event for its effect
  dominant ~ estate whose owner enjoys the benefit of the easement
  ~ at will one that can be created only by express contract
  ~ by sufferance one in which a person rightfully upon the land remains after the expiration of his term without his landlord's consent
  ~ for years one for a determinable time
  ~ in fee simple estate free of any encumbrance or condition; ownership in perpetuity

~ in fee tail estate of inheritance limited to the donee and the heirs of his body in a direct line of descent
~ pur autre vie estate for the life of another
freehold ~ estate for life or in fee simple
life ~ (for life) estate whose duration is limited to the life of a person
residuary ~ that part of an estate of a testator that remains after all legal dues have been satisfied and all devises, grants, and bequests are made

estoppel impediment which precludes allegation or denial of a fact because of previous conduct

estovers lessee's right to use timber on the premises

exception legal objection; exclusion from effect or operation

execution
stay of ~ a period in which no execution of a judgment can be issued

exterritoriality (extraterritoriality) operation of the laws of a state beyond the territorial limits of that state

extortion obtaining money unlawfully under cover of office; unlawful exaction of money by threat of force

F

fait accompli act done and irreversible

fee fixed charge for governmental or professional services; estate of inheritance without condition
~ simple (see **estate in fee simple**)
~ tail (see **estate in fee tail**)

felony any of several crimes more serious than misdemeanors
misprision of ~ failure to prevent the commission of a felony or to inform the authorities of a felony one has witnessed or known about
to compound a ~ to accept compensation for refraining from prosecuting a felony

feme covert married woman

feme sole unmarried woman

feoffment conveying title to land by delivery of actual possession

fiduciary person in a position of trust and confidence; founded upon trust or confidence; legally defined duty

fieri facias (see **writ of fieri facias**)

finding judicial statement of a conclusion of fact or law

foreclosure termination of a mortgagor's right to reclaim his estate

forfeiture deprivation of rights or interest as a penalty for nonperformance of obligation

frame-up plot to incriminate on false evidence

fraud intentional deceit which induces another to part with something of value

friend
next ~ a person who sues on behalf of an infant or other person legally disabled to act for himself

fund
sinking ~ sums of money set aside for a special purpose such as extinguishment of a debt
stabilization ~ government fund used to control its currency on the foreign exchange
trust ~ fund legally held for carrying out a specific purpose
to earmark funds to set aside funds for a specific purpose

fungibles movable goods which are interchangeable, such as grain or money

G

garnishment process of attaching money or goods owed to defendant but in the hands of a third party
gravamen material part of a charge or grievance; gist
guardian ad litem. protective authority given to someone by law to manage the person or property of one who is legally incompetent

H

habeas corpus (see **writ of habeas corpus**)
hearing preliminary judicial examination of an issue
hearsay evidence derived from what a witness heard repeated by another; rumor
hereditaments all things that may be inherited
holder
bona fide ~ one taking title by delivery and endorsement
~ in due course holder who accepted a bill of exchange in good faith and without notice of claim against it
homologation approbation; confirmation
housebreaking forcing an entry into a dwelling with felonious intent
hue and cry notice of a felon's escape from prison, requiring cooperation in his recapture; disturbance; shouts of alarm
hush-money money paid to assure secrecy

I

immunity exemption from duty, obligation, or penalty, as exemption of witnesses from prosecution for compiling testimony
impulse
irresistible ~ impulse to commit a crime which is uncontrollable because of some form of mental disease
in camera in private with spectators excluded
in curia before the court; in court
indefeasible incapable of being nullified or voided
indenture deed executed by both or all parties
indictment formal written accusation presented by a grand jury or initiating the trial of a criminal offense
to dismiss, quash an ~ to throw out an indictment and give it no further consideration
inducement motive; incentive; explanatory introduction to the principal allegations of a pleading
in extremis at the point of death; in very difficult circumstances
in flagrante delicto in the act of committing a crime
information accusation of crime on which an accused is brought to trial
upon ~ and belief formula indicating that the witness does not have direct knowledge of the facts
injunction (see **writ of injunction**)
in limine litis at the beginning of the suit; preliminarily
in pari delicto equally culpable
in personam against a specific person
inquest legal inquiry, especially by a jury
in re in the matter of

in rem against a thing
in statu quo in the existing state; unchanged
insurance
 liability ~ insurance covering an employer against liability resulting from injury to his employees
 workmen's compensation ~ insurance against damages for work-related injuries received by workmen while in the employ of the insured's employer
intendment true legal intention or meaning
interest
 accrued ~ interest which has accumulated but is not yet paid
 affected with a public ~ concerning the legal rights, liabilities or interests of the community at large
 compound ~ new principal created from original principal sum plus accrued interest
 vested ~ absolute, indefeasible interest
interpleader proceeding to enable a person to force two parties who make the same claim against him to litigate between themselves
intestacy condition of dying without having made a will

J

jeopardy
 double, former, prior ~ defense that a person shall not be tried twice for the same offense
joinder of parties uniting parties as plaintiffs or defendants in a suit
judge
 ~ advocate officer serving as prosecutor in a court martial
 ~ advocate general legal adviser to the military establishment
judgment
 arrest of ~ act of staying or refusing to render judgment in criminal cases, after verdict, for legal cause
 ~ creditor creditor who has obtained a judgment in his favor against a judgment debtor
 to quash (vacate) a ~ to annul or make void a judgment
judicature administration of justice; functions of those administering justice; the judiciary; a court of justice
juridical relating to the office or administration of a judge or to law in general
jurisconsult jurist; legal expert
jurisdiction
 summary ~ jurisdiction to give a judgment without referral to another body, as to commit to a prison for contempt
jury
 grand ~ jury investigating crimes committed in the country, hearing evidence and bringing an indictment if it finds sufficient evidence for trial by an ordinary jury
 hung ~ jury whose opinions are so split that they cannot reach a verdict
 packing a ~ improper, corrupt selection of a jury
 petit ~ ordinary twelve-man jury for the trial of civil and criminal cases
 struck ~ selection of a jury of twelve from a panel returned by the proper officer
 to challenge a juror to object to the presence of a summoned juror or to the seating of a prospective juror

to charge a ~ to instruct the jury on points of law
to impanel a ~ to select a jury
to labor a ~ to interfere with a jury to influence a verdict
to poll a ~ to question jurors individually with regard to their concurrence in the verdict

jus law; right
~ belli law of war
~ cogens law which is binding regardless of the will of the parties
~ gentium law of nations
~ sanguinis law of the place of one's parents; right of blood
~ soli law of the place of one's birth

K

kleptomania irresistible neurotic impulse to steal for no economic reasons
knowledge
constructive ~ knowledge inferred to a party by virtue of the existence of established facts or the following of an established procedure
'Know all men by these presents' formal introduction to written instruments

L

laches negligent delay in claiming a legal right or observing a duty
larceny taking away another's personalty and converting or intending to convert it to one's own use
grand ~ larceny where the goods stolen are above a certain value
petit ~ larceny where the goods stolen are below a certain value
law
adjective ~ law relating to remedies, procedure
anti-trust ~ law to protect trade and commerce from unfair monopolies
case ~ body of law derived from judicial decisions
due process of ~ (law of the land) due course of law through its regular administration in the courts of justice; fundamental fairness
natural ~; law of nature law which exists universally and independently of positive of enacted law; fundamental law
private-international ~; conflict of laws branch of law which deals with the adjustment of the conflict of laws between different juridictions or states
prize ~ law relating to the capture of prize at sea
substantive ~ law that regulates rights as distinguished from adjective or remedial law
legacy bequest; gift of personal property by will
legatee
residuary ~ one to whom the residue of the personal estate of a testator has been bequeathed after payment of legacies mentioned in the will
letters
~ of administration documents accrediting a diplomat and certifying his appointment
~ patent government instruments conveying a right, privilege or authority to a person
~ rogatory court request to courts of another jurisdiction to examine a witness resident therein

~ **testamentary** instruments authorizing an executor to discharge duties of his office

levee, levy en masse spontaneous, unorganized resort to arms by people of a territory upon threat of invasion

lex law

~ **ferenda** law desirable to establish

~ **fori** law of the forum

~ **lata** law in force

~ **loci (rei sitae)** law of the place, situs

~ **talionis** law of retaliation based on the doctrine of 'an eye for an eye', a tooth for a tooth'

liability

joint and several ~ liability for which the parties may be sued individually or all together

libel malicious, defamatory publication; plaintiff's statement of cause of action in an admiralty or ecclesiastical court case

licensee a person permitted but not expressly invited to enter property; person to whom a license has been granted

lien claim on a person's property as security for a debt

mechanic's ~ a lien held by a person who has not been paid for work or materials supplied

lis pendens pending suit

lockout employer's withholding of work to coerce employees to make more satisfactory concessions

locus delicti place where something is alleged to have happened

locus standi right of appearance in court on a certain question; standing in court

logrolling union of minority interests, often corrupt, to secure legislation; exchange of favors by legislators for mutual benefit

M

magistracy body of public officers who administer the law; body of judicial officers of the lowest rank

maintenance unlawful interference in a law suit, as by furnishing money or advice; support of livelihood

malfeasance illegal act; performance of an illegal act

malice

~ **aforethought** premeditation to commit an illegal acts without justification

malicious mischief willful destruction of personal property

malicious prosecution action for harm resulting from prosecution to injure defendant without probable cause

malum in se inherently wrong; wrong in itself, as commiting murder

malum prohibitum offense only because it is forbidden by law, as violating parking ordinance

malversation misbehavior or corruption in office

mandamus (see **writ of mandamus**)

manslaughter unlawful killing of a human being without malice or deliberation

mare clausum closed sea

marshal an officer with duties similar to those of a sheriff or constable

mayhem intentional maiming or depriving a person of the use of his members

meeting of the minds agreement essential to a valid contract

memorial rough draft of court order; petition presented to an executive or legislative body
mens rea criminal intent
miscegenation inter-racial cohabitation or marriage
misfeasance misuse of lawful authority; wrongful performance of a lawful act
misrepresentation
fraudulent ~ misrepresentation by a person in full knowledge of its falsehood and with intention to mislead
money
blood ~ reward offered for the apprehension and conviction of an alleged felon; price paid for causing the death of a person
liquid ~ ready money
mortgage conveyance of property as security for a debt
mortmain inalienable possession of land or tenements by any corporation
motion application to a court for a ruling or order
~ for a directed verdict motion made when there is a variance or insufficient evidence
~ for a judgment non obstante veredicto motion used when the case is decided on an immaterial issue; motion sought for a judgment from the court notwithstanding the jury verdict
~ for a new trial motion based on matters off the record, such as newly discovered evidence
~ for a repleader one used when a verdict has been given on an issue joined on an immaterial fact
~ for a venire facias de novo one which seeks a new trial before another jury
~ to dismiss one which lies for an error apparent on the face of the record
~ to vacate a judgment motion to set aside a judgment for good cause, such as lack of jurisdiction
to carry a ~ to have a motion approved
murder
first degree ~ unlawful killing of a human being with premeditation or accompanying a serious felony
second degree ~ murder committed spontaneously without forethought
mutatis mutandis with necessary changes

N

ne exeat (see **writ of ne exeat**)
negligence
comparative ~ doctrine that plaintiff may recover if his negligence was slight and the negligence of the defendant was gross
contributory ~ negligence on the part of the plaintiff combining with that of the defendant to cause injury
negotiable instrument instrument as evidence of debt, such as bills and notes and checks
nolens volens whether willing or unwilling; willy-nilly
nolle prosequi recorded decision not to prosecute further
non liquet doctrine that in certain cases the court cannot decide
nonsuit termination of a suit for any of several causes
notice document from a court or administrative body notifying a party of the date of a hearing or trial; notification; warning; attention; observation; information; knowledge

to take judicial ~ of to take cognizance of the truth of certain known facts without proof
novation agreed substitution of a new contract for an existing one
nuisance
abatement of a ~ remedy allowing an injured party to remove a nuisance
attractive ~ something which is dangerous but attractive to children
nulla poena sine lege there should be no punishment without a law fixing the penalty
nunc pro tunc order made at present to have effect at an earlier time, such as one correcting clerical errors after judgment

O

obiter dictum collateral judicial opinion not essential for the judgment
offset; set-off counterbalance; counterclaim; deduction
order
interim ~ provisional order
~ nisi conditional order
point of ~ question raised about proper procedure
restraining, stay ~ order enjoining someone not to do a given act
standing ~ order directing the use of procedure in force until specifically repealed
superior ~ (s) doctrine according to which an official of superior rank must assume responsibility for orders given to an official of inferior rank
overt act act carrying an intent or purpose, as to do harm or commit a crime

P

pacta sunt servanda contracts and other agreements are binding
Pandects a 50-volume collection on the Roman civil law
paper
accommodation ~ bill or note by which one party lends to another without consideration
working ~ a basic information paper used to assist conferees
parcener joint heir
pari delicto equal in fault; in a similar offense
pari passu equally, without preference
partition division of jointly held property; apportionment; dividing barrier
party an opposing litigant in a judicial proceeding; one engaged in a transaction or who has made an agreement
accommodation ~ person who signs an accommodating paper
charter ~ contract leasing a ship, or part of one, to a merchant to carry cargo
~ of the first part indispensable party
~ ticket program of the party
~ wall wall partly on one person's land, partly on that of his neighbor, for the common benefit of both
passage
innocent ~ right of a ship to put into a foreign port in case of emergency without being subject to its jurisdiction
pendente lite during litigation
per curiam according to the court
performance
specific ~ equitable remedy compelling a party to perform a contract as distin-

guished from an action for damages for nonperformance
per stirpes by the roots; by right of representing an ancestor
plea answer to a petition, declaration or complaint
dilatory ~ plea by the defense based on an objection to something other than the right of action
~ in abatement one aiming to defeat the declaration because of a defect
~ in bar one showing ground for defeating plaintiff's action
~ in confession and avoidance plea admitting plaintiff's cause of action, but declaring that it has been discharged
~ in mitigation of damages plea aiming to reduce the amount of damage sought
~ plea in suspension plea requesting the court to delay judgment
~ puis darrein continuance plea of events occuring subsequent to original pleadings
~ to the jurisdiction plea challenging the jurisdiction of the court
policy
good neighbor ~ policy of friendly cooperation with and non-interference in another country's affairs
open door ~ policy of gaining free and equal opportunities for commercial and other intercourse to all countries alike
possession
adverse ~ method of acquiring title by possession for a statutorily set period of time under a claim of right
postliminium (postliminy) the rule that a person who has been captured and later returned to his own state regains all his former rights, and that property captured in war vests in the state from which it was captured at the conclusion of hostilities
power
~ of attorney instrument of authorization for another to act as one's agent
delegation of ~ (s) granting powers to the federal government by the United States constitution, to administrative bodies by the legislature
pre-emption settler's exclusive right to buy his tract of land; a state's right of detention of foreign merchandise to afford preference of purchase by its nationals
prescription sovereignty or title acquired through long-continued possession
presentment grand jury notice of an offense without an indictment; presentation of a note for payment
presents, by these by this instrument
privateering government-authorized piracy against a belligerent
privity of contract special relation between parties based on mutuality of interest
prize belligerent goods seized at sea
probate (of a will) proof of the validity of a will
proceeding(s) all methods of obtaining court action; any step in the action taken by a court
adversary ~ a contested proceeding
ancillary ~ subordinate proceeding in aid of a primary action
stay of ~ temporary suspension of regular proceedings at the court's discretion
process court writ; summons
~ server person who serves legal documents, especially those requiring court appearance
program
austerity ~ government program of economic controls which aims to improve national economy

prolixity superfluous statement of facts in pleading or evidence; verbosity
property
  community ~ property owned by a marriage partnership
  industrial ~ intangible rights of property such as ownership of trademarks, patents or copyrights
  literary ~ right which entitles an author and his heirs to the sole use and profit of his composition
  real ~ lands and tenements and the rights connected with them
proscription condemnation to exile or death; banishment; outlawing; prohibition
'The prosecution rests' conclusion of the case for the prosecution
protest notarial act for want of payment of a note; master's renunciation of liability for the loss of his vessel
pursuit
  hot ~ pursuit across jurisdictional boundaries; in law of arrest pursuit with no interruption after offense or issuance of warrant

Q

quantum meruit how much he has earned; as much as he deserves
question
  catch ~ misleading question designed to detect an error
  leading ~ question which suggests to a witness a desired answer
quid pro quo fair compensation; mutual consideration
quitclaim renunciation of a right; relinquishment of a claim; release; acquittance
quo warranto (see **writ of quo warranto**)

R

rebus sic stantibus implied treaty condition that its validity depends upon no fundamental change in the circumstances in which the treaty was concluded
rebutter defendant's answer to plaintiff's surrejoinder
recidivist habitual criminal; a repeating or persistent offender
recognizance recorded obligation or debt
recoupment reduction of plaintiff's damages; repayment; discount; recovery
recovery legal restoration or vindication of a right or of property
recusation challenge to judge or jurors on grounds of prejudice
redemption process of revoking, cancelling or annuling
  right of ~ agreement by which the seller reserves the right to take back the thing sold by return of the price paid
referee legal officer appointed by the court to take testimony and report to the court; person referred to for settlement or recommendation
rejoinder defendant's answer to plaintiff's replication; response; retort
remainder an interest, estate which takes effect at the end of another estate
  contingent ~ estate in remainder which may never take effect
  vested ~ one which a person is ready to take when and as determined by the preceding estate
remedies
  election of ~ choice of one of several means for enforcement of a right
  exhaustion of local ~ international law doctrine that all local remedies must be utilized when so provided before courts will act or international law may be involved

extraordinary legal ~ remedies which are found in writs rather than by action
renvoi doctrine according to which a court adopts the rules of the foreign law in case of conflicts of laws
replevin (see **action of replevin**)
replication step in pleading that follows defendant's plea or, in equity, defendant's answer
reply plaintiff's answer to a set-off or counterclaim; in equity, plaintiff's pleading to allegations of fact in defendant's plea
report official account of findings or proceedings
to table a ~ to lay a report on the table to remove it from consideration (U.S.); to present a report (U.K.)
representation principle of inheriting **per stirpes**
reprieve suspension of sentence
repugnancy contradictory or inconsistent statements on a material point in a pleading
res communes thing common to all but which cannot be acquired by any
res gestae all things incidental to a transaction; things done
res inter alios acta acts between other parties
res ipsa loquitur the thing speaks for itself
res judicata matter judicially and therefore finally decided
res nullius property belonging to nobody
respondeat superior master's liability for a servant's fault
respondent defendant, especially in appellate and divorce cases; person who answers in a proceeding
retorsion retaliation; reprisal
return short account of execution of a writ
reversal voiding of a judgment by a superior court
reversion residue of an estate left by law in the grantor; future return of estate to grantor; right of redemption of land mortgaged or adjudged for payment of debt; return to former condition of owner
rider addition attached to a completed document; amendment attached to a bill
right
inchoate ~ incipient right; right not yet specifically vested
prescriptive ~ right based on long, continued enjoyment
right of asylum right to receive protection
right of visit ans search right of a belligerent to examine neutral vessels at sea
to waive one's right(s) to abdicate or give up one's right(s)
rights
precarious ~ granted rights which the grantor may revoke at will
riparian ~ particular rights connected with the ownership of lands on the banks of water courses
state's ~ rights of every state of the United States in contrast to rights of the federal government
vested ~ absolute, unconditional rights protected by government
robbery stealing personal property from a person by force, intimidation or stealth
Roe, Richard fictitious name sometimes used in court cases
rule nisi (order to show cause) rule which becomes final unless cause can be shown against it
ruling court decision on a point of law

S

sabotage obstruction of industry by workers to coerce employers; willful damage to hinder war effort; effort to prevent something by indirect means
safe-conduct permit guarantying safety in enemy territory
salvage compensation for voluntary assistance in preserving a ship; cargo or other property in danger; property salvaged; saving from destruction
scienter knowledge; knowingly; in full awareness of the consequences
scire facias (see **writ of scire facias**)
seizin actual or constructive legal possession
sequestration attachment; depositing property pending litigation; seizure of property for government purposes; separation
service execution of process; delivery of a writ or other legal communication
  return of ~ officer's endorsement of a delivered writ
servitude charge upon an estate to benefit another
severance termination of a joint tenancy
shop
  bucket ~ dishonest brokerage house where buying and selling are fictitious
  closed ~ establishment where union membership is a necessary condition for employment
  open ~ establishment in which union and non-union men are employed indiscriminately
  union ~ establishment in which only union members may continue employment
similiter the like; a written statement expressing a party's acceptance of an issue in his adversary's pleading
seriatim in a series; one by one
sine die without setting a day to appear again
sina qua non indispensable requisite; necessity
solicitation asking, enticing, requesting, or inviting another to commit a crime or sexual act
specialty contract under seal
stare decisis adherence to court precedents
statute
  disabling ~ statute restraining and regulating exercise of a certain right of power
  Statutes at Large annual collection of congressional law of the United States
  ~ of Frauds statute designed to prevent fraud and perjury by requiring that certain causes of action be verified in writing by the person charged
  ~ of Limitations statute that limits the period within which an action will lie
stipulation agreement between opposing lawyers; definite condition to an agreement; provision
subpoena duces tecum writ compelling a person to produce specific evidence in court
subrogation substitution, as of one person for another as creditor
sui generis of his own kind
sui juris of his own right
summation opposing counsel's final presentation of argument; judge's resumé before jury deliberation
summons (see **writ of summons**)
suretyship contractual relation resulting in liability for another's obligations
surrebutter plaintiff's plea following defendant's rebutter
surrejoinder plaintiff's plea responding to defendant's rejoinder
survivorship right of the person who lives longer than others concerned

T

taint conviction of felony; stain of disgrace or corruption
tenancy (see **also estate**), a holding; tenure
~ **at will** a letting of land without a determinate estate
~ **by the entirety** a tenancy by the husband and wife without the power of serving it
tenement thing of permanent nature that may be legally held
dominant ~ tenement which benefits from an easement
servient ~ tenement subject to the bonus of an easement
terra nullius land belonging to no particular state
testament will
testate having left a valid will
title
chain of ~ successive devolution of title from its origin to its present holder
cloud on ~ impairment of title which may be proved invalid by evidence
inchoate ~ imperfect title; title not yet legally vested
tortfeasor one who is guilty of a tort; wrongdoer
traverse denial of an allegation
treason
high ~ treason against the sovereign of the state
misprision of ~ knowledge and concealment of treason, while not participating therein
trover (see **action of trover**)
trust
cestui que ~ beneficiary of a trust
constructive ~ one imposed by law as a remedy for fraud, although contrary to the intent of the parties
resulting ~ trust created by construction of law
spendthrift ~ one which provides for a beneficiary's maintenance but secures it against his own improvidence
trusteeship state of being invested with a trust; function of a trustee

U

ultra vires something beyond the scope of authorized powers
union
personal ~ union of two independent sovereign states subject to the same ruler
real ~ one in which the international relations of two states are undertaken by the Union
usufruct right of enjoying the profit of another's property

V

variance discrepance between pleading and proof
venue neighborhood; place; scene of trial or injury
verdict
directed ~ one which the jury returns as instructed by the court
general ~ one which states 'guilty' or not 'guilty'
partial ~ one by which the jury acquits defendant of part of the accusation and finds him guilty of the rest
special ~ one in which the jury finds only the facts

suspended ~ one made temporarily inoperative; postponed verdict
visit and search the right of an officer of a belligerent state to inspect foreign vessels in time of war on suspicion of illegal acts
vis major act of God; irresistible force; force majeure
voir dire preliminary examination to ascertain the competence of a witness or juror

W

waiver voluntary relinquishment of a right; abandonment; renunciation
warrant
bench ~ warrant issued by a judge for the apprehension of a person
search ~ magistrate's warrant authorizing an officer to search suspected premises
will
holographic ~ one signed by testator and written in his handwriting
nuncupative ~ one declared orally in the presence of witnesses
writ process of mandatory direction from a court of law
~ of attachment writ by which an attachment may be levied after judgment on goods, chattels, and credits to enforce obedience to a court order
~ of capias writ ordering seizure of property or person
~ of certiorari appellate writ for the re-examination of action by a lower court and, in certain cases, to review the action of administrative boards
~ of detainer judicial order authorizing arrest and detention
~ of error appellate writ for the examination of a concluded case of alleged error of law
~ of fieri facias writ of execution relating to chattels and realty
writ of habeas corpus writ to discover whether a prisoner is lawfully detained or to give a citizen protection from illegal imprisonment
~ of injunction writ restraining persons from committing specific acts
~ of mandamus writ by a superior court to compel performance of an official duty
~ of ne exeat writ to prevent defendant from leaving the court's jurisdiction until authorized to do so
~ of prohibition writ from a superior court commanding inferior court cesse of prosecution
~ of quo warranto writ to text the validity of a claim to hold office
~ of scire facias writ requiring a party to show cause why the record should be enforced, annulled, or vacated
~ of summons writ directing the sheriff or other officer to order a party to appear in court
~ of supersedeas process to supersede or stay; enforcement of a lower court judgment

Appendix II
Law Dictionaries

1. Selected Bilingual and Multilingual Dictionaries

Aglion, R. Dictionnaire juridique, anglais-français. New York, Brentano, 1947. 246 p.
Anderson, R.J.B. French-English glossary of French legal terms in European treaties . . . London, Sweet and Maxwell, 1972.
Anspach, L.E.F. and A.M. Coutanche. Dictionary of Anglo-Belgian Law. London, Sweet and Maxwell, 1920. 181 p.
Antolinez, C. Juristisches Wörterbuch, deutsch-spanisch, spanisch-deutsch. Köln, Heymann, 1970. 185 p.
Basedow, K.H. Wörterbuch der Rechtssprache, Deutsch-English und English-Deutsch. Hamburg, W. Heldt, 1947-1948. 2 v.
Bean, M.E. Handbook of Spanish-English and English-Spanish legal words and phrases. New York, Appleton, 1933. 257 p.
Becker, U. Rechtswörterbuch für die gewerbliche Wirtschaft, Deutsch-Englisch-Französisch. Frankfurt a. Main, 1966. 424 p.
Beseler, D. An English-German and German-English pocket dictionary of law and business terminology. Berlin, W. de Gruyter, 1947. 2nd ed., 271 p.
Cassidy, C.D.T. Deutsch-englisches juristisches Fachwörterbuch. Graz, Querschnitt-Verlag, 1947. 105 p.
Comité international de droit comparé Catalogue des sources de documentation juridique dans le monde. Paris, UNESCO, 1963. 362 p.
Conference terminology A manual for conference members and interpreters in Arabic, English and French. New York, Elsevier Publishing Co., 1962. 57 p.
Crew, A. and K.W.A. Gibson. Dictionary of medico-legal terms. London, Pitman and Sons, 1937. 80 p.
Dalrymple, A.W. French-English and English-French dictionary of legal words and phrases. London, Stevens, 1951. 2nd ed., 218 p.
Daum, V.G., Haensch and M.M. Garcia. Terminología jurídica, español y alemán. Munich, M. Hueber, 1970. 351 p.
Department of State, Language Services Division (USA). English-French glossary of treaty and conference terminology not found in most dictionaries. Washington, 1963, 337 p.; revised edition, 1976, 645 p.
Doucet, M. Wörterbuch der deutschen und französischen Rechtssprache. 2. Auflage, Munich, Berlin, Beck, 1960-1963. 2v.
Egbert, L.D. Law Dictionary- English-Español-Français-Deutsch. New York, Fallon, 1949. 637 p.
Egbert, L.D., H.M. Chevalier and C.D. MacIntosh. Glossary of legal terms: English-French, French-English. Nuremberg, International Military Tribunal, 1946. 66 p.
Elsevier's Dictionary of Criminal Science in English/American, French, Italian, Spanish, Portuguese, Dutch, Swedish and German. Comp. by J. Adler. New York, Elsevier, 1960. 1460 p.
Erdsiek, G. Wörterbuch für Recht, Wirtschaft und Politik. Hamburg, O. Meissner, 1964-1968. 2 v.
Fehner, P. Nouveau dictionnaire juridique et administratif: Français-allemand, allemand-français. Paris, UNESCO, 1963. 362 p.

Fernand-Laurent, C.J. and G. Dumas. Dictionnaire juridique anglais-français et français-anglais. Paris, Rousseau, 1927. 227 p.

Glossary of legal terms appearing in the French texts of the treaties establishing the European Coal and Steel Community, and the European Economic Community, and related documents. London, H.M. Stationery Office, 1965. 2nd ed., 61 p.

Haensch, F. Wörterbuch der internationalen Beziehungen und der Politik. Deutsch-englisch-französisch-spanish. Munich, M. Hueber, 1965. 638 p.

Herbst, R. Dictionary of commercial, financial and legal terms . . . English, German, French. Lucerne, Thali, 2nd ed., 1966. 3 v.

Homburg, R. Vocabulaire juridique en français, anglais, allemand. Paris, Dalloz, 1950. 66 p.

Horn, S.F. Glossary of financial terms in English/American, French, Spanish, German. New York, Amsterdam, London, Elsevier, 1965. 271 p.

Jéraute, J. Vocabulaire français-anglais et anglais-français de termes et locutions juridiques. Paris, Librairie générale de droit et de jurisprudence, 1953. 414 p.

Jordana de Pozas, L. and O. Merlin. Dictionnaire juridique, français-español, español-français. Paris, Editions de Navarre, 1968. 299 p.

Kerkoven, C.L.M. Conference languages, English and German. Alphen aan den Rijn, 1956. 362 p.

Kettridge, J.O. French-English and English-French dictionary of commercial and financial terms, phrases, and practices. London, Routledge and Kegan Paul, 1965. 647 p.

Kniepkamp, H.P. Rechtswörterbuch: English-Deutsch, Deutsch-Englisch. Berlin, Colloquium-Verlag, 4th ed., 1968. 216 p.

Langstaff, A.M. French-English, English-French law dictionary. Montreal, Wilson and Lafleur, 1937. 141 p.

Lapousse, C. Vocabulario jurídico francés-español. Buenos Aires, Abeledo-Perrot, 1960. 87 p.

Moreno Pacheco, M. Economic Terminology: English-Spanish, Spanish-English. Munich, Max Hueber, 1967. 479 p.

Nichols, P. Vocabulaire anglais-français de terminologie économique et juridique, Paris. Librairie générale de droit et de jurisprudence, 1971. 104 p.

Olver, G.T.W.A. French-English dictionary of legal and commercial terms. London, Stevens, 1925. 170 p.

Picard, R.E. Thilo and E. Steiner. Rechtswörterbuch, französisch-deutsch und deutsch-französisch. Zurich, Schulthess, 1950. 596 p.

Quemer, T.A. Dictionaire juridique; français-anglais, anglais-français: droit, finances, commerce, douanes, administration. Paris, Editions de Navarre, 1974. 323 p.

Quemner, T.A. and H. Neumann. Dictionnaire juridique: français-allemand, allemand-français. Paris, Editions de Navarre, 1960. 592 p.

Renner, R. Rechtssprache englisch-deutsch. Legal terminology English-German. Munich, Hueber, 1971. 526 p.

Renner, R., G. Haensch and M.C. de Kostine. Französisch-deutsche Rechtssprache. Munich, Hueber, 1966. 460 p.

Renner, R., R. Sachs and J. Foxberry. German-English economic terminology. Munich, M. Hueber Verlag, 1965. 556 p.

Robayo, L.A. Spanish-English, English-Spanish technical, legal, and commercial dictionary. Montreal, Dictionary Pub. Company, 1952. 334 p.

Robb, L.A. Diccionario de términos legales: Español-Inglés, Inglés-español. México, Editorial Limusa Wiley, S.A., 1967. 228 p.

Schreiber, A. Terminologie juridique, français-allemand, allemand-français. Droit pénal et procédure pénale. Geneva, Georg, 1949. 158 p.

Sell, L.L. English-Spanish comprehensive specialist's dictionary for insurance, law, labor, politics, business. New York International Dictionary Co., 1956. 536 p.

Tejada y Sainz, J. de D. Spanish and English legal and commercial dictionary. Cuba, Santa Maria de Rosario, 1945. 2nd ed., 124, 158 p.

The European Communities. A glossary of legal terms. London, H.M. Stationery Office, 1962. 27 p.

The European Communities. A glossary of legal terms appearing in French texts of the treaties establishing the European Atomic Energy Community, the European Coal and Steel Community, and the European Economic Community. London, H.M. Stationery Office, 1965. 61 p.

Union Académique Internationale. Dictionnaire de la terminologie du droit international. English, Spanish, German, Italian. Paris, Sirey, 1960. 755 p.

Van Hoof H., Economic Terminology. English-French. Munich, Max Hueber Verlag, 1967, 771 p.

World Bank Glossary. English-French-Spanish, 1977, 136 p.

2. General Law Dictionaries

Association of American Law Schools, Law Books Recommended for Librraries, No. 16, Dictionaries. Fred B. Rothman and Company. South Hackensack, New Jersey, 1966.

Europa-Glossar der Rechts- und Verwaltungssprache. Berlin, Munich, Zurich, Langenscheidt-Verlag, 1961. 63 p.

3. American/English Law Dictionaries

Ballentine's law dictionary. Rochester, New York, Lawyer's Cooperative Pub. Company; San Francisco, California, Bancroft-Whitney, 3rd ed., 1969. 1429 p.

Black's law dictionary. St. Paul, Minnesota, West Pub. Company, 4th ed., 1968. 1882 p.

Bouvier's law dictionary. Kansas City, Missouri, Vernon Law Book Company; St. Paul, Minnesota, West Pub. Company, 8th ed., 1914. 2 v. 3504 p.

Corpus Juris Secundum. Brooklyn, New York, American Law Book Company, 1936-1958. 101 v.

Jowitt, W.A. The dictionary of English law. London, Sweet and Maxwell, 1959. 2 v.

Saunders, John B. Words and phrases legally defined. London, Buttersworth, 1969-70, 5 v.

4. French Law Dictionaries

Capitant, H. Vocabulaire juridique. Parks, Les Presses Universitaires de France, 1930-1936. 15 fasciscules.

Dalloz Dictionnaire de droit. Paris, Librairie Dalloz. 2nd ed., 2 v.

Perraud-Charmantier, A. Petit dictionnaire de droit. Paris, Librairie générale de droit et de jurisprudence, 1938. 264 p.

Sirey Dictionnaire de la terminologie du droit international. Paris, Sirey, 1960. 755 p.

Soufflier, C. Vocabulaire de droit. Paris, M. Giard, 2nd ed., 1926. 1028 p.

5. Spanish Law Dictionaries

Capitant, H. Vocabulario jurídico. Buenos Aires, Ediciones Depalms, 1961. 630 p.
Couture, E.J. Vocabulario jurídico, Montevideo, 1960. 606 p.
Enciclopedia jurídica española. Barcelona, F. Seix, 1911-1923. 15 v.
Enciclopedia jurídica OMEBA. Buenos Aires, Editorial Bibliográfica Argentina, 1954. 268 v.
Fernandes de León, G. Diccionario jurídico. Buenos Aires, Editorial Abece, 1961. 4 v.

6. German Dictionaries

Creifelds, C. Rechtswörterbuch, Munich, C.H. Beck'sche Verlagsbuchhandlung, 1968. 1315 p.
Curtius, H. and K. Curtius. Keyser Rechtslexion für Alle. Heidelberg, 1951. 480 p.
Erganzbares Lexikon des Rechts. Neuwied am Rhein, Herman Luchterhand Verlag, 1955. (loose-leaf).
Kost, E. Juristisches Wörterbuch. Bremen, Carl Schunemann Verlag, 1961. 774 p.
Ullstein. Lexikon des Rechts. Herausgegeben von Otto Gritschner. 1971 by Verlag Ullstein GmbH, Frankfurt am Main, Berlin, Wien. 535 p.

Appendix III
Selected References on Legal Literature

The few selected references given below, although far from being comprehensive, will provide the researcher with much useful documentation and lead him to many other sources. The references include bibliographies; guides to the law and legal literature; handbooks, including legal materials; yearbooks; a reference book on constitutions; and law journals. There is also a brief comment on codes, ordinances and statutes.

The Harvard Law School Library has published, since 1960, an *Annual Legal Bibliography* with monthly supplements containing references on bibliography; general studies, including a collection of laws, statutes and reports; and a wide coverage of common law, civil law, and both private and public international law subjects. The first eight volumes contain indexes in English, French, German and Spanish; since 1969 the only index is in English.

A *Bibliography on Foreign and Comparative Law,* compiled and annotated by Charles Szladits, was published by Oceana Publications in New York in three volumes covering the years 1960-1965, with Supplements issued annually. It includes references to books and articles in English on private law, commercial law, labor law, law and procedure, criminal law and procedure, public law, and private international law. There is also a geographic index and an author index. The same author is the general editor of a series published by Oceana for the Parker School of Foreign and Comparative Law, Columbia University, entitled *Guide to Foreign Legal Materials.* Three have been published to date, covering French, German and Swiss; Italian; and Belgian, Luxembourg and Netherlands sources.

The United Nations Office in Geneva publishes a monthly list of selected articles, with references on public international law, private international law, and national legislation of various countries; also a monthly list of books catalogued in its library, including law books.

The United Nations in New York publishes a bibliography on subjects of concern to the United Nations, including legal questions. It appeared semiannually from 1965-1970 as *Current Issues*; since January 1971 it has appeared semi-monthly under the title *Current Bibliographical Information.*

The International Association of Law Libraries published a *Bibliography of Legal Encyclopedias* in 1963.

The American Association of Law Libraries has published the *Index to Foreign Legal Periodicals* in cooperation with the Institute of Advanced Legal Studies, University of London, since 1960. The *Index* appears quarterly and is cumulated annually and again in volumes covering three years. It includes a list of the periodicals indexed; subject headings; a classification of subjects; a subject index; a geographical index; a book review index; and an author index.

The Association of American Law Schools published in 1968 a series entitled *Law Books Recommended for Libraries,* with broad coverage of the various fields of law and the law of many countries and systems of law, including Roman law, African law, Latin American law, Islamic law, and Russian (Soviet) law. Number 45 of this series is on foreign law and Number 46 on international law.

Law Books in Print, a two volume compilation by Meira G. Pimsleur and J. Myron Jacobstein, was published by Glanville Publishers, Inc., in Dobbs Ferry, New York, in 1965; a 1970 edition appeared in three volumes. Glanville also publishes a quarterly to supplement *Law Books in Print,* entitled *Law Books Published.*

The Library of Congress has published a useful series of *Guides* to the law and literature of most of the Latin American countries, with various editors including two former Law Librarians, Edwin M. Borchard and John T. Vance, and the former Chief of the Hispanic Law Division of the Law Library, Helen L. Clagett. The *Guides* include references on legislation, periodicals, history and philosophy of law, court reports and digests, general works, legal education, general jurisprudence, legal history, Roman law, civil and commercial codes, judicial organization and procedure, criminal codes and codes of criminal procedure, constitutional law, administrative law, public international law and private international law. A *Guide to the Law and Legal Literature of Central American* Republics, by Edward Schuster of New York, was published in 1937. Chapter 1 deals with general and comparative literature of Central America. In Chapters 2 to 7 there are sections for each of the Central American Republics on bibliography, legislation, court reports and digests, general works, legal history, civil law, criminal law, judicial organization and civil procedure, notarial law and practice, criminal procedure, constitutional law, administrative law, military law, public international law, and private international law. There are also *Guides* to the law and literature of Spain and of Germany.

In each of the 25 volumes of *Handbooks of Latin American Studies*, 1937-1963, published by the Library of Congress, there is a chapter on legal literature prepared by Helen L. Clagett.

Various yearbooks offer a store of information in many fields for lawyers in countries throughout the world. Among these are the *Yearbook of the United Nations*, published by the UN Office of Public Information in New York; the *Yearbook of the International Law Commission*: the *Yearbook of International Associations*, published in Brussels by the Union of International Associations: and the *European Yearbook*, published in The Hague by Martinus Nijhoff.

A useful reference on the constitutions of many countries is found in Amos J. Peaslee's *Constitutions of Nations*, published in The Hague by Martinus Nijhoff, 4th edition, 1974.

Important sources of international and comparative law documentation are provided by the international law journals now published in many countries. The American Society of International Law, which has published the *American Journal of International Law* since 1907, has added another valuable source of legal documentation, *International Legal Materials*, which has appeared bi-monthly since 1962.

In view of the amendments frequently made to codes, ordinances, and statutes, it is important to examine the most current edition. The great law libraries, like the Law Library of Congress in the United States and some of the larger law school libraries, can provide much needed assistance in obtaining current material.

An American Series of Foreign Penal Codes, published by Fred M. Rothman and Company of South Hackensack, New Jersey (57 Lenning Street) under the direction of Gerhard O.W. Mueller now includes over 20 codes. In 1937 a *Code pénal international en 1314 articles* was prepared by F. Consentini.

Additional research sources may be found at The Legal Center in New York City (866 U.N. Plaza) and at the Centre de la Terminologie de Droit in Paris (28 rue St. Guillaume).

Appendix IV

1. Members of the United Nations*	1. Membres des Nations Unies

Afghanistan
Republic of ~
  Afghan
	Afghanistan
	République d'~
	  afghan

Albania
People's Socialist Republic
  of ~
  Albanian
	Albanie
	République socialiste populaire
	  d'~
	  albanais

Algeria
Democratic and Popular
Republic of ~
  Algerian
	Algérie
	République algérienne
	démocratique et populaire
	  algérien

Angola
The People's Republic
of Angola
  Angolan
	Angola
	République populaire
	d'Angola
	  angolais

Argentina
Argentine Republic
  Argentine
	Argentine
	République ~
	  argentin

Australia
Commonwealth of ~
  Australian
	Australie
	Commonwealth d'~
	  australien

Austria
Republic of ~
  Austrian
	Autriche
	République d' ~
	  autrichien

Bahamas
Commonwealth of the ~
  Bahamian
	Bahamas
	Commonwealth des ~
	  bahamien

Bahrain
Bahrain
  Bahraini
	Bahreïn
	Etat de ~
	  bahreïnite

Bangladesh
People's Republic of ~
  (of) ~
	Bangladesh
	République populaire de ~
	  du ~

Barbados
  Barbadian
	Barbado
	  barbadien

* As of May 1977.

1. Miembros de las Naciones Unidas

Afganistán
República del ~
afgano

Albania
República Socialista Popular
de ~
albanés

Argelia
República Argelina
Democrática y Popular
argelina, Argel

Angola
República Popular
de Angola
angoleño

Argentina
República ~
argentino

Australia
Commonwealth de ~
australiano

Austria
República de ~
austríaco

Bahamas
Commonwealth de las ~
bahamiano, bahamés

Bahrein
Estado de ~
de ~

Bangladesh
República Popular del ~
de ~

Barbados
barbadense

1. Mitgliede der Vereinten Nationen

Afghanistán
Republik ~
afghanisch, Afghan/e

Albanien
Sozialistische Volksrepublik ~
albanisch, Albaner

Algerien
Demokratische Volksrepublik ~
algerisch, Algerier

Angola
Volksrepublik ~

angolaner

Argentinien
Argentinische Republik
argentinisch, Argentinier

Australien
Australischer Bund
australisch, Australier

Österreich
Republik ~
österreichisch, Österreicher

Bahamas
Bund der ~
bahamaisch, Behamaer

Bahrain
Staat ~
bahrainisch, Bahrainer

Bangladesh
Volksrepublik ~

Barbados
barbadisch, Barbadier

1. Members of the United Nations	1. Membres des Nations Unies
Belgium Kingdom of ~ Belgian	Belgique Royaume de ~ belge
Benin People's Republic of ~ Beninese	Benin la République populaire du ~ beninois
Bhutan Kingdom of ~ Bhutanese	Bhoutan Royaume du ~ bhoutanais
Bolivia Republic of ~ Bolivian	Bolivie République de ~ bolivien
Botswana Republic of ~ (of) ~	Botswana République de ~ du ~
Brazil Federative Republic of ~ Brazilian	Brésil République fédérative du ~ brésilien
Bulgaria People's Republic of ~ Bulgarian	Bulgarie République populaire de ~ bulgare
Burma Socialist Republic of the Union of ~ Burmese	Birmanie République socialiste de l'Union birmane birman
Burundi Republic of ~ (of) ~	Burundi République du ~ burundais
Byelorussia Byelorussian Soviet Socialist Republic Byelorussian	Biélorussie République socialiste soviétique de Biélorussie biélorussien

Cambodia (see Democratic Kampuchea, the name adopted by Cambodia)

Cameroon United Republic of ~ Cameroonian	Cameroun République-Unie du ~ camerounais
Canada Canadian	Canada canadien

1. Miembros de las Naciones Unidas	1. Mitgliede der Vereinten Nationen
Bélgica Reino de ~ belga	Belgien Königreich ~ belgisch, Belgier
Benin la República Popular de ~ beninés	Benin Volksrepublik ~ Bewohner oder Staatsbürger von ~
Bhután Reino de ~ bhutanés	Bhutan Königreich ~ bhutanisch, Bhutaner
Bolivia República de ~ boliviano	Bolivien Republik ~ bolivianisch, Bolivianer
Botswana República de ~ botswanés	Botsvana Republik ~ botsvanisch, Botsvaner
Brasil República Federativa del ~ brasileño	Brasilien Foderative Republik ~ brasilianisch, Brasilianer
Bulgaria República Popular de ~ búlgaro	Bulgarien Volksrepublik ~ bulgarisch, Bulgare
Birmania República Socialista de la Unión Birmania birmano	Birma Sozialistische Republik Birmanische Union birmanisch, Birmane
Burundi República de ~ burundiano	Burundi Republik Burundi burundisch, Burundier
Bielorusia República Socialista Soviótica de Bielorusia bielorruso	Weissrussland Weissrussische Sozialistische Sowietrepublik weissrussisch, Weissrusse
Camerún República Unida del ~ camerunés	Kamerun Vereinigte Republik ~ kamerunisch, Kameruner
Canadá canadiense	Kanada kanadisch, Kanadier

1. Members of the United Nations	1. Membres des Nations Unies
Cape Verde Republic of ~ Cape Verdean	Cap Vert République du ~ du ~
Central African Empire (of the) ~	Empire centroafricain centrafricain
Chad Republic of ~ (of) ~	Tchad République du ~ tchadien
Chile Republic of ~ Chilean	Chili République du ~ chilien
China People's Republic of ~ Chinese	Chine République populaire de ~ chinois
Colombia Republic of ~ Colombian	Colombie République de ~ colombien
Comoros Comorian	Comores comorien
Congo People's Republic of the ~ Congolese	Congo République populaire du ~ congolais
Costa Rica Republic of ~ Costa Rican	Costa Rica République de ~ costa-ricien
Cuba Republic of ~ Cuban	Cuba République de ~ cubain
Cyprus Republic of Cypriot	Chypre République de ~ chypriote
Czechoslovakia Czechoslovak Socialist Republic Czechoslovak	Tchecoslovaquie République socialiste tchécoslovaque tchécoslovaque

Dahomey (see Benin, the name adopted by Dahomey)

1. Miembros de las Naciones Unidas	1. Mitgliede der Vereinten Nationen
Cabo Verde República de ~ caboverdiano	Kap Verde Republik ~ kapverdisch
República Centroafricana centroafricano	Zentralafrikanisches Kaiserreich zentralafrikanisch, Zentralafrikaner
Chad República del ~ chadiano	Tschad Republik ~ tschadisch, Tschader
Chile República de ~ chileno	Chile Republik ~ chilenisch, Chilene
China República Popular de ~ chino	China Volksrepublik ~ chinesisch, Chinese
Colombia República de ~ colombiano	Kolumbien Republik ~ kolumbianisch, Kolumbianer
Comoras comorano	Komoren Bewohner oder Staatsburger von ~
Congo Républica Popular del ~ congoleño	Kongo Volksrepublik ~ kongolesisch, Kongolese
Costa Rica República de ~ costarricense	Costa Rica Republik ~ costaricanisch, Costaricaner
Cuba República de ~ cubano	Kuba Republik ~ kubanisch, Kubaner
Chipre República de ~ chipriota	Zypern Republik ~ zyprisch, Zyprer
Checoslovaquia República Socialista Checoslovaca checoslovaco	Tschechoslowakei Tschechoslowakische Sozialistische Republik Tschechoslowake, tschechisch

1. Members of the United Nations	**1. Membres des Nations Unies**
Democratic Kampuchea (of) ~ ~	Kampuchea Démocratique du ~ ~
Democratic Yemen (see Yemen)	
Denmark Kingdom of ~ Danish, a Dane	Danemark Royaume du ~ danois
Dominican Republic Dominican	République Dominicaine dominicain
Ecuador Republic of ~ Ecuadorian	Equateur République de l' ~ equatorien
Egypt Arab Republic of ~ Egyptian	Egypte République arabe d' ~ egyptien
El Salvador Republic of ~ Salvadorian	El Salvador République d' ~ salvadorien
Equatorial Guinea Republic of ~ (of) ~	Guinée equatoriale Republique de ~ de la ~
Ethiopia Ethiopian	Ethiopie ethiopien
Fiji (of Fiji), Fijian	Fidji de ~, fidjien
Finland Republic of ~ Finnish, a Finn	Finlande République de ~ finlandais
France French Republic Frenchman, the French	France République française français
Gabon Gabonese Republic Gabonese	Gabon République gabonaise gabonais
Gambia Republic of ~ Gambian	Gambie République de ~ gambien

1. Miembros de las Naciones Unidas	**1. Mitgliede der Vereinten Nationen**
Kampuchea Democrática de ~ ~	Demokratisches Kampuchea Kampucheaner
Dinamarca Reino de ~ danés, dinamarqués	Dänemark Königreich ~ dänisch, Däne
República Dominicana dominicano	Dominikanische Republik dominikanisch, Dominikaner
Ecuador República del ~ ecuatoriano	Ecuador Republik ~ ecuadorianisch, Ecuadorianer
Egipto República Arabe de ~ egipcio	Ägypten Arabische Republik ~ ägyptisch, Agypter
El Salvador República de ~ salvadoreño	El Salvador Republik ~ salvadorianisch, Salvadorianer
Guinea Ecuatorial República de ~ guineano	Äquatorialguinea Republik ~ aequatorialguineisch, Äquatorialguineer
Etiopía etíope	Äthiopien äthiopisch, Athiopier
Fiji de ~, vitiano	Fidschi fidschianisch, Fidschianer
Finlandia República de ~ finlandés	Finnland Republik ~ finnisch, Finne
Francia República Francesa francés	Frankreich Französische Republik französisch, Franzose
Gabón República Gabonesa gabonés	Gabun Republik ~ gabunisch, Gabuner
Gambia República de ~ gambiano	Gambia Republik ~ gambisch, Gambier

1. Members of the United Nations	1. Membres des Nations Unies
German Democratic Republic of the ~	République démocratique d'Allemagne de la ~
Germany, Federal Republic of ~ of the ~	République fédérale d'Allemagne de la ~
Ghana Republic of ~ Ghanian	Ghana République du ~ ghanéen
Greece Hellenic Republic of ~ Greek	Grece République héllenique de ~ grec (fém. grecque)
Grenada Grenadian	la Grenade de ~
Guatemala Republic of ~ Guatemalan	Guatemala République du ~ guatemalien, guatemalteque
Guinea Republic of ~ Guinean	Guineé République de ~ guineen
Guinea-Bissau Republic of ~ (of) ~	Guinée-Bissau République de ~ de la ~
Guyana Republic of ~ Guyanese	Guyane République de ~ guyanais
Haiti Republic of ~ Haitian	Haïti République d' ~ haïtien
Honduras Republic of ~ Honduran	Honduras République du ~ hondurien
Hungary Hungarian People's Republic Hungarian	Hongrie République populaire hongroise hongrois

1. Miembros de las Naciones Unidas	1. Mitgliede der Vereinten Nationen
República Democrática de Alemania de la ~	Deutsche Demokratische Republik deutsch, Deutscher
República Federal de Alemania de la ~	Bundesrepublik Deutschland deutsch, Deutscher
Ghana República de ~ ghanés	Ghana Republik ~ ghanisch, Ghanaer
Grecia República Helénica griego	Griechenland Republik ~ griechisch, Grieche
Granada granadino	Grenada grenadisch, Grenader
Guatemala República de ~ guatemalteco	Guatemala Republik ~ gualtemaltekisch, Gualtemalteke
Guinea República de guineo	Guinea Republik ~ guinoisch, Guineer
Guinea-Bissau República de ~ de ~	Guinea-Bissau Republik ~ guineisch, Guineer
Guyana República de ~ guyanés	Guyana Republik ~ guyanisch, Guyaner
Haití República de ~ haitiano	Haiti Republik ~ haitianisch, Haitianer
Hondúras República de ~ hondureño	Honduras Republik ~ honduranisch, Honduraner
Hungria República Popular Húngara húngaro	Ungarn Ungarische Volksrepublik ungarisch, Ungar

1. Members of the United Nations	1. Membres des Nations Unies
Iceland Republic of ~ Icelandic, an Icelander	Islande République d' ~ islandais
India Republic of India Indian	Inde République de l' ~ indien
Indonesia Republic of ~ Indonesian	Indonesie République d' ~ indonesien
Iran Empire of ~ Iranian	Iran Empire d' ~ iranien
Iraq Republic of ~ Iraqui	Irak République d' ~ irakien
Ireland Irish, Irishman	Irlande irlandais
Israel State of ~ Israeli	Israël Etat d' ~ israélien
Italy Italian Republic Italian	Italie République italienne italien
Ivory Coast Republic of the ~ (of the) ~	Côte d'Ivoire République de ~ ivoirien
Jamaica Jamaican	Jamaïque jamaïquain
Japan Japanese	Japon japonais
Jordan Hashemite Kingdom of ~ Jordanian	Jordanie Royaume hachemite de ~ jordanien
Kenya Republic of ~ Kenyan	Kenya République du ~ kényen

1. Miembros de las Naciones Unidas

Islandia
República de ~
islandés

India
República de la ~
indio

Indonesia
República de ~
indonesio

Iran
Imperio del ~
irani

Iraq
República del ~
Iraquí

Irlanda
irlandés

Israel
Estado de ~
israelí

Italia
República Italiania
italiano

Costa de Marfil
República de la ~
marfilense

Jamaica
jamaiquino

Japon
japonés

Jordania
Reino Hachemito de ~
jordano

Kenya
República de ~
keniano

1. Mitgliede der Vereinten Nationen

Island
Republik ~
islandisch, Islander

Indien
Republik ~
indisch, Inder

Indonesien
Republik ~
indonesisch, Indonesier

Iran
Kaiserreich ~
iranisch, Iraner

Irak
Republik ~
irakisch, Iraker

Irland
irish, Ire

Israel
Staat ~
israelisch, Israeli

Italien
Italienische Republik
italienisch, Italiener

Elfenbeinküste
Republik ~
elfenbeinisch, Elfenbeiner

Jamaika
jamaikanisch, Jamaikaner

Japan
japanisch, Japaner

Jordanien
Haschemitisches Königreich ~
jordanisch, Jordaner

Kenia
Republik ~
kenianisch, Kenianer

1. Members of the United Nations

Kuwait
State of ~
Kuwaiti

Laos
Lao People's
Democratic Republic
Lao, a Lao, the Lao

Lebanon
Lebanese Republic
Lebanese

Lesotho
Kingdom of ~
(of) ~, Basotho

Liberia
Republic of ~
Liberian

Libyan Arab Jamahiriya
Libyan

Luxembourg
Grand Duchy of ~
(of) ~

Madagascar
Democratic Republic of ~
Malagasy

Malawi
Republic of ~
Malawian

Malaysia
Malaysian

Maldives
Republic of the ~
Maldivian

Mali
Republic of ~
Malian

Malta
Republic of ~
Maltese

1. Membres des Nations Unies

Koweït
Etat du ~
koweitien

Laos
République démocratique
populaire lao
lao, un Lao, les Lao

Liban
République libanaise
libanais

Lesotho
Royaume du ~
du ~, bassouto

Libéria
République du ~
libérien

Jamahiriya arabe libyenne
libyen

Luxembourg
Grand-Duché de ~
luxembourgeois

Madagascar
République démocratique de ~
malgache

Malawi
République du ~
malawien

Malaisie
malaisien

Maldives
République des ~
maldivien

Mali
République du ~
malien

Malte
République de ~
maltais

1. Miembros de las Naciones Unidas

Kuwait
Estado de ~
kuwaiti

Laos
República Democrática
Popular Lao
lao, un lao, los lao

Libano
República Libanesa
libanés

Lesotho
Reino de ~
de ~

Liberia
República de
liberiano

Jamahiriya Arabe Libia
libio

Luxemburgo
Gran Ducado de ~
luxemburgués

Madagascar
República Democrática de ~
malgache

Malawi
República de ~
malawiano

Malasia
malasio

Maldivas
República de las ~
maldivo

Mali
República de ~
maliense

Malta
República de ~
maltés

1. Mitgliede der Vereinten Nationen

Kuwait
Staat ~
kuwaitisch, Kuwaiter

Laos
Laotische Volksdemokratische
Republik
laotisch, Laote

Libanon
Libanesische Republik
libanesisch, Libanese

Lesotho
Königreich ~
lesothisch, Lesother

Liberia
Republik ~
liberianisch, Liberianer

Libysche Arabische Jamahiriya
libysch, Libyer

Luxemburg
Grossherzogtum ~
luxemburgisch, Luxemburger

Madagaskar
Volksrepublik ~
madagassisch, Madagasse

Malawi
Republik ~
malawisch, Malawier

Malaysia
malaysisch, Malaysier

Malediven
Republik der ~
maledivisch, Malediver

Mali
Republik ~
malisch, Malier

Malta
Republik ~
maltesisch, Malteser

1. Members of the United Nations	1. Membres des Nations Unies
Mauritania Islamic Republic of ~ Mauritanian	Mauritanie République islamique de ~ mauritanien
Mauritius Mauritian	Maurice mauricien
Mexico United Mexican States Mexican	Mexique Etats-Unis du ~ mexicain
Mongolia Mongolian People's Republic Mongolian	Mongolie République populaire mongole mongole
Morocco Kingdom of ~ Moroccan	Maroc Royaume du ~ marocain
Mozambique People's Republic of ~ Mozambican	Mozambique République populaire du ~ mozambicain
Nepal Kingdom of ~ Nepalese	Népal Royaume du ~ népalais
Netherlands Kingdom of the ~ Netherlands, Netherlander	Pays-Bas Royaume des ~ néerlandais
New Zealand of ~, a New Zealander	Nouvelle-Zélande neo-zélandais
Nicaragua Republic of ~ Nicaraguan	Nicaragua République du ~ nicaraguayen
Niger Republic of the ~ (of the) ~, Nigerian	Niger République du ~ nigérien, du ~
Nigeria Federal Republic of ~ Nigerian	Nigéria République fédérale du ~ nigérian

1. Miembros de las Naciones Unidas	1. Mitgliede der Vereinten Nationen
Mauritania República Islámica de ~ mauritano	Mauretanien Islamische Republik ~ mauretanisch, Mauretanier
Mauricio mauriciano	Mauritius mauritisch, Mauritier
Mexico Estados Unidos Mexicanos mexicano	Mexiko Vereinigte Mexikanische Staaten mexikanisch, Mexikaner
Mongolia República Popular Mongola mongol	Mongolei Mongolische Volksrepublik mongolisch, Mongole
Marruecos Reino de ~ marroquí	Marokko Königreich ~ marokkanisch, Marokkaner
Mozambique República Popular de ~ mozambiqueño	Mosambik Volksrepublik ~ Bewohner oder Staatsbürger von ~
Nepal Reino de ~ nepalés	Nepal Königreich ~ nepalesisch, Nepalese
Países Bajos Reino de los ~ neerlandés	Niederlande Königreich der ~ niederländisch, Niederländer
Nueva Zelandia neozelandés	Neuseeland neuseelandisch, Neuseelander
Nicaragua República de ~ nicaragüense	Nicaragua Republik ~ nicaragunisch, Nicaraguaner
Níger República del ~ nigerino	Niger Republik ~ nigrisch, Nigrer
Nigeria República Federal de ~ nigeriano	Nigeria Bundesrepublik ~ nigerianisch, Nigerianer

1. Members of the United Nations	**1. Membres des Nations Unies**
Norway	Norvège
Kingdom of ~	Royaume de ~
Norwegian	norvégien
Oman	Oman
Sultanate of ~	Sultanat d' ~
Omani	omanais
Pakistan	Pakistan
Islamic Republic of ~	République Islamique de ~
Pakistani	pakistanais
Panama	Panama
Republic of ~	République du ~
Panamanian	panamion, panaméen
Papua New Guinea	Papouasie-Nouvelle-Guinée
(of) ~, Papua New Guinean	papouan-néo-guinéen
Paraguay	Paraguay
Republic of ~	République du ~
Paraguayan	paraguayen
Peru	Pérou
Republic of ~	République du ~
Peruvian	péruvien
Philippines	Philippines
Republic of the ~	la République des ~
Philipine, a Filipino	philippin
Poland	Pologne
Polish People's Republic	République populaire de ~
Polish, a Pole	polonais
Portugal	Portugal
Portuguese Republic	République portugaise
Portuguese	portugais
Qatar	Qatar
State of ~	Etat du ~
(of) ~	qatarien
Romania	Roumanie
Socialist Republic of ~	République socialiste de ~
Romanian	roumain
Rwanda	Rwanda
Rwandese Republic	République rwandaise
Rwandese	rwandais

1. Miembros de las Naciones Unidas	1. Mitgliede der Vereinten Nationen
Noruega Reino de ~ noruego	Norwegen Königreich ~ norwegisch, Norweger
Omán Sultanía de ~ omaní	Oman Sultanat ~ omanisch, Omaner
Pakistán República Islámica del ~ pakistaní	Pakistan Islamische Republik ~ pakistanisch, Pakistaner
Panamá República de ~ panameño	Panama Republik ~ panamaisch, Panamaer
Papua Nueva Guinea de ~	Papua-Neuguinea Bewohner oder Staatsbürger von ~
Paraguay República del ~ paraguayo	Paraguay Republik ~ paraguayisch, Paraguayer
Perú República del ~ peruano	Peru Republik ~ peruanisch, Peruaner
Filipinas República de ~ filipino	Philippinen Republik der ~ philippinisch, Philippiner
Polonia República Popular Polaca polaco	Polen Volksrepublik ~ polonisch, Pole
Portugal República Portuguesa portugués	Portugal Portugiesische Republik portugiesisch, Portugiese
Qatar Estado de ~ de ~	Katar Staat ~ katarisch, Katarer
Rumania República Socialista de ~ rumano	Rumänien Sozialistische Republik ~ rumänisch, Rumäne
Rwanda República Rwandesa rwandés	Ruanda Republik ~ ruandisch, Rwander

1. Members of the United Nations

Samoa
Independent State of
Western Samoa
Samoan

Sao Tome and Principe
Democratic Republic of ~
(of) ~

Saudi Arabia
Kingdom of ~
Saudi Arabian

Senegal
Republic of
Senegalese

Seychelles
Republic of ~
(of) ~

Sierra Leone
Republic of ~
Sierra Leonean

Singapore
Republic of ~
Signaporean

Somalia
Somalia Democratic Republic
Somali

South Africa
Republic of ~
South African

Spain
Spanish State
Spanish, a Spaniard

Sri Lanka
Republic of ~
(of) ~

Sudan
Democratic Republic of the ~
Sudanese

1. Membres des Nations Unies

Samoa
Etat indépendent du
Samoa occidental
samoan

Sao Tomé-et-Principe
République démocratique de ~
de ~

Arabie Saoudite
Royaume d' ~
saoudien

Sénégal
République du ~
sénégalais

les Seychelles
la République des ~
seychellois

Sierra Leone
République de ~
sierra-léonien

Singapour
République de ~
singapourien

Somalie
République démocratique ~
somali

Afrique du Sud
République sud-africaine
sud-africain

Espagne
Etat Espagnol
espagnol

Sri Lanka
République de ~
sri-lankais

Sudan
République démocratique
du ~
soudanais

1. Miembros de las Naciones Unidas

Samoa
Estado Independiente
de Samoa Occidental
samoano

Santo Tomé y Príncipe
República Democrática de ~
de ~

Arabia Saudita
Reino de ~
árabe saudita

Senegal
República del ~
senegalés

Las Seychelles
La República de ~
de ~

Sierra Leona
República de ~
sierraleonés

Singapur
República de ~
singapurense

Somalia
República Democrática ~
somali

Sudafrica
República de ~
sudafricano

España
Estado Español
español

Sri Lanka
República de ~
de ~

Sudan
República democrática
del ~
sudanés

1. Mitgliede der Vereinten Nationen

Samoa
Unabhängiger Staat ~

Samoaner

Santo Tomé und Principe
Demokratische Republik ~
von ~

Saudi-Arabien
Königreich ~
saudiarabisch, Saudiaraber

Senegal
Republik ~
senegalesisch, Senegalese

die Seychelles
Republik ~
von ~

Sierra Leone
Republik ~
sierraleonisch, Sierraleone

Singapur
Republik ~
singapurisch, Singapurer

Somalia
Demokratische Republik ~
somalisch, Somalier

Südafrika
Republik ~
südafrikanisch, Südafrikaner

Spanien
Spanischer Staat
spanisch, Spanier

Sri Lanka
Republik ~
lankaisch, Lankaer

Sudan
Demokratische Republik ~
sudanesisch, Sudanese

1. Members of the United Nations

Surinam
Republic of ~
  Surinamese

Swaziland
Kingdom of ~
  Swazu

Sweden
Kingdom of ~
  Swedish, a Swede

Syria
Syrian Arab Republic
  Syrian

Tanzania
United Republic of ~
  Tanzanian

Thailand
Kingdom of ~
  Thai

Togo
Togolese Republic
  Togolese

Trinidad and Tobago
  of ~

Tunisia
Republic of ~
  Tunisian

Turkey
Repubiic of ~
  Turkish, a Turk

Uganda
Republic of ~
  Ugandan

Ukraine
Ukrainian Soviet
Socialist Republic
  Ukrainian

1. Membres des Nations Unies

le Surinam
République du ~
  surinamais

Souasziland
Royaume du ~
  souazi

Suède
Royaume de la ~
  suédois

Syrie
République arabe syrienne
  syrien

Tanzanie
République-Unie de ~
  tanzanien

Thaïlande
Royaume de ~
  thaïlandais

Togo
République togolaise
  togolais

Trinité-et-Tobago
  de la ~

Tunisie
République tunisienne
  tunisien

Turquie
République turque
  Turc

Ouganda
République de l' ~
  ougandais

Ukraine
République socialiste
soviétique d'Ukraine
  ukrainien

1. Miembros de las Naciones Unidas	1. Mitgliede der Vereinten Nationen
Surinam República de ~ surinamés	Surinam Republik ~ Bewohner oder Staatsbürger von ~
Swazilandia Reino de ~ swazi	Swasiland Königreich ~ swasilandisch, Swasi
Suecia Reino de ~ sueco	Schweden Königreich ~ schwedisch, Schwede
Siria República Arabe Siria sirio	Syrien Arabische Republik Syrien syrisch, Syrer
Tanzania República Unida de ~ tanzaniano	Tansania Vereinigte Republik ~ tansanisch, Tansanier
Tailandia Reino de ~ tailandés	Thailand Königreich ~ thailändisch, Thailänder
Togo República Togolesa togolés	Togo Republik ~ togoisch, Togoer
Trinidad y Tobago de ~	Trinidad und Tobago von ~
Túnez República de ~ tunecino	Tunesien Tunesische Republik tunesisch, Tunesier
Turquia República de ~ turco	Türkei Republik ~ türkisch, Türke
Uganda República de ~ ugandés	Uganda Republik ~ ugandisch, Ugander
Ucrania República Socialista Soviética de Ucrania ucranio	Ukraine Ukrainische Sozialistische Sowjetrepublik ukranisch, Ukrainer

1. **Members of the United Nations**	1. **Membres des Nations Unies**
USSR Union of Soviet Socialist Republics (of the) USSR, Soviet Union, Soviet	URSS Union des Républiques socialistes soviétiques de ~, l'union soviétique soviétique
United Arab Emirates of the ~	Emirats arabes unis des ~
United Kingdom United Kingdom of Great Britain and Northern Ireland (of the) ~, British	Royaume-Uni Royaume-Uni de Grande Bretagne et d'Irlande du Nord du ~, britannique
United Republic of Cameroon (see Cameroon)	
United Republic of Tanzania (see Tanzania)	
United States the United States of America (of the) ~, American	Etats-Unis les Etats-Unis d'Amérique des ~, américain
Upper Volta Republic of ~ (of the) ~	Haute-Volta République de ~ voltaïque
Uruguay Eastern Republic of ~ Uruguayan	Uruguay République orientale de l' ~ uruguayen
Venezuela Republic of ~ Venezuelan	Venezuela République de ~ vénézuelien
Yemen Democratic ~ the People's Democratic Republic of ~ (of) Democratic ~	Yémen le Yémen démocratique la République démocratique populaire du ~ du Yémen démocratique
Yemen Yemen Arab Republic Yemeni, a Yemenite	Yémen République arabe du ~ yémenite
Yugoslavia Socialist Federal Republic of ~ Yugoslav	Yugoslavie République fédérative socialiste de ~ yougoslave

1. Miembros de las Naciones Unidas	1. Mitgliede der Vereinten Nationen
URSS Union de Repúblicas Socialistas Soviéticas de la ~, Union Soviética, soviético	UdSSR Union der Sozialistischen Sowjetrepubliken sowjetisch, Sowjetbürger
Emiratos Arabes Unidos de los ~	Vereinigte Arabische Emirate
Reino Unido Reino Unido de Gran Bretaña e Irlanda del Norde británico	Vereinigtes Königreich Vereinigtes Königreich Grossbritannien und Nordirland britisch, Brite
Estados Unidos los Estados Unidos de America estadounidense, norteamericano	Vereinigte Staaten Vereinigte Staaten von Amerika amerikanisch, Amerikaner
Alto Volta República del ~ altovoltaico	Obervolta Republik ~ obervoltaisch, Obervoltaer
Uruguay República Oriental del ~ uruguayo	Uruguay Republik ~ uruguayisch, Uruguayer
Venezuela República de ~ venezolano	Venezuela Republik ~ venezolanisch, Venezolaner
Yemen el Yemen Democrático la República Democrática Popular del ~ del Yemen Democrático	Jemen Demokratischer ~ Demokratische Volksrepublik ~ jemenitisch, Jemenit
Yemen República Arabe del ~ yemenita	Jemen Arabische Republik ~ jemenitisch, Jemenit
Yugoslavia República Federativa Socialista de ~ yugoslavo	Jugoslawien Sozialistische Föderative Republik ~ jugoslawisch, Jugoslawe

1. Members of the United Nations	1. Membres des Nations Unies
Zaire Republic of ~ Zairian	Zaïre République du ~ zaïrois
Zambia Republic of ~ Zambian	Zambie République de ~ zambien

1. Miembros de las Naciones Unidas

Zaire
República del ~
zairense

Zambia
República de ~
zambiano

1. Mitgliede der Vereinten Nationen

Zaire
Republik ~
zairisch, Zairer

Sambia
Republik ~
sambisch, Sambier

2. **United Nations Organizations and Related Agencies**

Principle United Nations Organs

General Assembly
Main Committees
First Committee (Political and Security)
Special Political Committee
Second Committee (Economic and Financial)
Third Committee (Social, Humanitarian and Cultural)
Fourth Committee (Trusteeship, including Non-Self Governing Territories)
Fifth Committee (Administrative and Budgetary)
Sixth Committee (Legal)
Procedural Committees
Credentials Committee
General Committee
Standing Committee
Advisory Committee on Administrative and Budgetary Questions
Committee on Contributions
Subsidiary Bodies
International Civil Service Advisory Board (ICSAB)
Office of United Nations High Commissioner for Refugees (UNHCR)
Trade and Development Board
United Nations Children's Fund (UNICEF)
United Nations Conference on Trade and Development (UNCTAD)
United Nations Development Programme (UNDP)
United Nations Emergency Force
United Nations Institute for Training and Research (UNITAR)
United Nations Joint Staff Pension Fund
United Nations Organization for Industrial Development (UNIDO)
United Nations Relief and Works Agency for Palestine Refugees in the Near East (UNRWA)
United Nations Research Institute for Social Development (UNRISD)
World Food Programme
United Nations Administrative Tribunal
Security Council
Disarmament Commission
Military Staff Committee
United Nations Force in Cyprus
United Nations Military Observer Group in India and Pakistan
United Nations Truce Supervision Organization in Palestine

International Court of Justice
Trusteeship Council
Economic and Social Council
Functional Commissions
Commission for Social Development
Commission for Human Rights
Sub-Commission on Prevention of Discrimination and Protection of Minorities
Commission on Narcotic Drugs

Population Commission
Statistical Commission

Regional Economic Commissions

Ecomic Commission for Africa (ECA)
Economic Commission for Asia and the Far East (ECAFE)
Economic Commission for Europe (ECE)
Economic Commission for Latin America (ECLA)

Administrative Committee on Coordination

Inter-Agency Consultative Board of the United Nations Development Programme

International Atomic Energy Agency (AIEA)

Secretariat

Administrative Management Service
Department of Economic and Social Affairs
Department of Political and Security Council Affairs
Department of Trusteeship and Non-Self-Governing Territories
Economic and Social Office in Beirut
Executive Office of the Secretary-General
General Assembly Affairs
Office of Conference Services
Office of General Services
Office of Inter-Agency Affairs
Office of Legal Affairs
Office of Personnel
Office of Public Information
Office of the Controller
Office of the Under-Secretary-General for Administration and Management
Office of the Under-Secretary-General for Special Political Affairs
United NationsOffice at Geneva

The Specialized Agencies

Food and Agriculture Organization of the United Nations (FAO)
Inter-Government Maritime Consultative Organization (IMCO)
International Bank for Reconstruction and Development (WORLD BANK)
International Civil Aviation Organization (ICAO)
International Development Association (IDA)
International Finance Corporation (IFC)
International Labour Organization (ILO)
International Monetary Fund (FUND)
International Telecommunication Union (ITU)
International Trade Organization: General Agreement on Tariffs and Trade (GATT)
United Nations Educational, Scientific and Cultural Organization (UNESCO)
Universal Postal Union (UPU)
World Health Organization (WHO)
World Meteorological Organization (WMO)

2. L'ONU et les organisations connexes

Les organes principaux

L'Assemblée Générale
Commissions principales
Première Commission (Questions politiques et de sécurité)
Commission Politique Spéciale
Deuxième Commission (Questions économiques et financières)
Troisième Commission (Questions sociales, humanitaires et culturelles)
Quatrième Commission (Tutelle, y compris les territoires non autonomes)
Cinquième Commission (Questions administratives et budgétaires)
Sixième Commission (Questions juridiques)
Comités de procédure
Commission de vérification des pouvoirs
Comité général
Comités permanents
Comité consultatif pour les questions administratives et budgétaires
Comité des contributions
Organes subsidiaires
Comité consultatif de la fonction publique internationale (CCFPI)
Haut Commissariat des Nations Unies pour les réfugiés
Conseil de commerce et du développement
Fonds des Nations Unies pour l'enfance (FISE)
Conférence des Nations Unies sur le commerce et le développement (CNUCED)
Programme des Nations Unies pour le développement industriel
Fonds d'équipment des Nations Unies
Institut des Nations Unies pour la formation et la recherche
Caisse commune des pensions du personnel des Nations Unies
Organisation des Nations Unies pour le développement industriel
Office de secours et de travaux des Nations Unies pour les refugiés de Palestine
Institut de recherche des Nations Unies pour le développement social
Programme alimentaire mondiale
Tribunal Administratif des Nations Unies
Conseil de Sécurité
Commission du désarmement
Comité d'état-major
Force des Nations Unies chargée du maintien de la paix à Chypre
Groupe d'observateurs militaires des Nations Unies pour l'Inde et le Pakistan
Organisme des Nations Unies chargé de la surveillance de la trêve en Palestine

Cour Internationale de Justice
Conseil de Tutelle
Conseil Economique et Sociale
Commissions techniques
La Commission des questions sociales
La Commission des droits de l'homme
Sous-Commission de la lutte contre les mesures discriminatoires et de la protection des minorités
La Commission des Stupéfiants

La Commission de la population
La Commission de statistique
Commissions régionales
La Commission économique pour l'Afrique (CEA)
La Commission économique pour l'Asie et l'Extrême-Orient (CEAEO)
La Commission économique pour l'Europe (CEE)
La Commission économique pour l'Amérique latine (CEPAL)
Comité Administratif de Coordination
Bureau Consultatif Interorganisations du Programme des Nations Unies pour le Développement
Agence internationale de l'énergie atomique (AIEA)
Secrétariat
Service de gestion administrative
Le Département des affaires économiques et sociales
Le Département des affaires politiques et des affaires du Conseil de Sécurité
Le Département de la tutelle et des renseignements relatifs aux territoires non autonomes
Bureau économique et social des Nations Unies à Beyrouth
Le Cabinet du Secrétaire général
Affaires de l'Assemblée générale
Le Service des conférences
Les Services généraux
Bureau des affaires interorganisations
Le Service juridique
Le Service du personnel
Le Service financier
Cabinet du Secrétaire général adjoint à l'administration et à la gestion
Cabinet du Secrétaire général adjoint aux affaires politiques spéciales
L'Office des Nations Unies à Genève
Institutions spécialisées
Organisation des Nations Unies pour l'alimentation et l'agriculture (FAO)
Organisation intergouvernementale consultative de la navigation maritime (OMCI)
Banque internationale pour la reconstruction et le développement (BIRD)–Banque mondiale
Organisation de l'aviation civile internationale (OACI)
Association internationale pour le développement (AID)
Société financière internationale (SFI)
Organisation internationale du travail (OIT)
Fonds monétaire international (FMI)
Union internationale des télécommunications (UIT)
Accord général sur les tarifs douaniers et le commerce (GATT)
Organisation des Nations Unies pour l'éducation, la science et la culture (UNESCO)
Union postale universelle (UPU)
Organisation mondiale de la santé (OMS)
Organisation météorologique mondiale (OMM)

2. **Las Naciones Unidas y los Organos Vinculados**

Los Organos Principales

Asamblea General

Comisiones principales

Primera Comisión (Política y de Seguridad)
Segunda Comisión (Asuntos económicos y financieros)
Tercera Comisión (Asuntos sociales, humanitarios y culturales)
Cuarta Comisión (Administración fiduciaria, incluyendo los territorios no autónomos)
Quinta Comisión (Asuntos administrativos y de presupuesto)
Sexta Comisión (Asuntos jurídicos)

Comisiones procesales

Comisión de Verificación de Poderes
Comisión General

Comisiones permanentes

Comisión Consultativa en Asuntos Administrativos y de Presupuesto
Comisión de Cuotas

Organos subsidiarios

Junta Consultativa de Administración Pública Internacional
Alto Comisionado de las Naciones Unidas para los Refugiados
Junta de Comercio y Desarrollo
Fondo de las Naciones Unidas para la Infancia
Fondo de las Naciones Unidas para el Desarrollo de la Capitalización
Programa de las Naciones Unidas para el Desarrollo
Fuerza de Emergencia de las Naciones Unidas
Instituto de las Naciones Unidas para Formación Profesional e Investigaciones
Caja Común de Pensiones del Personal de las Naciones Unidas
Organismo de Obras Públicas y Socorro de las Naciones Unidas para los Refugiados de Palestina
Instituto de Investigaciones de las Naciones Unidas para el Desarrollo Social
Programa Mundial de Alimentos

Tribunal Administrativo de las Naciones Unidas

Consejo de Seguridad

Comisión de Desarme
Comité de Estado Mayor
Fuerza de las Naciones Unidas para el Mantenimiento de la Paz en Chipre
Grupo de Observadores Militares de las Naciones Unidas para la India y el Paquistán
Organismo de Vigilancia de la Tregua en Palestina

Corte Internacional de Justicia

Consejo de Tutela

Consejo Económico y Social

Comisiones técnicas

Comisión de Asuntos Sociales
Comisión de Derechos Humanos
Subcomisión de Prevención de Discriminaciones y Protección a las Minorías
Comisión de Estupefacientes

Comisión de Población
Comisión de Estadística
Comisiones regionales económicas
Comisión Económica para Africa
Comisión Económica para Asia y el Lejano Oriente
Comisión Económica para Europa
Comisión Económica para América Latina
Comité de Vivienda, Construcción y Planificación
Comité Asesor sobre la Aplicación de la Ciencia y la Tecnología al Desarrollo
Organismo Internacional de Energía Atómica
Secretaría
Servicio de Gestión Administrativa
Departamento de Asuntos Económicos y Sociales
Departamento de Asuntos Políticos y de Asuntos del Consejo de Seguridad
Departamento de Administración Fiduciaria y Territorios no Autónomos
Oficina de Asuntos Políticos y Sociales en Beirut
Oficina Ejecutiva del Secretario General
Asuntos de la Asamblea General
Oficina de Servicios de Conferencias
Oficina de Servicios Generales
Oficina de Asuntos entre Organismos
Oficina de Asuntos Jurídicos
Oficina de Personal
Oficina de Información Pública
Oficina del Contralor
Oficina del Secretario General Adjunto de Administración y Gestión
Oficina de Subsecretario para Asuntos Políticos Especiales
Oficina de las Naciones Unidas en Ginebra
Organismos Especializados
Organización de las Naciones Unidas para la Agricultura y la Alimentación (FAO)
Organización Consultiva Marítima Intergubernamental (OCMI)
Banco Internacional de Reconstrucción y Fomento (BANCO MUNDIAL)
Organización de Aviación Civil Internacional (OACI)
Asociación Internacional de Fomento (AIF)
Corporación Financiera Internacional (CFI)
Organización Internacional del Trabajo (OIT)
Fondo Monetario Internacional (FMI)
Union Internacional de Telecomunicaciones (UIT)
Organización Internacional de Comercio: Acuerdo General sobre Aranceles Aduaneros y Comercio (GATT)
Organización de las Naciones Unidas para la Educación, la Ciencia y la Cultura (UNESCO)
Unión Postal Universal (UPU)
Organización Mundial de la Salud (OMS)
Organización Meteorológica Mundial (OMM)

2. Die Vereinten Nationen und Ihre Sonderorganisationen

Hauptorgane der Vereinten Nationen

Generalversammlung
Hauptausschüsse
Erster Ausschuss (für Fragen betreffend Politik und Sicherheit)
Politischer Sonderausschuss
Zweiter Ausschuss (für Wirtschafts- und Finanzfragen)
Dritter Ausschuss (für soziale, humanitäre und kulturelle Fragen)
Vierter Ausschuss (für Treuhandschaftsfragen, einschliesslich solcher, die Gebiete ohne Selbstregierung betreffen)
Fünfter Ausschuss (Verwaltungs- und Haushaltsfragen)
Sechster Ausschuss (Rechtsfragen)
Verfahrensauschüsse
Ausschuss für Beglaubigungsschreiben
Lenkungsausschuss
Ständige Ausschüsse
Ausschuss für Mitgliedsbeiträge
Beratungsausschuss für Verwaltungs- und Budgetfragen
Hilfsorgane
Beirat für internationale Verwaltung
Amt des Hohen Kommissars der Vereinten Nationen für Flüchtlinge
Handels- und Entwicklungsrat
Weltkinderhilfswerk der Vereinten Nationen
Konferenz der Vereinten Nationen für Handel- und Entwicklung
Entwicklungsprogramm der Vereinten Nationen
Truppen der Vereinten Nationen für Ausnahmefälle
Ausbildung- und Forschungsinstitut der Vereinten Nationen
Pensionsfonds der Vereinten Nationen
Organisation der Vereinten Nationen für industrielle Entwicklung
Hilfswerk der Vereinten Nationen für die Palästina Flüchtlinge
Komitee für Soziale Entwicklung
Welternährungsprogramm
Verwaltungs-Gerichtshof der Vereinten Nationen
Sicherheitsrat
Abrüstungskommission
Ständiger Militärausschuss
Hilfskorps der Vereinten Nationen in Zypern
Militärische Mission der Vereinten Nationen in Indien und Pakistan
Organisation der Vereinten Nationen für die Kontrolle des Waffenstillstandes in Palästina
Internationaler Gerichtshof
Treuhandschaftsrat
Wirtschafts- und Sozialrat
Funktionelle Kommissionen
Die Kommission für Soziale Fragen
Die Kommission für die Menschenrechte
Unterkommission zur Verhütung der Diskriminierung und zum Schuts der Minderheiten
Die Rauschgiftkommission

Die Kommission für Bevölkerungsfragen
Die statistische Kommission

Regionale Wirtschaftskommission

Die Wirtschaftskommission für Afrika
Die Wirtschaftskommission für Asien und den Fernen Osten
Die Wirtschaftskommission für Europa
Die Wirtschaftskommission für Lateinamerika

Verwaltungsausschuss für Zusammenarbeit

Zwischenamtliche Beratungsstelle für das Entwicklungsprogramm der Vereinten Nationen

Internationale Atomenergie Organisation

Sekretariat

Organisationsabteilung der Verwaltung
Abteilung für Wirtschafts- und Sozialfragen
Abteilung für Treuhandschaft und Gebiete ohne Selbstregierung
Büro für Wirtschafts- und Sozialfragen in Beirut
Exekutivbüro des Generalsekretärs
Vollversammlungsangelegenheiten
Konferenzdienststelle
Dienststelle für allgemeine Verwaltung
Dienststelle für Rechtsfragen
Dienststelle für Personalfragen
Dienststelle für Information der Öffentlichkeit
Dienststelle für Finanzkontrolle
Kanzleien der Unter-Generalsekretäre für besondere politische Angelegenheiten
Kanzleien der Vereinten Nationen in Genf

Die Sonderorganisationen

Organisation der Vereinten Nationen für Ernährung und Landwirtschaft
Zwischenstaatliche beratende Seeschiffahrts-Organisation
Internationale Bank für Wiederaufbau und Entwicklung – (Welt Bank)
Internationale Zivilluftfahrt Organisation
Internationale Entwicklungsorganisation
Internationale Finanz-Corporation
Internationale Arbeitsorganisation
Internationale Währungsfonds
Internationale Fernmeldeunion
Internationale Handelorganisation: Allgemeines Abkommen über Zolltarife und Handel
Organisation der Vereinten Nationen für Erziehung, Wissenschaft und Kultur
Weltpostverein
Weltgesundheitsorganisation
Weltorganisation für Meteorologie